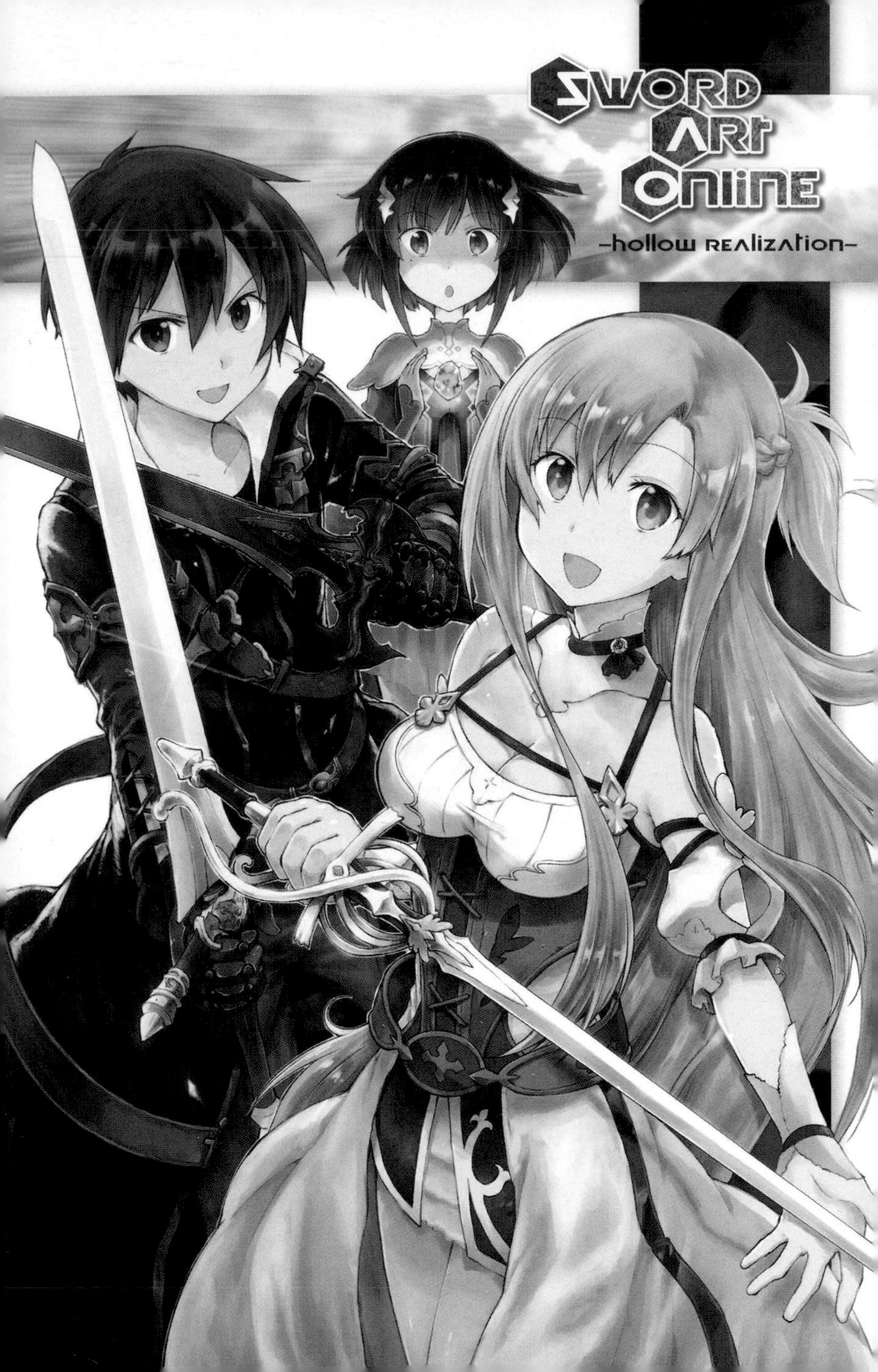
SWORD ART ONLINE
-hollow realization-

SWORD ART ONLINE
—HOLLOW REALIZATION—

002

CONTENTS

I'm Back
in Kincradl

#04: Silica's New Path

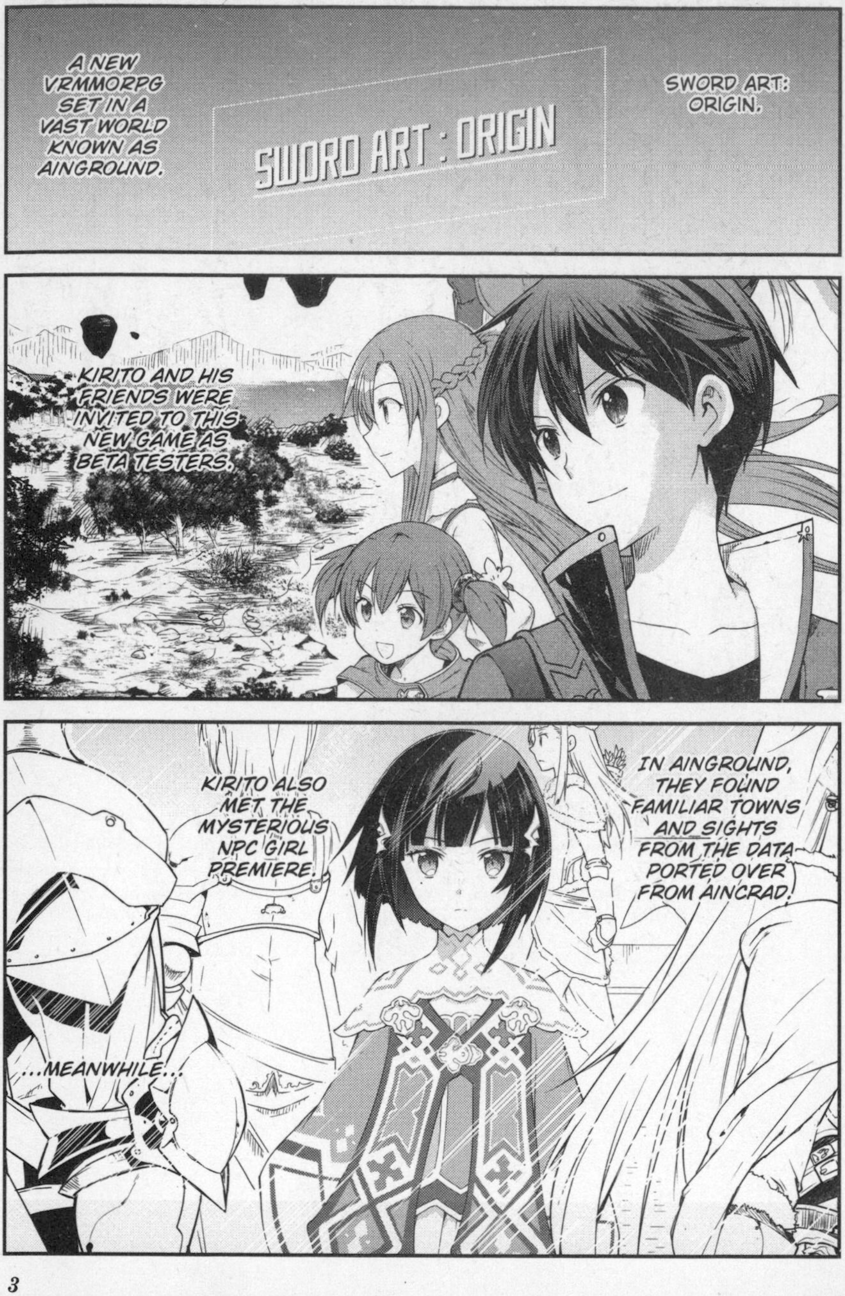
SWORD ART: ORIGIN.
SWORD ART : ORIGIN
A NEW VRMMORPG SET IN A VAST WORLD KNOWN AS AINGROUND.
KIRITO AND HIS FRIENDS WERE INVITED TO THIS NEW GAME AS BETA TESTERS.
IN AINGROUND, THEY FOUND FAMILIAR TOWNS AND SIGHTS FROM THE DATA PORTED OVER FROM AINCRAD.
KIRITO ALSO MET THE MYSTERIOUS NPC GIRL PREMIERE.
...MEANWHILE...

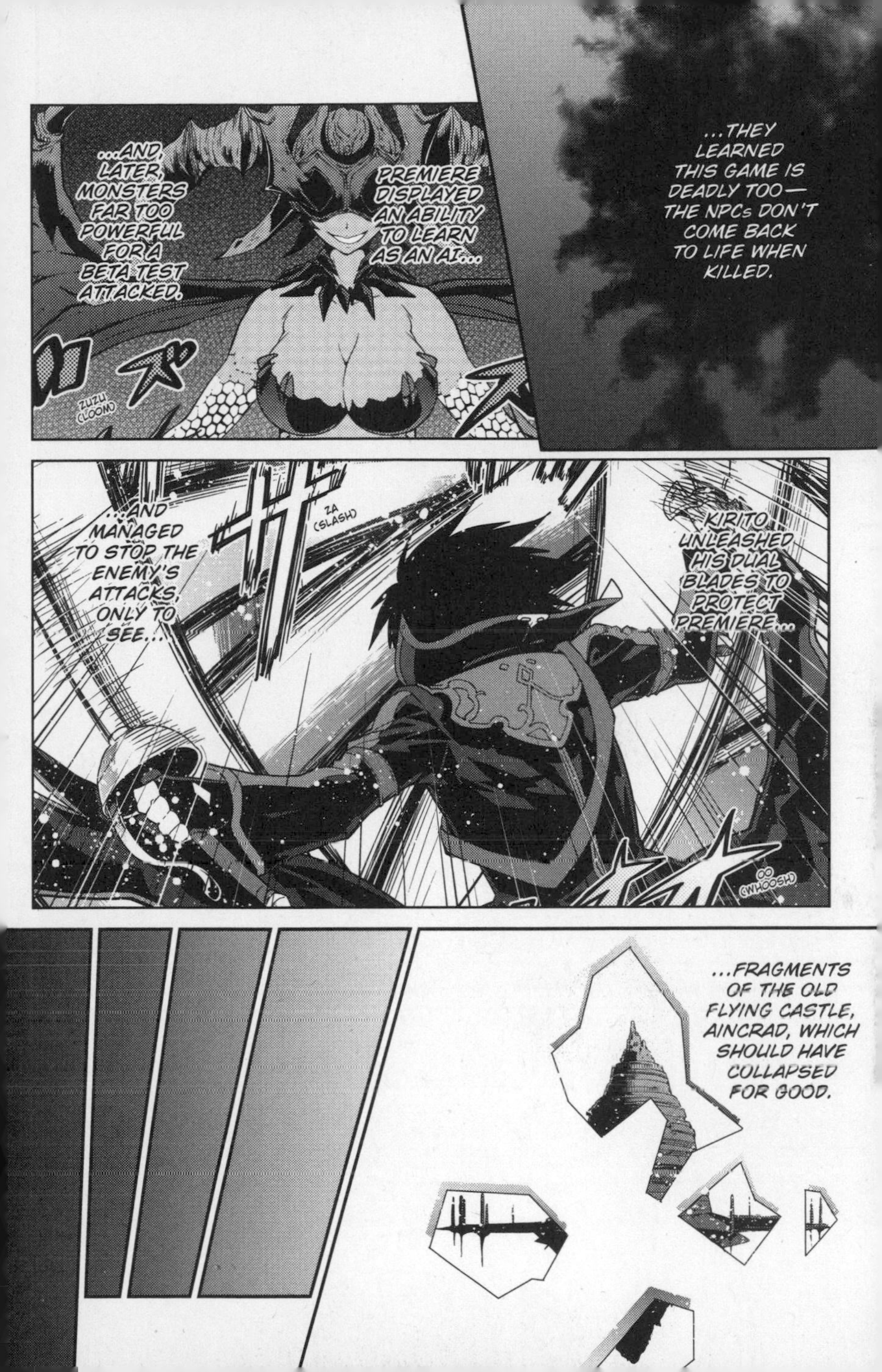
...THEY LEARNED THIS GAME IS DEADLY TOO— THE NPCs DON'T COME BACK TO LIFE WHEN KILLED.
PREMIERE DISPLAYED AN ABILITY TO LEARN AS AN AI...
...AND, LATER, MONSTERS FAR TOO POWERFUL FOR A BETA TEST ATTACKED.
ZUZU (LOOM)
KIRITO UNLEASHED HIS DUAL BLADES TO PROTECT PREMIERE...
ZA (SLASH)
...AND MANAGED TO STOP THE ENEMY'S ATTACKS, ONLY TO SEE...
OO (WHOOSH)
...FRAGMENTS OF THE OLD FLYING CASTLE, AINCRAD, WHICH SHOULD HAVE COLLAPSED FOR GOOD.

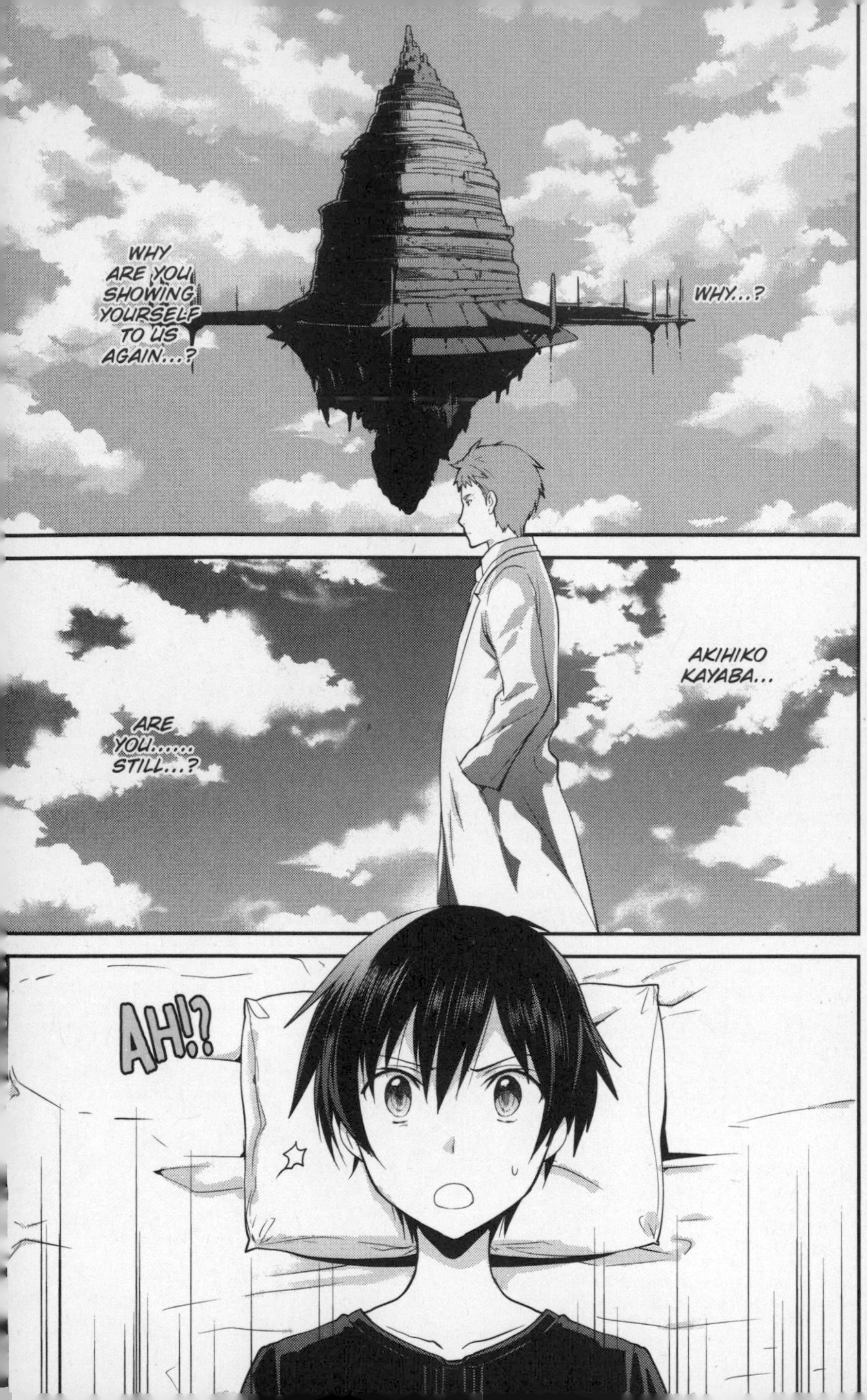
WHY...?
WHY ARE YOU SHOWING YOURSELF TO US AGAIN...?
AKIHIKO KAYABA...
ARE YOU...... STILL...?
AH!?

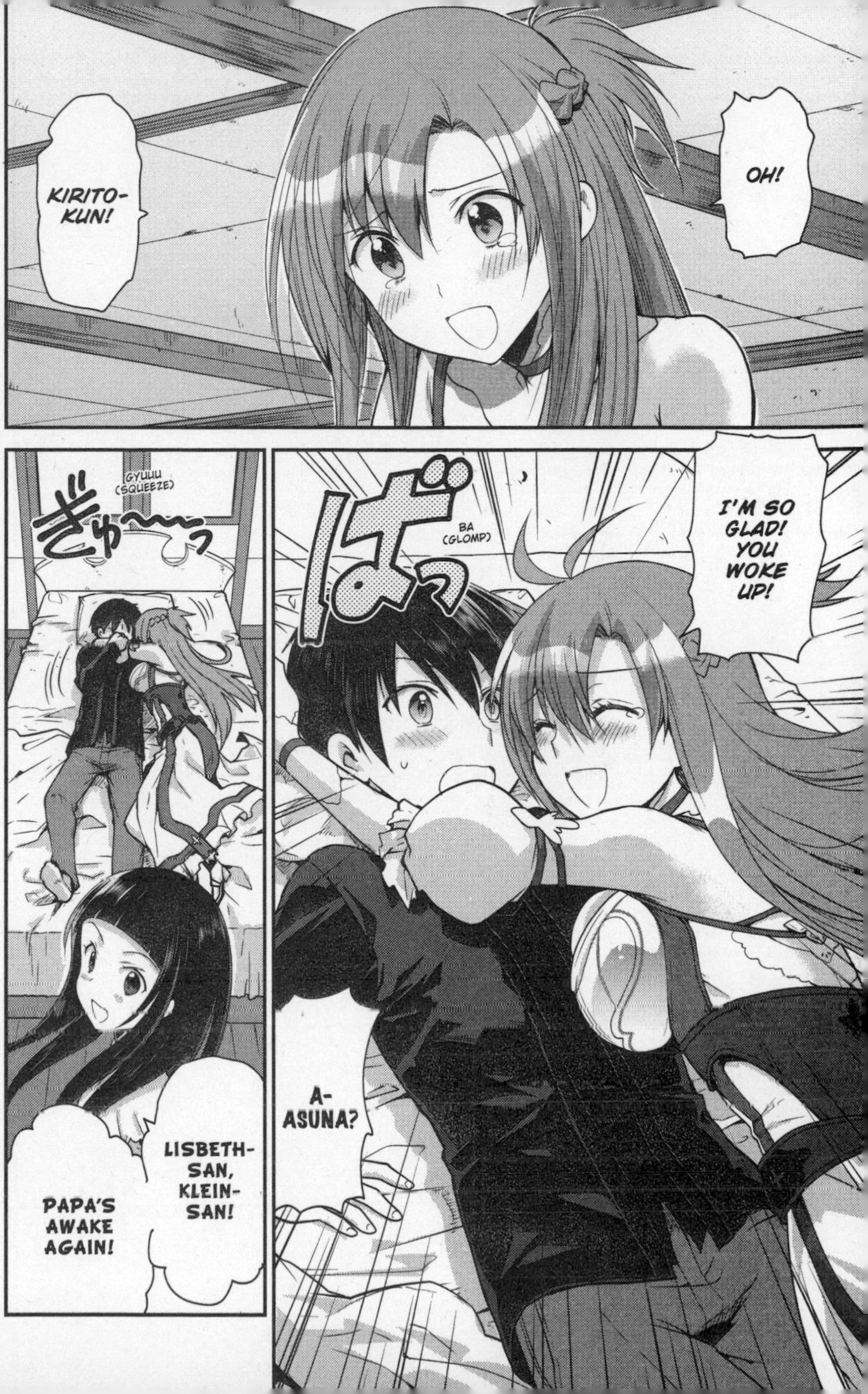
OH!
KIRITO-KUN!
I'M SO GLAD! YOU WOKE UP!
ぱっ
BA (GLOMP)
A- ASUNA?
ぎゅ〜〜っ
GYUUU (SQUEEZE)
LISBETH-SAN, KLEIN-SAN!
PAPA'S AWAKE AGAIN!

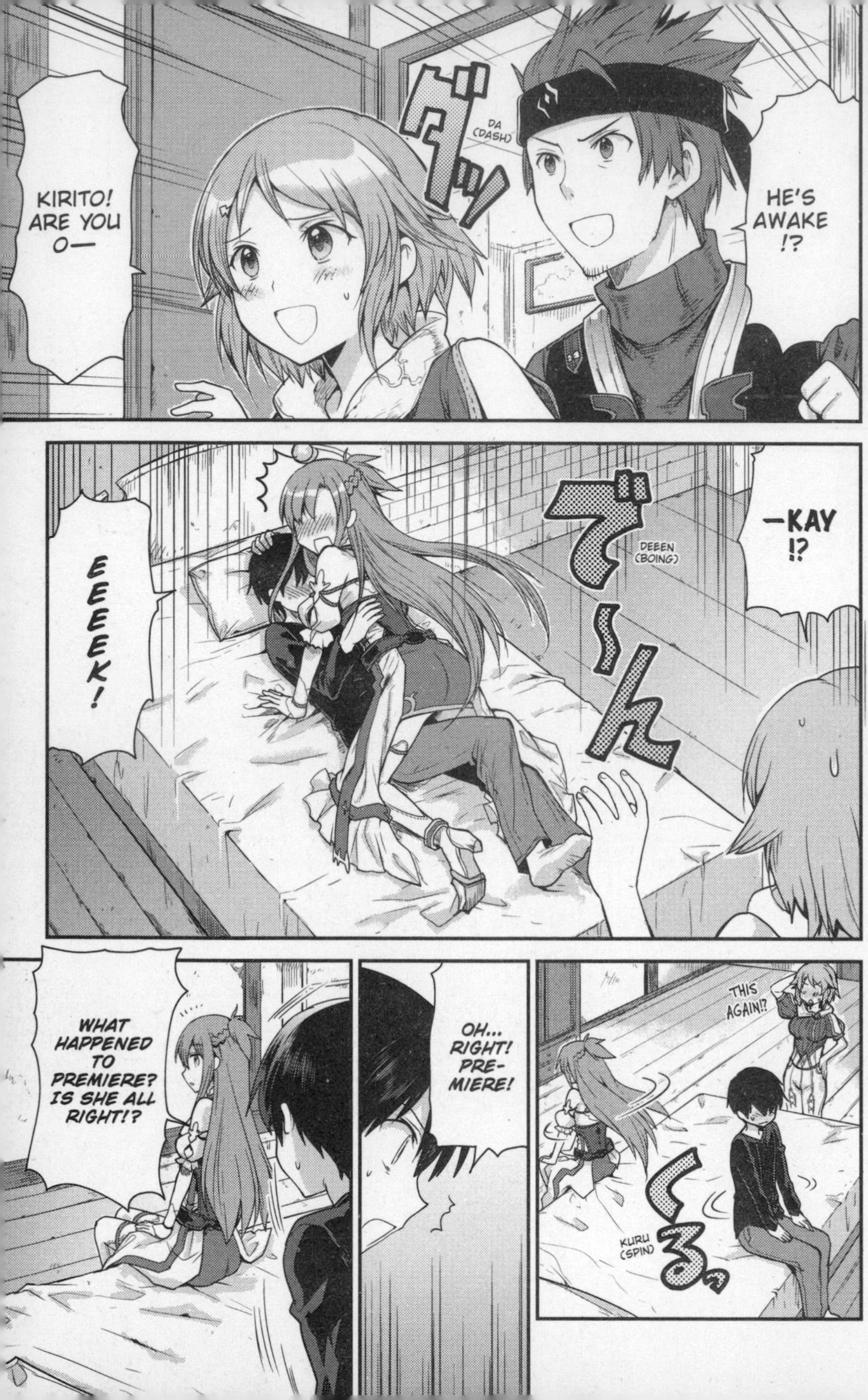
HE'S AWAKE !?
ダッ
DA (DASH)
KIRITO! ARE YOU O—
—KAY !?
でーん
DEEEN (BOING)
EEEEEK!
THIS AGAIN!?
くる
KURU (SPIN)
OH... RIGHT! PRE-MIERE!
WHAT HAPPENED TO PREMIERE? IS SHE ALL RIGHT!?

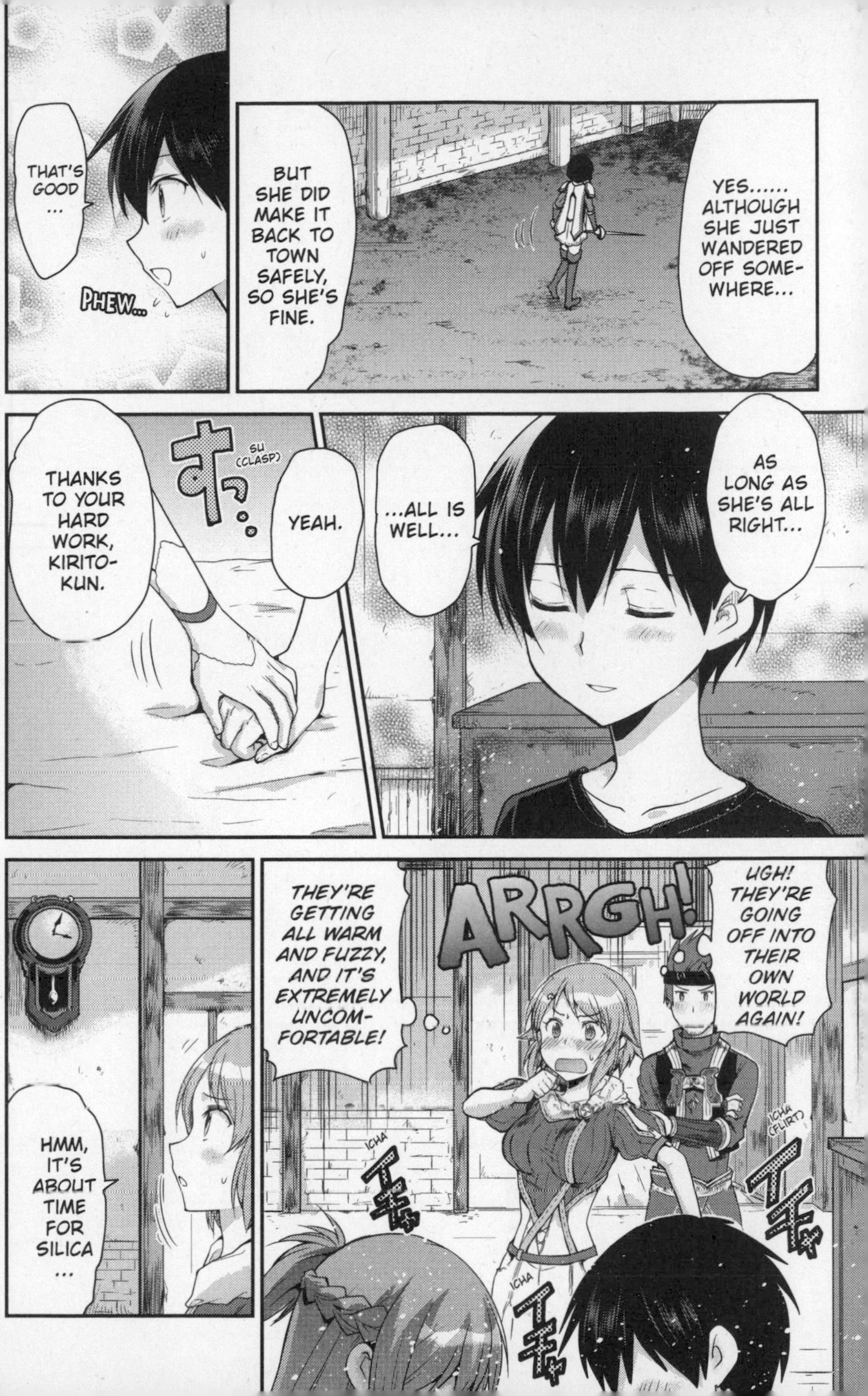
YES...... ALTHOUGH SHE JUST WANDERED OFF SOME-WHERE...
BUT SHE DID MAKE IT BACK TO TOWN SAFELY, SO SHE'S FINE.
THAT'S GOOD ...
PHEW...
AS LONG AS SHE'S ALL RIGHT...
...ALL IS WELL...
SU (CLASP)
YEAH.
THANKS TO YOUR HARD WORK, KIRITO-KUN.
UGH! THEY'RE GOING OFF INTO THEIR OWN WORLD AGAIN!
ARRGH!
THEY'RE GETTING ALL WARM AND FUZZY, AND IT'S EXTREMELY UNCOM-FORTABLE!
ICHA (FLIRT)
ICHA
ICHA
HMM, IT'S ABOUT TIME FOR SILICA ...

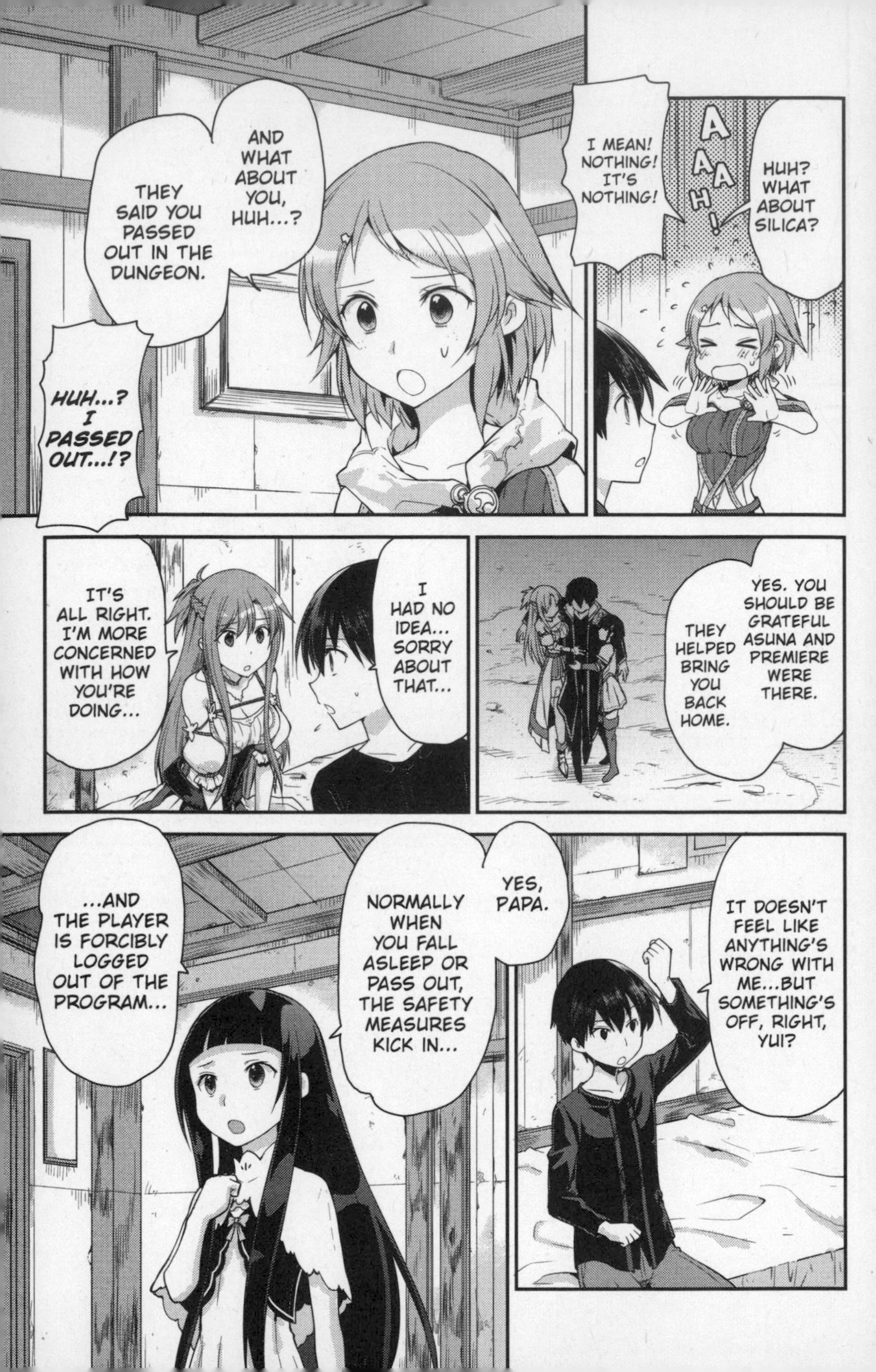
HUH? WHAT ABOUT SILICA?
AAAH!
I MEAN! NOTHING! IT'S NOTHING!
AND WHAT ABOUT YOU, HUH...?
THEY SAID YOU PASSED OUT IN THE DUNGEON.
HUH...? I PASSED OUT...!?
YES. YOU SHOULD BE GRATEFUL ASUNA AND PREMIERE WERE THERE.
THEY HELPED BRING YOU BACK HOME.
I HAD NO IDEA... SORRY ABOUT THAT...
IT'S ALL RIGHT. I'M MORE CONCERNED WITH HOW YOU'RE DOING...
IT DOESN'T FEEL LIKE ANYTHING'S WRONG WITH ME...BUT SOMETHING'S OFF, RIGHT, YUI?
YES, PAPA.
NORMALLY WHEN YOU FALL ASLEEP OR PASS OUT, THE SAFETY MEASURES KICK IN...
...AND THE PLAYER IS FORCIBLY LOGGED OUT OF THE PROGRAM...

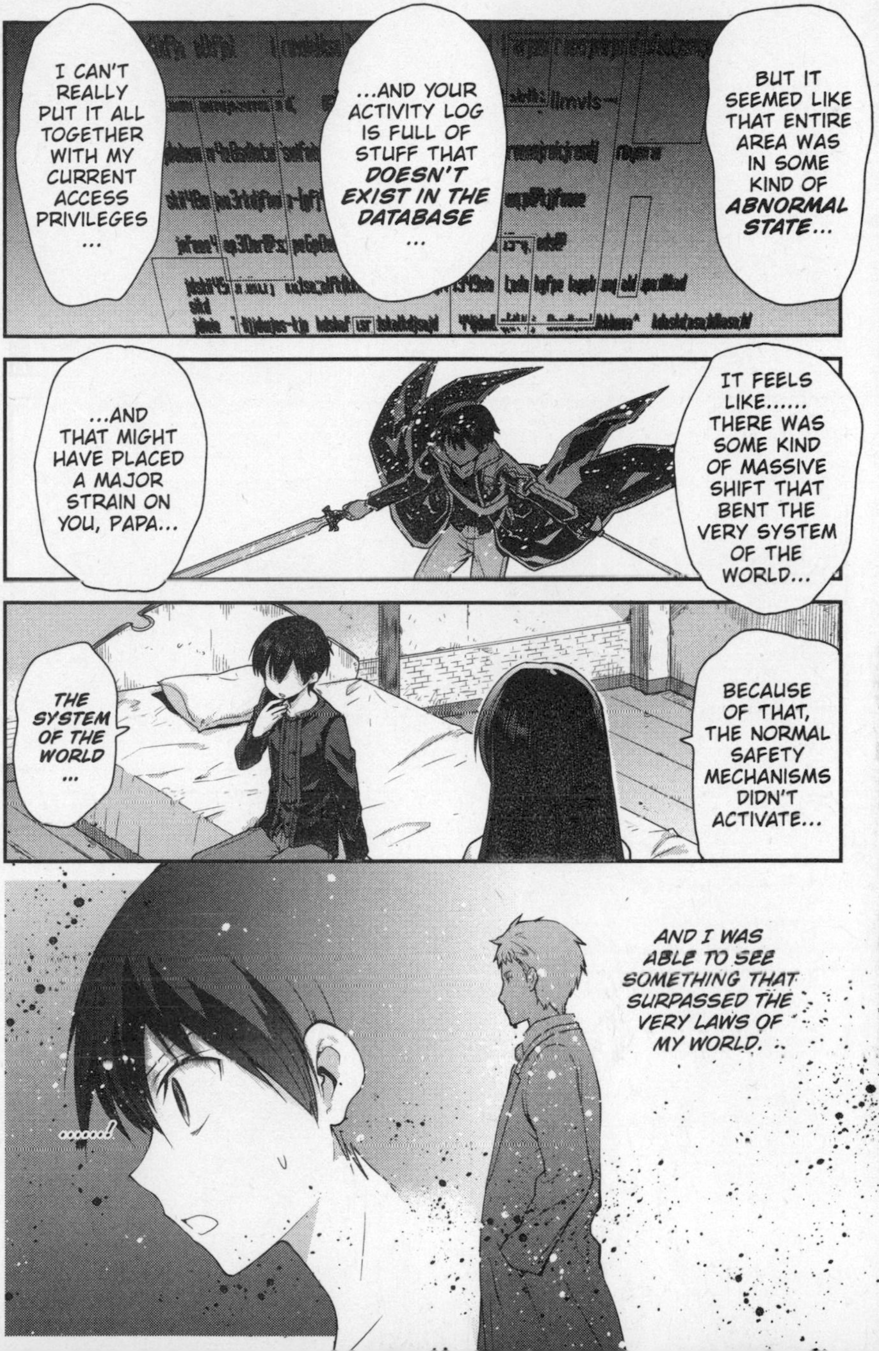
BUT IT SEEMED LIKE THAT ENTIRE AREA WAS IN SOME KIND OF ABNORMAL STATE...
...AND YOUR ACTIVITY LOG IS FULL OF STUFF THAT DOESN'T EXIST IN THE DATABASE...
I CAN'T REALLY PUT IT ALL TOGETHER WITH MY CURRENT ACCESS PRIVILEGES...
IT FEELS LIKE...... THERE WAS SOME KIND OF MASSIVE SHIFT THAT BENT THE VERY SYSTEM OF THE WORLD...
...AND THAT MIGHT HAVE PLACED A MAJOR STRAIN ON YOU, PAPA...
BECAUSE OF THAT, THE NORMAL SAFETY MECHANISMS DIDN'T ACTIVATE...
THE SYSTEM OF THE WORLD...
AND I WAS ABLE TO SEE SOMETHING THAT SURPASSED THE VERY LAWS OF MY WORLD.

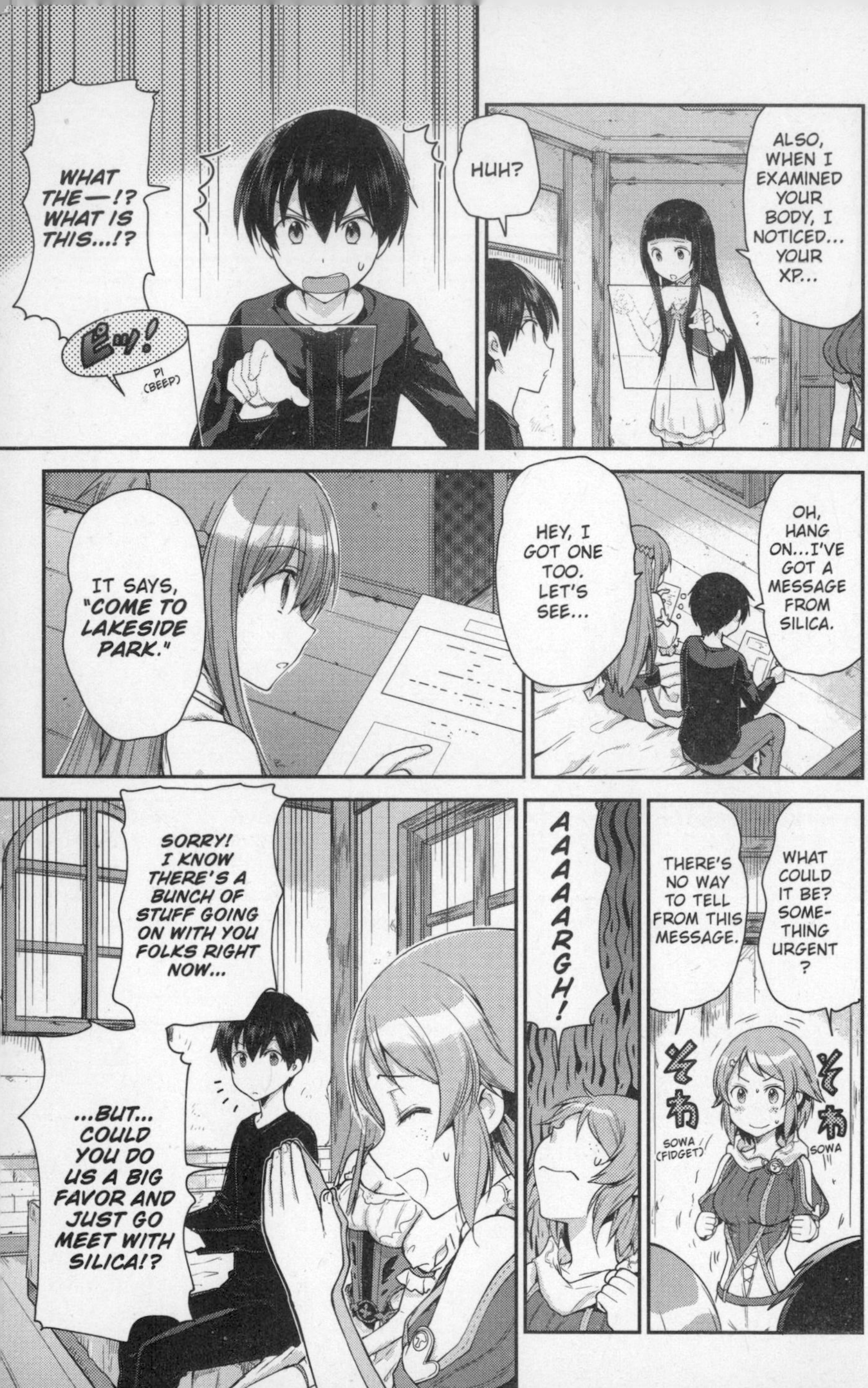
ALSO, WHEN I EXAMINED YOUR BODY, I NOTICED... YOUR XP...
HUH?
WHAT THE—!? WHAT IS THIS...!?
ピッ!
PI (BEEP)
OH, HANG ON...I'VE GOT A MESSAGE FROM SILICA.
HEY, I GOT ONE TOO. LET'S SEE...
IT SAYS, "COME TO LAKESIDE PARK."
WHAT COULD IT BE? SOME-THING URGENT?
THERE'S NO WAY TO TELL FROM THIS MESSAGE.
そわ
SOWA
そわ
SOWA (FIDGET)
AAAAAARGH!
SORRY! I KNOW THERE'S A BUNCH OF STUFF GOING ON WITH YOU FOLKS RIGHT NOW...
...BUT... COULD YOU DO US A BIG FAVOR AND JUST GO MEET WITH SILICA!?

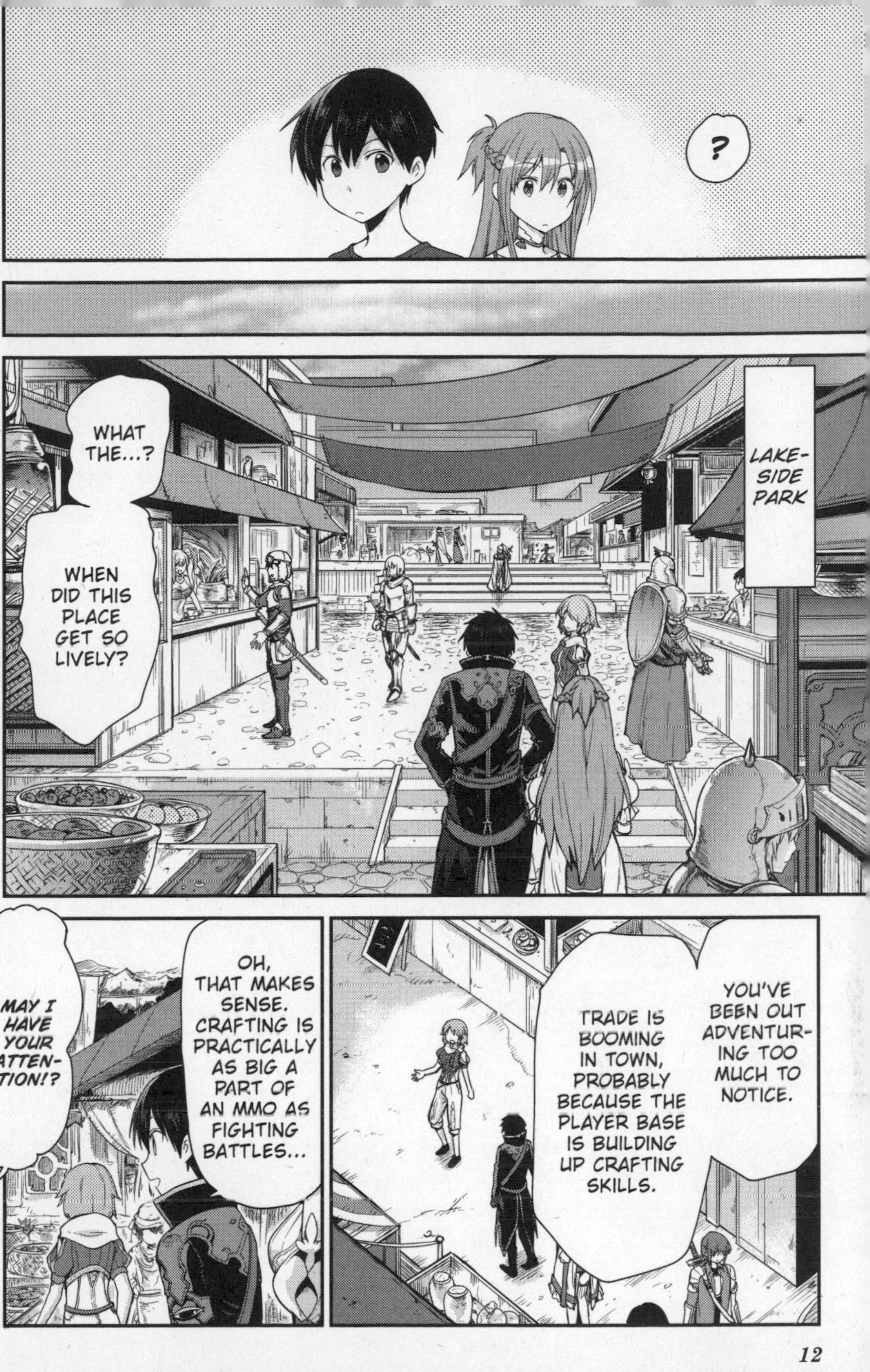
?
LAKESIDE PARK
WHAT THE...?
WHEN DID THIS PLACE GET SO LIVELY?
YOU'VE BEEN OUT ADVENTURING TOO MUCH TO NOTICE.
TRADE IS BOOMING IN TOWN, PROBABLY BECAUSE THE PLAYER BASE IS BUILDING UP CRAFTING SKILLS.
OH, THAT MAKES SENSE. CRAFTING IS PRACTICALLY AS BIG A PART OF AN MMO AS FIGHTING BATTLES...
MAY I HAVE YOUR ATTENTION!?

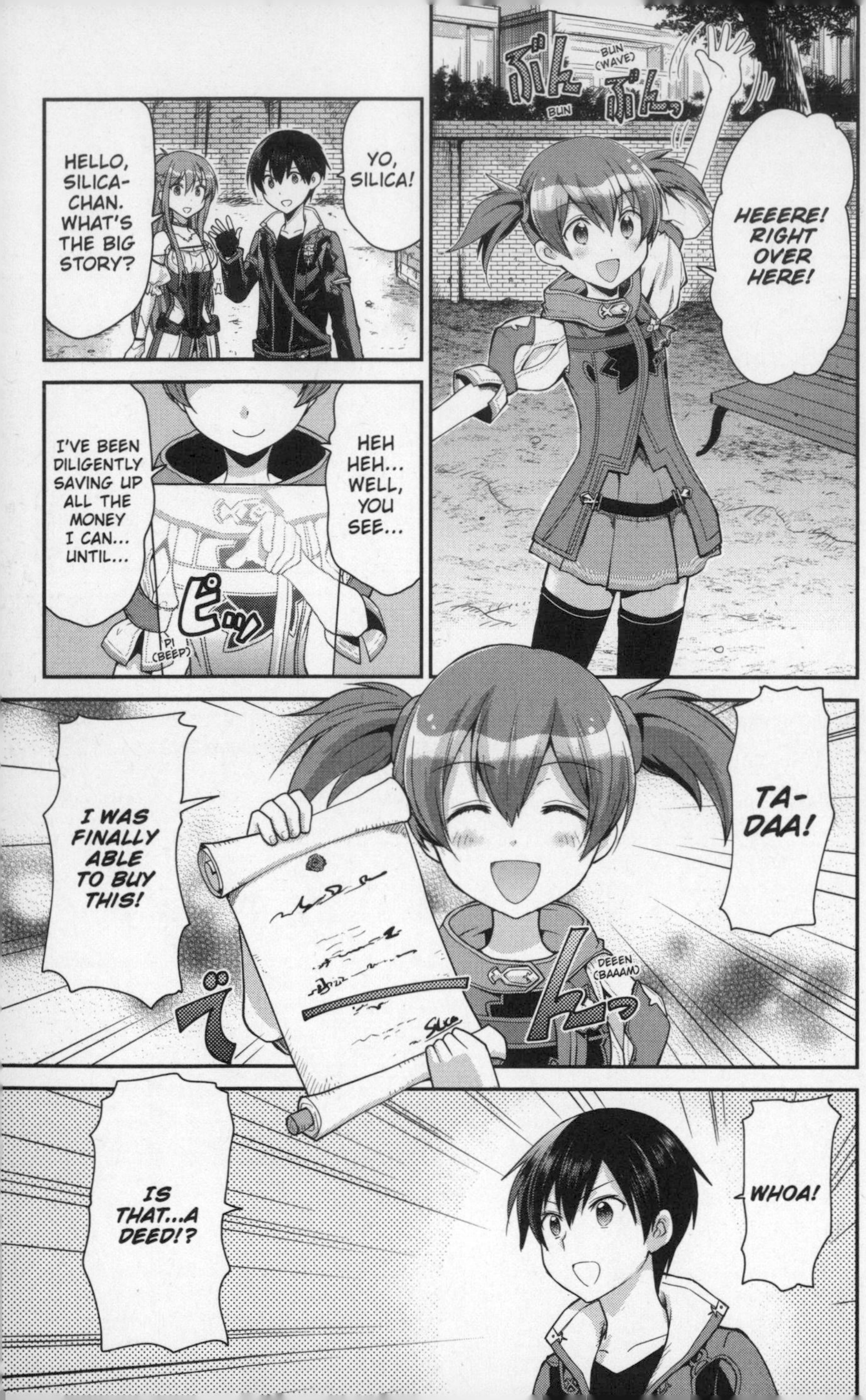
BUN (WAVE)
BUN
HEEERE! RIGHT OVER HERE!
YO, SILICA!
HELLO, SILICA-CHAN. WHAT'S THE BIG STORY?
HEH HEH... WELL, YOU SEE...
I'VE BEEN DILIGENTLY SAVING UP ALL THE MONEY I CAN... UNTIL...
PI (BEEP)
TA-DAA!
DEEEN (BAAAM)
I WAS FINALLY ABLE TO BUY THIS!
WHOA!
IS THAT...A DEED!?

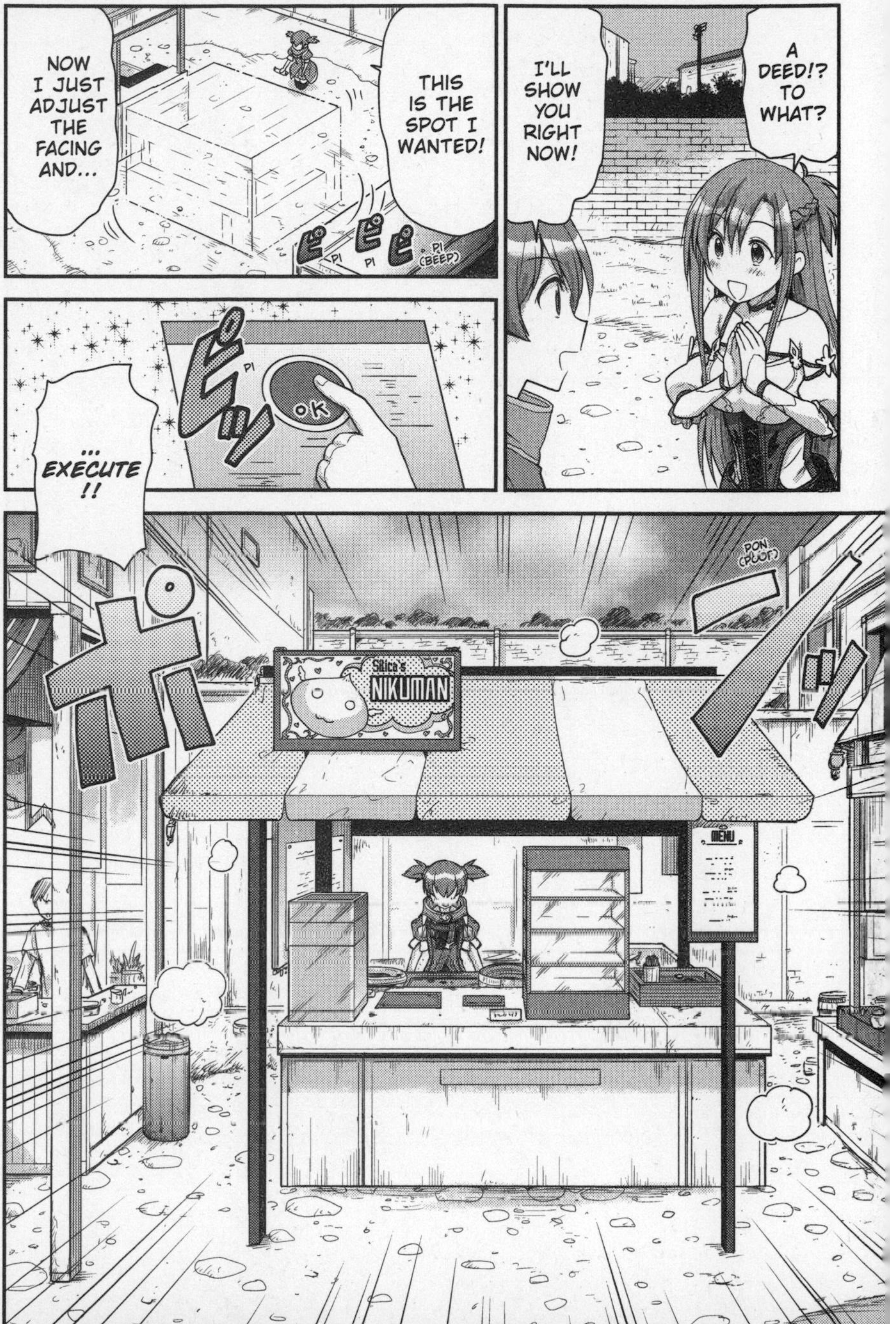
A DEED!? TO WHAT?
I'LL SHOW YOU RIGHT NOW!
THIS IS THE SPOT I WANTED!
NOW I JUST ADJUST THE FACING AND...
PI PI PI (BEEP)
PI
OK
...EXECUTE!!
PON (POOF)
Silica's NIKUMAN
MENU

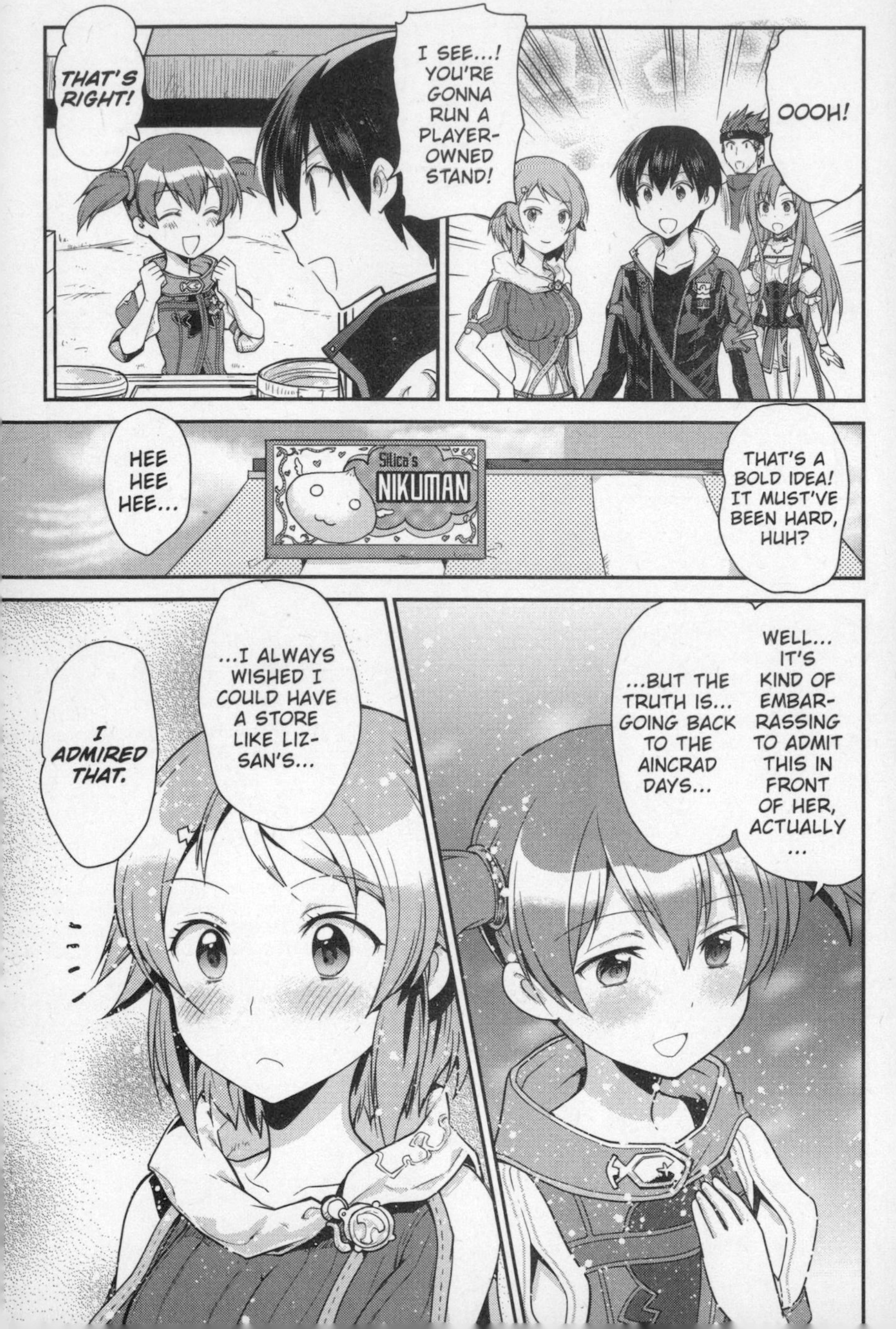
OOOH!
I SEE...! YOU'RE GONNA RUN A PLAYER-OWNED STAND!
THAT'S RIGHT!
THAT'S A BOLD IDEA! IT MUST'VE BEEN HARD, HUH?
Silica's NIKUMAN
HEE HEE HEE...
WELL... IT'S KIND OF EMBAR-RASSING TO ADMIT THIS IN FRONT OF HER, ACTUALLY...
...BUT THE TRUTH IS... GOING BACK TO THE AINCRAD DAYS...
...I ALWAYS WISHED I COULD HAVE A STORE LIKE LIZ-SAN'S...
I ADMIRED THAT.

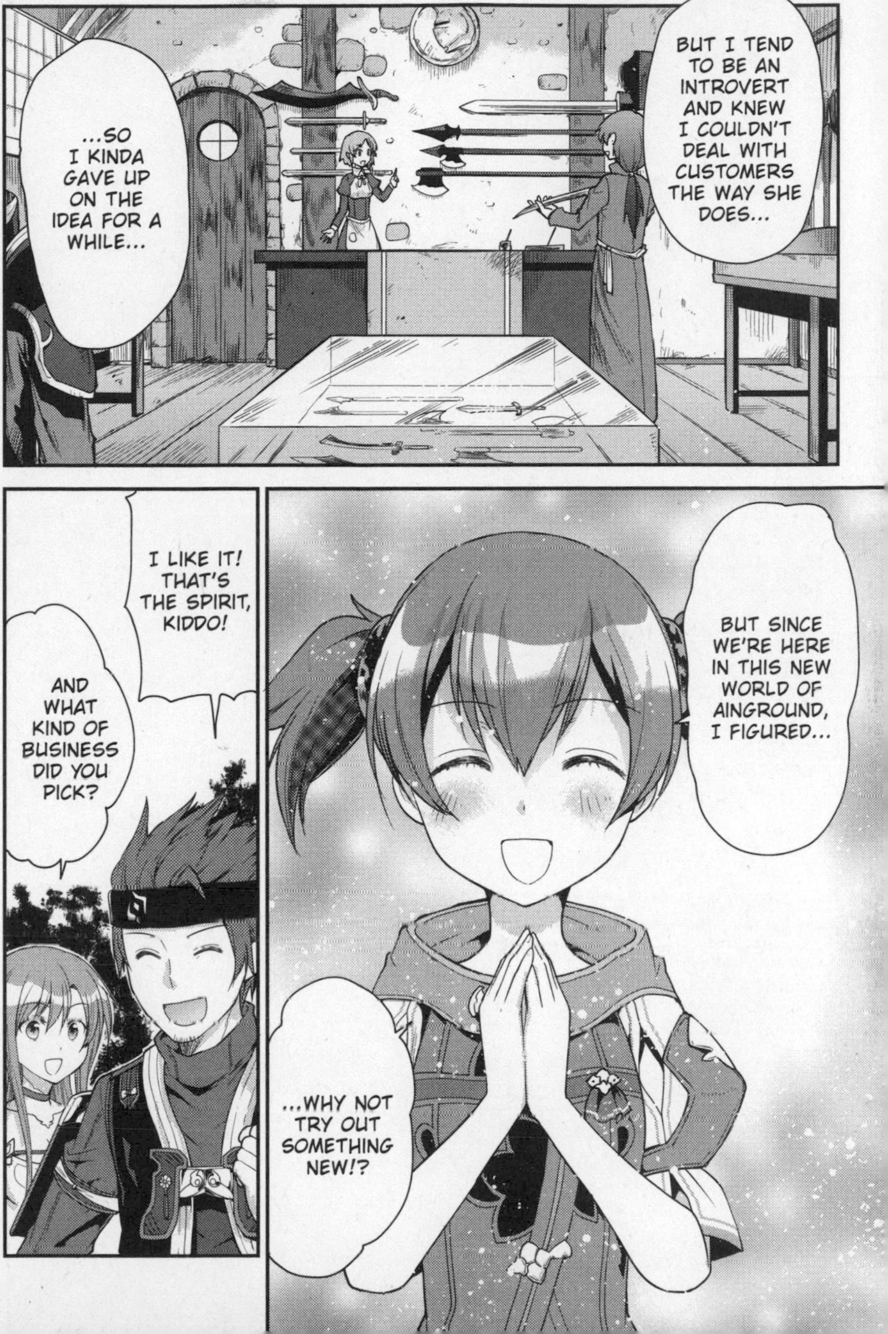
BUT I TEND TO BE AN INTROVERT AND KNEW I COULDN'T DEAL WITH CUSTOMERS THE WAY SHE DOES...
...SO I KINDA GAVE UP ON THE IDEA FOR A WHILE...
BUT SINCE WE'RE HERE IN THIS NEW WORLD OF AINGROUND, I FIGURED...
...WHY NOT TRY OUT SOMETHING NEW!?
I LIKE IT! THAT'S THE SPIRIT, KIDDO!
AND WHAT KIND OF BUSINESS DID YOU PICK?

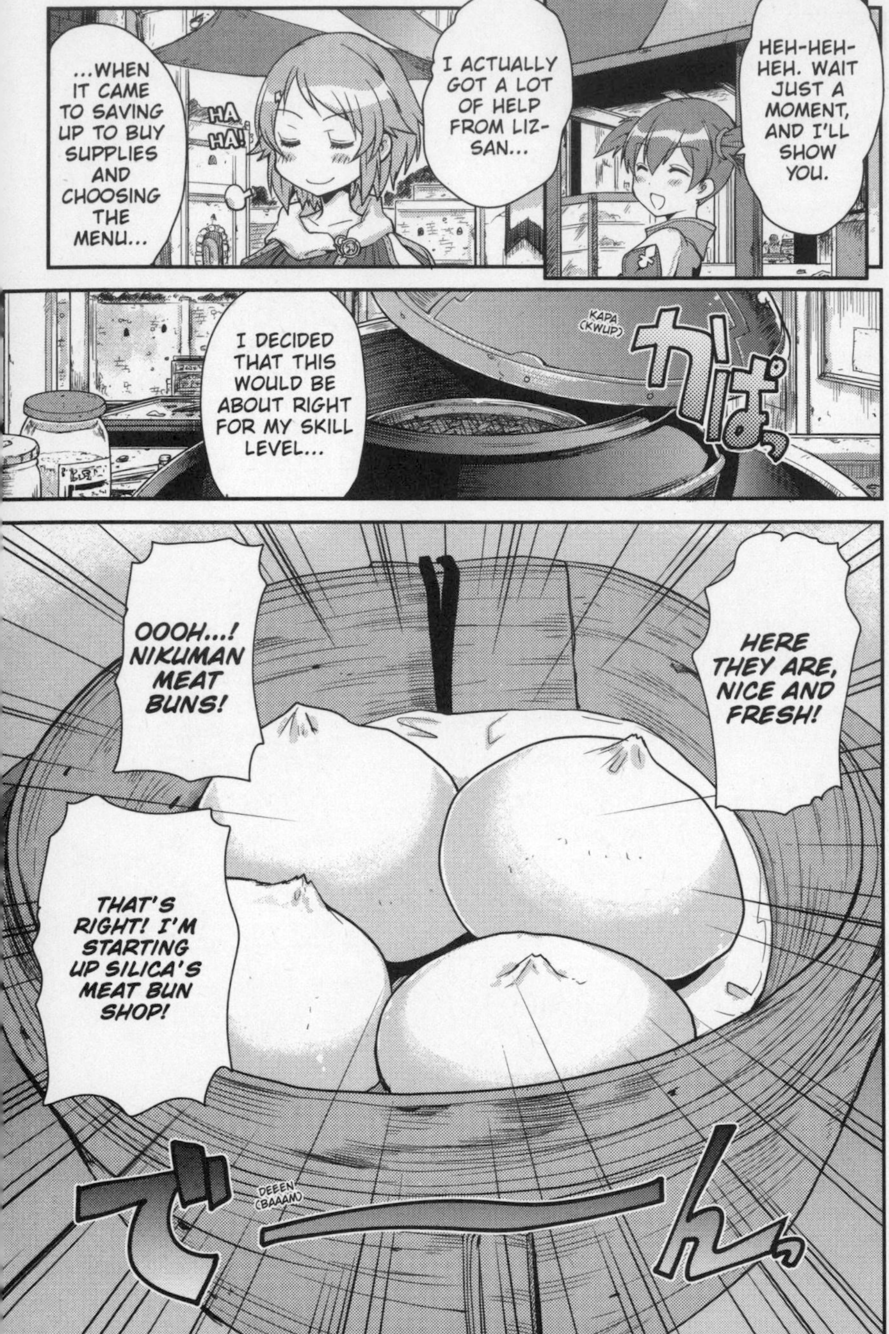
HEH-HEH-HEH. WAIT JUST A MOMENT, AND I'LL SHOW YOU.
I ACTUALLY GOT A LOT OF HELP FROM LIZ-SAN...
HA HA!
...WHEN IT CAME TO SAVING UP TO BUY SUPPLIES AND CHOOSING THE MENU...
かぱ
KAPA (KWUP)
I DECIDED THAT THIS WOULD BE ABOUT RIGHT FOR MY SKILL LEVEL...
HERE THEY ARE, NICE AND FRESH!
OOOH...! NIKUMAN MEAT BUNS!
THAT'S RIGHT! I'M STARTING UP SILICA'S MEAT BUN SHOP!
でーーん
DEEEN (BAAAM)

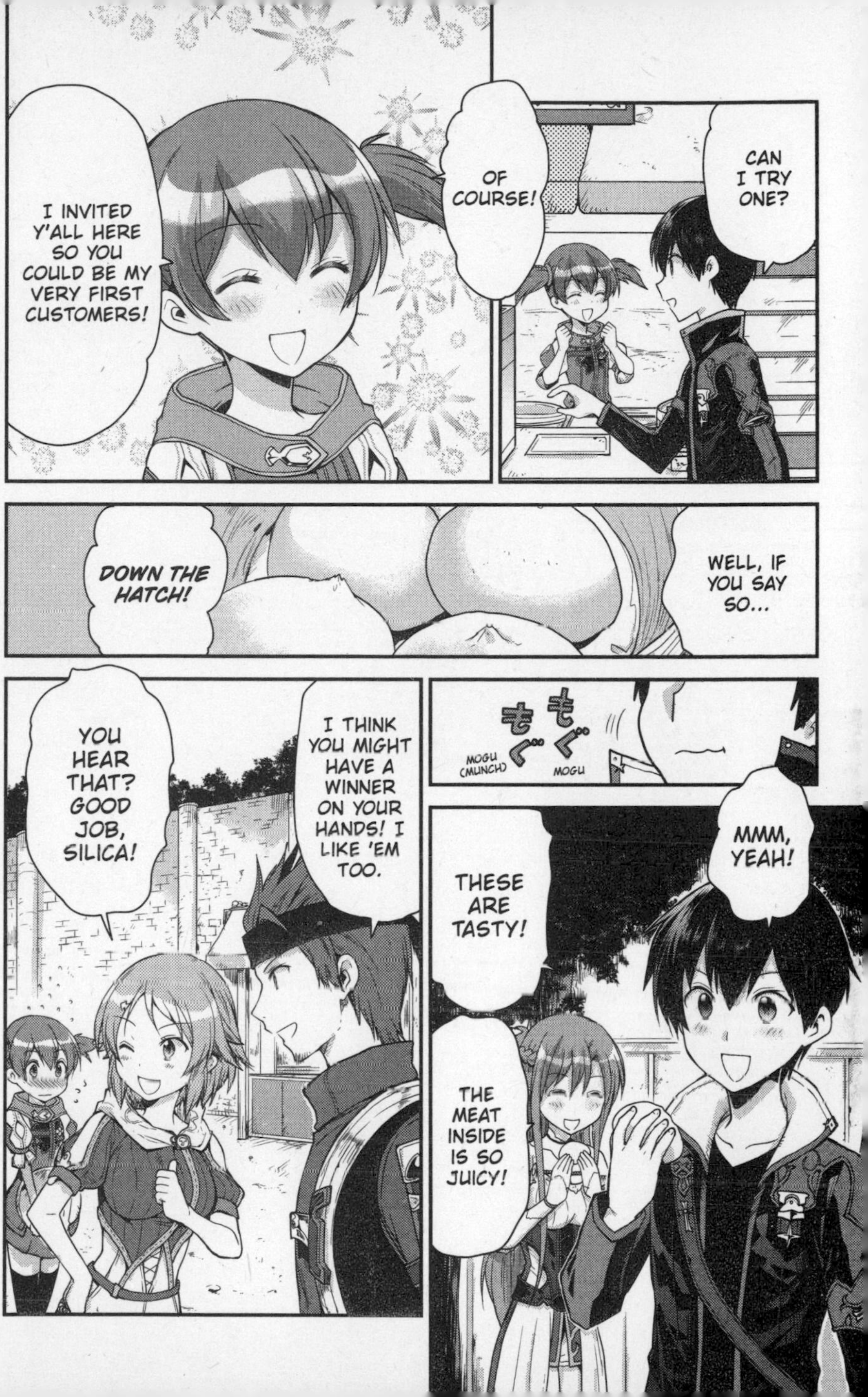
CAN I TRY ONE?
OF COURSE!
I INVITED Y'ALL HERE SO YOU COULD BE MY VERY FIRST CUSTOMERS!
WELL, IF YOU SAY SO...
DOWN THE HATCH!
もぐ
MOGU
もぐ
MOGU (MUNCH)
MMM, YEAH!
THESE ARE TASTY!
THE MEAT INSIDE IS SO JUICY!
I THINK YOU MIGHT HAVE A WINNER ON YOUR HANDS! I LIKE 'EM TOO.
YOU HEAR THAT? GOOD JOB, SILICA!

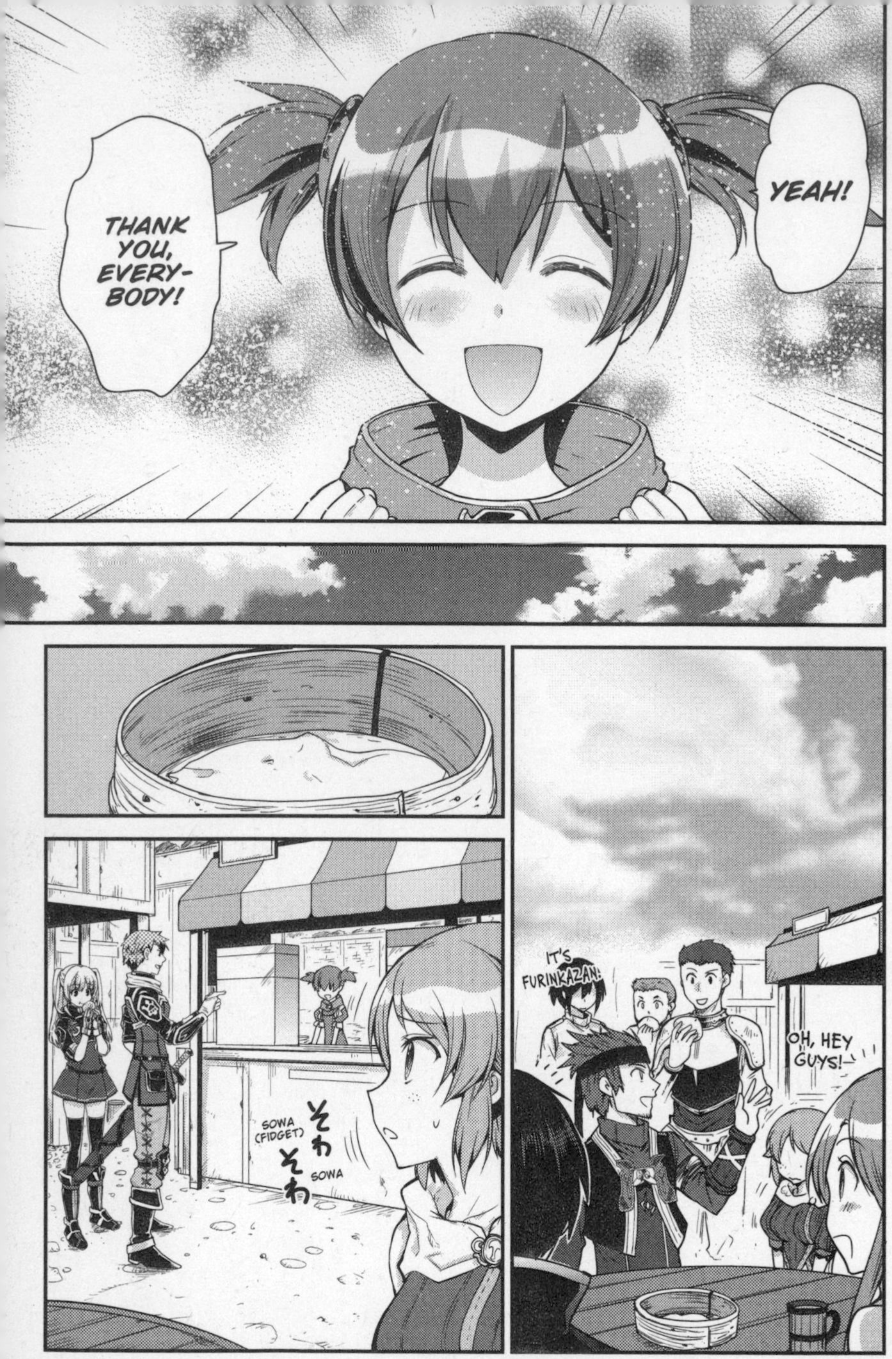
YEAH!
THANK YOU, EVERY-BODY!
IT'S FURINKAZAN!
OH, HEY GUYS!
そわ
SOWA (FIDGET)
そわ
SOWA

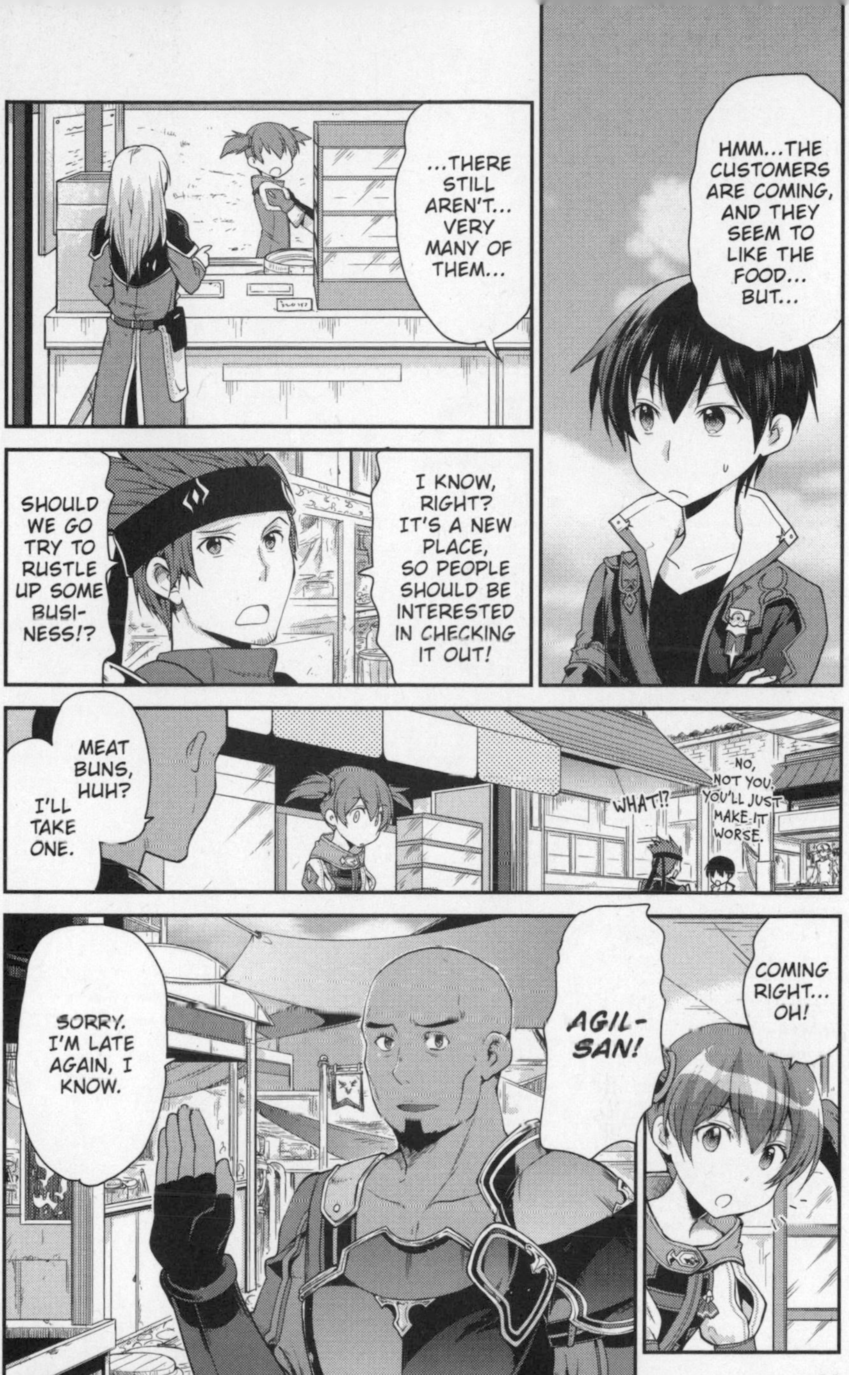
HMM...THE CUSTOMERS ARE COMING, AND THEY SEEM TO LIKE THE FOOD... BUT...
...THERE STILL AREN'T... VERY MANY OF THEM...
I KNOW, RIGHT? IT'S A NEW PLACE, SO PEOPLE SHOULD BE INTERESTED IN CHECKING IT OUT!
SHOULD WE GO TRY TO RUSTLE UP SOME BUSI-NESS!?
NO, NOT YOU. YOU'LL JUST MAKE IT WORSE.
WHAT!?
MEAT BUNS, HUH? I'LL TAKE ONE.
COMING RIGHT... OH!
AGIL-SAN!
SORRY. I'M LATE AGAIN, I KNOW.

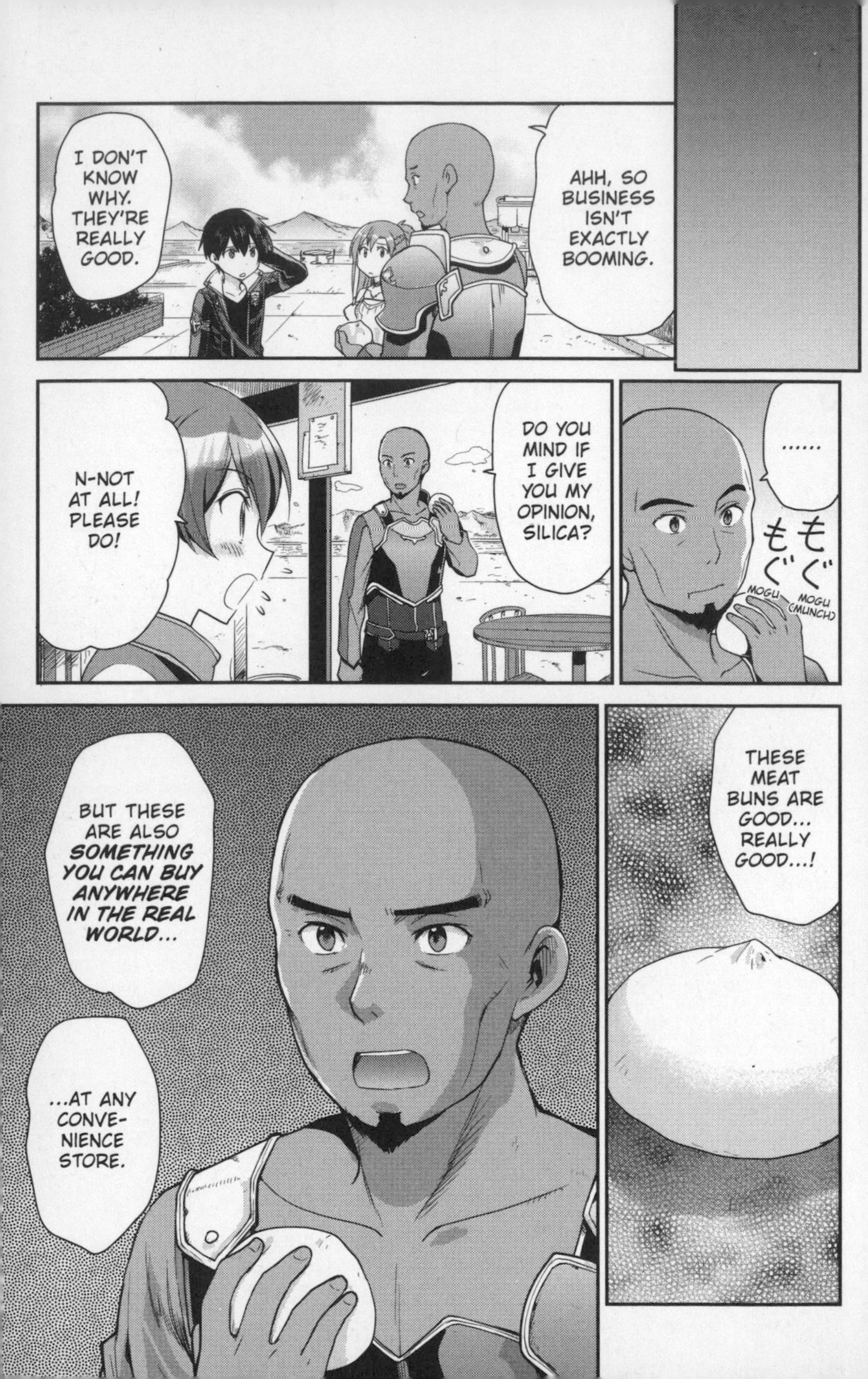
AHH, SO BUSINESS ISN'T EXACTLY BOOMING.
I DON'T KNOW WHY. THEY'RE REALLY GOOD.
......
もぐもぐ
MOGU MOGU (MUNCH)
DO YOU MIND IF I GIVE YOU MY OPINION, SILICA?
N-NOT AT ALL! PLEASE DO!
THESE MEAT BUNS ARE GOOD... REALLY GOOD...!
BUT THESE ARE ALSO *SOMETHING YOU CAN BUY ANYWHERE IN THE REAL WORLD*...
...AT ANY CONVE-NIENCE STORE.

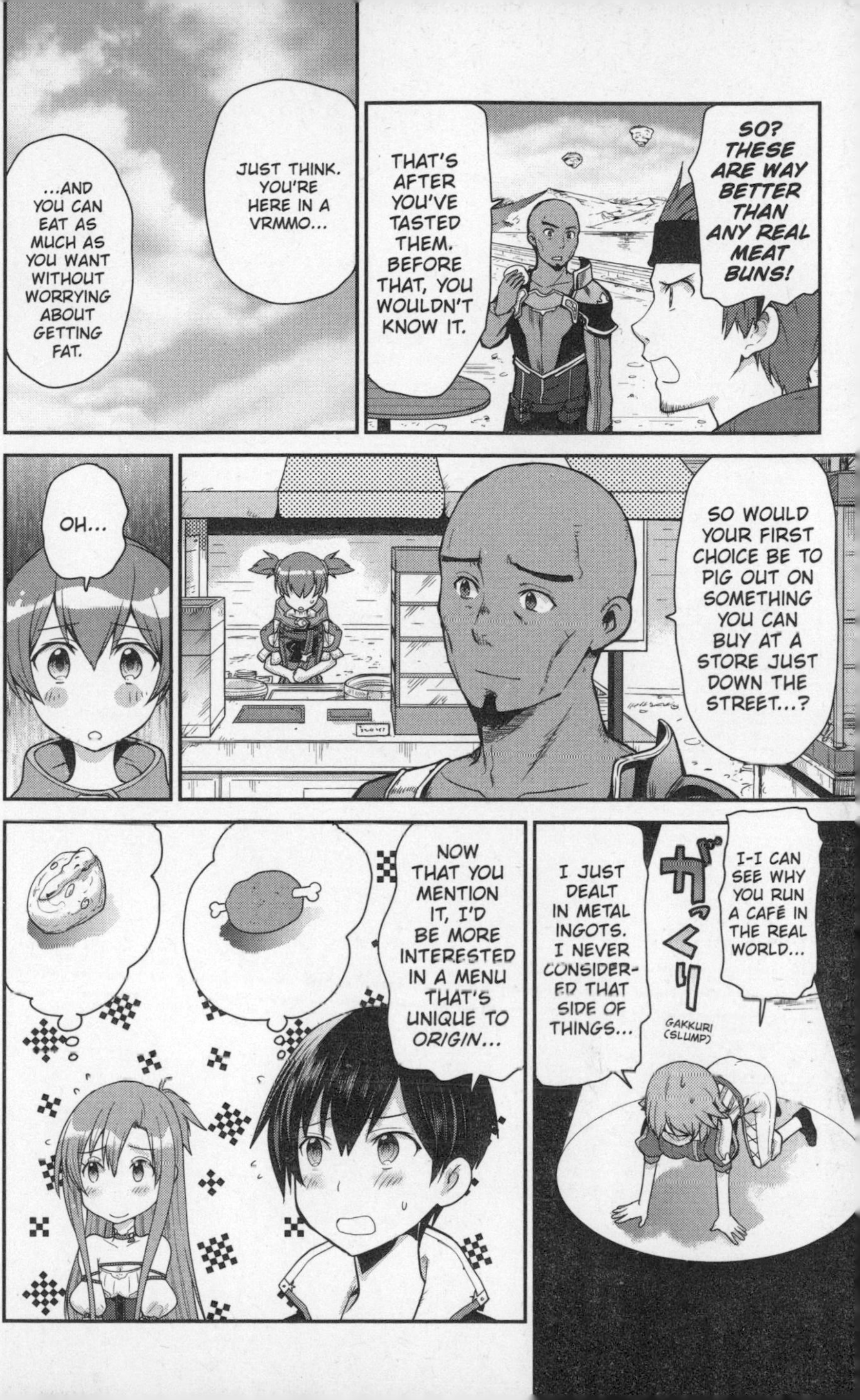
SO? THESE ARE WAY BETTER THAN ANY REAL MEAT BUNS!
THAT'S AFTER YOU'VE TASTED THEM. BEFORE THAT, YOU WOULDN'T KNOW IT.
JUST THINK. YOU'RE HERE IN A VRMMO...
...AND YOU CAN EAT AS MUCH AS YOU WANT WITHOUT WORRYING ABOUT GETTING FAT.
SO WOULD YOUR FIRST CHOICE BE TO PIG OUT ON SOMETHING YOU CAN BUY AT A STORE JUST DOWN THE STREET...?
OH...
I-I CAN SEE WHY YOU RUN A CAFÉ IN THE REAL WORLD...
I JUST DEALT IN METAL INGOTS. I NEVER CONSIDERED THAT SIDE OF THINGS...
GAKKURI (SLUMP)
NOW THAT YOU MENTION IT, I'D BE MORE INTERESTED IN A MENU THAT'S UNIQUE TO *ORIGIN*...

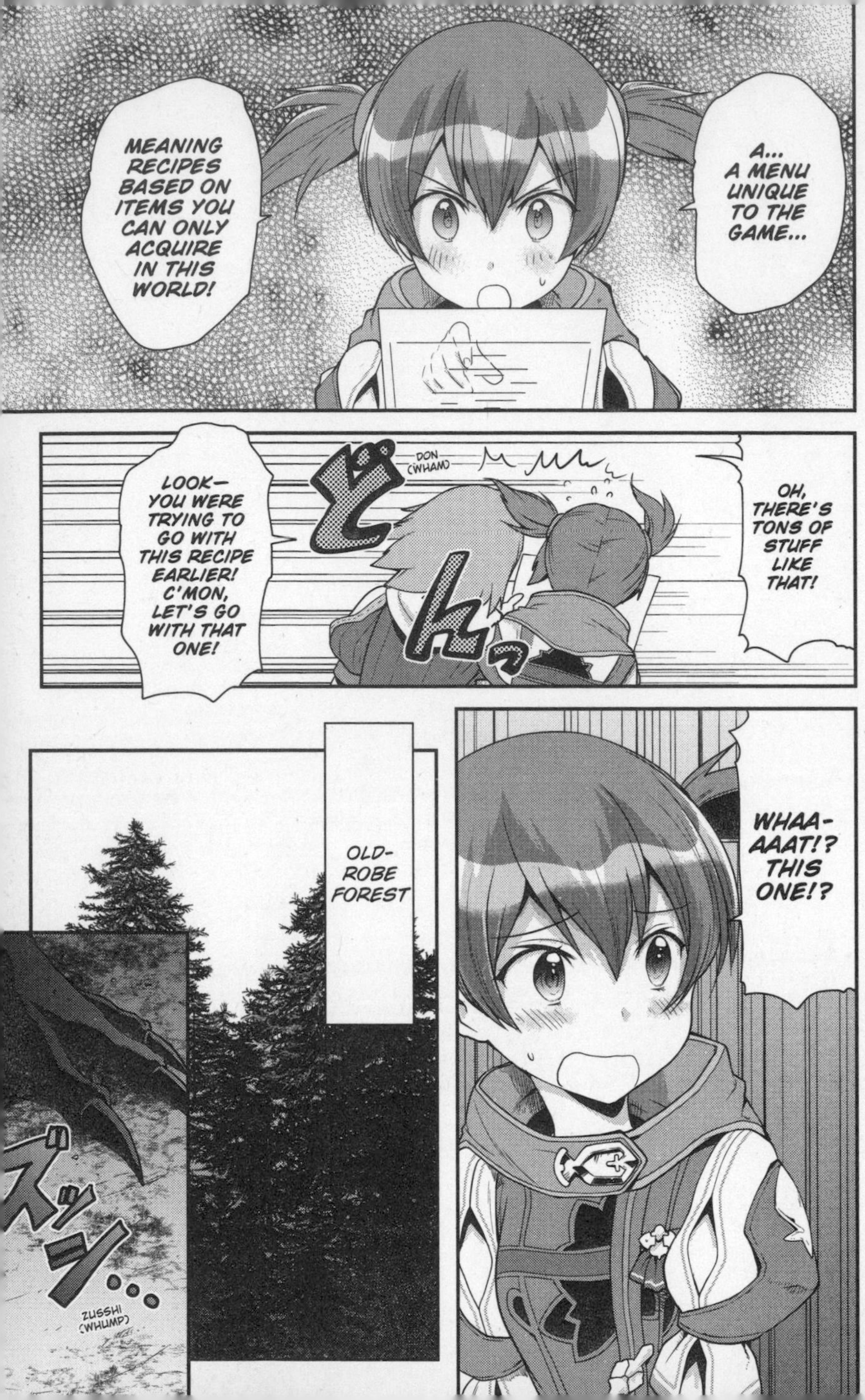
A... A MENU UNIQUE TO THE GAME...
MEANING RECIPES BASED ON ITEMS YOU CAN ONLY ACQUIRE IN THIS WORLD!
OH, THERE'S TONS OF STUFF LIKE THAT!
DON (WHAM)
LOOK— YOU WERE TRYING TO GO WITH THIS RECIPE EARLIER! C'MON, LET'S GO WITH THAT ONE!
WHAA-AAAT!? THIS ONE!?
OLD-ROBE FOREST
ZUSSHI (WHUMP)

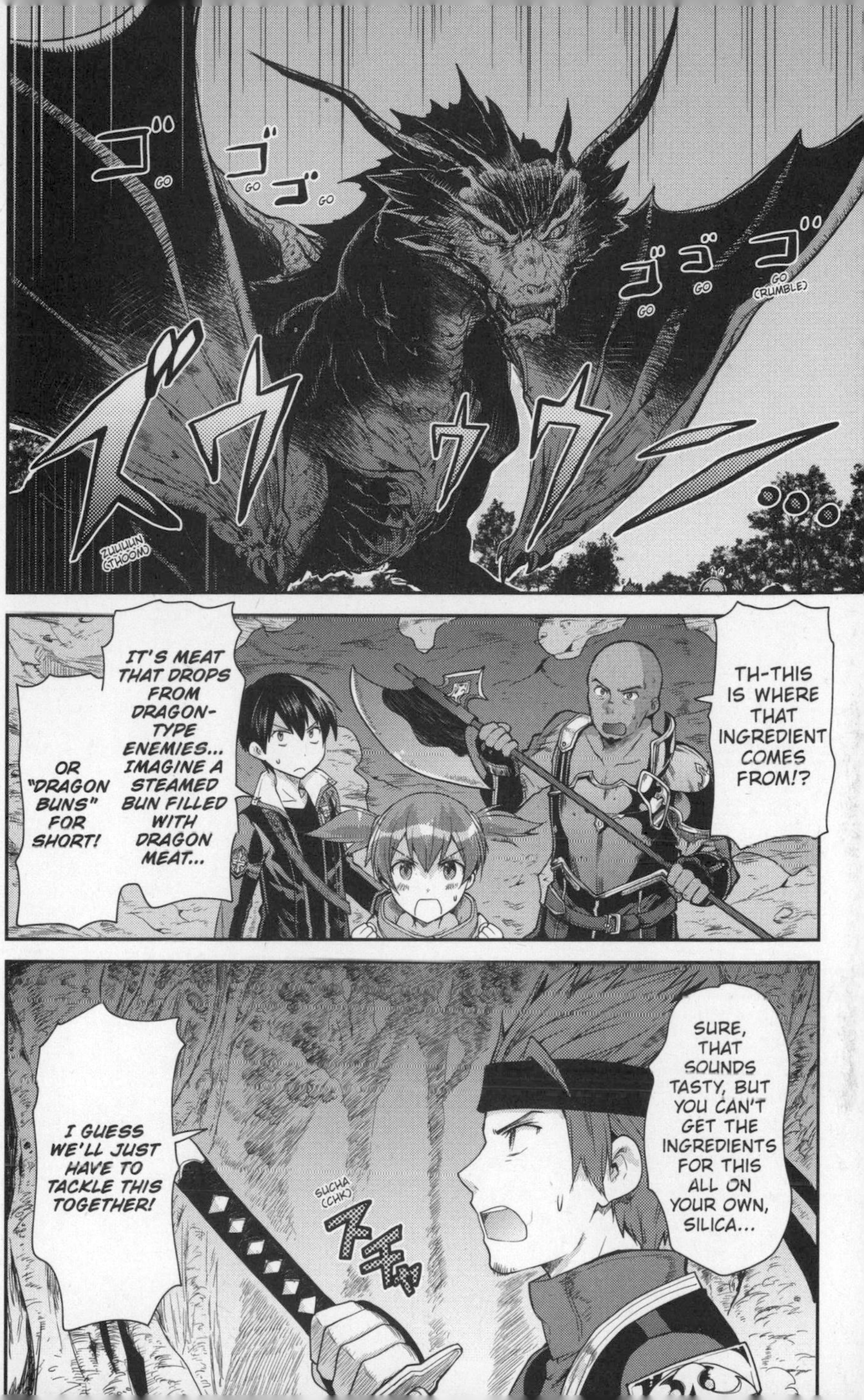
GO GO GO (RUMBLE)
GO GO GO
GO
ZUUUUN (THOOM)
TH-THIS IS WHERE THAT INGREDIENT COMES FROM!?
IT'S MEAT THAT DROPS FROM DRAGON-TYPE ENEMIES... IMAGINE A STEAMED BUN FILLED WITH DRAGON MEAT...
OR "DRAGON BUNS" FOR SHORT!
SURE, THAT SOUNDS TASTY, BUT YOU CAN'T GET THE INGREDIENTS FOR THIS ALL ON YOUR OWN, SILICA...
SUCHA (CHK)
I GUESS WE'LL JUST HAVE TO TACKLE THIS TOGETHER!

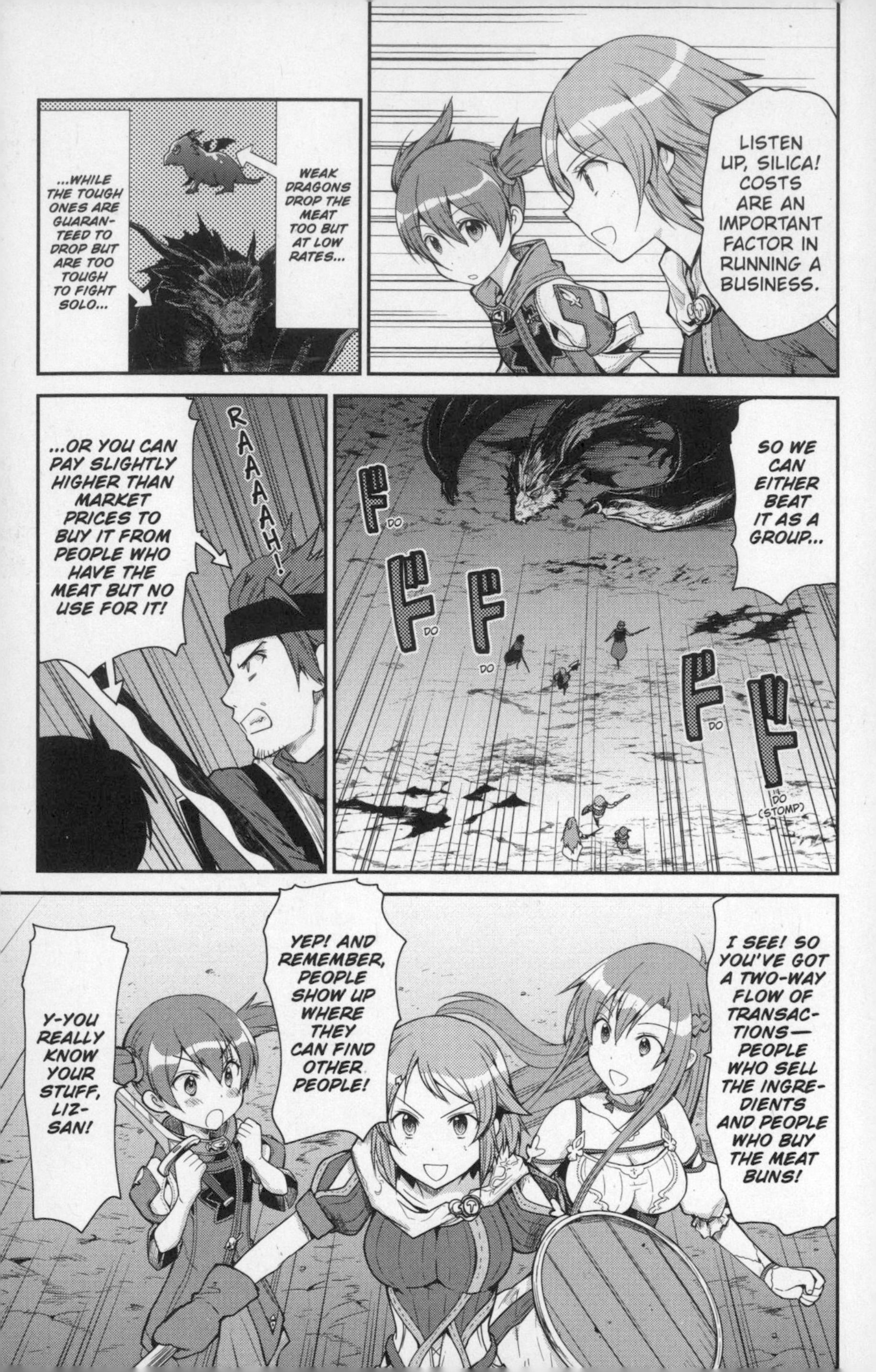
LISTEN UP, SILICA! COSTS ARE AN IMPORTANT FACTOR IN RUNNING A BUSINESS.
WEAK DRAGONS DROP THE MEAT TOO BUT AT LOW RATES...
...WHILE THE TOUGH ONES ARE GUARANTEED TO DROP BUT ARE TOO TOUGH TO FIGHT SOLO...
SO WE CAN EITHER BEAT IT AS A GROUP...
ド DO
ド DO
ド DO
ド DO
ド DO (STOMP)
RAAAAAH!
...OR YOU CAN PAY SLIGHTLY HIGHER THAN MARKET PRICES TO BUY IT FROM PEOPLE WHO HAVE THE MEAT BUT NO USE FOR IT!
I SEE! SO YOU'VE GOT A TWO-WAY FLOW OF TRANSACTIONS—PEOPLE WHO SELL THE INGREDIENTS AND PEOPLE WHO BUY THE MEAT BUNS!
YEP! AND REMEMBER, PEOPLE SHOW UP WHERE THEY CAN FIND OTHER PEOPLE!
Y-YOU REALLY KNOW YOUR STUFF, LIZ-SAN!

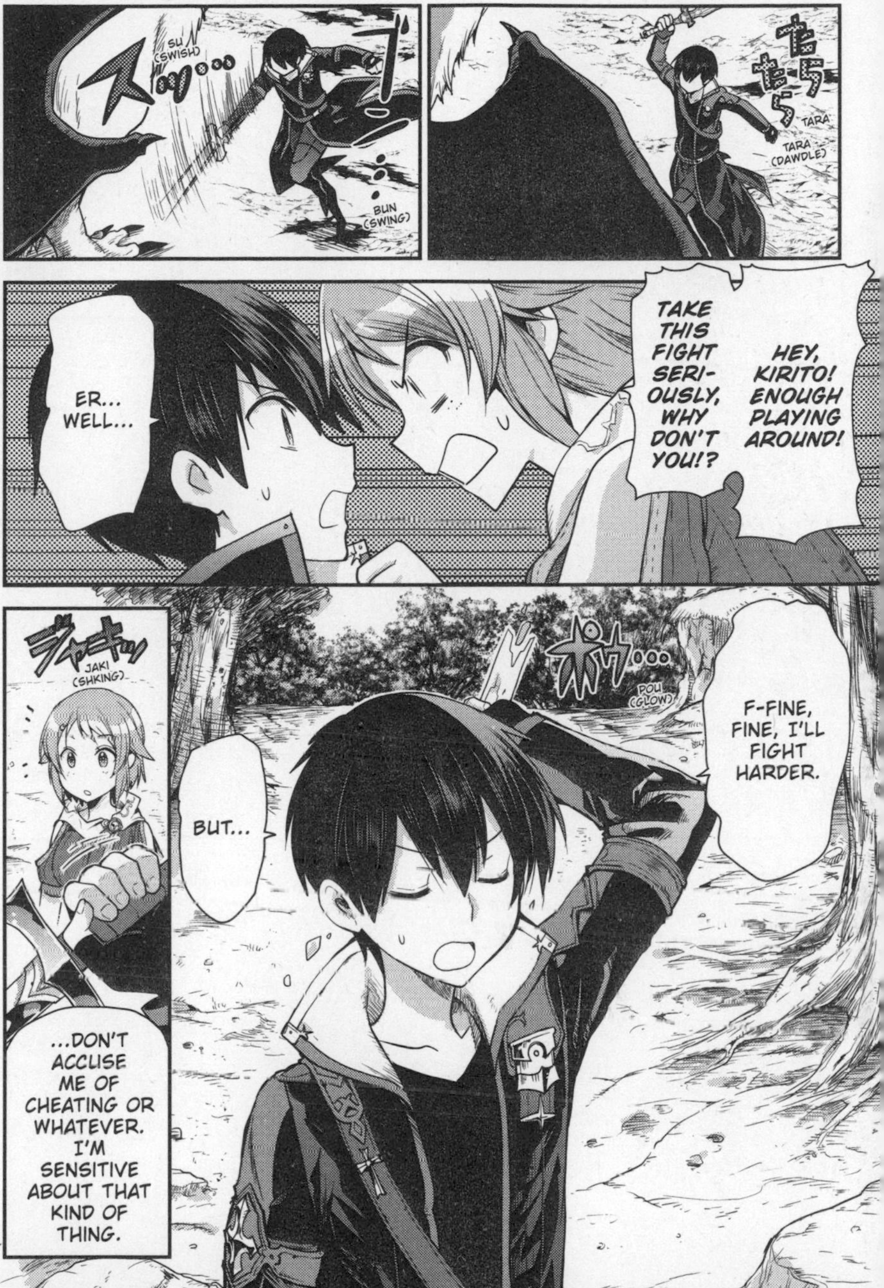
TARA
TARA
(DAWDLE)
SU
(SWISH)...
BUN
(SWING)
HEY, KIRITO! ENOUGH PLAYING AROUND!
TAKE THIS FIGHT SERI-OUSLY, WHY DON'T YOU!?
ER... WELL...
POU
(GLOW)
F-FINE, FINE, I'LL FIGHT HARDER.
BUT...
JAKI
(SHKING)
...DON'T ACCUSE ME OF CHEATING OR WHATEVER. I'M SENSITIVE ABOUT THAT KIND OF THING.

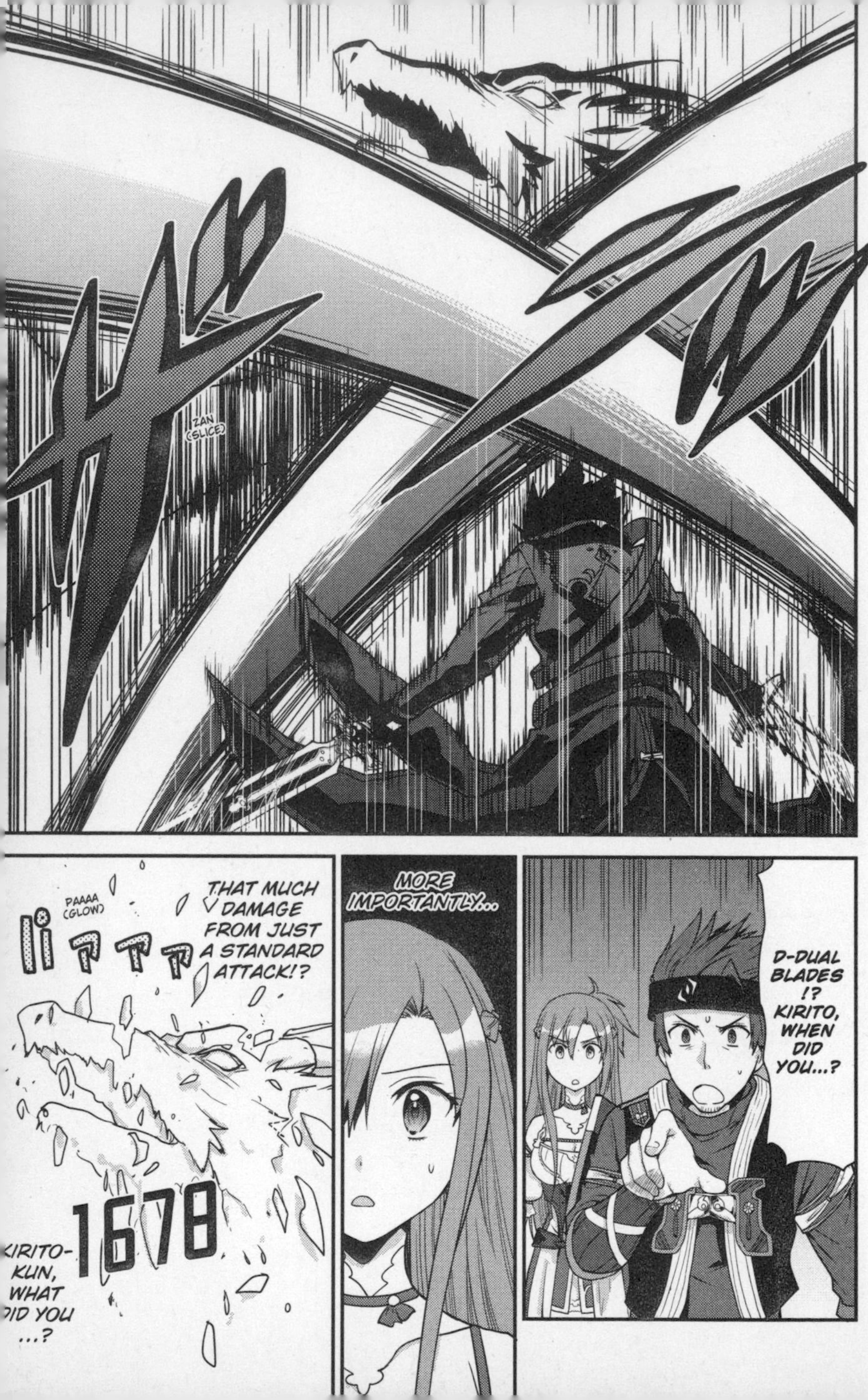
ZAN (SLICE)
D-DUAL BLADES!? KIRITO, WHEN DID YOU...?
MORE IMPORTANTLY...
THAT MUCH DAMAGE FROM JUST A STANDARD ATTACK!?
PAAAA (GLOW)
1678
KIRITO-KUN, WHAT DID YOU ...?

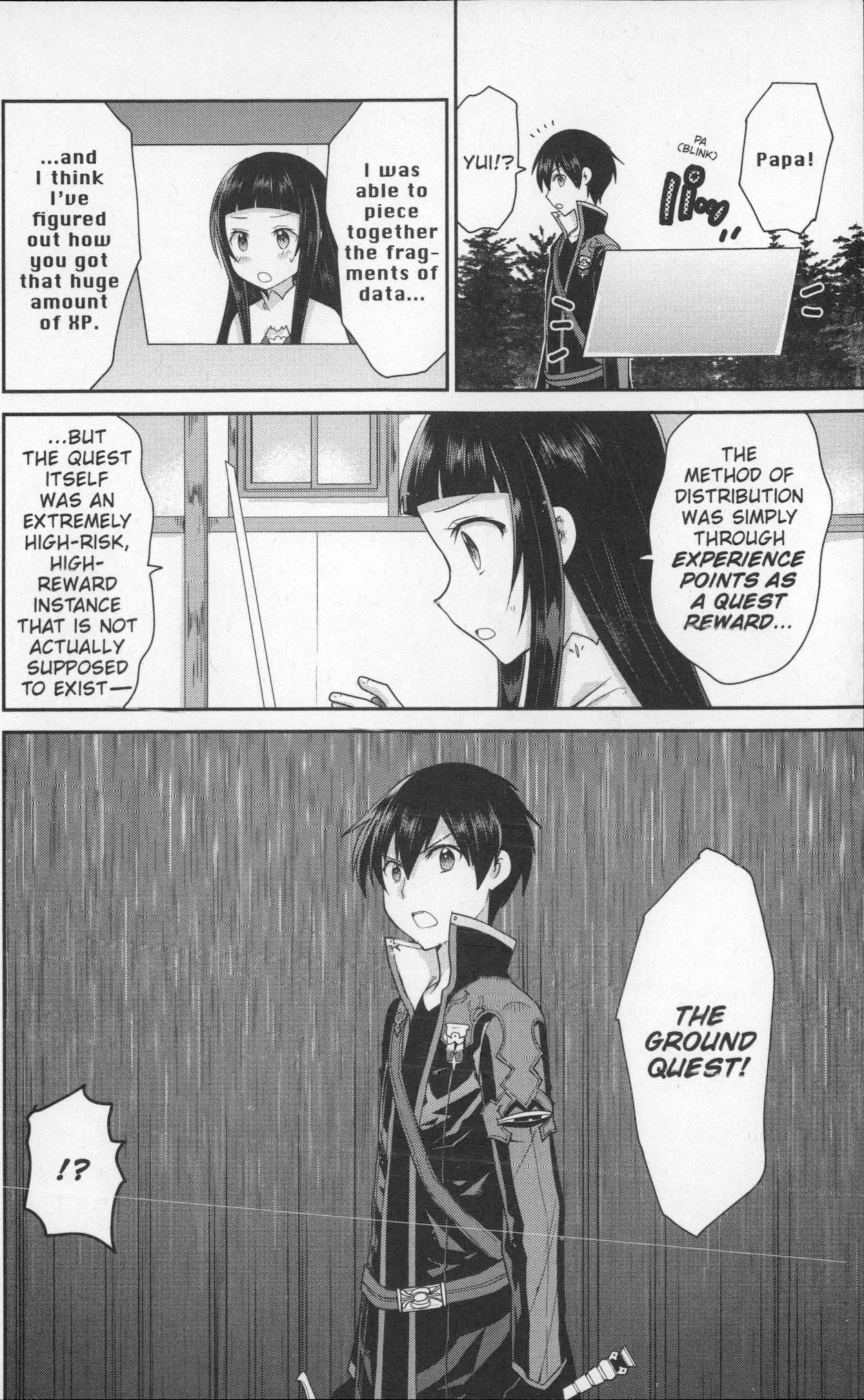
Papa!
PA (BLINK)
YUI!?
I was able to piece together the frag-ments of data...
...and I think I've figured out how you got that huge amount of XP.
THE METHOD OF DISTRIBUTION WAS SIMPLY THROUGH *EXPERIENCE POINTS AS A QUEST REWARD*...
...BUT THE QUEST ITSELF WAS AN EXTREMELY HIGH-RISK, HIGH-REWARD INSTANCE THAT IS NOT ACTUALLY SUPPOSED TO EXIST—
THE GROUND QUEST!
!?

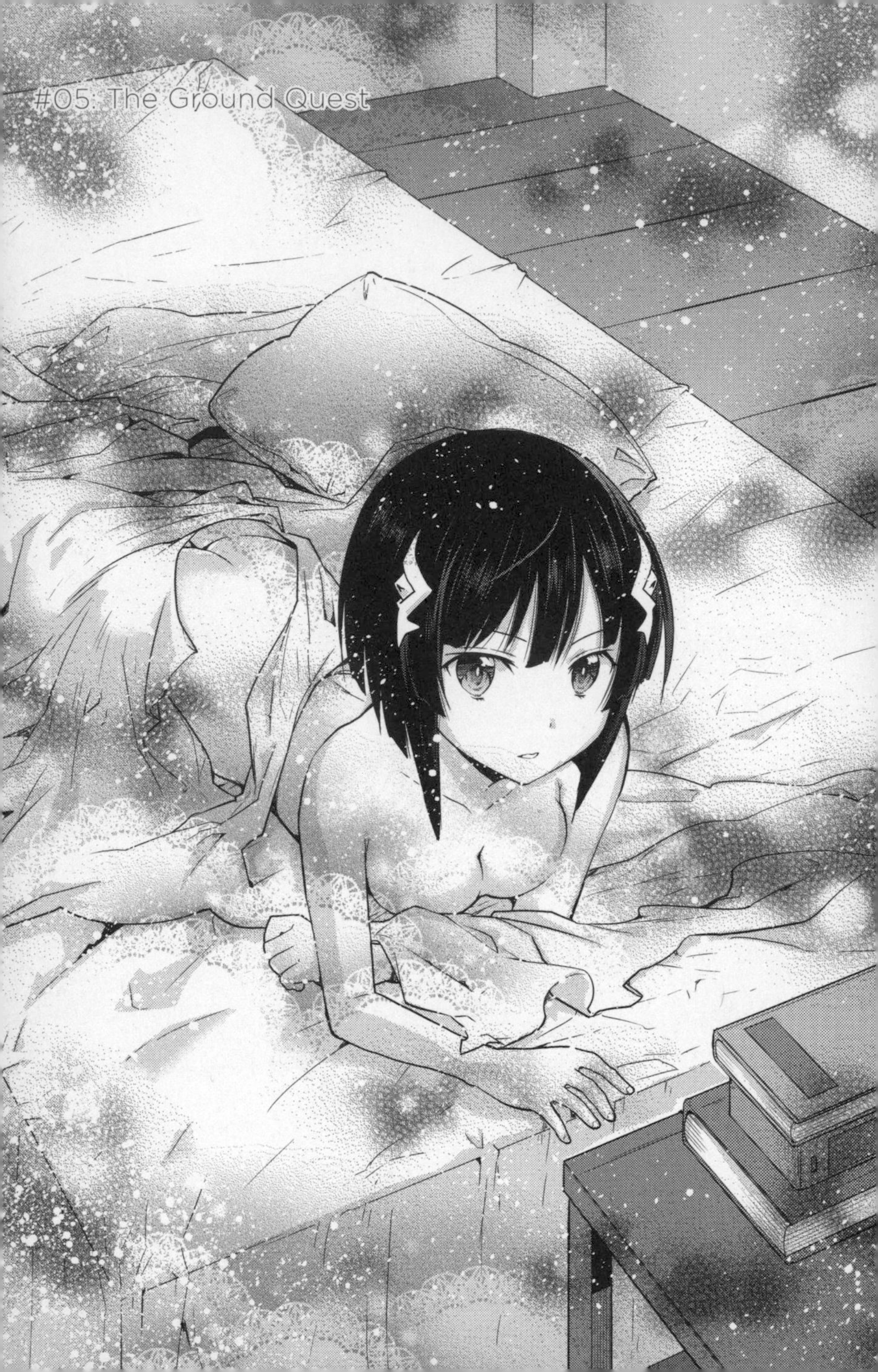
#05: The Ground Quest

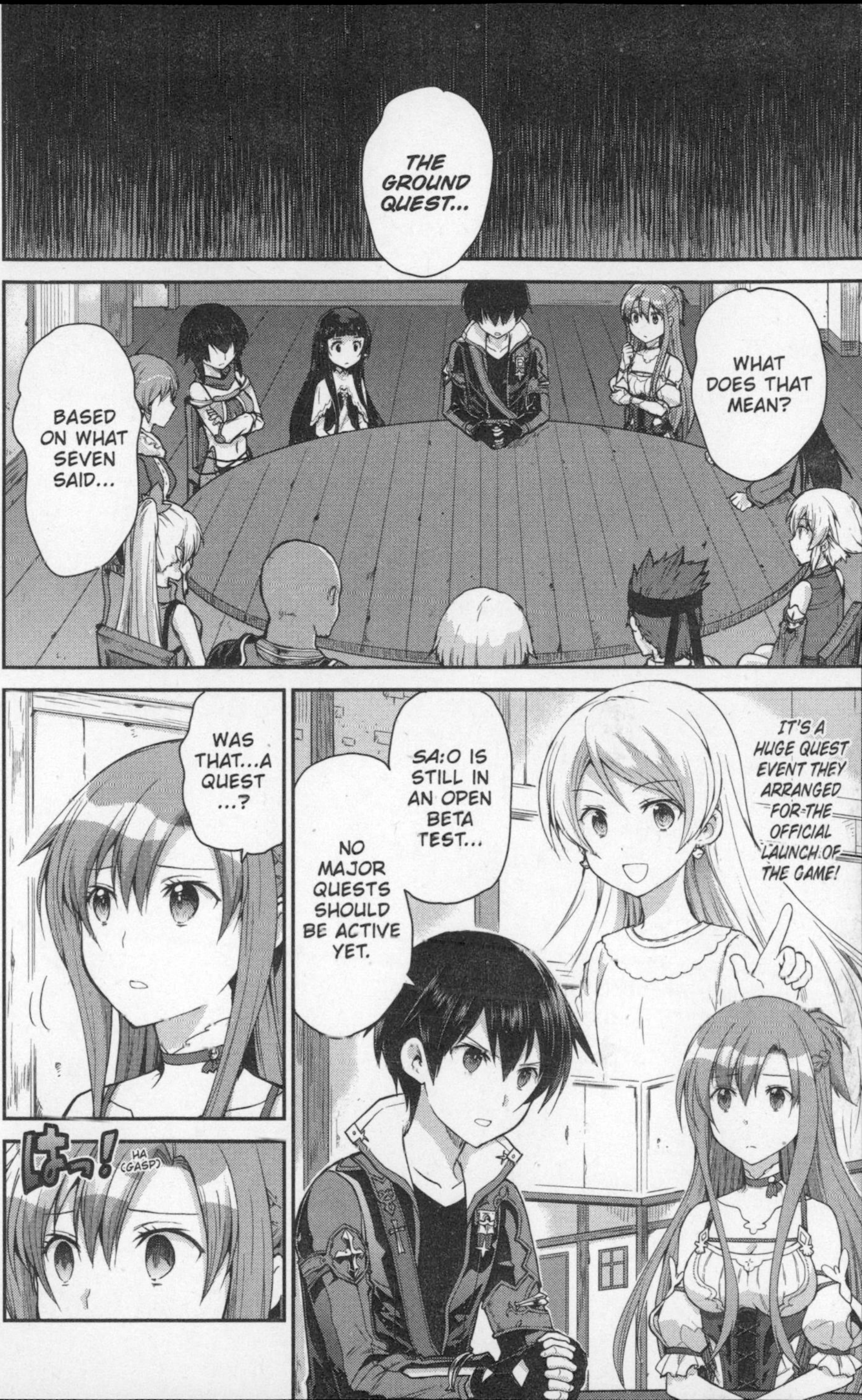
THE GROUND QUEST...
WHAT DOES THAT MEAN?
BASED ON WHAT SEVEN SAID...
IT'S A HUGE QUEST EVENT THEY ARRANGED FOR THE OFFICIAL LAUNCH OF THE GAME!
SA:O IS STILL IN AN OPEN BETA TEST...
NO MAJOR QUESTS SHOULD BE ACTIVE YET.
WAS THAT...A QUEST ...?
はっ!
HA (GASP)

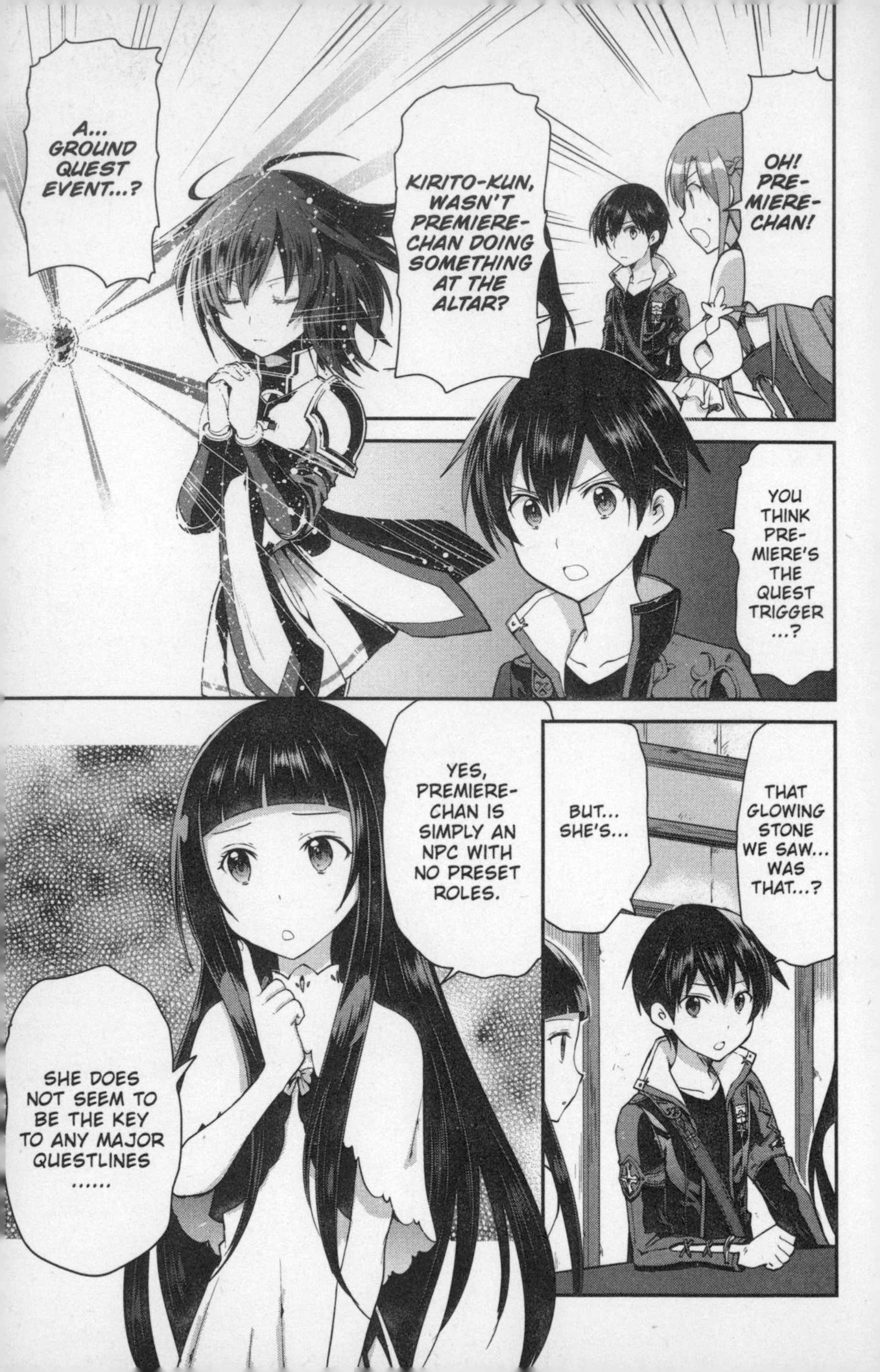
OH! PRE-MIERE-CHAN!
KIRITO-KUN, WASN'T PREMIERE-CHAN DOING SOMETHING AT THE ALTAR?
A... GROUND QUEST EVENT...?
YOU THINK PRE-MIERE'S THE QUEST TRIGGER ...?
THAT GLOWING STONE WE SAW... WAS THAT...?
BUT... SHE'S...
YES, PREMIERE-CHAN IS SIMPLY AN NPC WITH NO PRESET ROLES.
SHE DOES NOT SEEM TO BE THE KEY TO ANY MAJOR QUESTLINES ......

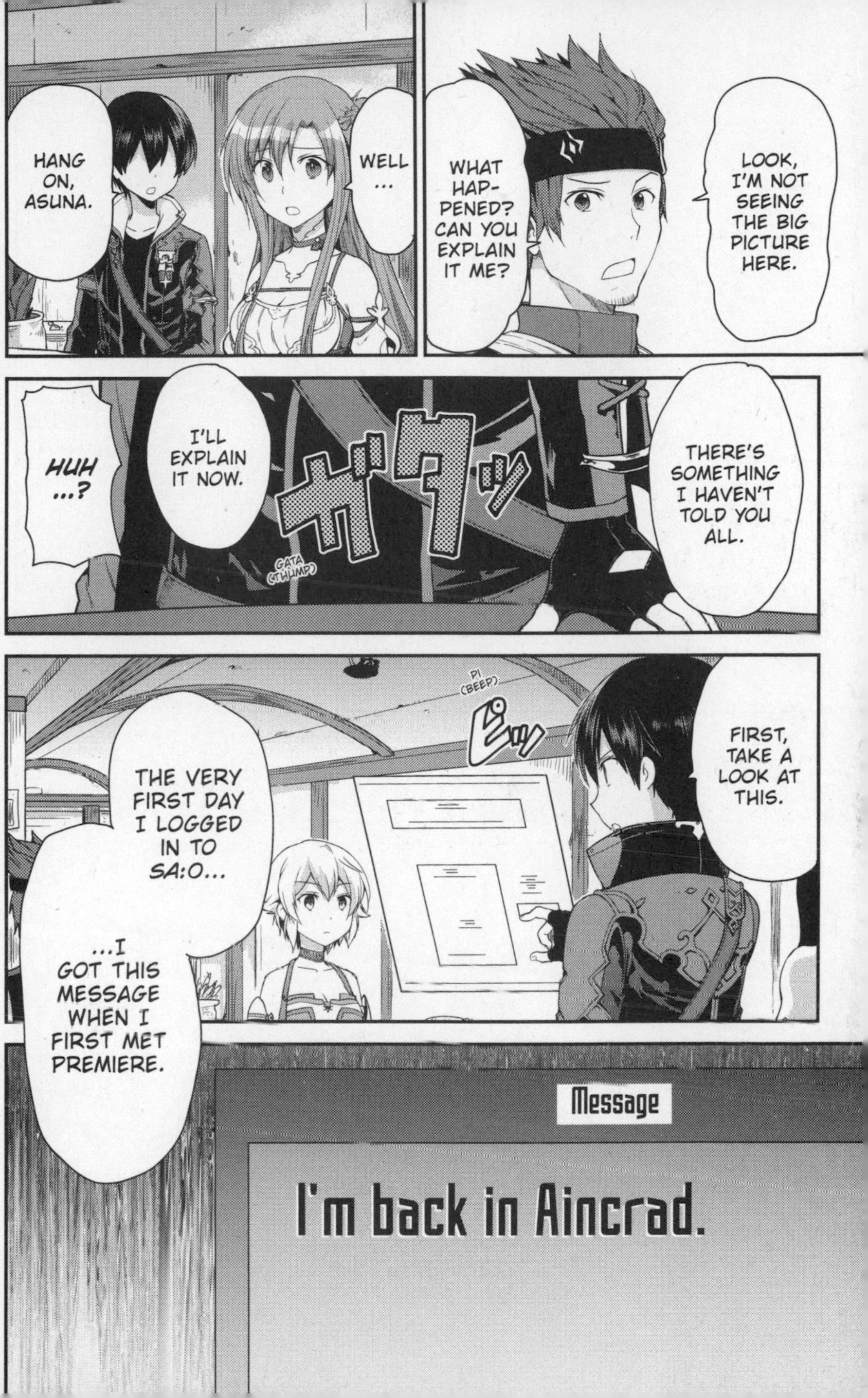
LOOK, I'M NOT SEEING THE BIG PICTURE HERE.
WHAT HAPPENED? CAN YOU EXPLAIN IT ME?
WELL...
HANG ON, ASUNA.
THERE'S SOMETHING I HAVEN'T TOLD YOU ALL.
GATA (THUMP)
I'LL EXPLAIN IT NOW.
HUH...?
PI (BEEP)
FIRST, TAKE A LOOK AT THIS.
THE VERY FIRST DAY I LOGGED IN TO SA:O...
...I GOT THIS MESSAGE WHEN I FIRST MET PREMIERE.
Message
I'm back in Aincrad.

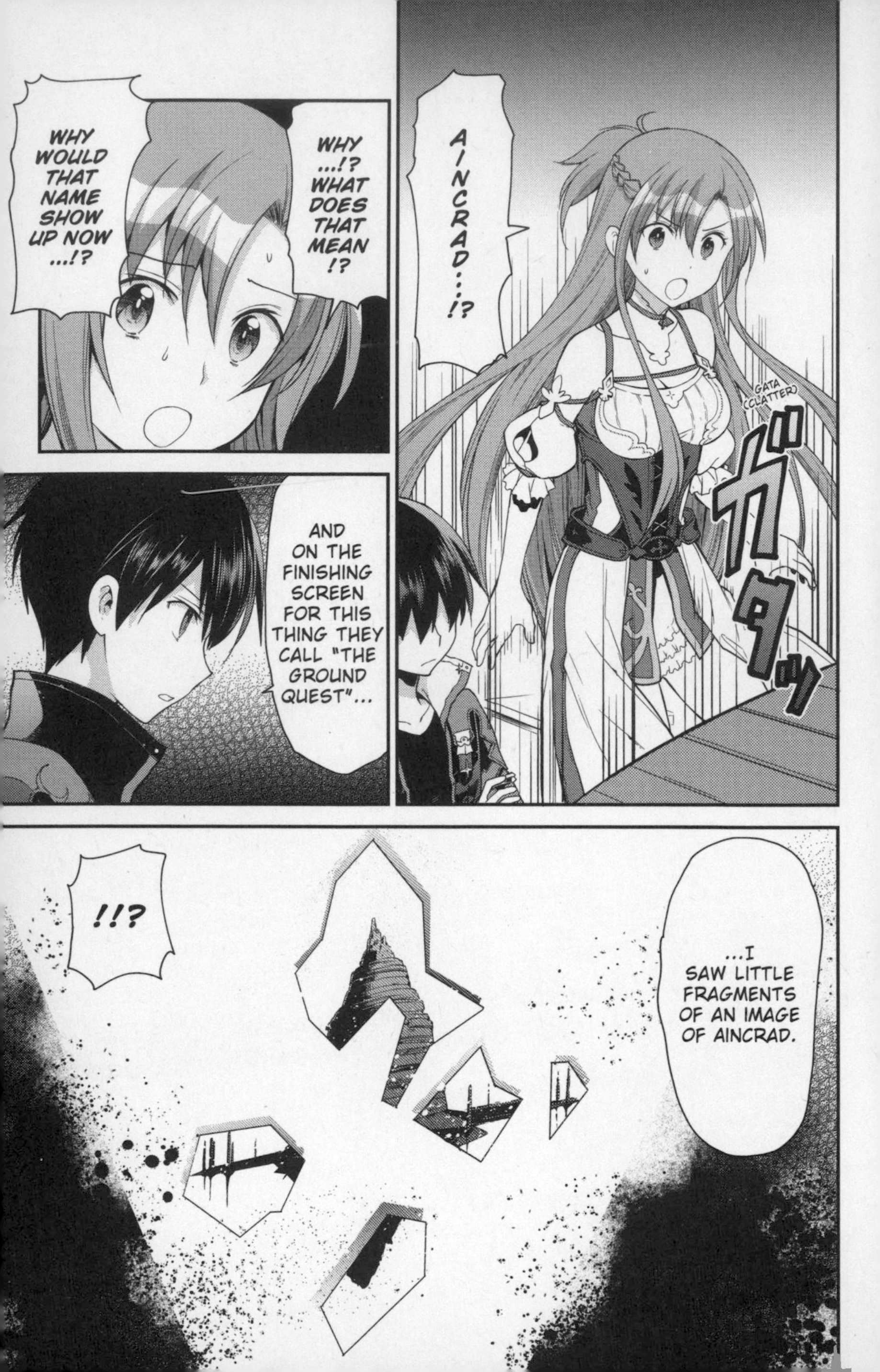
AINCRAD...!?
GATA (CLATTER)
ガタッ
WHY ...!? WHAT DOES THAT MEAN !?
WHY WOULD THAT NAME SHOW UP NOW ...!?
AND ON THE FINISHING SCREEN FOR THIS THING THEY CALL "THE GROUND QUEST"...
...I SAW LITTLE FRAGMENTS OF AN IMAGE OF AINCRAD.
!!?

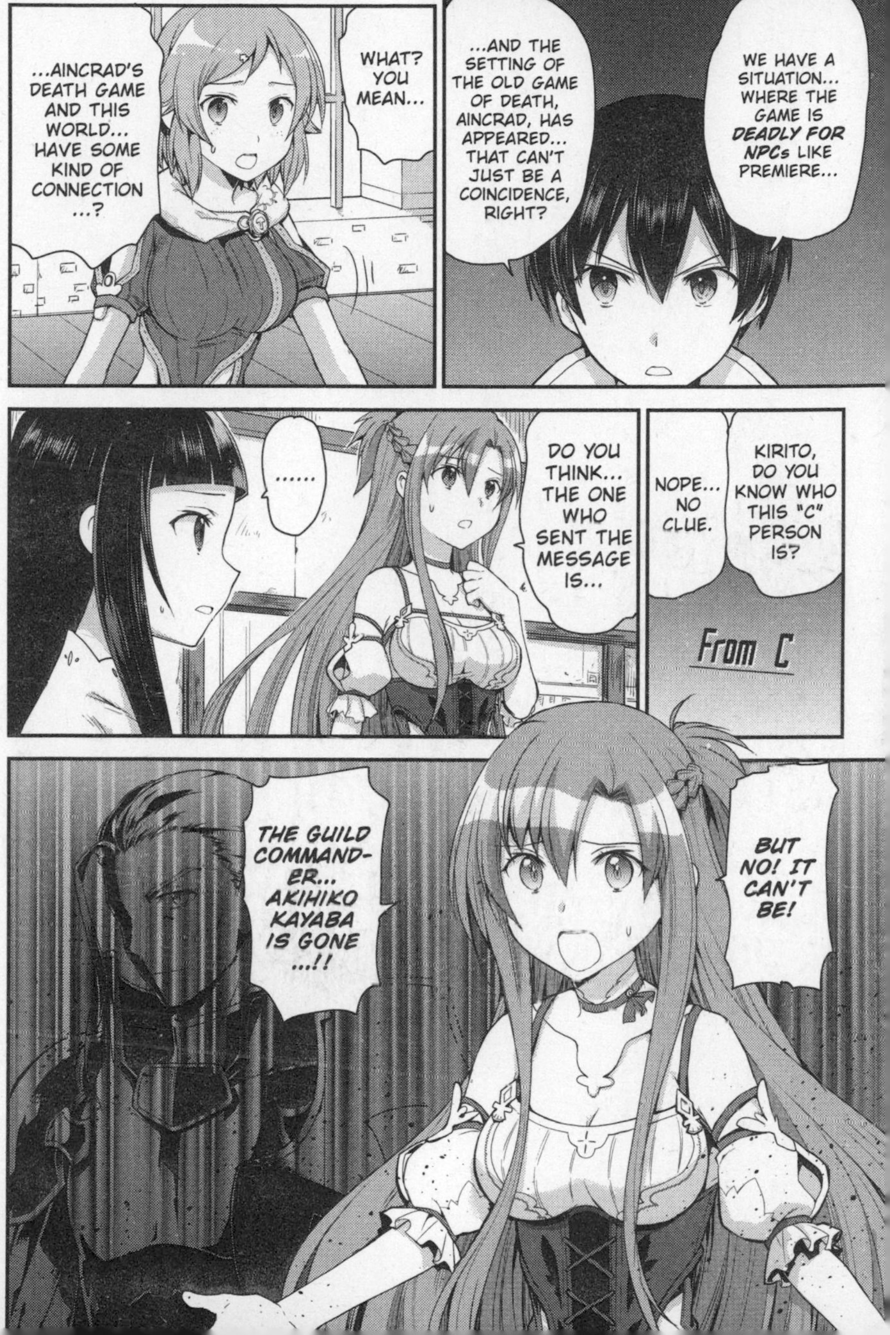
WE HAVE A SITUATION... WHERE THE GAME IS DEADLY FOR NPCs LIKE PREMIERE...
...AND THE SETTING OF THE OLD GAME OF DEATH, AINCRAD, HAS APPEARED... THAT CAN'T JUST BE A COINCIDENCE, RIGHT?
WHAT? YOU MEAN...
...AINCRAD'S DEATH GAME AND THIS WORLD... HAVE SOME KIND OF CONNECTION ...?
KIRITO, DO YOU KNOW WHO THIS "C" PERSON IS?
NOPE... NO CLUE.
From C
DO YOU THINK... THE ONE WHO SENT THE MESSAGE IS...
......
BUT NO! IT CAN'T BE!
THE GUILD COMMANDER... AKIHIKO KAYABA IS GONE ...!!

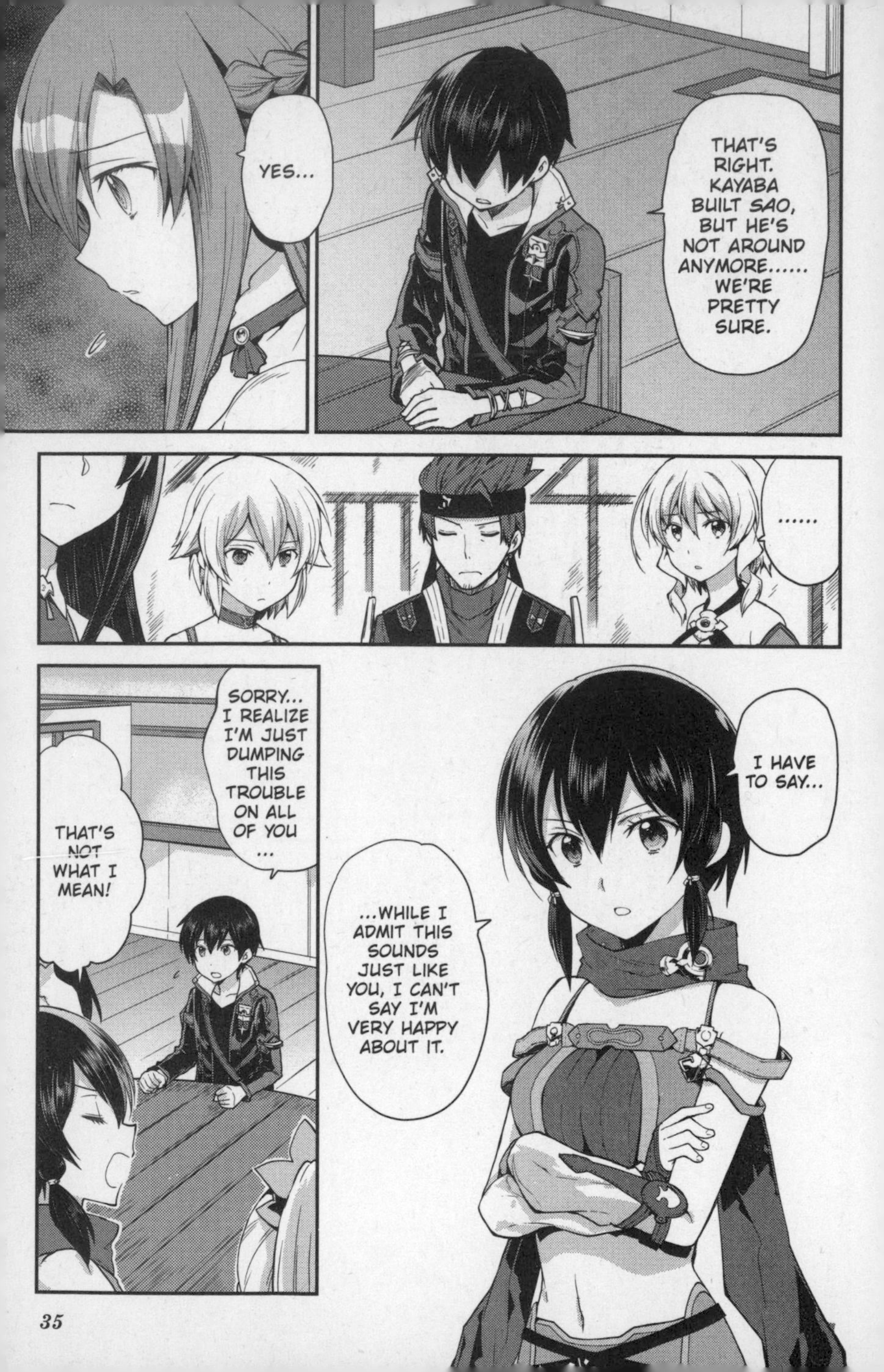
THAT'S RIGHT. KAYABA BUILT SAO, BUT HE'S NOT AROUND ANYMORE...... WE'RE PRETTY SURE.
YES...
......
I HAVE TO SAY...
...WHILE I ADMIT THIS SOUNDS JUST LIKE YOU, I CAN'T SAY I'M VERY HAPPY ABOUT IT.
SORRY... I REALIZE I'M JUST DUMPING THIS TROUBLE ON ALL OF YOU ...
THAT'S NOT WHAT I MEAN!

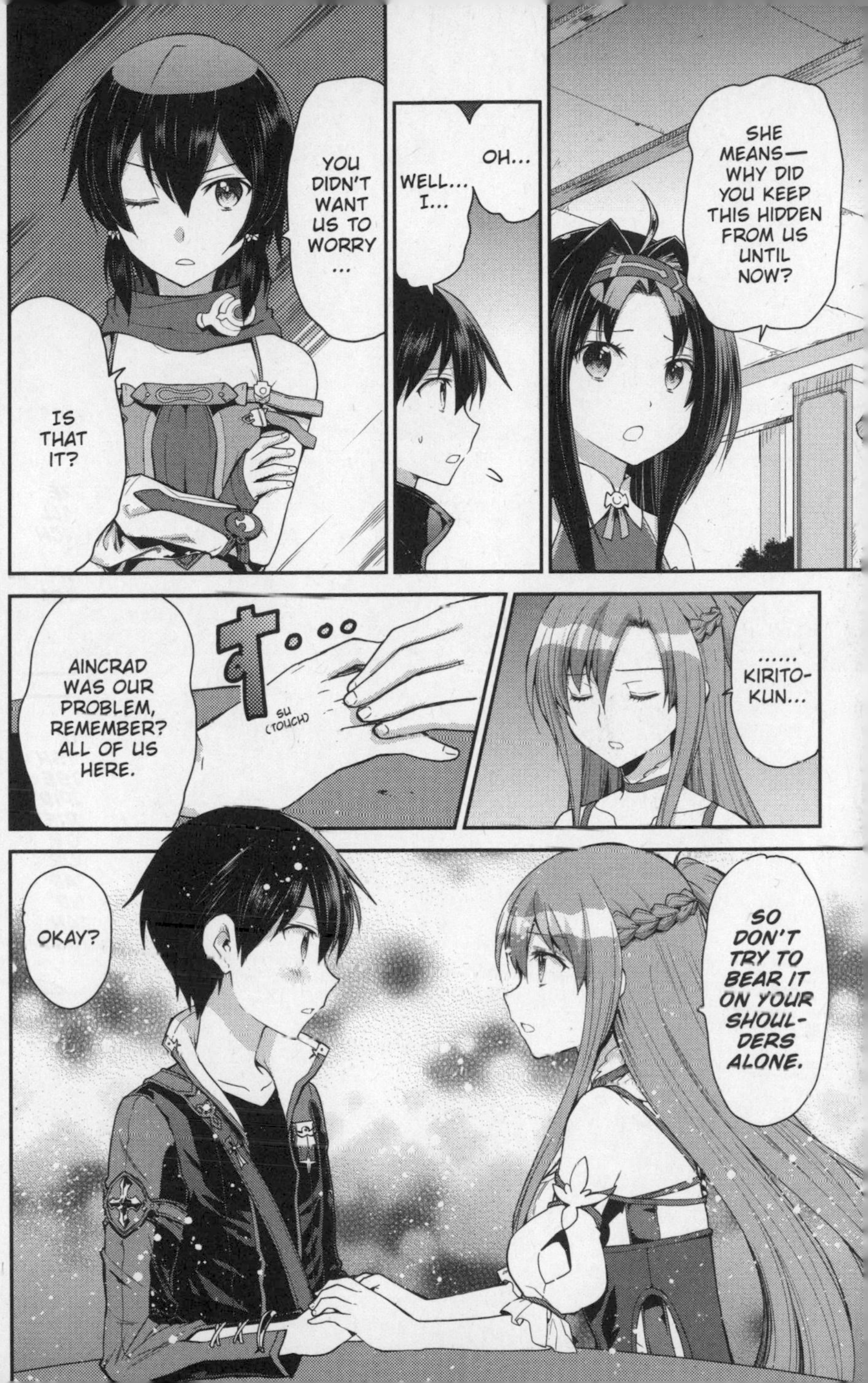
SHE MEANS—WHY DID YOU KEEP THIS HIDDEN FROM US UNTIL NOW?
OH...
WELL... I...
YOU DIDN'T WANT US TO WORRY ...
IS THAT IT?
...... KIRITO-KUN...
SU (TOUCH)
AINCRAD WAS OUR PROBLEM, REMEMBER? ALL OF US HERE.
SO DON'T TRY TO BEAR IT ON YOUR SHOUL-DERS ALONE.
OKAY?

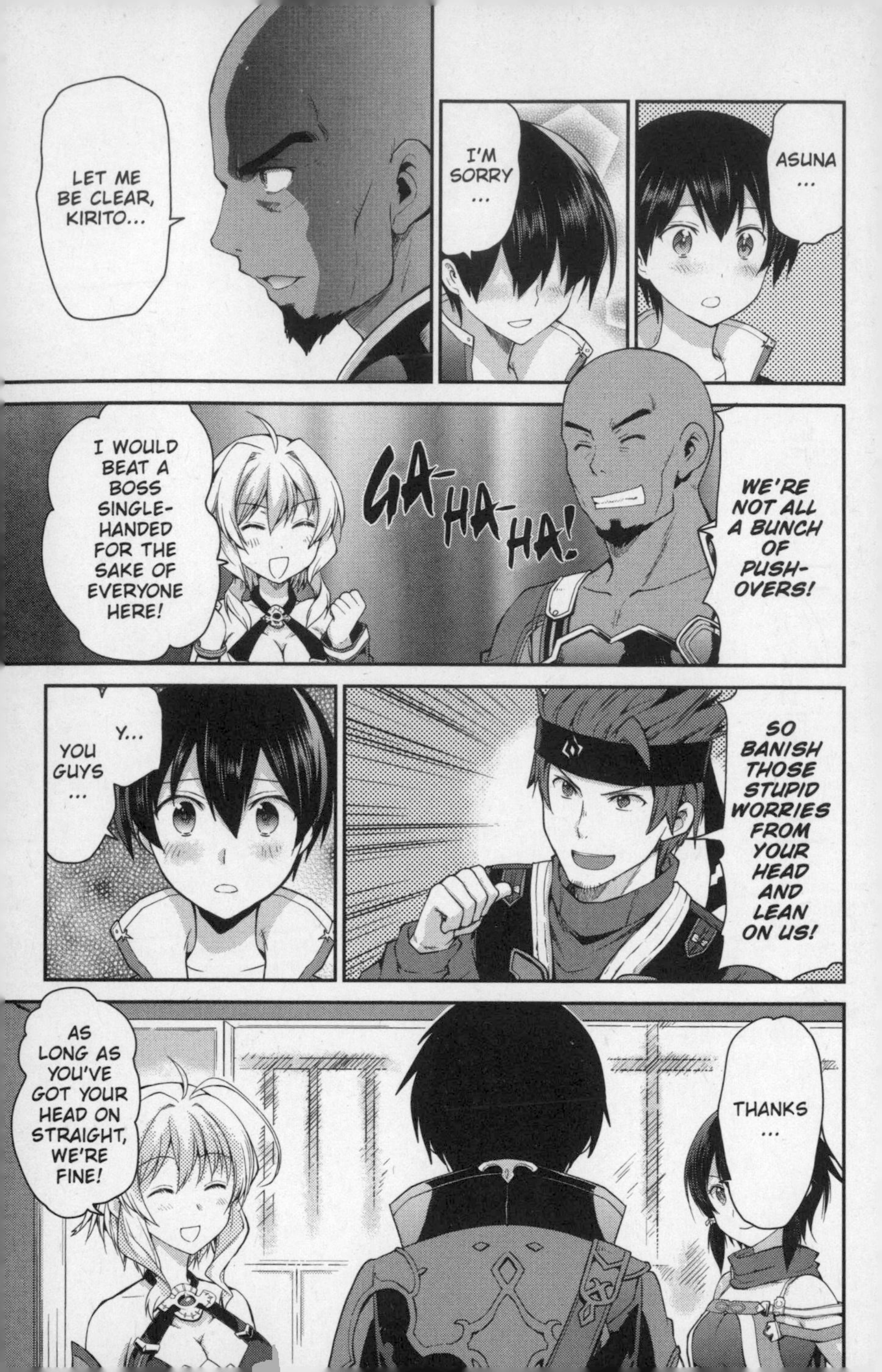
ASUNA ...
I'M SORRY ...
LET ME BE CLEAR, KIRITO...
WE'RE NOT ALL A BUNCH OF PUSH-OVERS!
GA-HA-HA!
I WOULD BEAT A BOSS SINGLE-HANDED FOR THE SAKE OF EVERYONE HERE!
SO BANISH THOSE STUPID WORRIES FROM YOUR HEAD AND LEAN ON US!
Y... YOU GUYS ...
THANKS ...
AS LONG AS YOU'VE GOT YOUR HEAD ON STRAIGHT, WE'RE FINE!

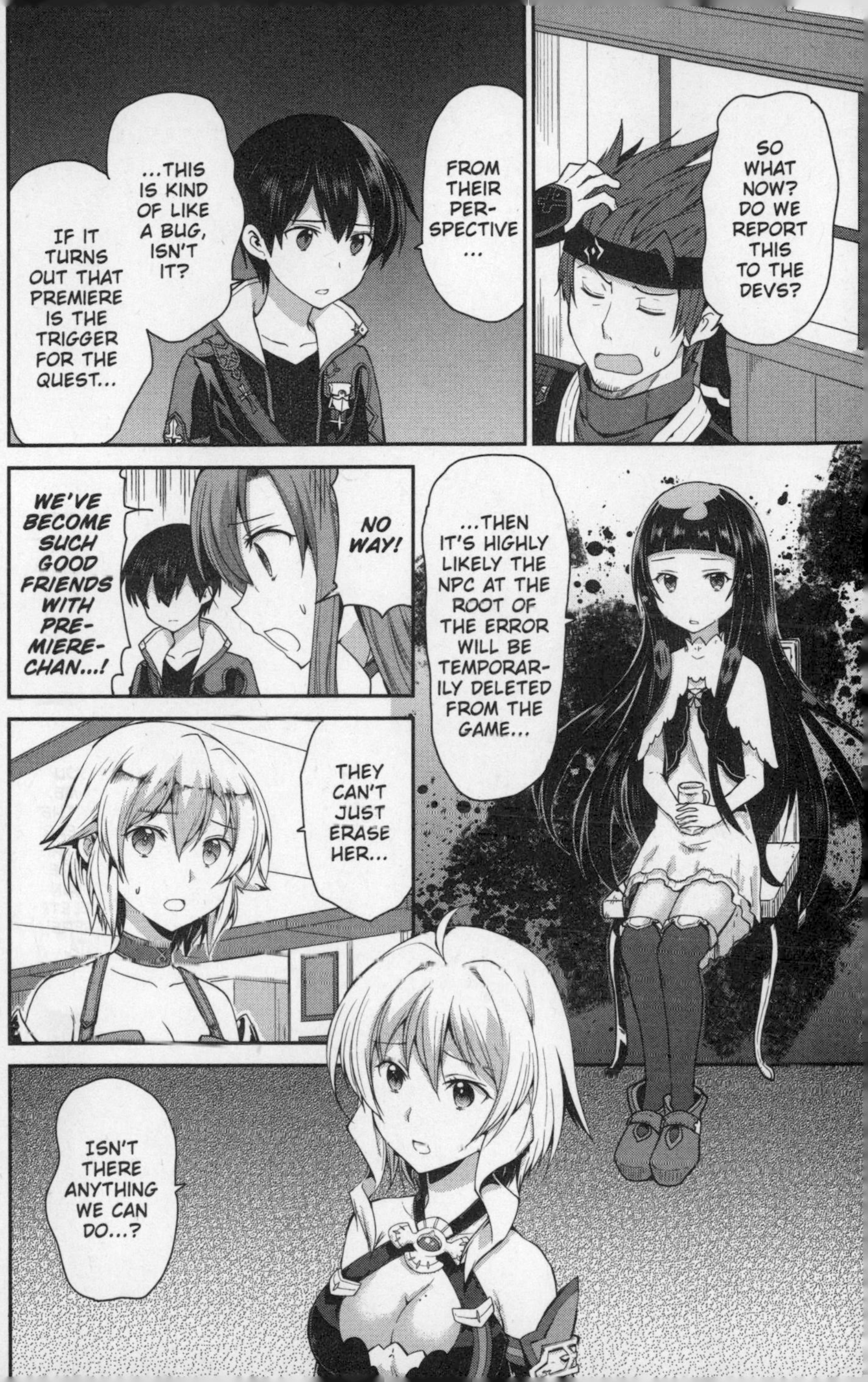
SO WHAT NOW? DO WE REPORT THIS TO THE DEVS?
FROM THEIR PER-SPECTIVE...
...THIS IS KIND OF LIKE A BUG, ISN'T IT?
IF IT TURNS OUT THAT PREMIERE IS THE TRIGGER FOR THE QUEST...
...THEN IT'S HIGHLY LIKELY THE NPC AT THE ROOT OF THE ERROR WILL BE TEMPORAR-ILY DELETED FROM THE GAME...
NO WAY!
WE'VE BECOME SUCH GOOD FRIENDS WITH PRE-MIERE-CHAN...!
THEY CAN'T JUST ERASE HER...
ISN'T THERE ANYTHING WE CAN DO...?

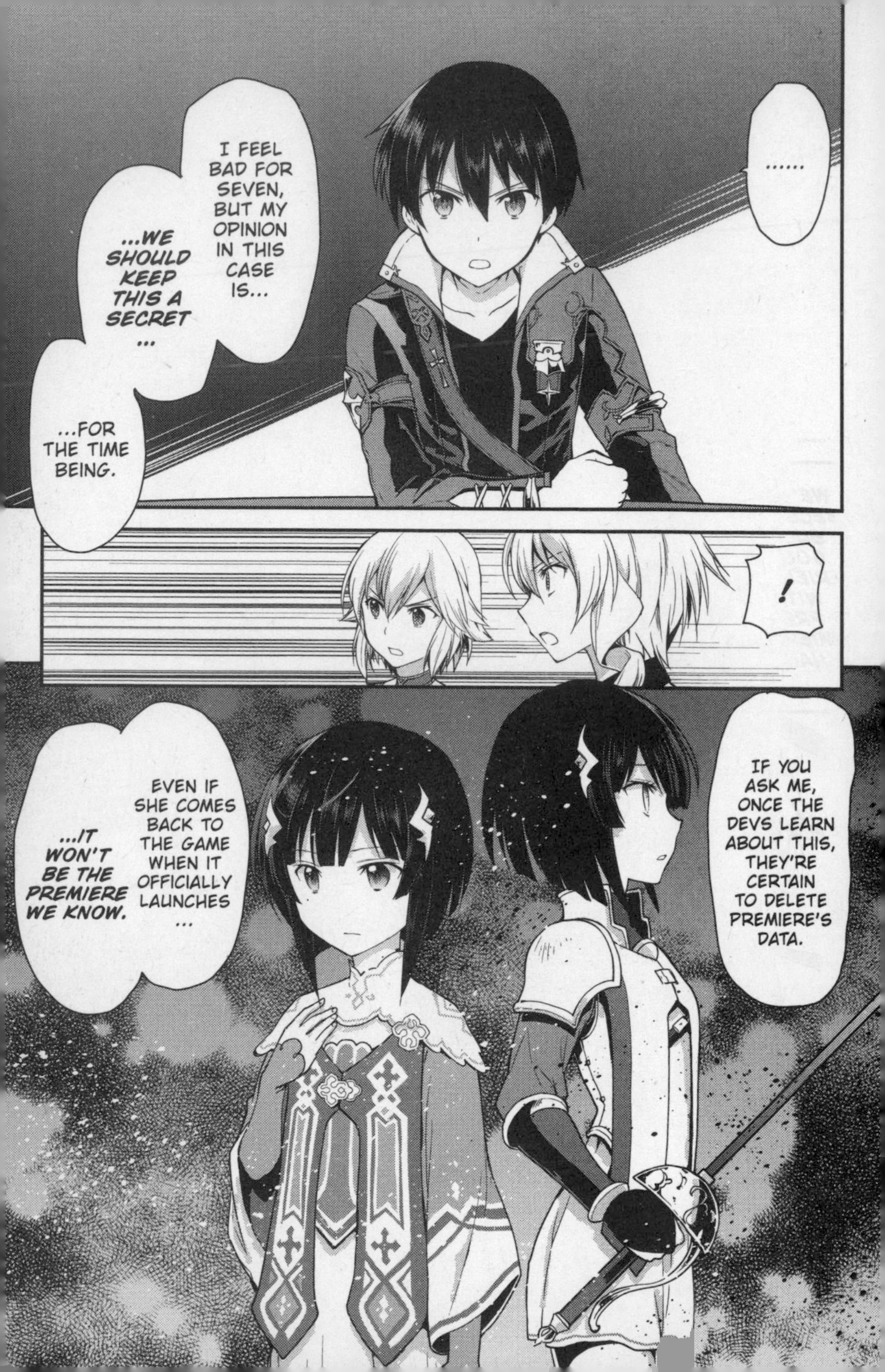
......
I FEEL BAD FOR SEVEN, BUT MY OPINION IN THIS CASE IS...
...WE SHOULD KEEP THIS A SECRET...
...FOR THE TIME BEING.
!
IF YOU ASK ME, ONCE THE DEVS LEARN ABOUT THIS, THEY'RE CERTAIN TO DELETE PREMIERE'S DATA.
EVEN IF SHE COMES BACK TO THE GAME WHEN IT OFFICIALLY LAUNCHES...
...IT WON'T BE THE PREMIERE WE KNOW.

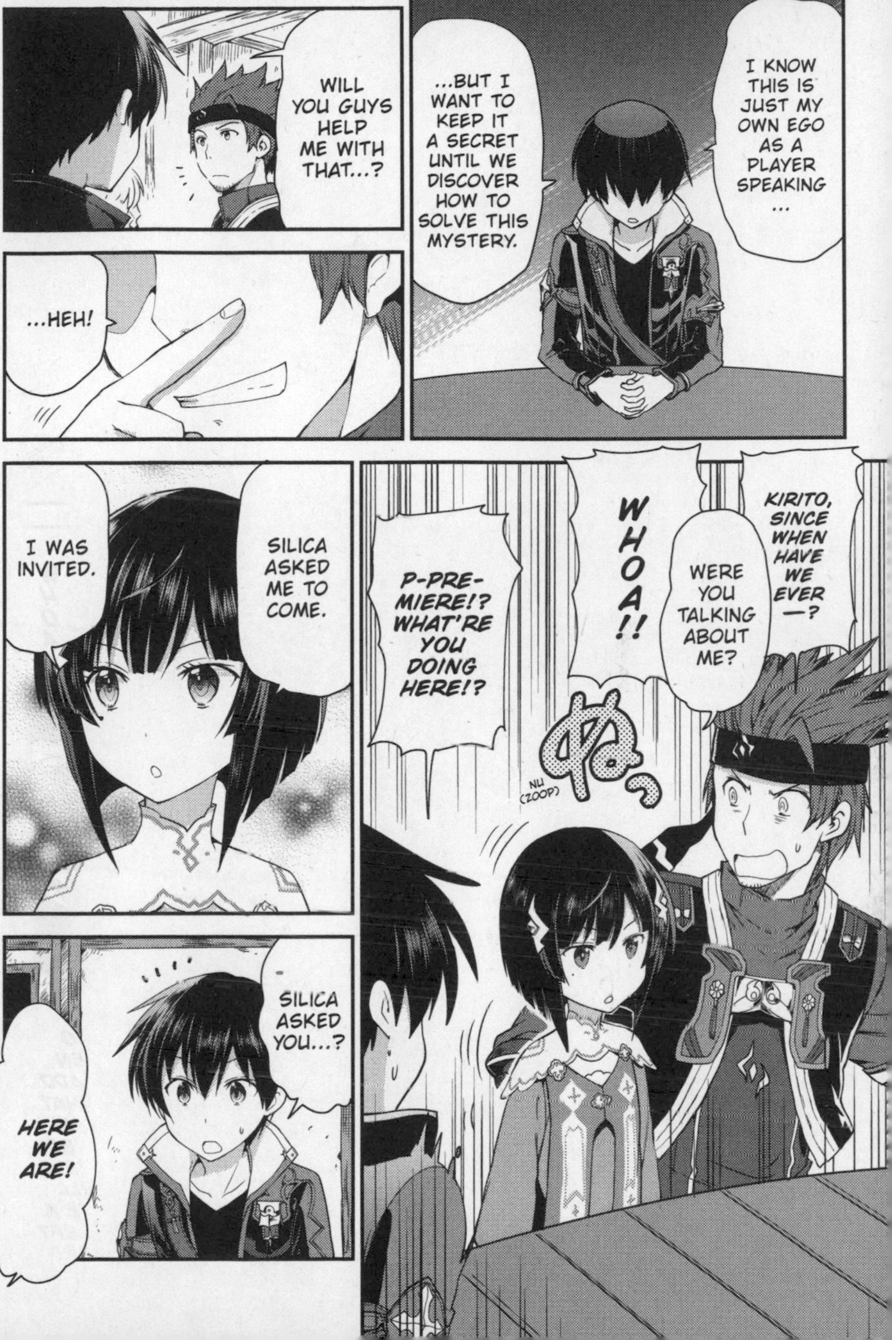
I KNOW THIS IS JUST MY OWN EGO AS A PLAYER SPEAKING...
...BUT I WANT TO KEEP IT A SECRET UNTIL WE DISCOVER HOW TO SOLVE THIS MYSTERY.
WILL YOU GUYS HELP ME WITH THAT...?
...HEH!
KIRITO, SINCE WHEN HAVE WE EVER—?
WERE YOU TALKING ABOUT ME?
WHOA!!
P-PREMIERE!? WHAT'RE YOU DOING HERE!?
NU (ZOOP)
SILICA ASKED ME TO COME.
I WAS INVITED.
SILICA ASKED YOU...?
HERE WE ARE!

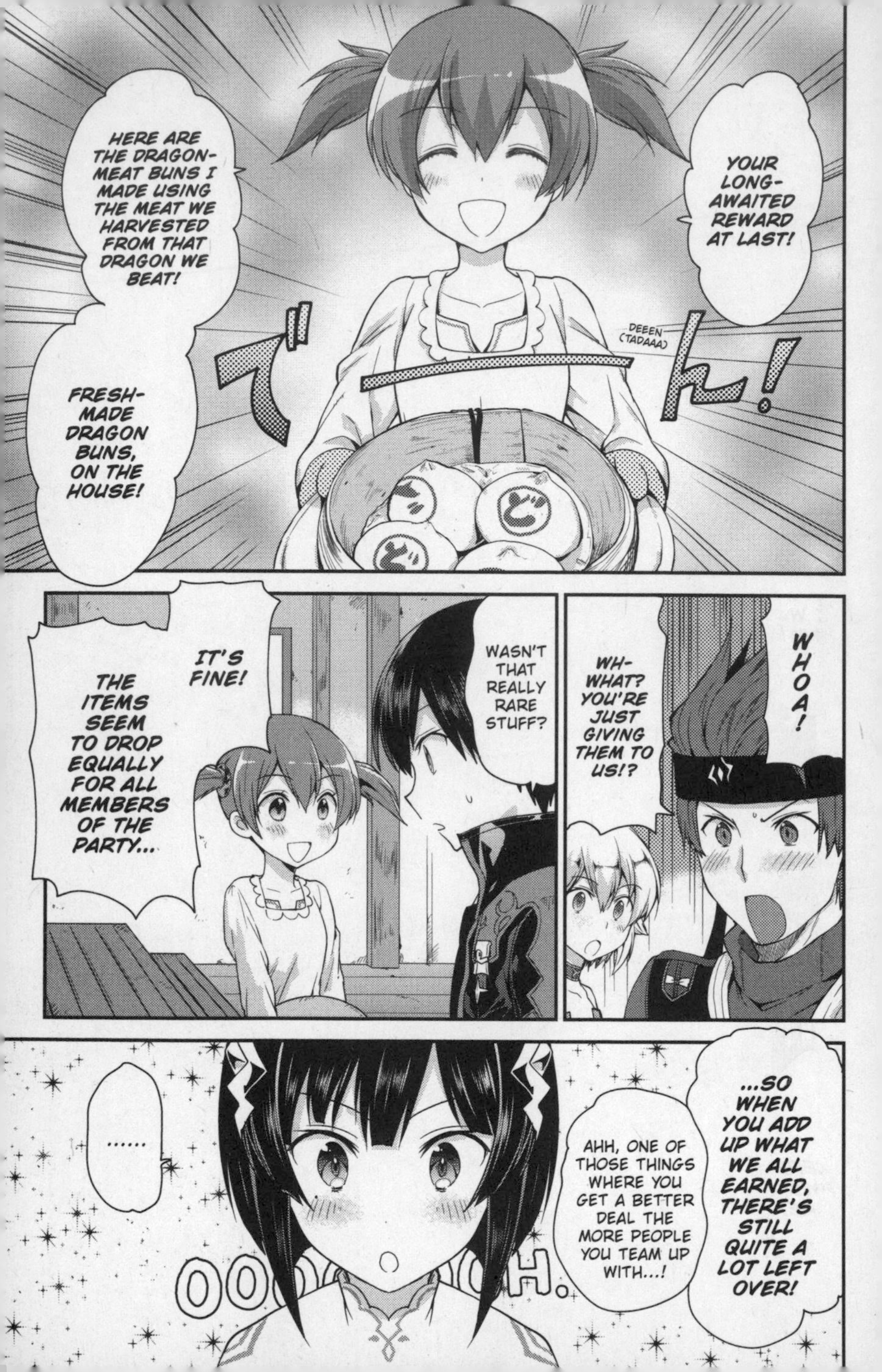
YOUR LONG-AWAITED REWARD AT LAST!
HERE ARE THE DRAGON-MEAT BUNS I MADE USING THE MEAT WE HARVESTED FROM THAT DRAGON WE BEAT!
DEEEN (TADAAA)
FRESH-MADE DRAGON BUNS, ON THE HOUSE!
WHOA!
WH-WHAT? YOU'RE JUST GIVING THEM TO US!?
WASN'T THAT REALLY RARE STUFF?
IT'S FINE!
THE ITEMS SEEM TO DROP EQUALLY FOR ALL MEMBERS OF THE PARTY...
...SO WHEN YOU ADD UP WHAT WE ALL EARNED, THERE'S STILL QUITE A LOT LEFT OVER!
AHH, ONE OF THOSE THINGS WHERE YOU GET A BETTER DEAL THE MORE PEOPLE YOU TEAM UP WITH...!
......

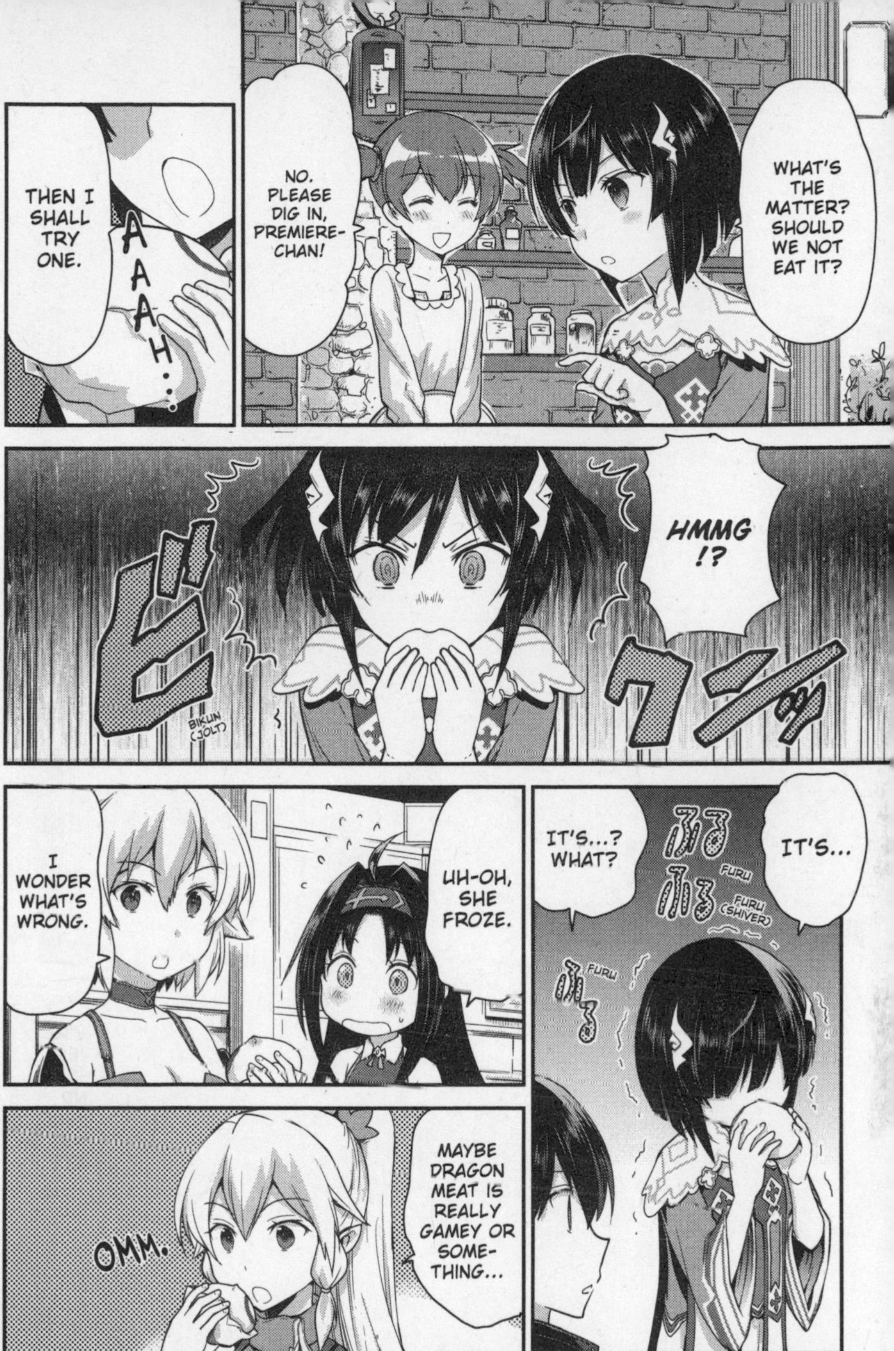
WHAT'S THE MATTER? SHOULD WE NOT EAT IT?
NO. PLEASE DIG IN, PREMIERE-CHAN!
THEN I SHALL TRY ONE.
AAAH...
HMMG!?
BIKUN (JOLT)
IT'S...
FURU FURU (SHIVER)
IT'S...? WHAT?
FURU
UH-OH, SHE FROZE.
I WONDER WHAT'S WRONG.
MAYBE DRAGON MEAT IS REALLY GAMEY OR SOME-THING...
OMM.

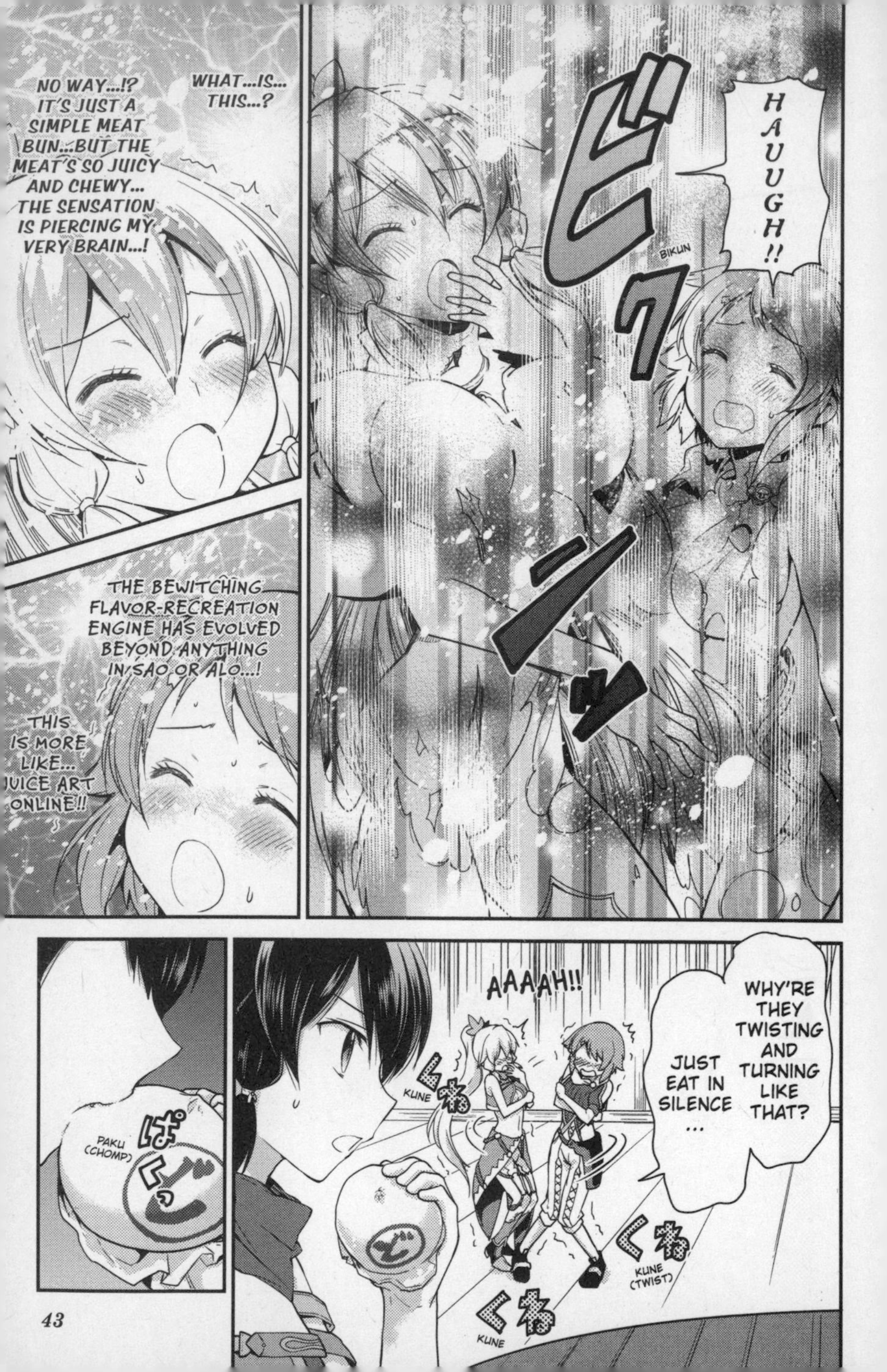
HAUUGH!!
BIKUN
WHAT...IS... THIS...?
NO WAY...!? IT'S JUST A SIMPLE MEAT BUN...BUT THE MEAT'S SO JUICY AND CHEWY... THE SENSATION IS PIERCING MY VERY BRAIN...!
THE BEWITCHING FLAVOR-RECREATION ENGINE HAS EVOLVED BEYOND ANYTHING IN SAO OR ALO...!
THIS IS MORE LIKE... JUICE ART ONLINE!!
WHY'RE THEY TWISTING AND TURNING LIKE THAT?
JUST EAT IN SILENCE ...
AAAAH!!
KUNE
KUNE (TWIST)
KUNE
PAKU (CHOMP)

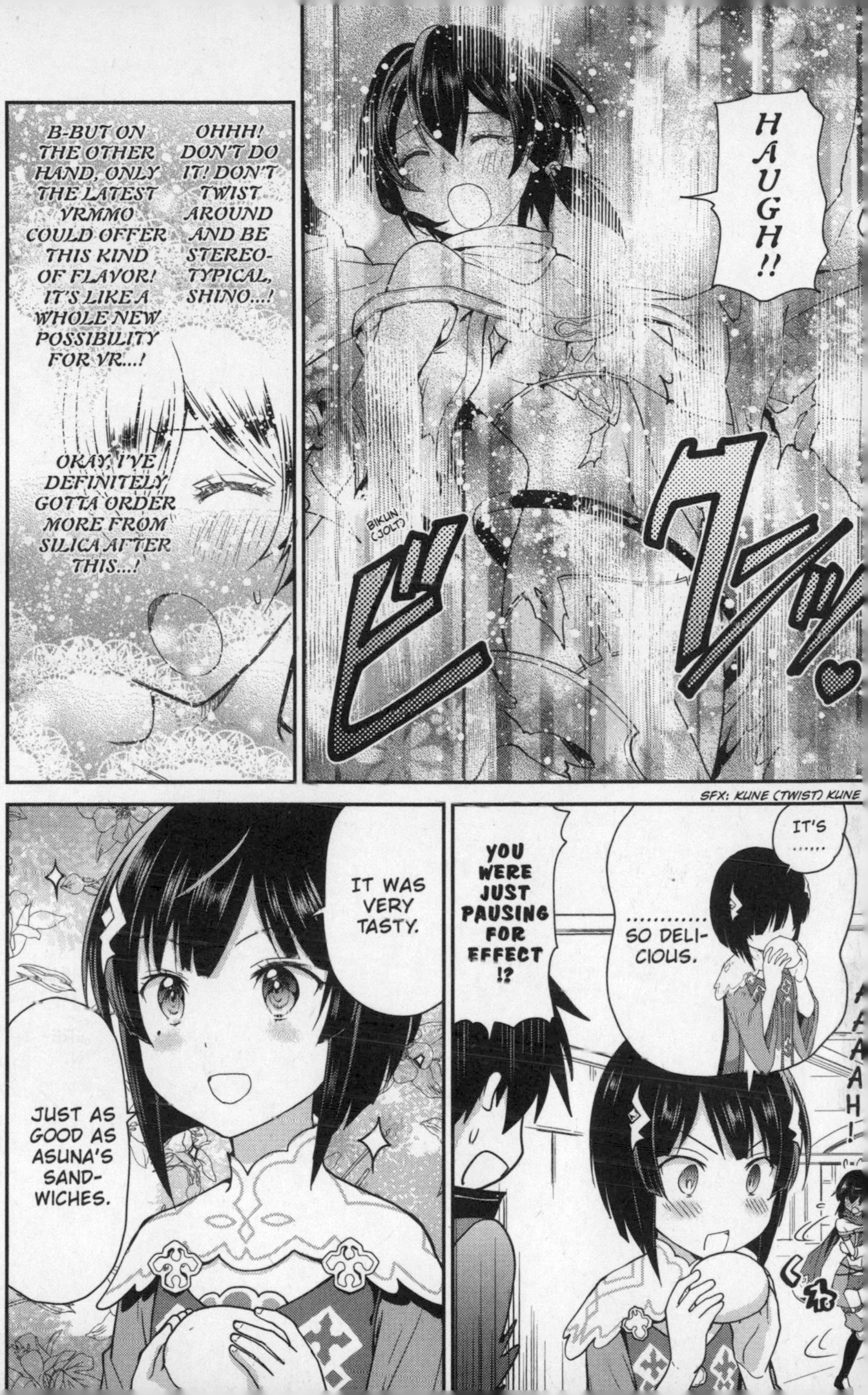
HAUGH!!
BIKUN (JOLT)
SFX: KUNE (TWIST) KUNE
OHHH! DON'T DO IT! DON'T TWIST AROUND AND BE STEREO-TYPICAL, SHINO...!
B-BUT ON THE OTHER HAND, ONLY THE LATEST VRMMO COULD OFFER THIS KIND OF FLAVOR! IT'S LIKE A WHOLE NEW POSSIBILITY FOR VR...!
OKAY, I'VE DEFINITELY GOTTA ORDER MORE FROM SILICA AFTER THIS...!
IT'S ......
.... SO DELI-CIOUS.
AAAAH!
YOU WERE JUST PAUSING FOR EFFECT !?
IT WAS VERY TASTY.
JUST AS GOOD AS ASUNA'S SAND-WICHES.

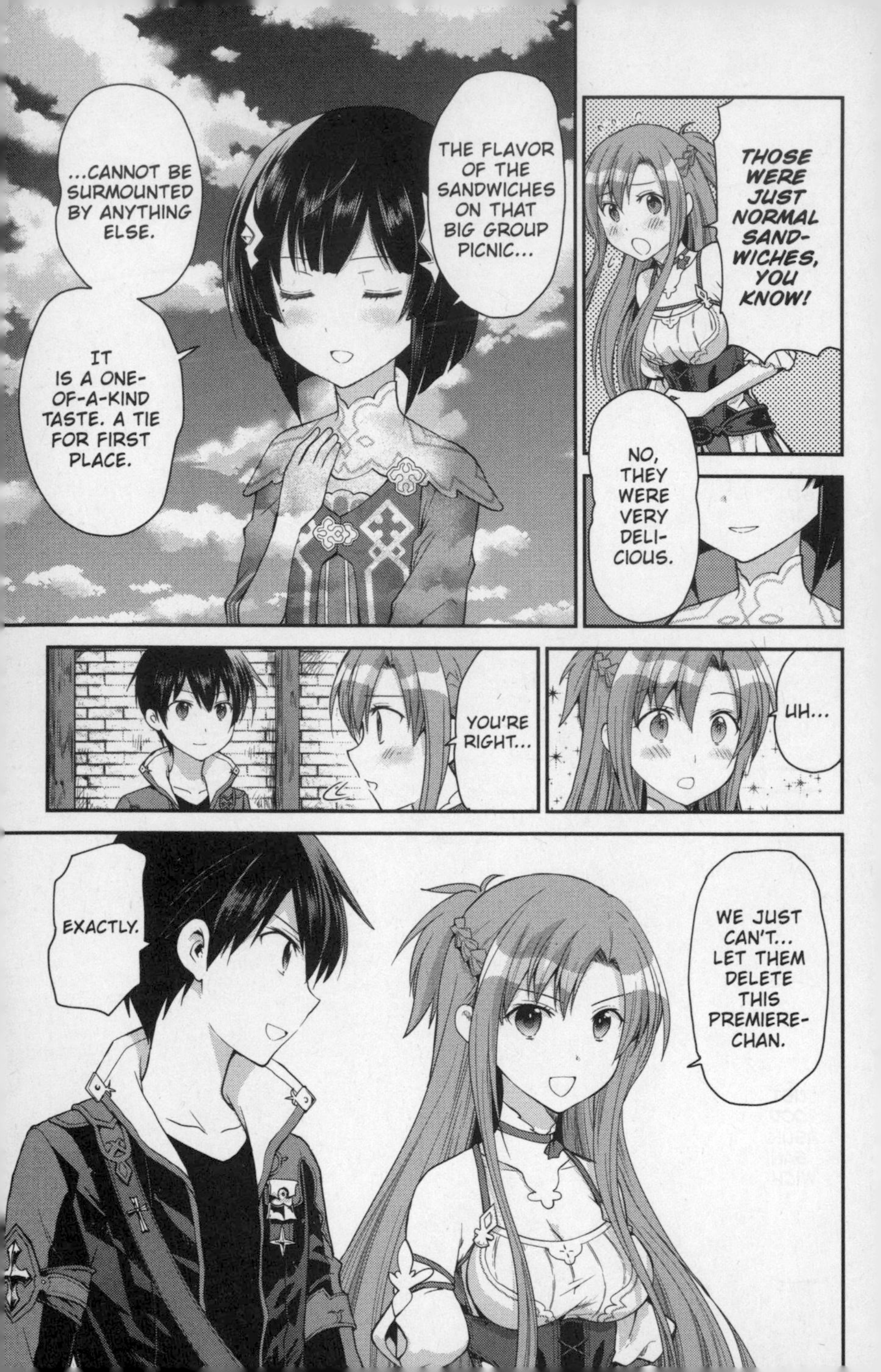
THOSE WERE JUST NORMAL SANDWICHES, YOU KNOW!
NO, THEY WERE VERY DELICIOUS.
THE FLAVOR OF THE SANDWICHES ON THAT BIG GROUP PICNIC...
...CANNOT BE SURMOUNTED BY ANYTHING ELSE.
IT IS A ONE-OF-A-KIND TASTE. A TIE FOR FIRST PLACE.
UH...
YOU'RE RIGHT...
WE JUST CAN'T... LET THEM DELETE THIS PREMIERE-CHAN.
EXACTLY.

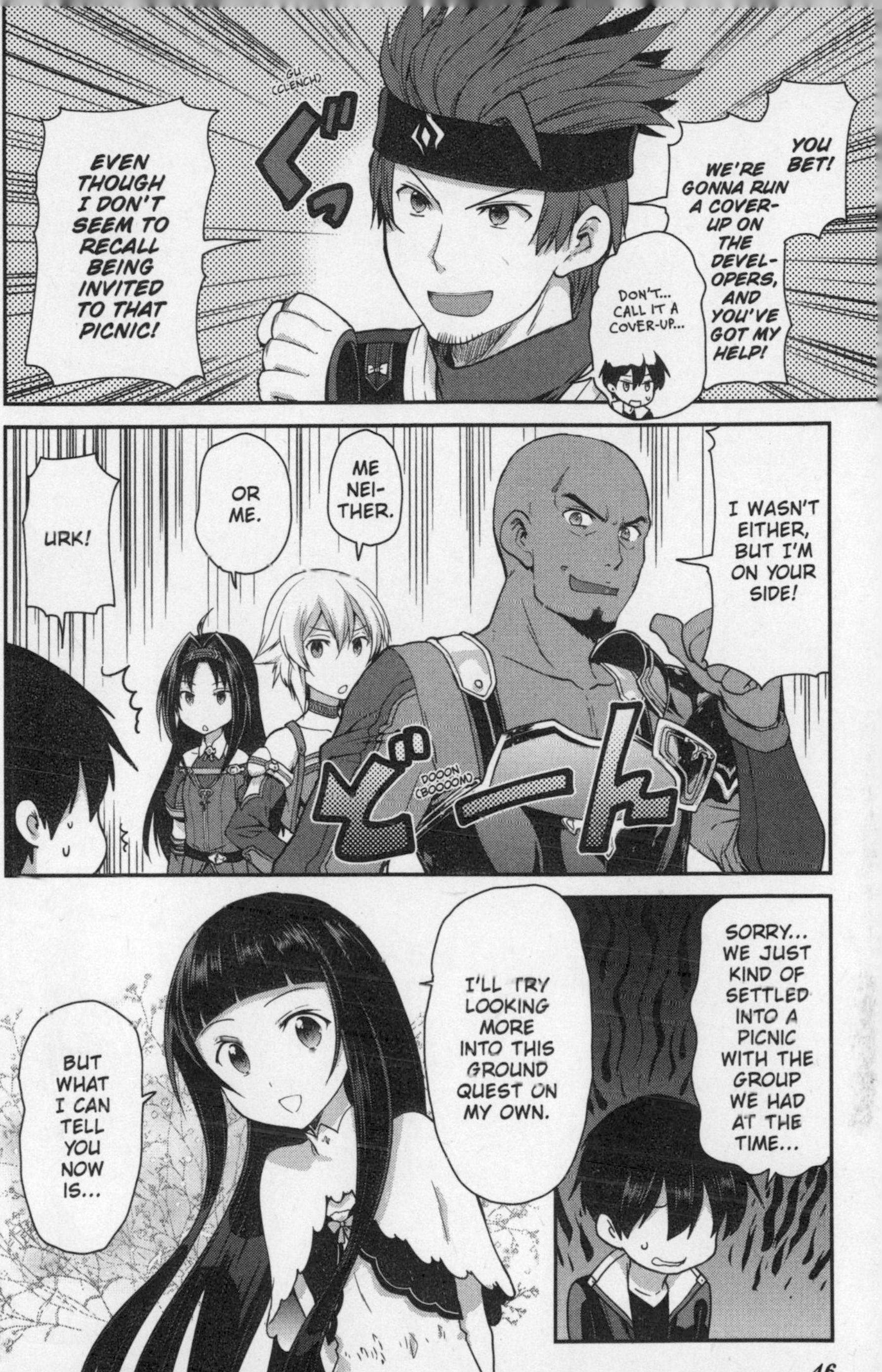
YOU BET! WE'RE GONNA RUN A COVER-UP ON THE DEVELOPERS, AND YOU'VE GOT MY HELP!
DON'T... CALL IT A COVER-UP...
GU (CLENCH)
EVEN THOUGH I DON'T SEEM TO RECALL BEING INVITED TO THAT PICNIC!
I WASN'T EITHER, BUT I'M ON YOUR SIDE!
ME NEI-THER.
OR ME.
URK!
DOOON (BOOOOM)
SORRY... WE JUST KIND OF SETTLED INTO A PICNIC WITH THE GROUP WE HAD AT THE TIME...
I'LL TRY LOOKING MORE INTO THIS GROUND QUEST ON MY OWN.
BUT WHAT I CAN TELL YOU NOW IS...

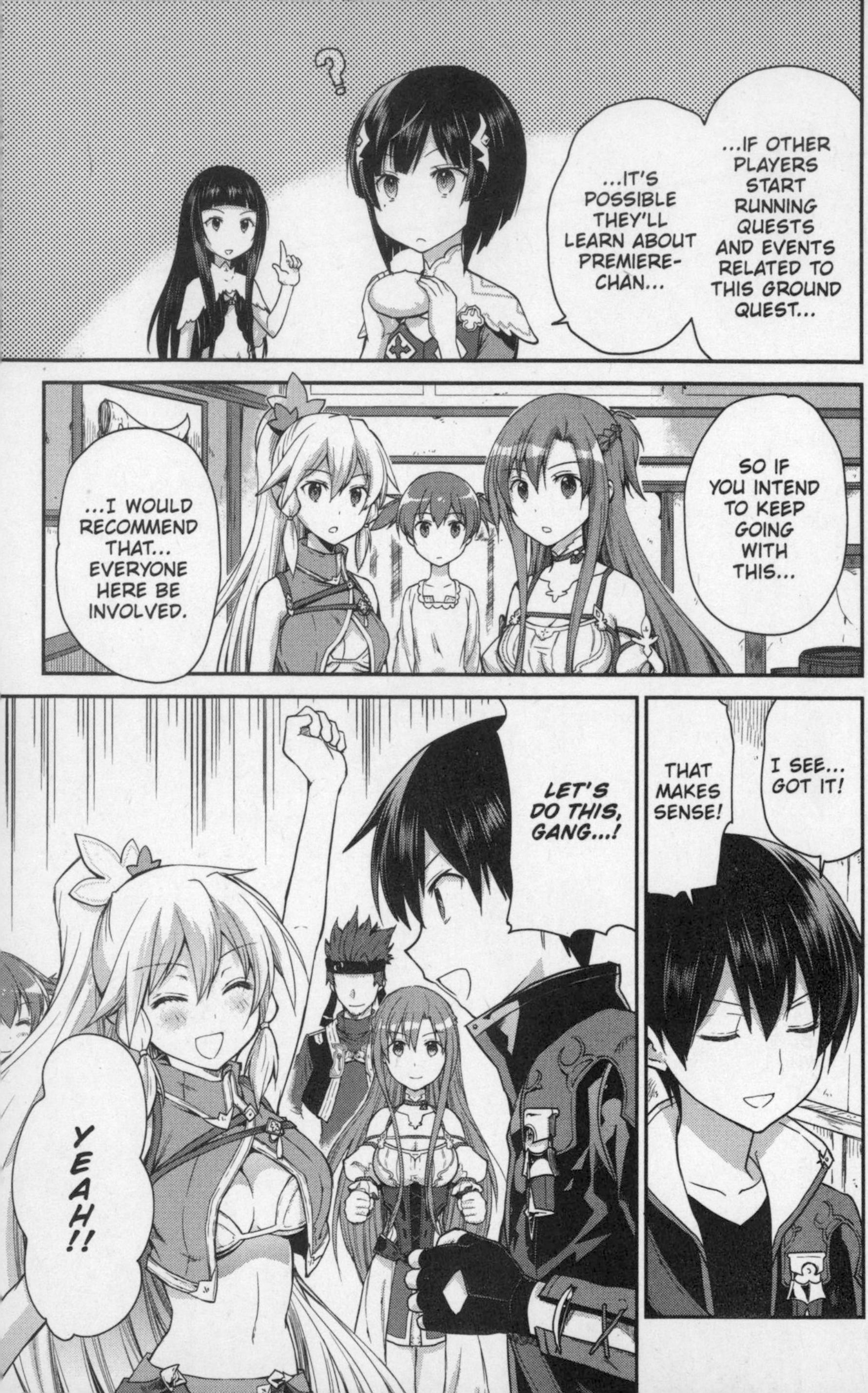
...IF OTHER PLAYERS START RUNNING QUESTS AND EVENTS RELATED TO THIS GROUND QUEST...
...IT'S POSSIBLE THEY'LL LEARN ABOUT PREMIERE-CHAN...
SO IF YOU INTEND TO KEEP GOING WITH THIS...
...I WOULD RECOMMEND THAT... EVERYONE HERE BE INVOLVED.
I SEE... GOT IT!
THAT MAKES SENSE!
LET'S DO THIS, GANG...!
YEAH!!

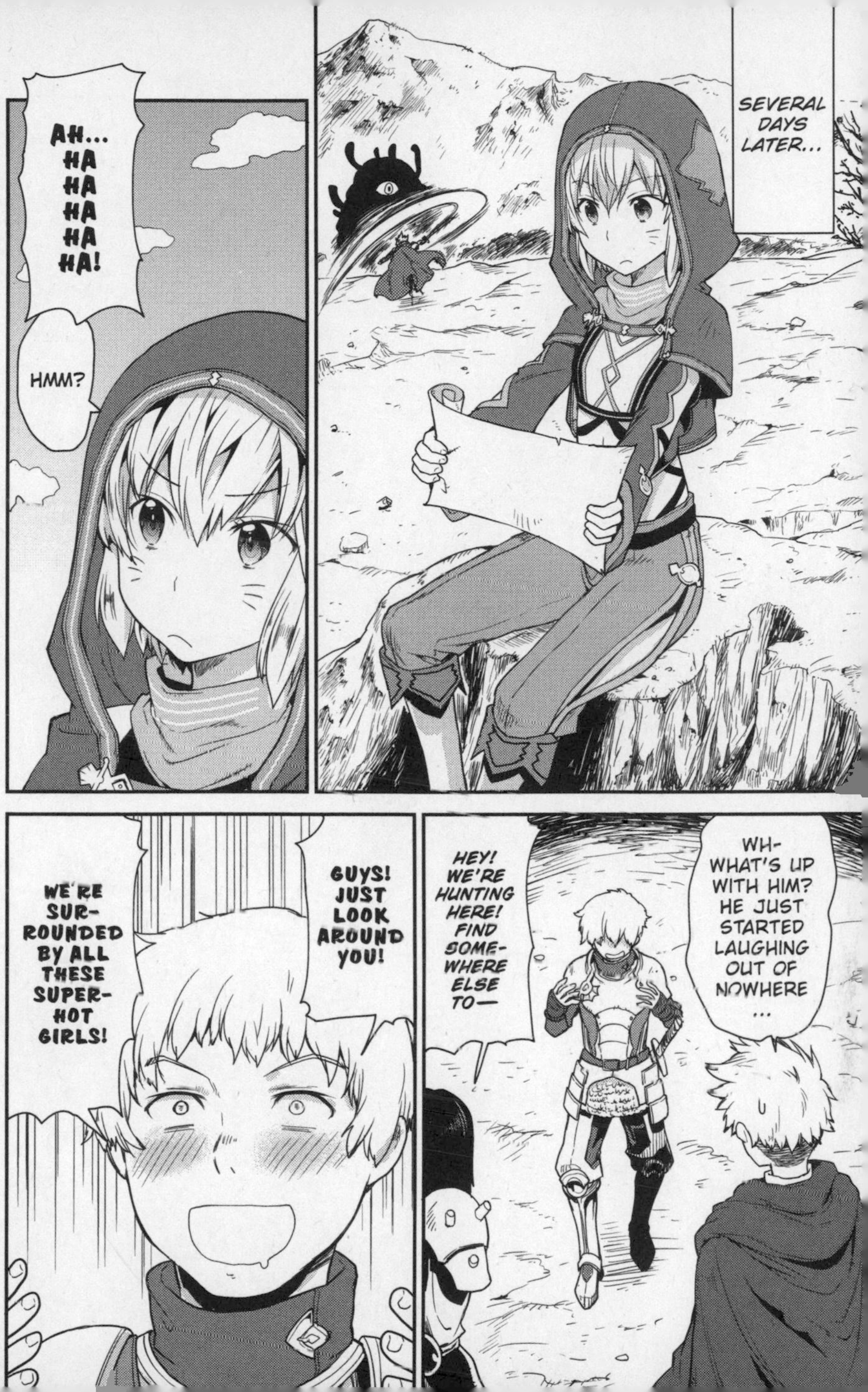
SEVERAL DAYS LATER...
AH... HA HA HA HA HA!
HMM?
WH-WHAT'S UP WITH HIM? HE JUST STARTED LAUGHING OUT OF NOWHERE...
HEY! WE'RE HUNTING HERE! FIND SOME-WHERE ELSE TO—
GUYS! JUST LOOK AROUND YOU!
WE'RE SUR-ROUNDED BY ALL THESE SUPER-HOT GIRLS!

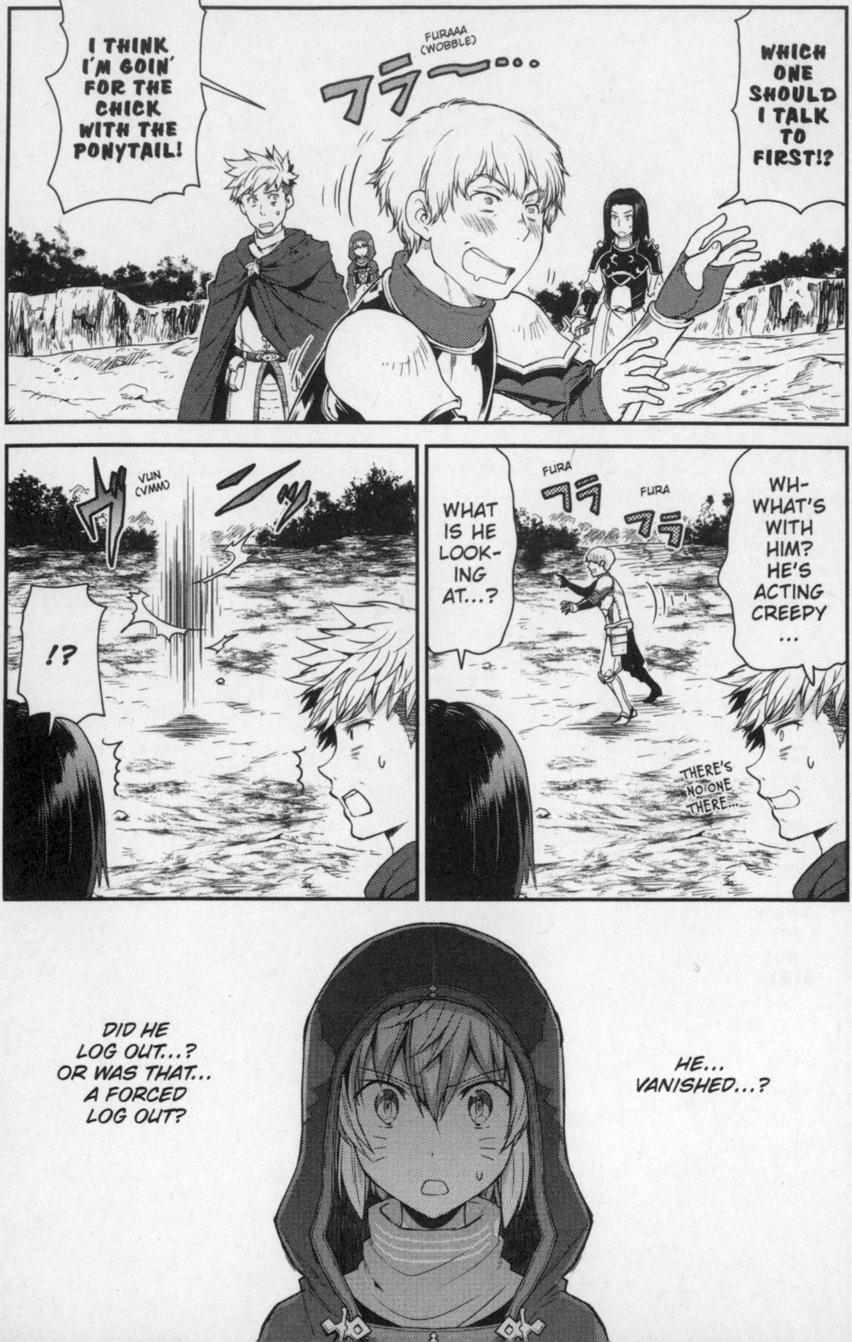
WHICH ONE SHOULD I TALK TO FIRST!?
FURAAA (WOBBLE)
フラ〜…
I THINK I'M GOIN' FOR THE CHICK WITH THE PONYTAIL!
WH-WHAT'S WITH HIM? HE'S ACTING CREEPY...
FURA
フラ
FURA
フラ
WHAT IS HE LOOKING AT...?
THERE'S NO ONE THERE...
VUN (VMM)
!?
HE... VANISHED...?
DID HE LOG OUT...? OR WAS THAT... A FORCED LOG OUT?

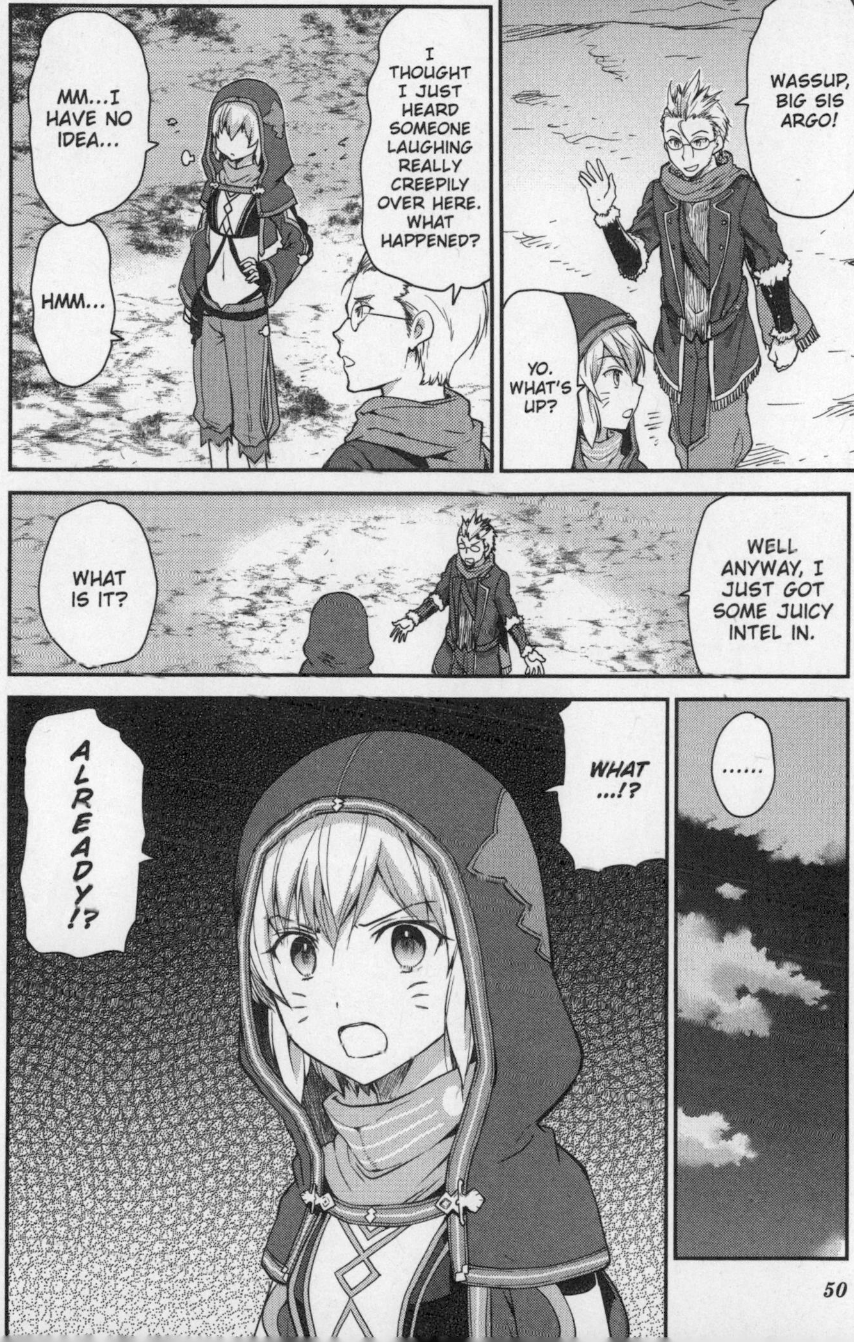
WASSUP, BIG SIS ARGO!
YO. WHAT'S UP?
I THOUGHT I JUST HEARD SOMEONE LAUGHING REALLY CREEPILY OVER HERE. WHAT HAPPENED?
MM...I HAVE NO IDEA...
HMM...
WELL ANYWAY, I JUST GOT SOME JUICY INTEL IN.
WHAT IS IT?
......
WHAT ...!?
ALREADY!?

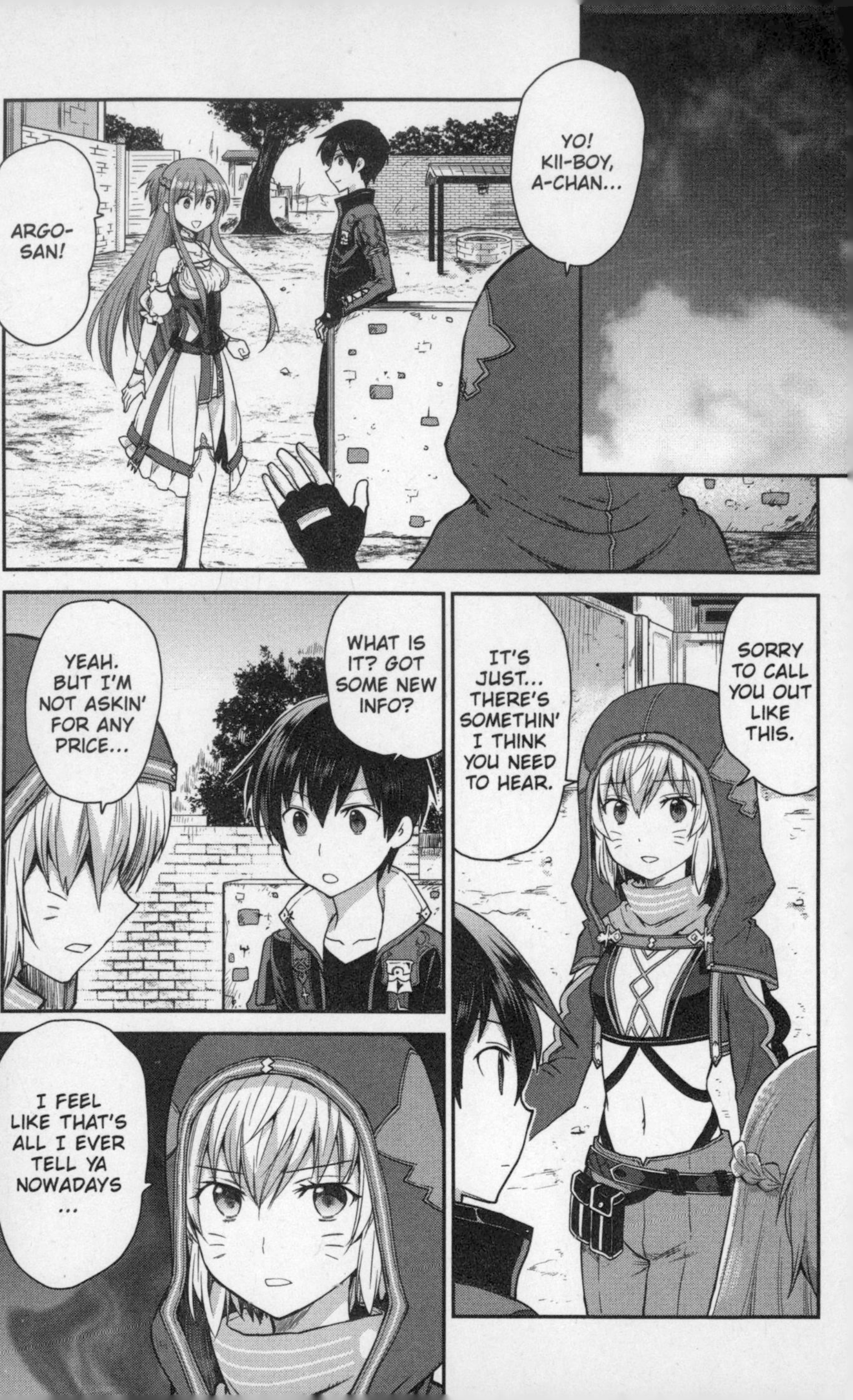
YO! KII-BOY, A-CHAN...
ARGO-SAN!
SORRY TO CALL YOU OUT LIKE THIS.
IT'S JUST... THERE'S SOMETHIN' I THINK YOU NEED TO HEAR.
WHAT IS IT? GOT SOME NEW INFO?
YEAH. BUT I'M NOT ASKIN' FOR ANY PRICE...
I FEEL LIKE THAT'S ALL I EVER TELL YA NOWADAYS ...

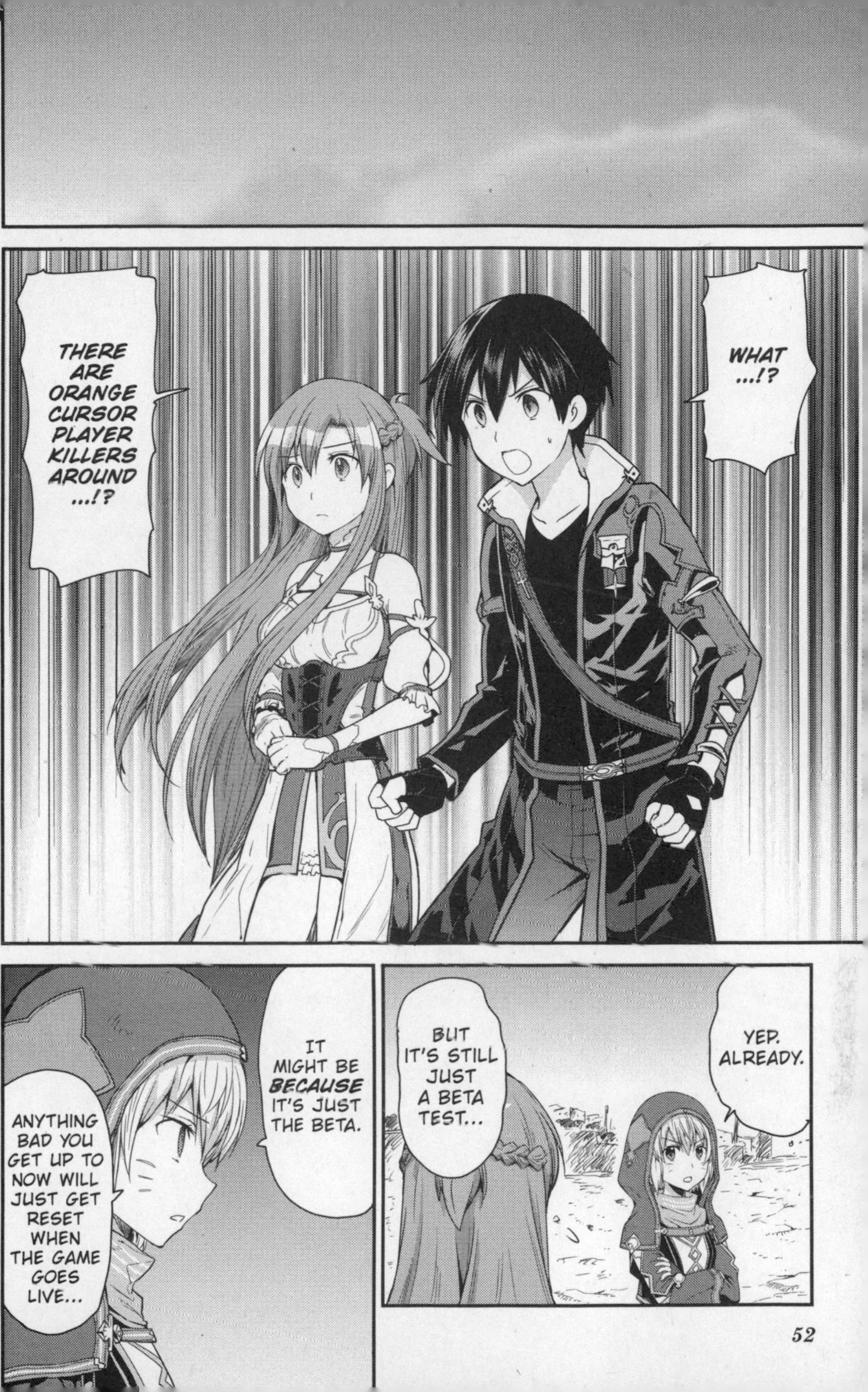
WHAT ...!?
THERE ARE ORANGE CURSOR PLAYER KILLERS AROUND ...!?
YEP. ALREADY.
BUT IT'S STILL JUST A BETA TEST...
IT MIGHT BE *BECAUSE* IT'S JUST THE BETA.
ANYTHING BAD YOU GET UP TO NOW WILL JUST GET RESET WHEN THE GAME GOES LIVE...

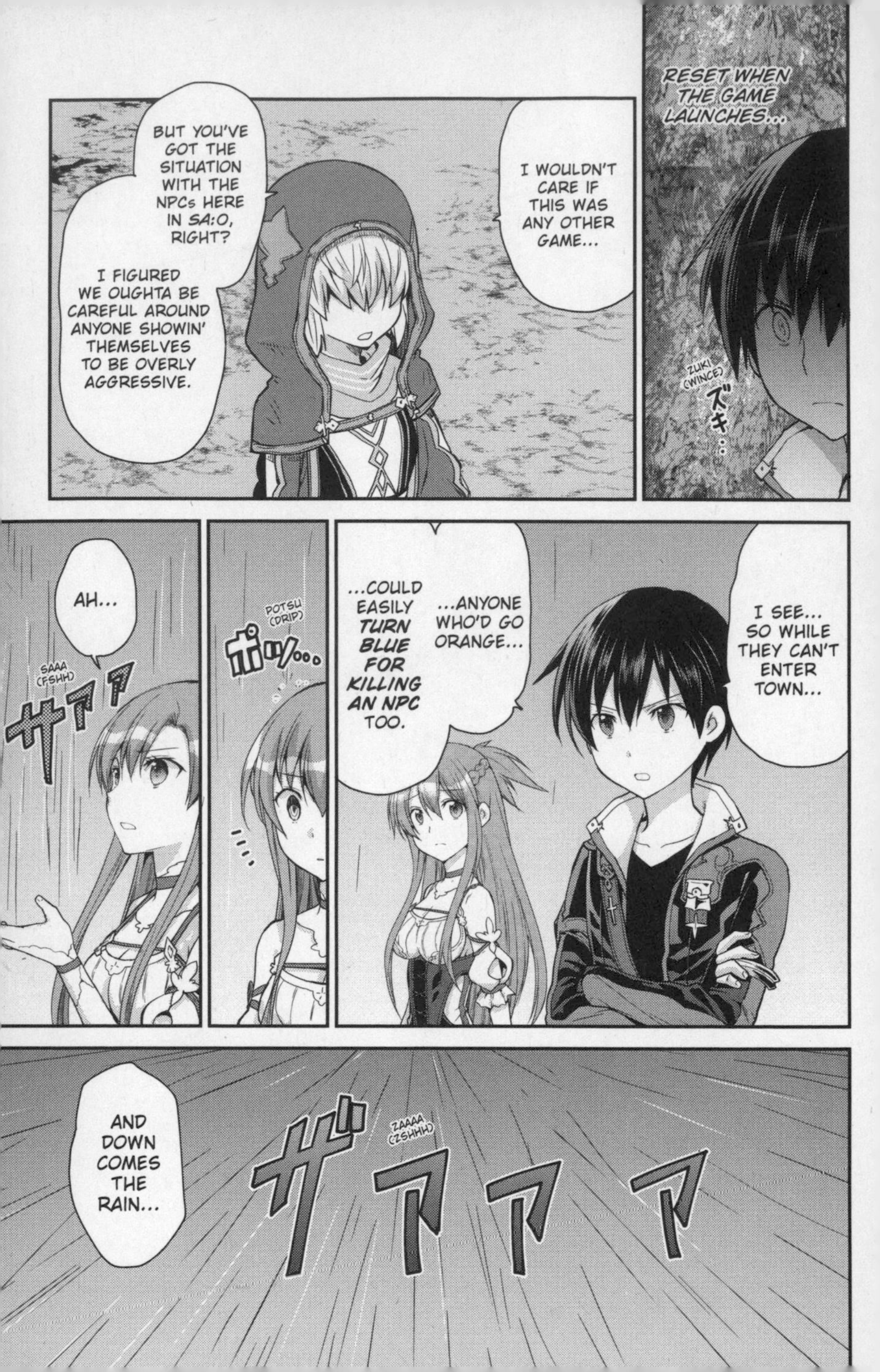
RESET WHEN THE GAME LAUNCHES...
ZUKI (WINCE)
ズキ…
I WOULDN'T CARE IF THIS WAS ANY OTHER GAME...
BUT YOU'VE GOT THE SITUATION WITH THE NPCs HERE IN SA:O, RIGHT?
I FIGURED WE OUGHTA BE CAREFUL AROUND ANYONE SHOWIN' THEMSELVES TO BE OVERLY AGGRESSIVE.
I SEE... SO WHILE THEY CAN'T ENTER TOWN...
...ANYONE WHO'D GO ORANGE...
...COULD EASILY TURN BLUE FOR KILLING AN NPC TOO.
POTSU (DRIP)
ポツ…
AH...
SAAA (FSHH)
サァァ
ZAAAA (ZSHHH)
ザァァァ
AND DOWN COMES THE RAIN...

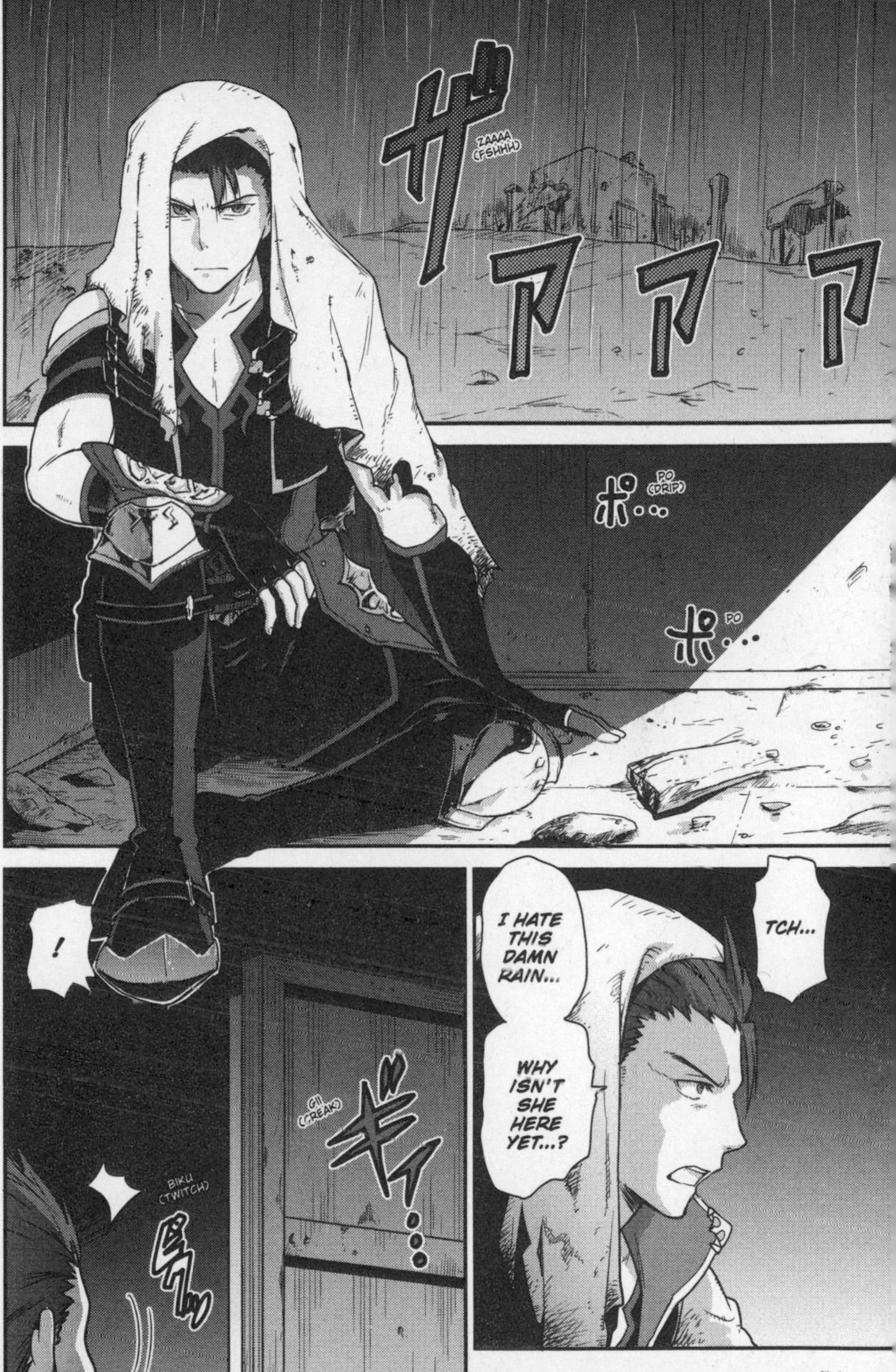
ZAAAA (FSHHH)
PO (DRIP)
PO
TCH...
I HATE THIS DAMN RAIN...
WHY ISN'T SHE HERE YET...?
!
GII (CREAK)
BIKU (TWITCH)

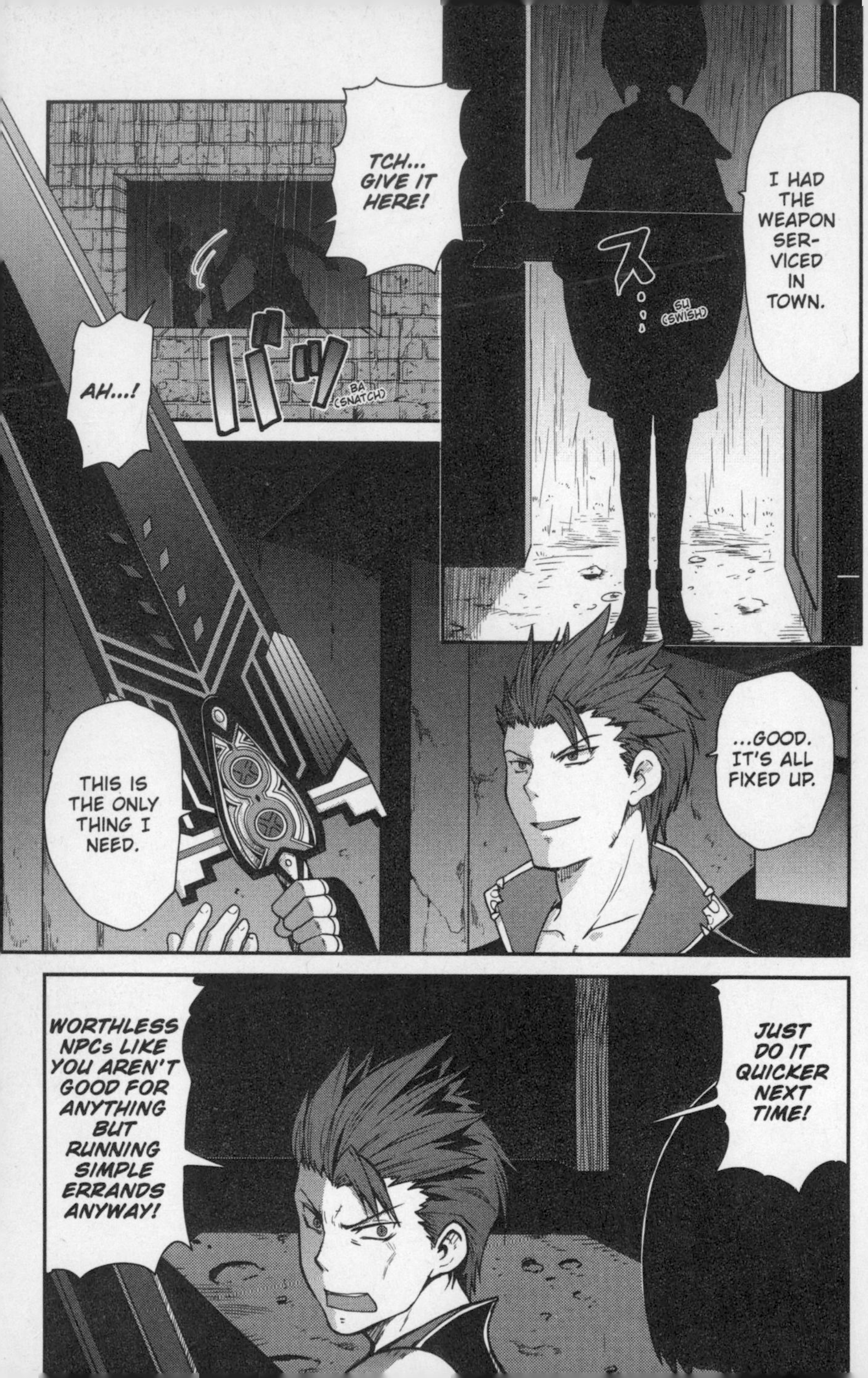
I HAD THE WEAPON SER-VICED IN TOWN.
SU (SWISH)
TCH... GIVE IT HERE!
BA (SNATCH)
AH...!
...GOOD. IT'S ALL FIXED UP.
THIS IS THE ONLY THING I NEED.
JUST DO IT QUICKER NEXT TIME!
WORTHLESS NPCs LIKE YOU AREN'T GOOD FOR ANYTHING BUT RUNNING SIMPLE ERRANDS ANYWAY!

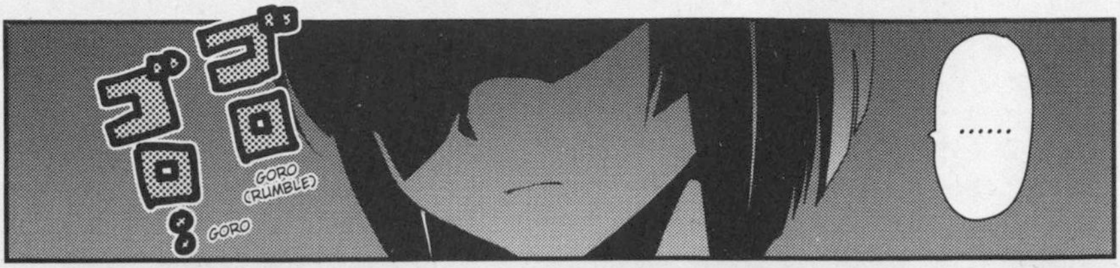
......
ゴロ
GORO (RUMBLE)
ゴロ
GORO
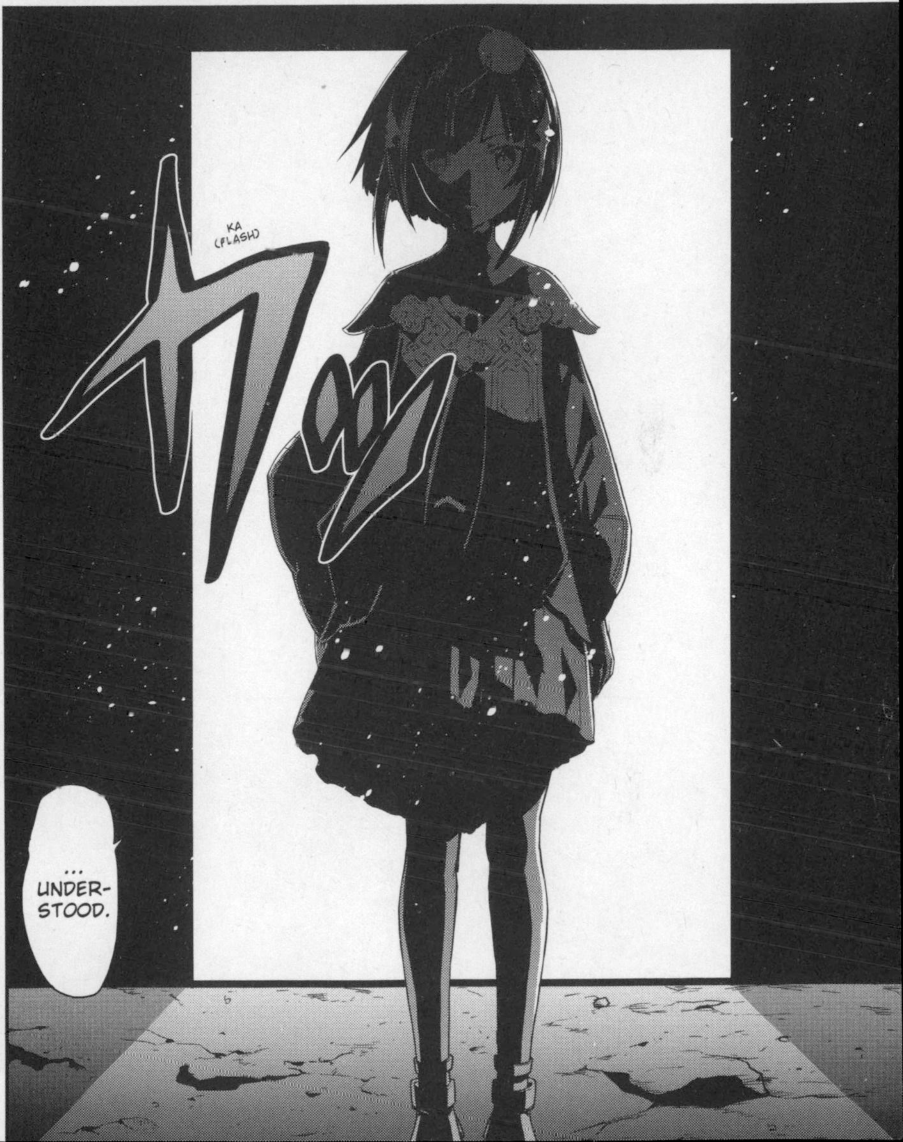
カッ
KA (FLASH)
... UNDER-STOOD.

#06: Proceed with Courage

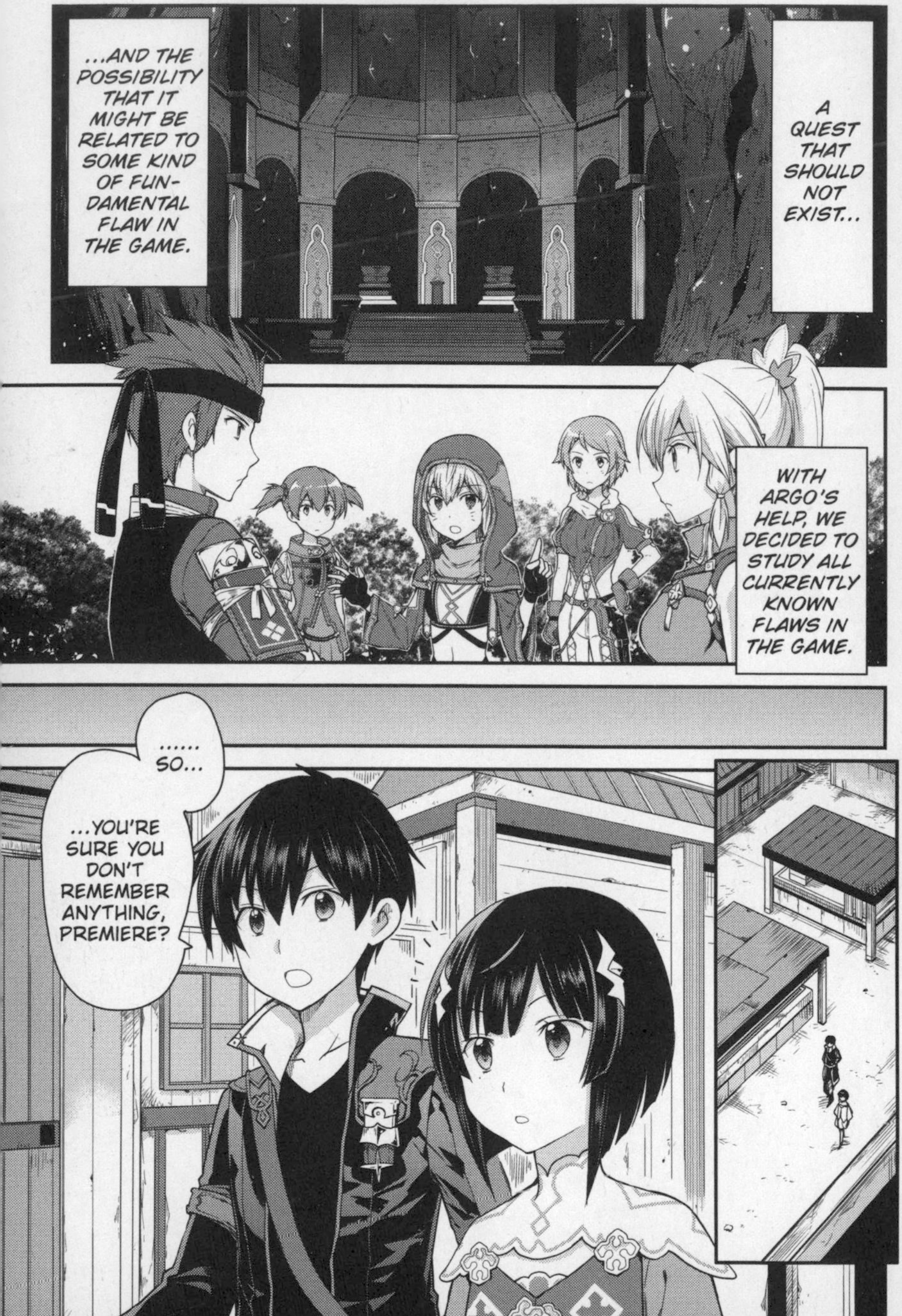
A QUEST THAT SHOULD NOT EXIST...
...AND THE POSSIBILITY THAT IT MIGHT BE RELATED TO SOME KIND OF FUN-DAMENTAL FLAW IN THE GAME.
WITH ARGO'S HELP, WE DECIDED TO STUDY ALL CURRENTLY KNOWN FLAWS IN THE GAME.
...... SO...
...YOU'RE SURE YOU DON'T REMEMBER ANYTHING, PREMIERE?

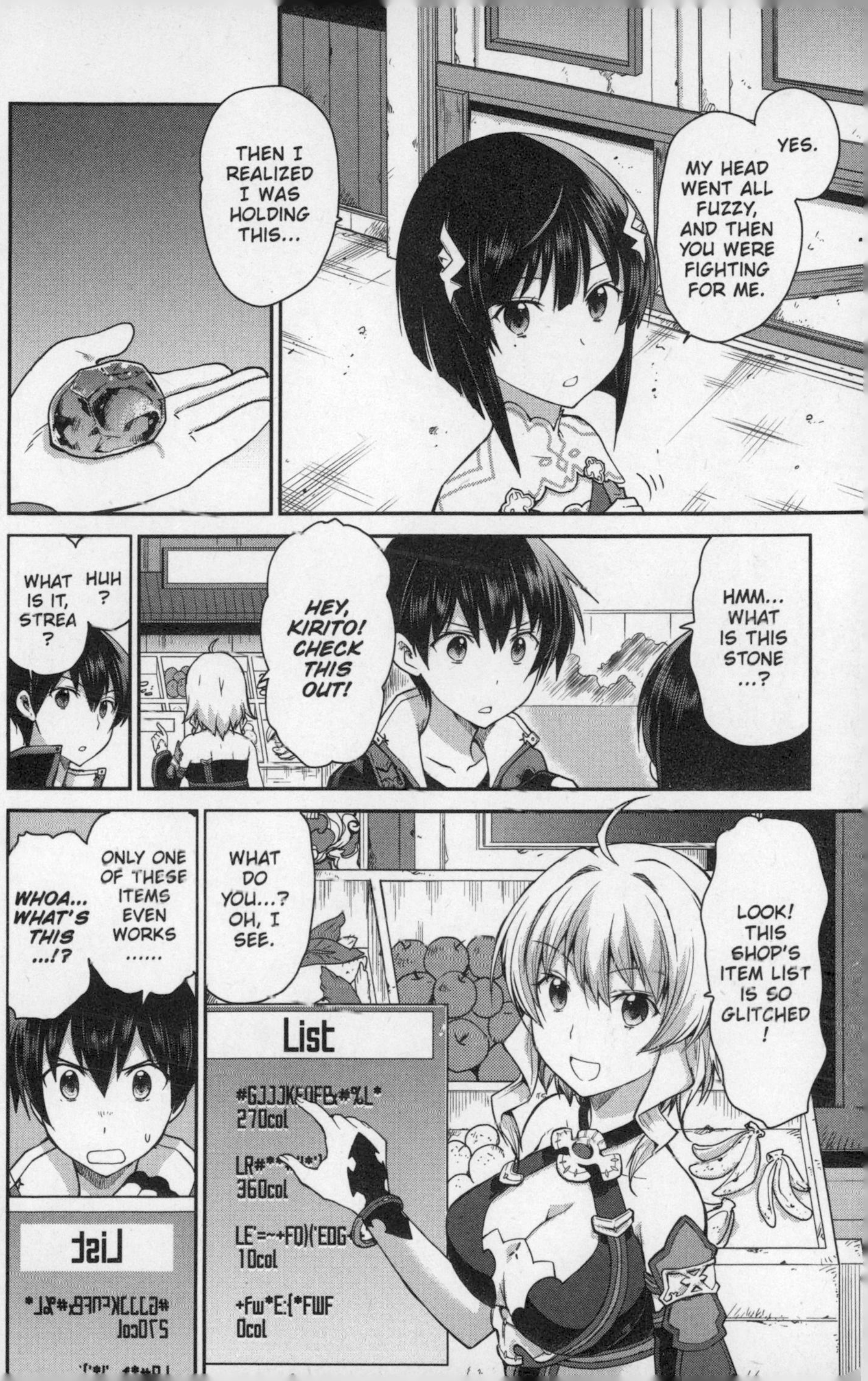
YES. MY HEAD WENT ALL FUZZY, AND THEN YOU WERE FIGHTING FOR ME.
THEN I REALIZED I WAS HOLDING THIS...
HMM... WHAT IS THIS STONE ...?
HEY, KIRITO! CHECK THIS OUT!
HUH?
WHAT IS IT, STREA?
LOOK! THIS SHOP'S ITEM LIST IS SO GLITCHED!
List
270col
360col
10col
+Fw*E:[*FWF
0col
WHAT DO YOU...? OH, I SEE.
ONLY ONE OF THESE ITEMS EVEN WORKS......
WHOA... WHAT'S THIS ...!?

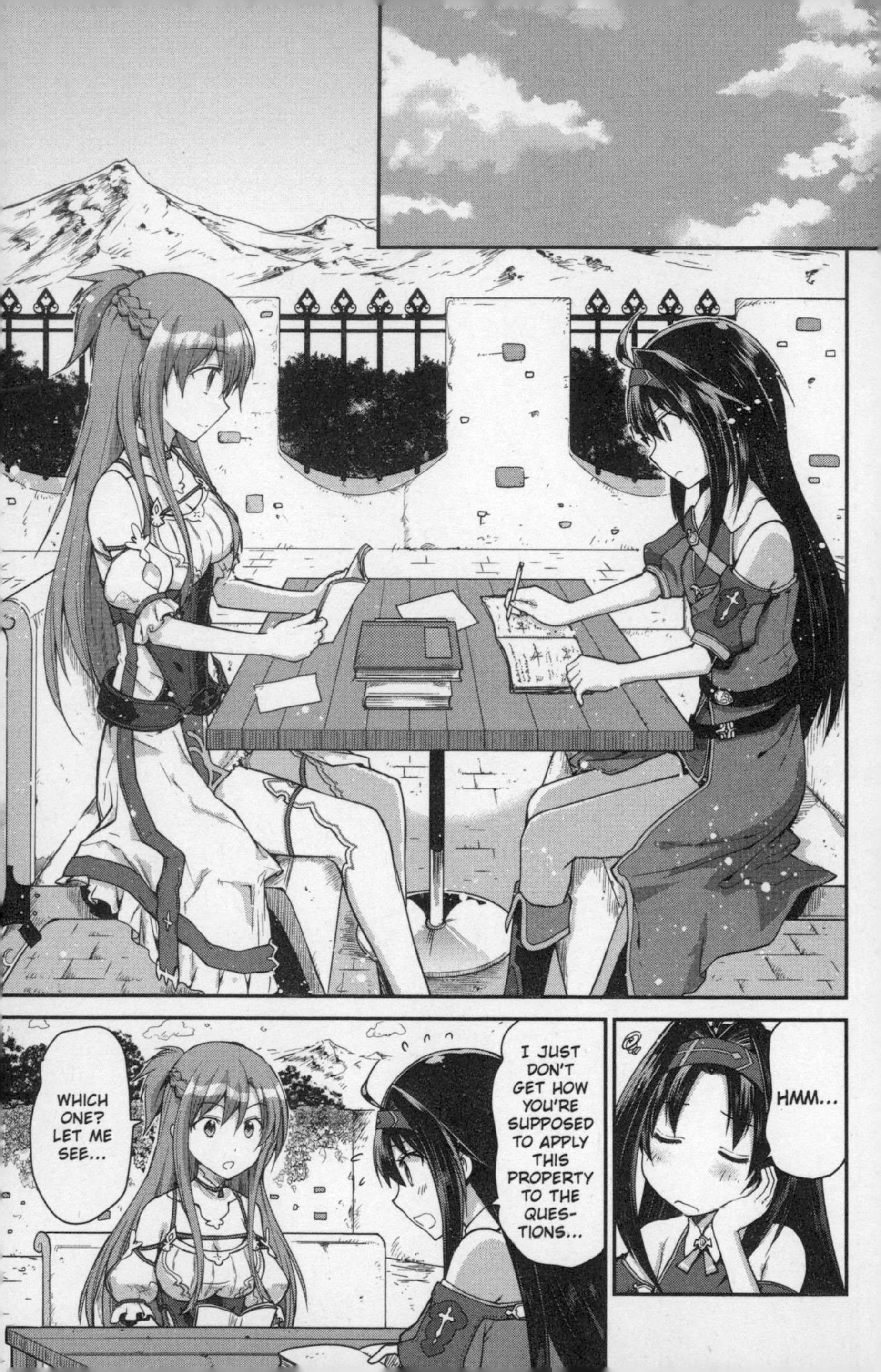
HMM...
I JUST DON'T GET HOW YOU'RE SUPPOSED TO APPLY THIS PROPERTY TO THE QUES-TIONS...
WHICH ONE? LET ME SEE...

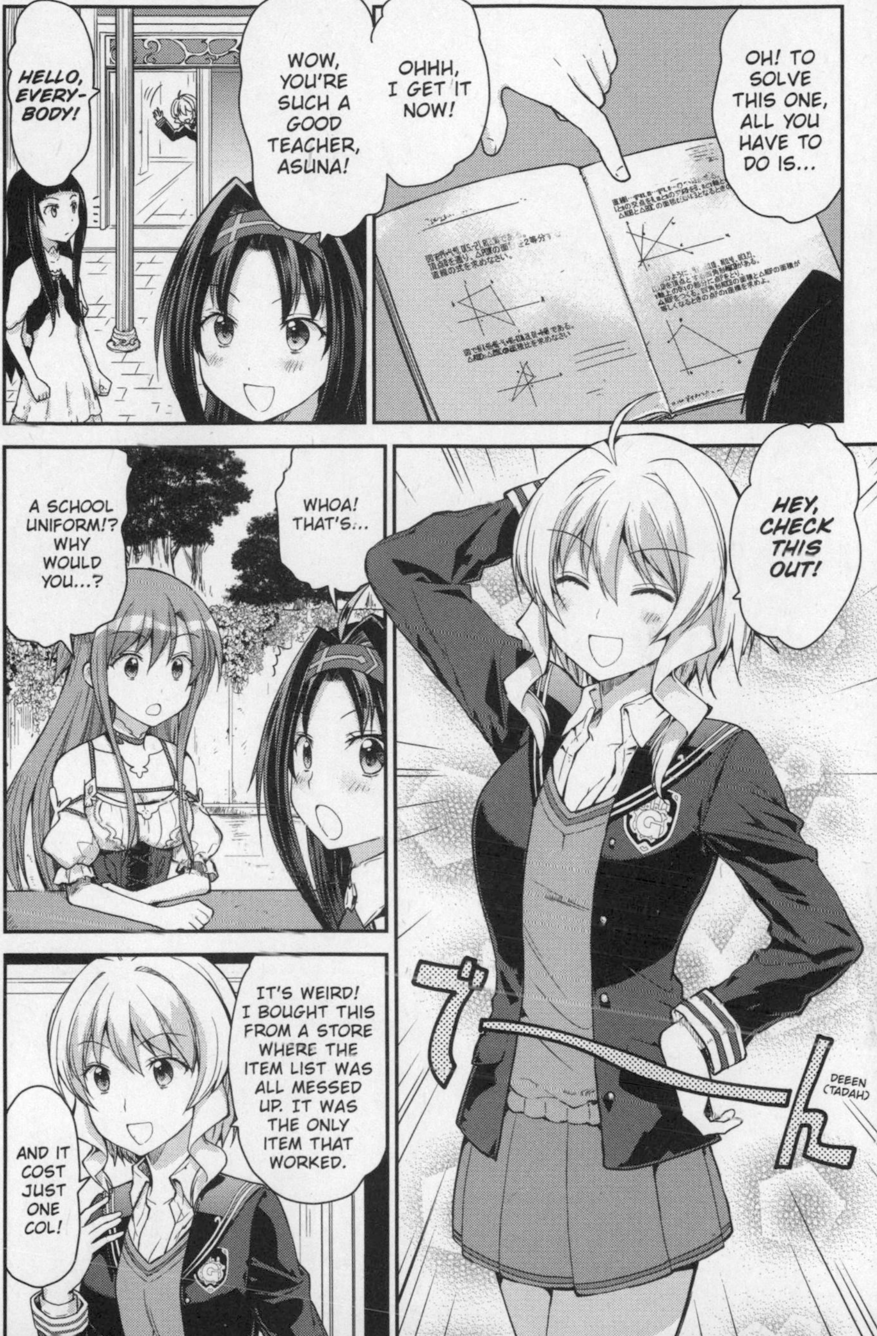
OH! TO SOLVE THIS ONE, ALL YOU HAVE TO DO IS...
OHHH, I GET IT NOW!
WOW, YOU'RE SUCH A GOOD TEACHER, ASUNA!
HELLO, EVERYBODY!
HEY, CHECK THIS OUT!
でーん
DEEEN (TADAH)
WHOA! THAT'S...
A SCHOOL UNIFORM!? WHY WOULD YOU...?
IT'S WEIRD! I BOUGHT THIS FROM A STORE WHERE THE ITEM LIST WAS ALL MESSED UP. IT WAS THE ONLY ITEM THAT WORKED.
AND IT COST JUST ONE COL!

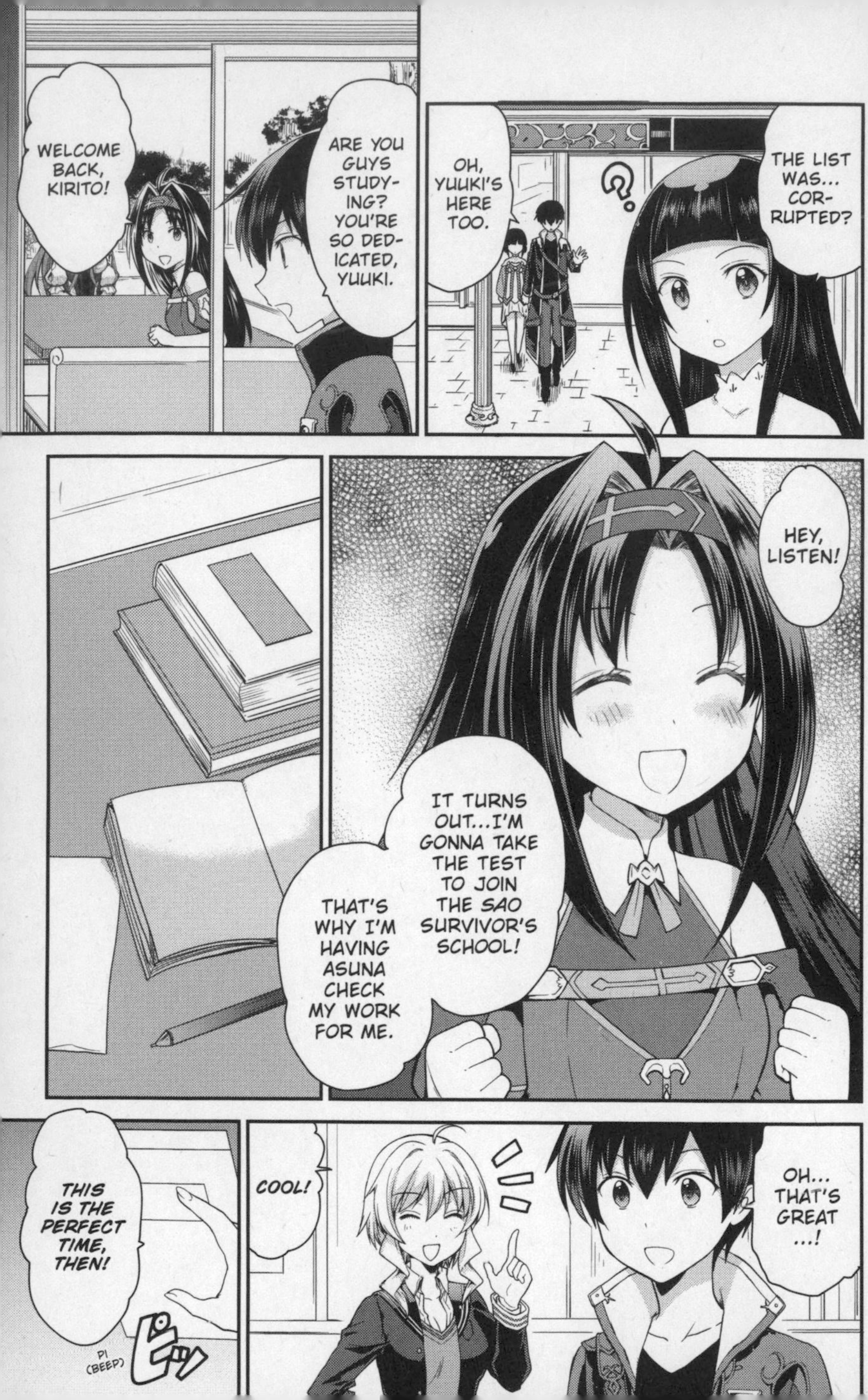
THE LIST WAS... COR-RUPTED?
OH, YUUKI'S HERE TOO.
ARE YOU GUYS STUDY-ING? YOU'RE SO DED-ICATED, YUUKI.
WELCOME BACK, KIRITO!
HEY, LISTEN!
IT TURNS OUT...I'M GONNA TAKE THE TEST TO JOIN THE SAO SURVIVOR'S SCHOOL!
THAT'S WHY I'M HAVING ASUNA CHECK MY WORK FOR ME.
OH... THAT'S GREAT ...!
COOL!
THIS IS THE PERFECT TIME, THEN!
PI (BEEP)

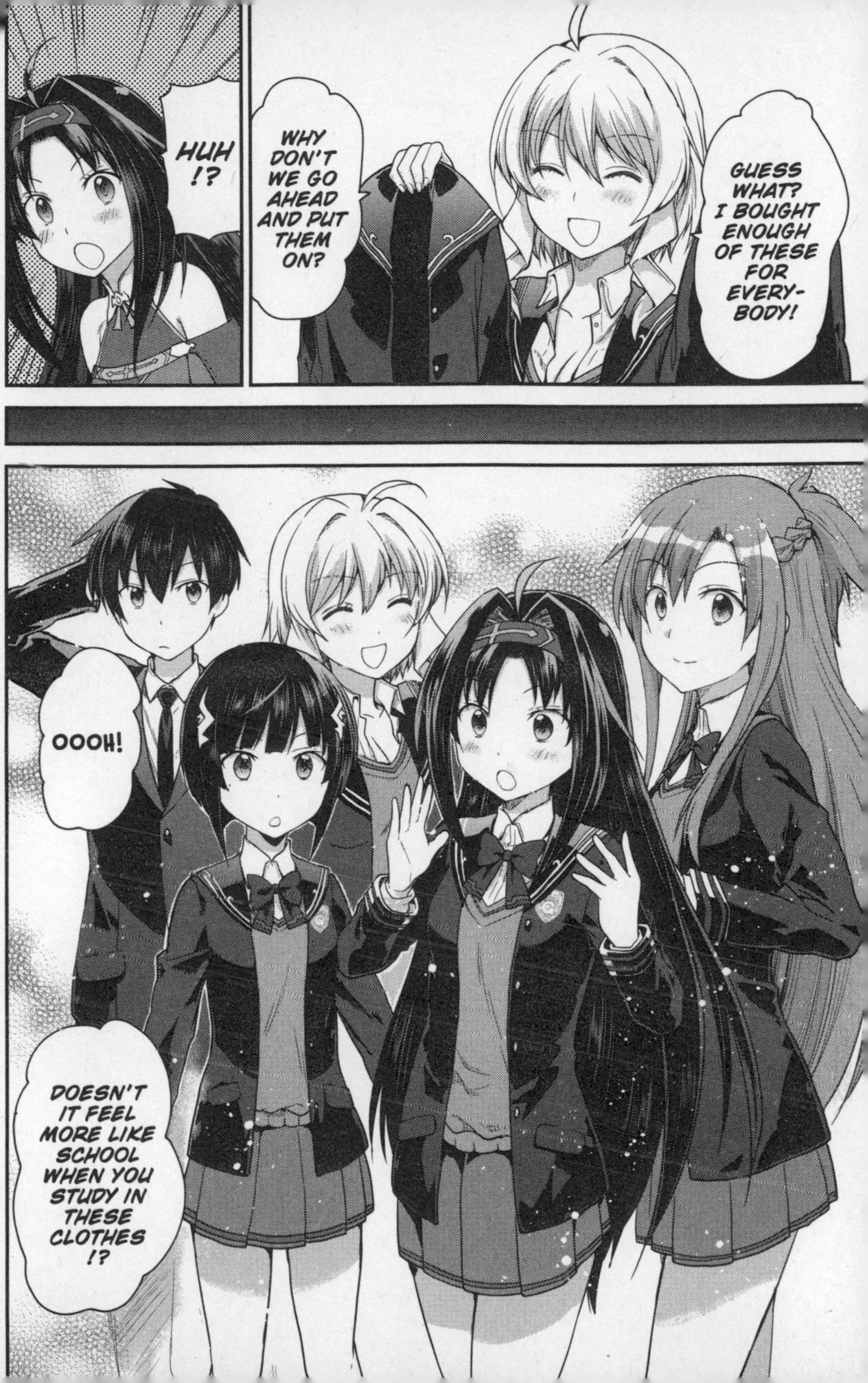
GUESS WHAT? I BOUGHT ENOUGH OF THESE FOR EVERY-BODY!
WHY DON'T WE GO AHEAD AND PUT THEM ON?
HUH !?
OOOH!
DOESN'T IT FEEL MORE LIKE SCHOOL WHEN YOU STUDY IN THESE CLOTHES !?

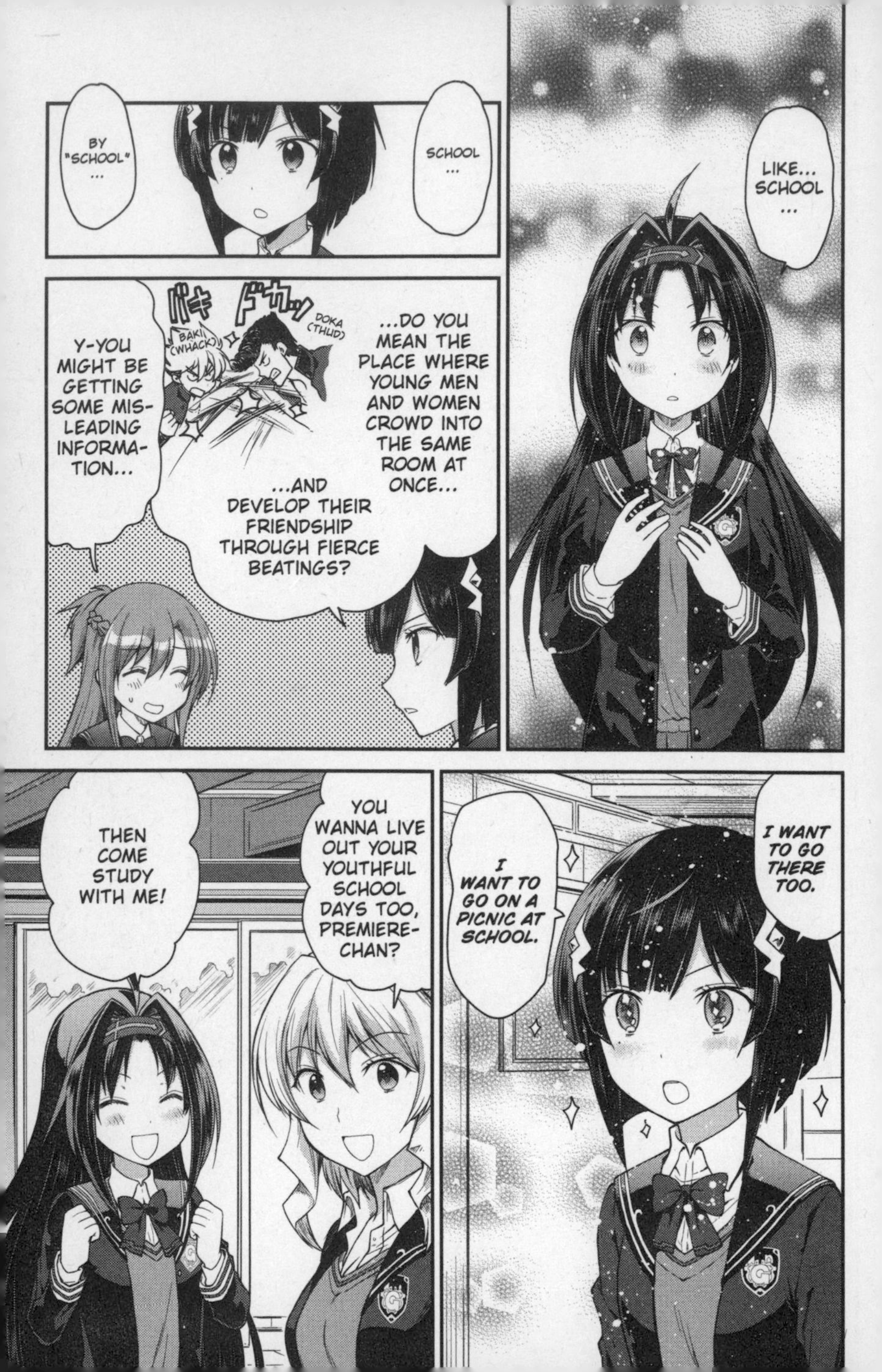
LIKE... SCHOOL ...
SCHOOL ...
BY "SCHOOL" ...
...DO YOU MEAN THE PLACE WHERE YOUNG MEN AND WOMEN CROWD INTO THE SAME ROOM AT ONCE...
ドカッ
DOKA (THUD)
パキ
BAKI (WHACK)
...AND DEVELOP THEIR FRIENDSHIP THROUGH FIERCE BEATINGS?
Y-YOU MIGHT BE GETTING SOME MIS-LEADING INFORMA-TION...
I WANT TO GO THERE TOO.
I WANT TO GO ON A PICNIC AT SCHOOL.
YOU WANNA LIVE OUT YOUR YOUTHFUL SCHOOL DAYS TOO, PREMIERE-CHAN?
THEN COME STUDY WITH ME!

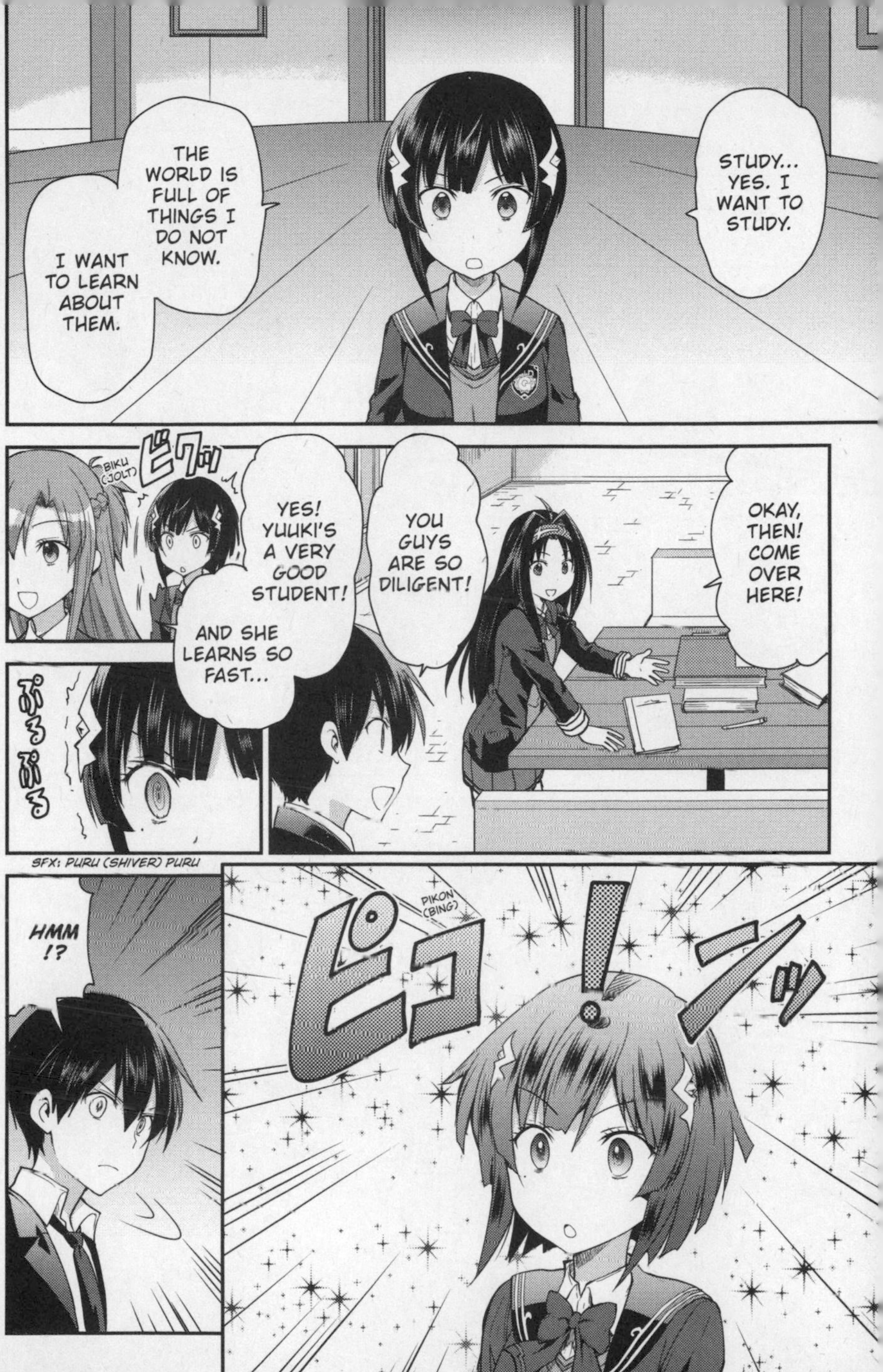
STUDY... YES. I WANT TO STUDY.
THE WORLD IS FULL OF THINGS I DO NOT KNOW.
I WANT TO LEARN ABOUT THEM.
OKAY, THEN! COME OVER HERE!
YOU GUYS ARE SO DILIGENT!
YES! YUUKI'S A VERY GOOD STUDENT!
BIKU (JOLT)
AND SHE LEARNS SO FAST...
ぷるぷる
SFX: PURU (SHIVER) PURU
PIKON (BING)
HMM !?

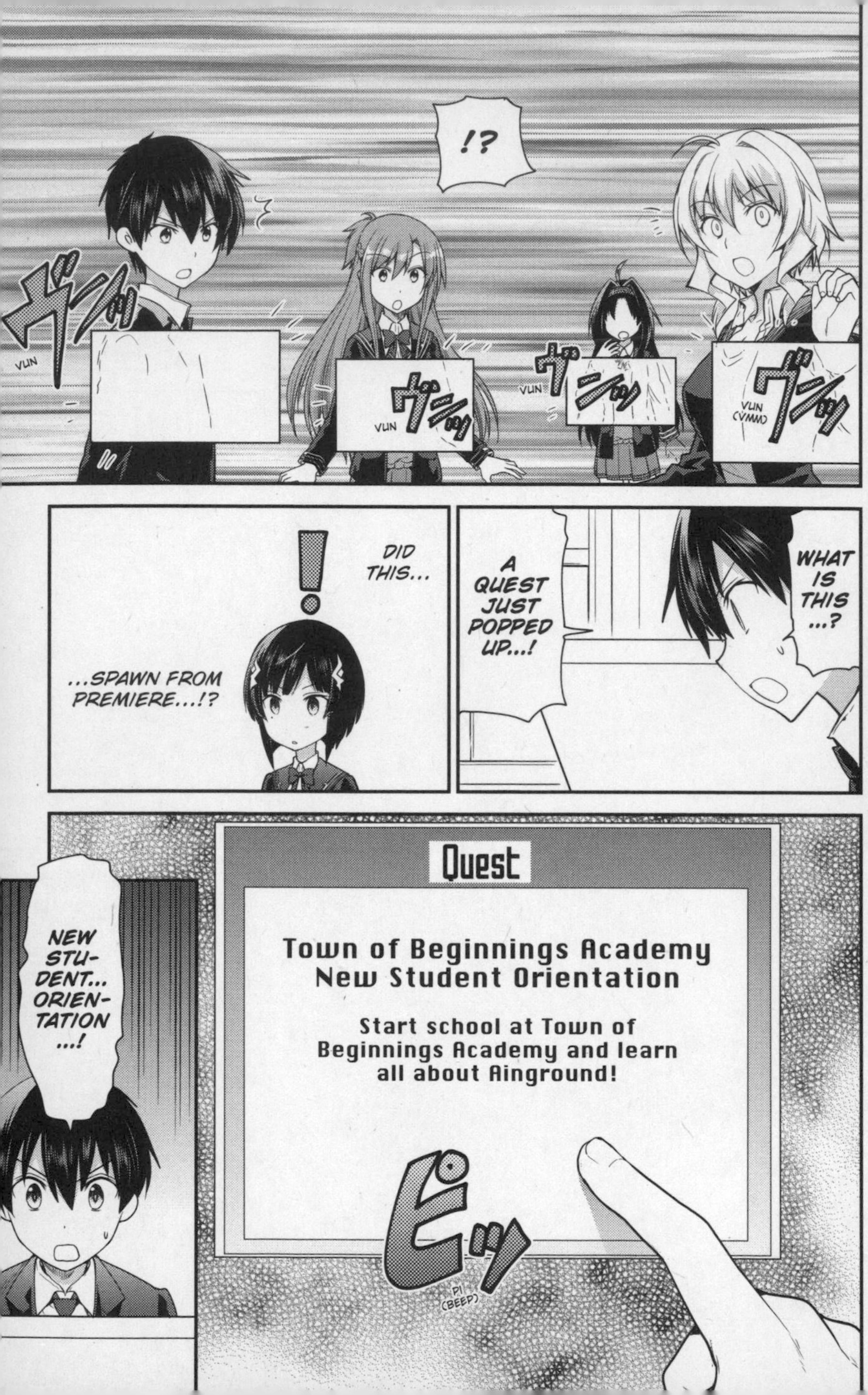
!?
VUN (VMM)
VUN
VUN
VUN
WHAT IS THIS ...?
A QUEST JUST POPPED UP...!
DID THIS...
...SPAWN FROM PREMIERE...!?
Quest
Town of Beginnings Academy
New Student Orientation
Start school at Town of Beginnings Academy and learn all about Ainground!
PI (BEEP)
NEW STUDENT... ORIENTATION ...!

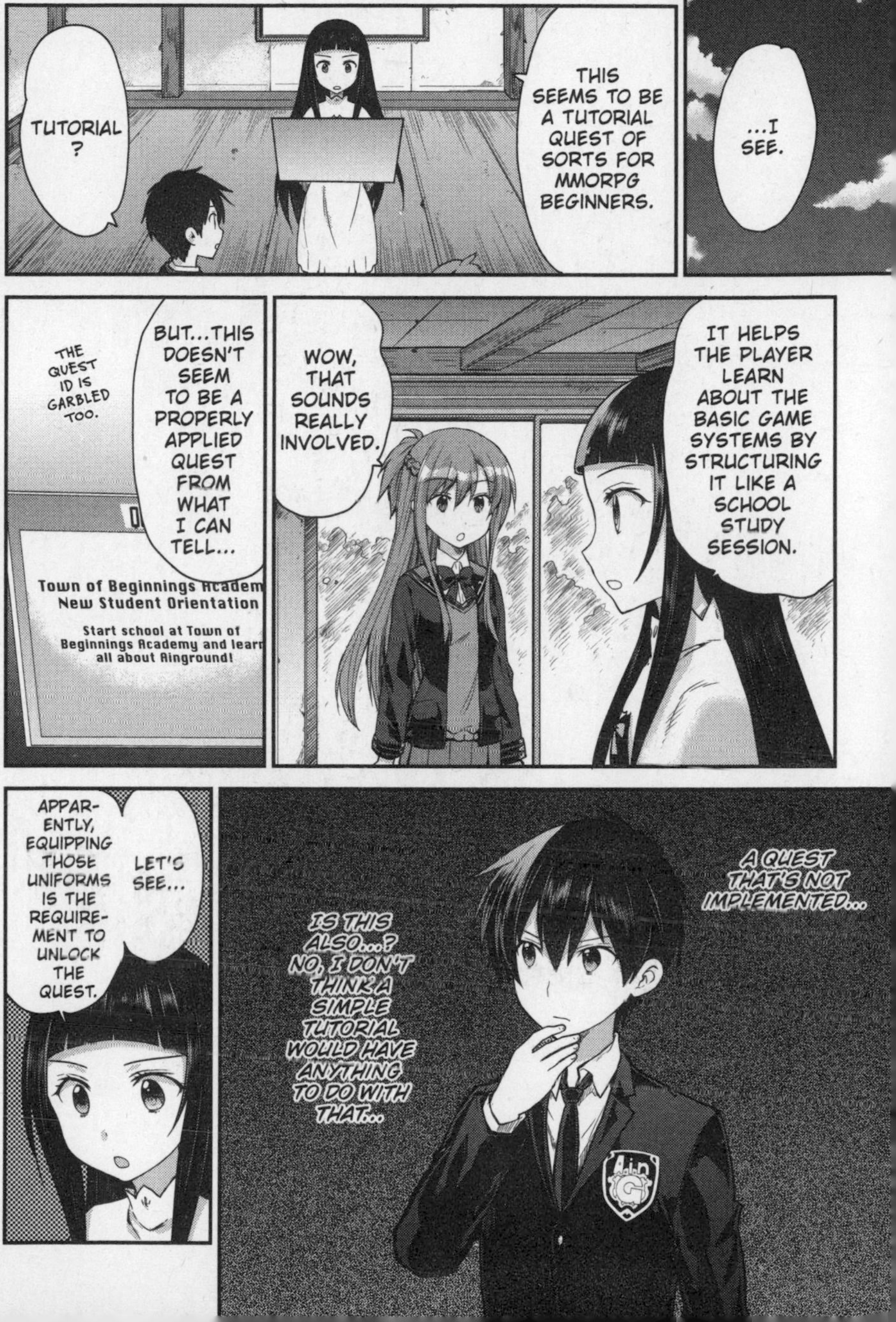
...I SEE.
THIS SEEMS TO BE A TUTORIAL QUEST OF SORTS FOR MMORPG BEGINNERS.
TUTORIAL?
IT HELPS THE PLAYER LEARN ABOUT THE BASIC GAME SYSTEMS BY STRUCTURING IT LIKE A SCHOOL STUDY SESSION.
WOW, THAT SOUNDS REALLY INVOLVED.
BUT...THIS DOESN'T SEEM TO BE A PROPERLY APPLIED QUEST FROM WHAT I CAN TELL...
THE QUEST ID IS GARBLED TOO.
Town of Beginnings Academ
New Student Orientation
Start school at Town of Beginnings Academy and learn all about Ainground!
A QUEST THAT'S NOT IMPLEMENTED...
IS THIS ALSO...? NO, I DON'T THINK A SIMPLE TUTORIAL WOULD HAVE ANYTHING TO DO WITH THAT...
LET'S SEE...
APPARENTLY, EQUIPPING THOSE UNIFORMS IS THE REQUIREMENT TO UNLOCK THE QUEST.

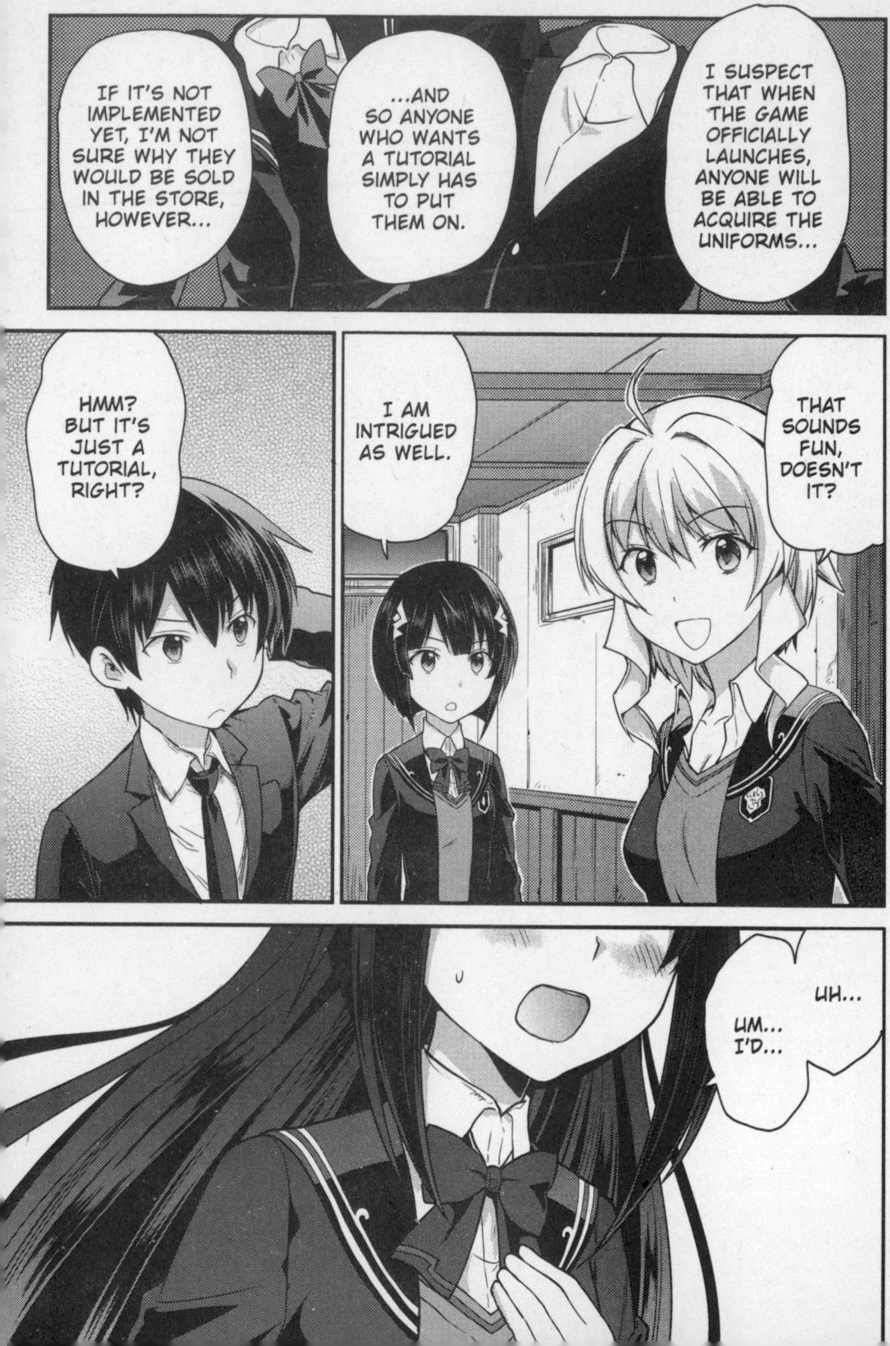
I SUSPECT THAT WHEN THE GAME OFFICIALLY LAUNCHES, ANYONE WILL BE ABLE TO ACQUIRE THE UNIFORMS...
...AND SO ANYONE WHO WANTS A TUTORIAL SIMPLY HAS TO PUT THEM ON.
IF IT'S NOT IMPLEMENTED YET, I'M NOT SURE WHY THEY WOULD BE SOLD IN THE STORE, HOWEVER...
THAT SOUNDS FUN, DOESN'T IT?
I AM INTRIGUED AS WELL.
HMM? BUT IT'S JUST A TUTORIAL, RIGHT?
UH...
UM... I'D...

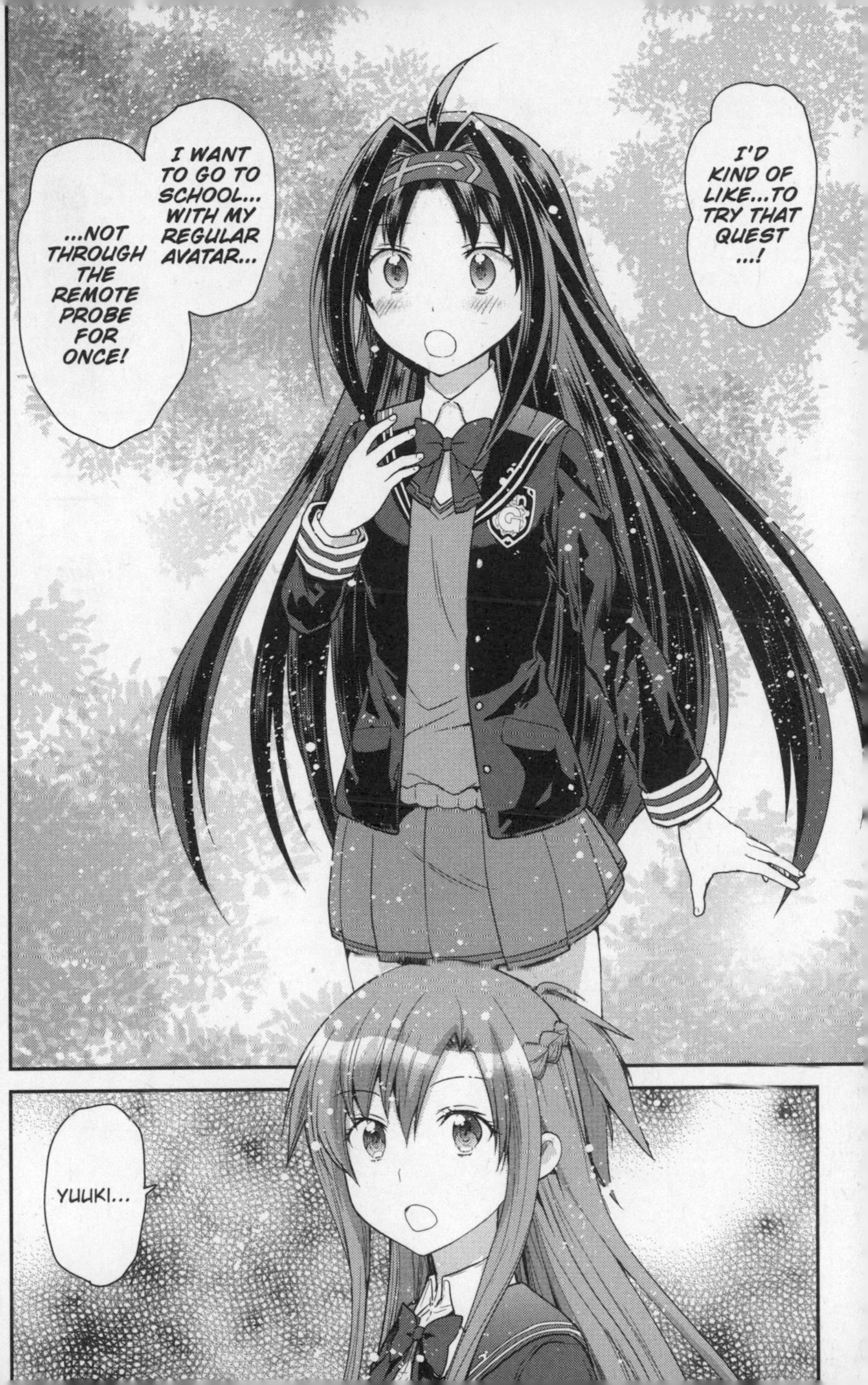
I'D KIND OF LIKE...TO TRY THAT QUEST ...!
I WANT TO GO TO SCHOOL... WITH MY REGULAR AVATAR...
...NOT THROUGH THE REMOTE PROBE FOR ONCE!
YUUKI...

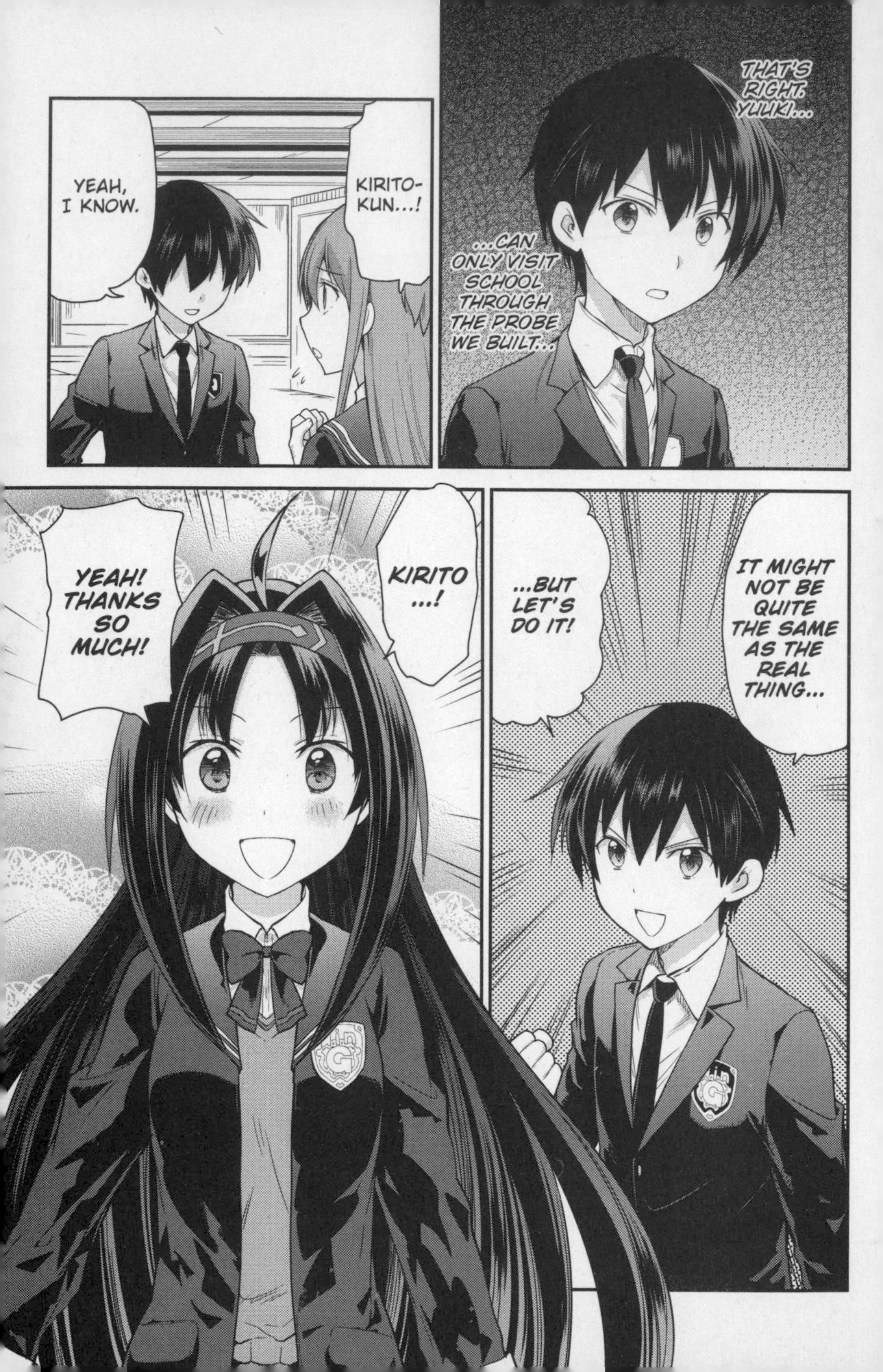
THAT'S RIGHT. YUUKI...
...CAN ONLY VISIT SCHOOL THROUGH THE PROBE WE BUILT...
KIRITO-KUN...!
YEAH, I KNOW.
IT MIGHT NOT BE QUITE THE SAME AS THE REAL THING...
...BUT LET'S DO IT!
KIRITO...!
YEAH! THANKS SO MUCH!

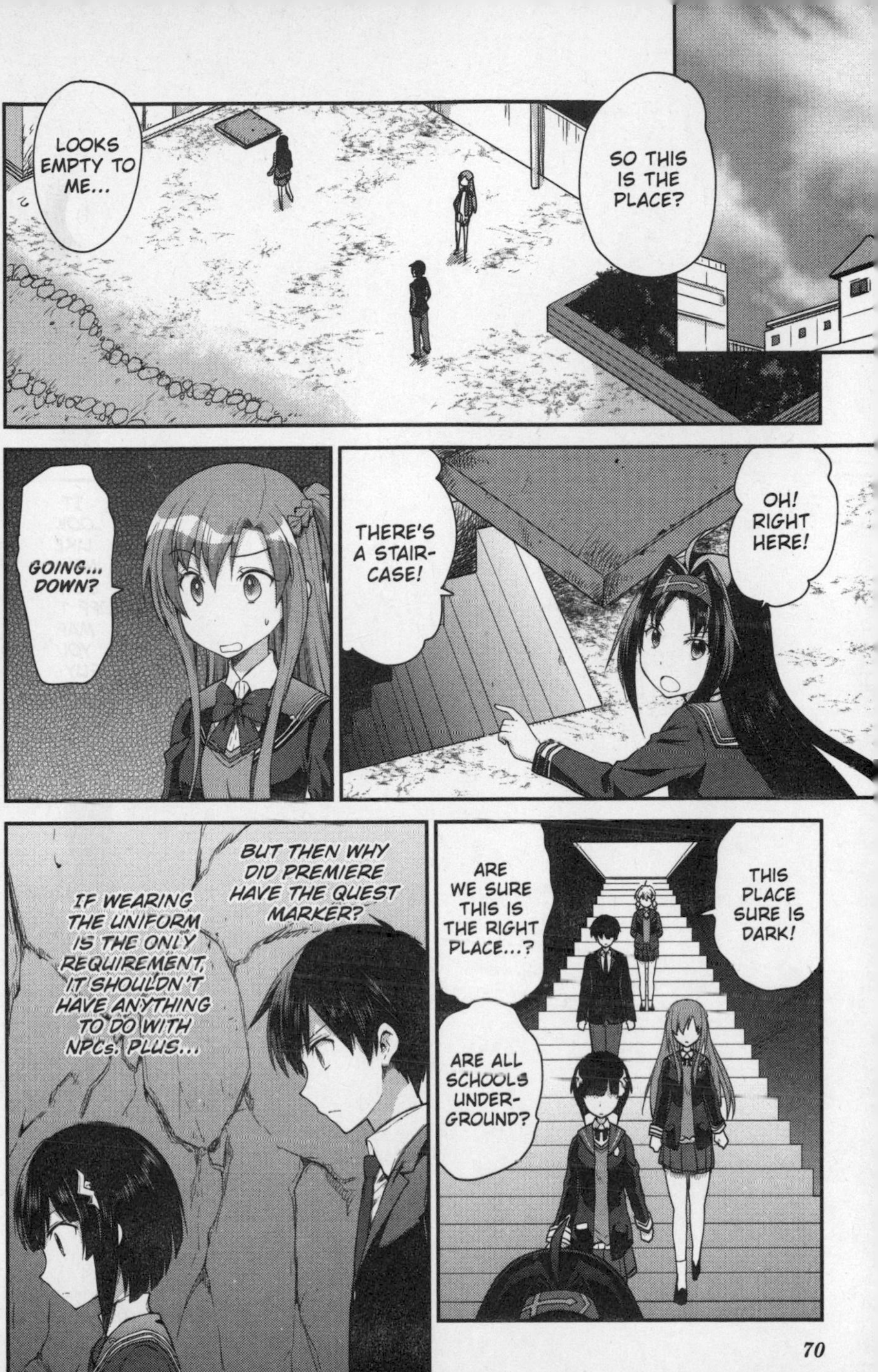
SO THIS IS THE PLACE?
LOOKS EMPTY TO ME...
OH! RIGHT HERE!
THERE'S A STAIR-CASE!
GOING... DOWN?
THIS PLACE SURE IS DARK!
ARE WE SURE THIS IS THE RIGHT PLACE...?
ARE ALL SCHOOLS UNDER-GROUND?
BUT THEN WHY DID PREMIERE HAVE THE QUEST MARKER?
IF WEARING THE UNIFORM IS THE ONLY REQUIREMENT, IT SHOULDN'T HAVE ANYTHING TO DO WITH NPCs. PLUS...

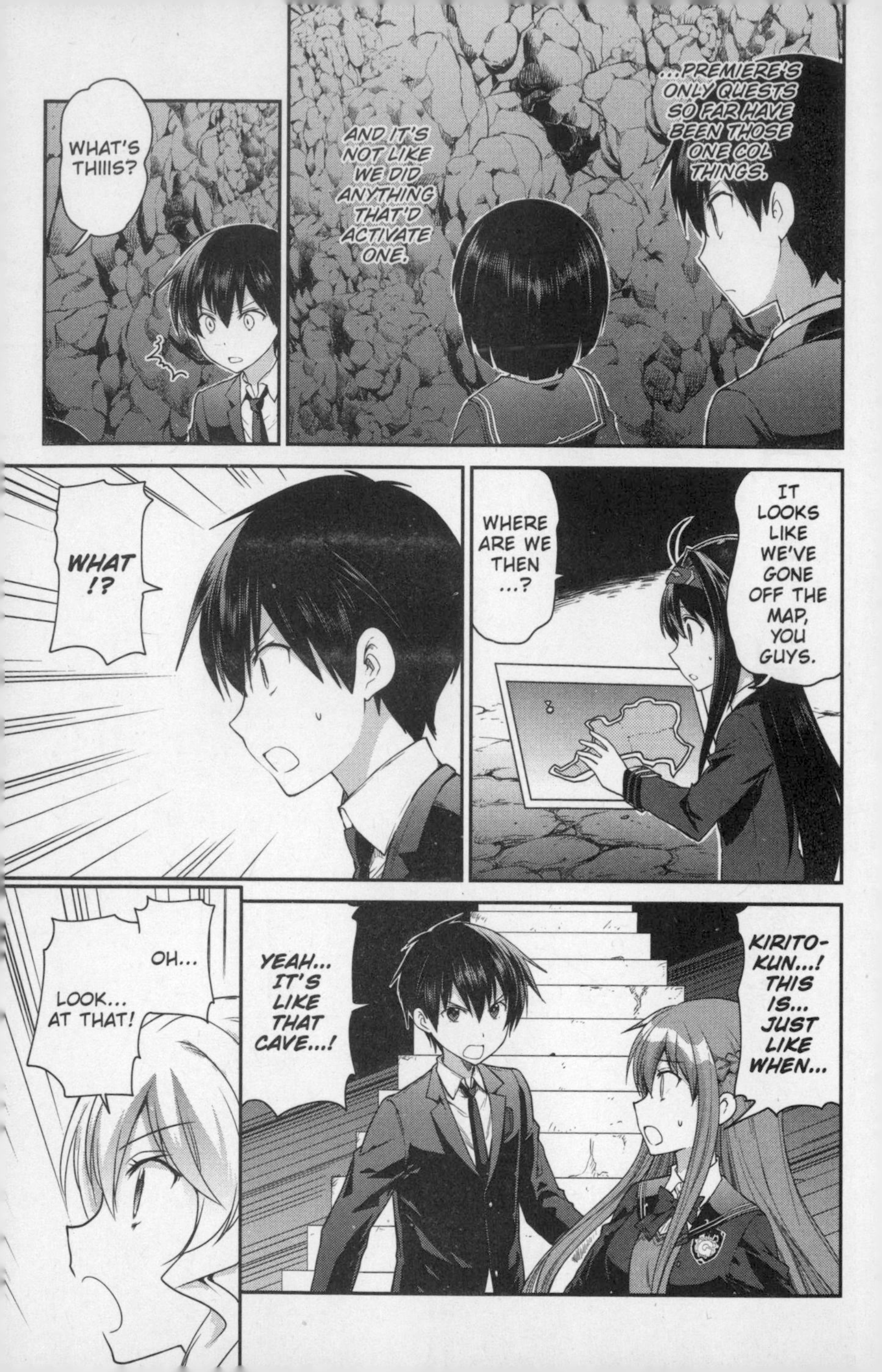
...PREMIERE'S ONLY QUESTS SO FAR HAVE BEEN THOSE ONE COL THINGS.
AND IT'S NOT LIKE WE DID ANYTHING THAT'D ACTIVATE ONE.
WHAT'S THIIIS?
IT LOOKS LIKE WE'VE GONE OFF THE MAP, YOU GUYS.
WHERE ARE WE THEN ...?
WHAT !?
KIRITO-KUN...! THIS IS... JUST LIKE WHEN...
YEAH... IT'S LIKE THAT CAVE...!
OH...
LOOK... AT THAT!

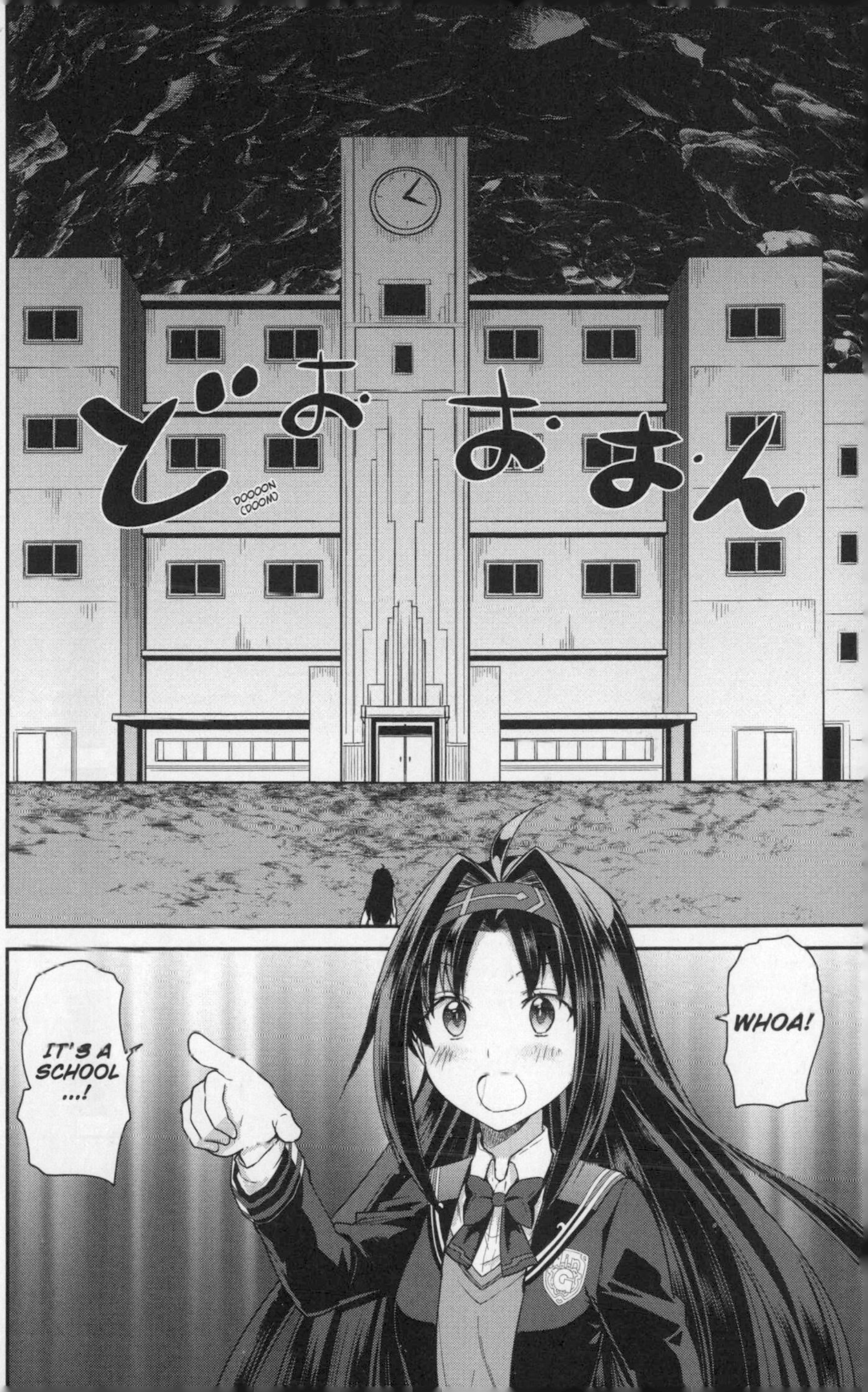
どおおん
DOOOON (DOOM)
WHOA!
IT'S A SCHOOL ...!

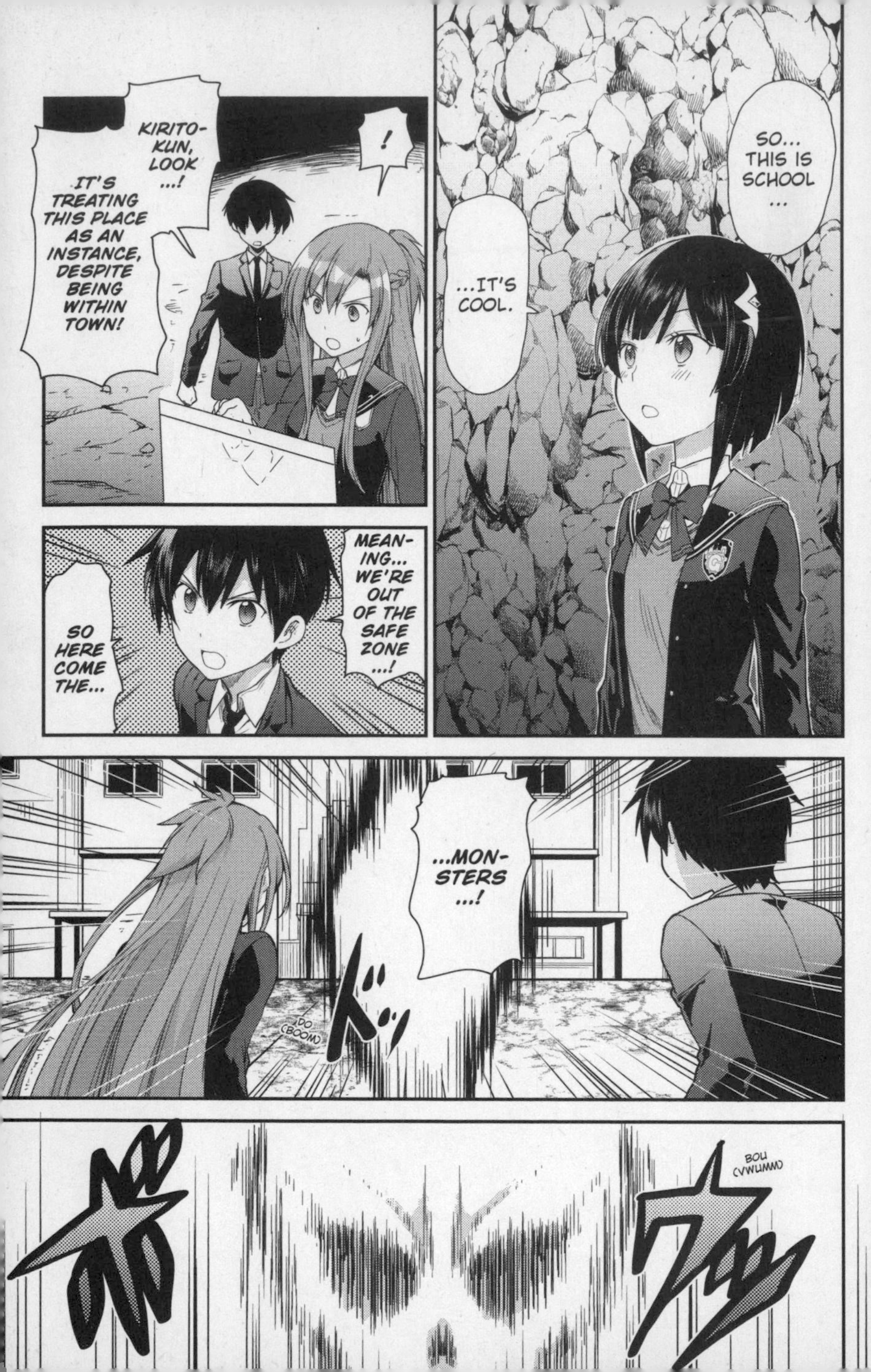
SO... THIS IS SCHOOL ...
...IT'S COOL.
!
KIRITO-KUN, LOOK ...!
IT'S TREATING THIS PLACE AS AN INSTANCE, DESPITE BEING WITHIN TOWN!
MEANING... WE'RE OUT OF THE SAFE ZONE ...!
SO HERE COME THE...
...MONSTERS ...!
ドッ
DO (BOOM)
ボワッ
BOU (VWUMM)

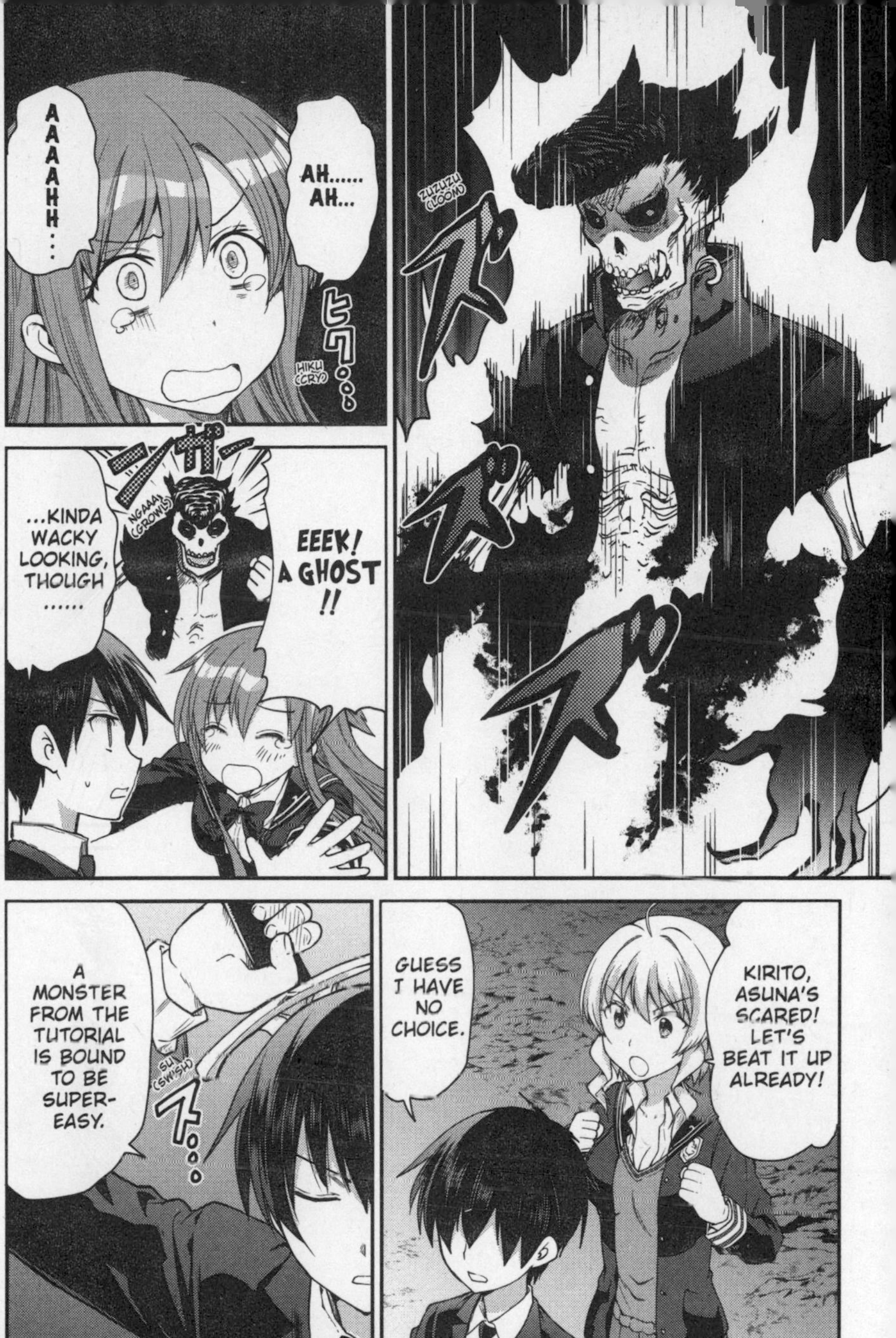
ZUZUZU (LOOM)
AH...... AH...
AAAAAHH...
HIKU (CRY)
EEEK! A GHOST!!
NGAAA (GROWLS)
...KINDA WACKY LOOKING, THOUGH......
KIRITO, ASUNA'S SCARED! LET'S BEAT IT UP ALREADY!
GUESS I HAVE NO CHOICE.
SU (SWISH)
A MONSTER FROM THE TUTORIAL IS BOUND TO BE SUPER-EASY.

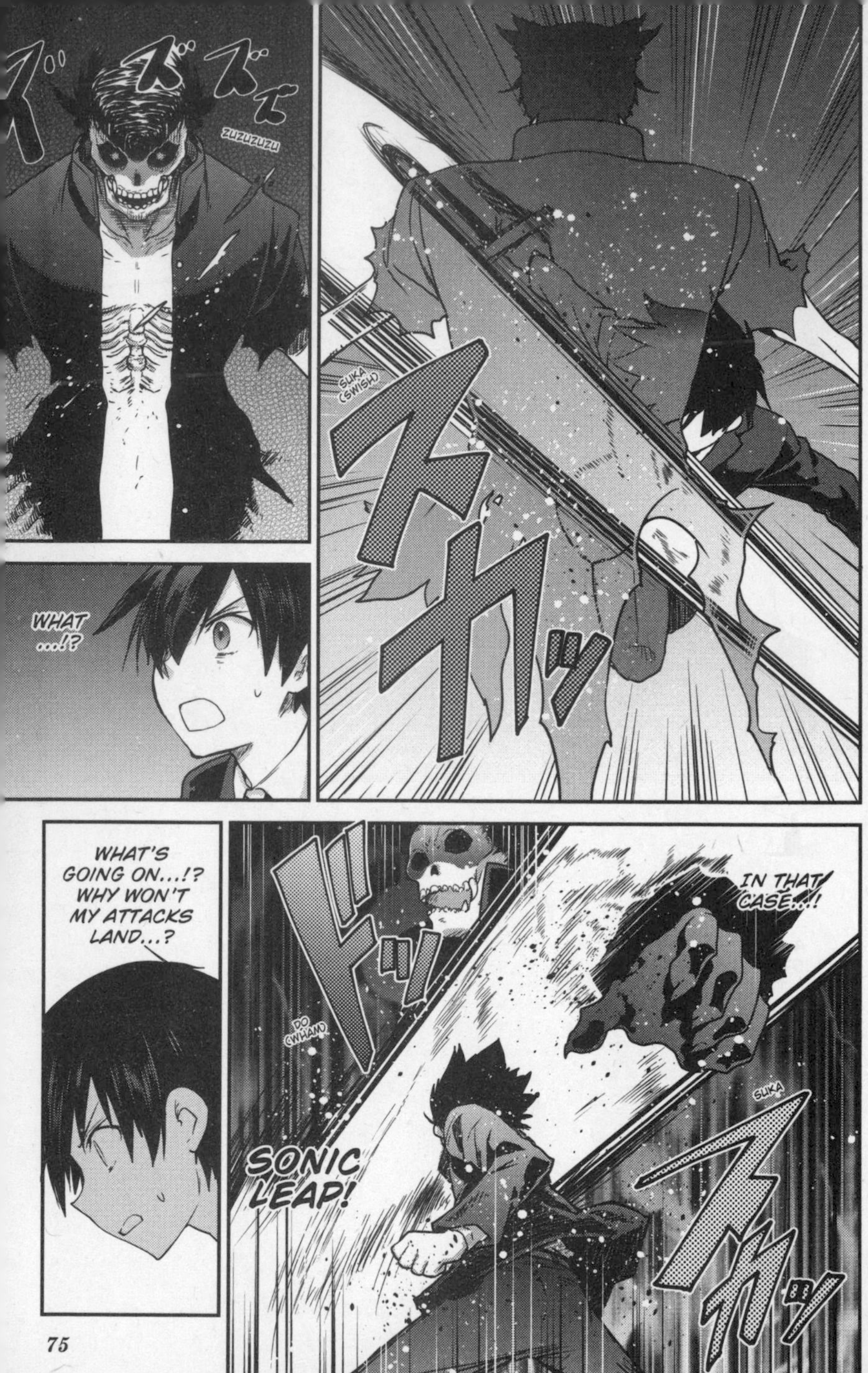
SUKA (SWISH)
ZUZUZUZU
WHAT ...!?
IN THAT CASE...!
DO (WHAM)
SUKA
SONIC LEAP!
WHAT'S GOING ON...!? WHY WON'T MY ATTACKS LAND...?

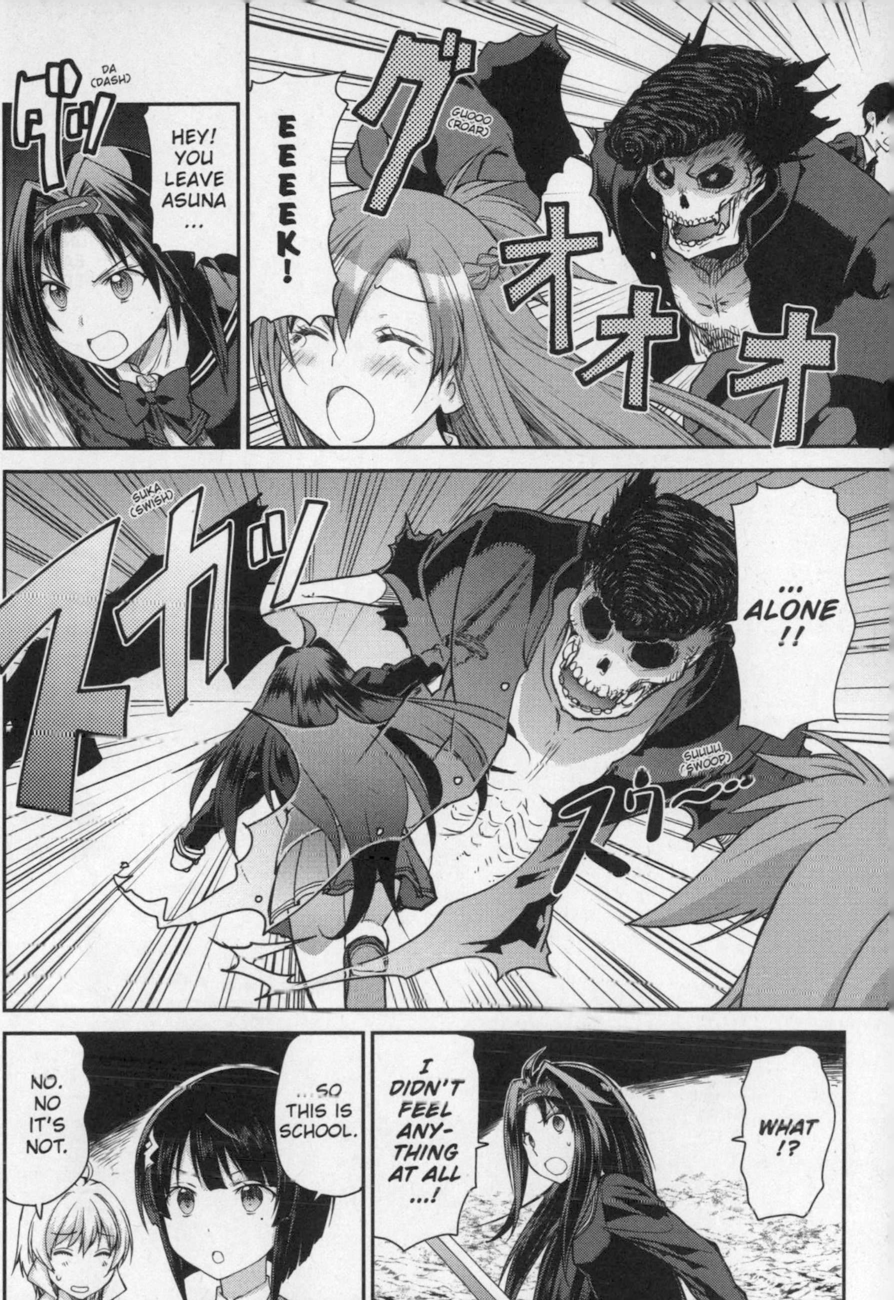
GUOOO (ROAR)
EEEEEK!
DA (DASH)
HEY! YOU LEAVE ASUNA ...
... ALONE !!
SUKA (SWISH)
SUUUU (SWOOP)
WHAT !?
I DIDN'T FEEL ANY-THING AT ALL ...!
... SO THIS IS SCHOOL.
NO. NO IT'S NOT.

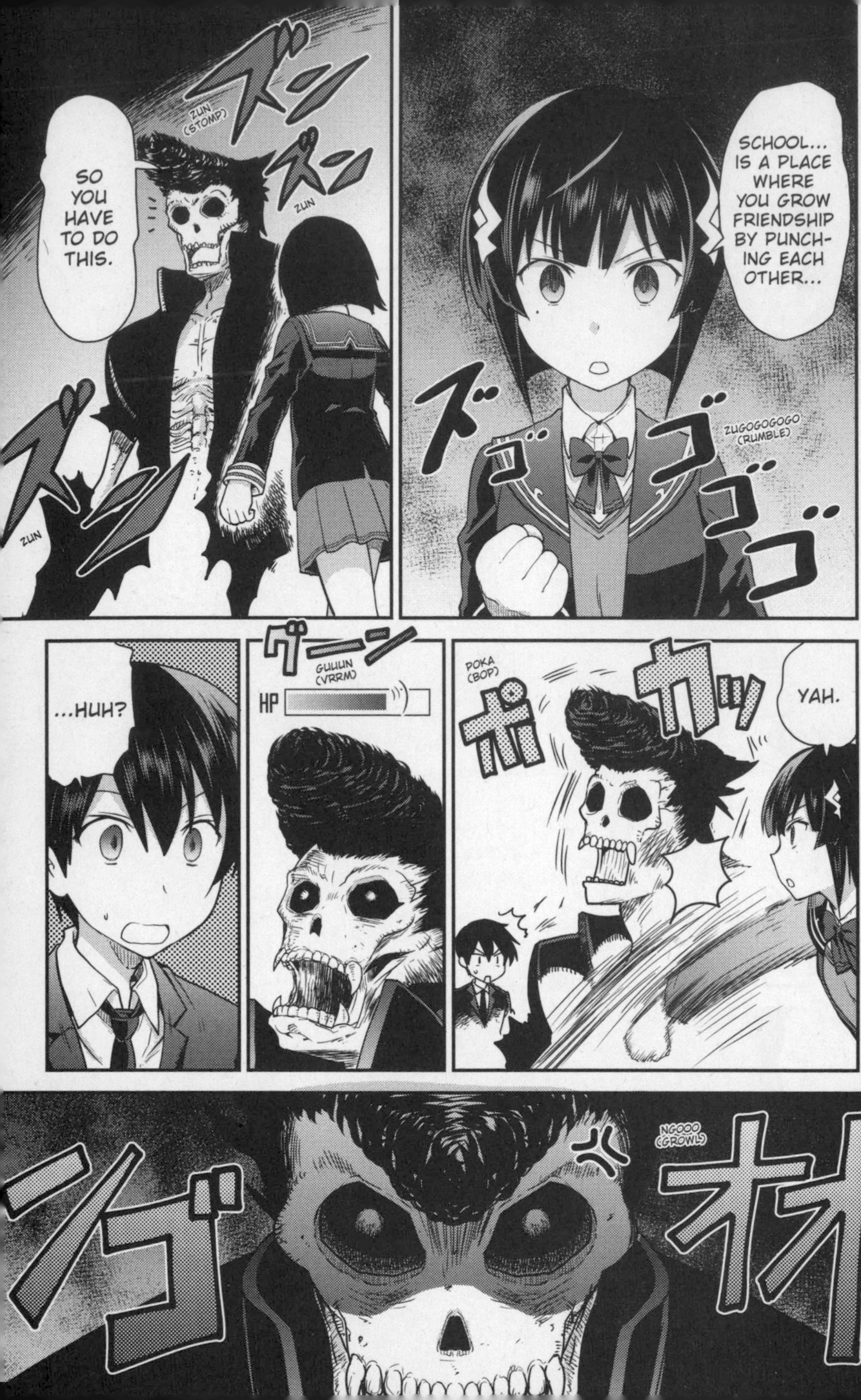
SCHOOL... IS A PLACE WHERE YOU GROW FRIENDSHIP BY PUNCH-ING EACH OTHER...
ZUGOGOGOGO (RUMBLE)
ZUN (STOMP)
SO YOU HAVE TO DO THIS.
ZUN
ZUN
YAH.
POKA (BOP)
GUHUN (VRRM)
HP
...HUH?
NGOOO (GROWL)

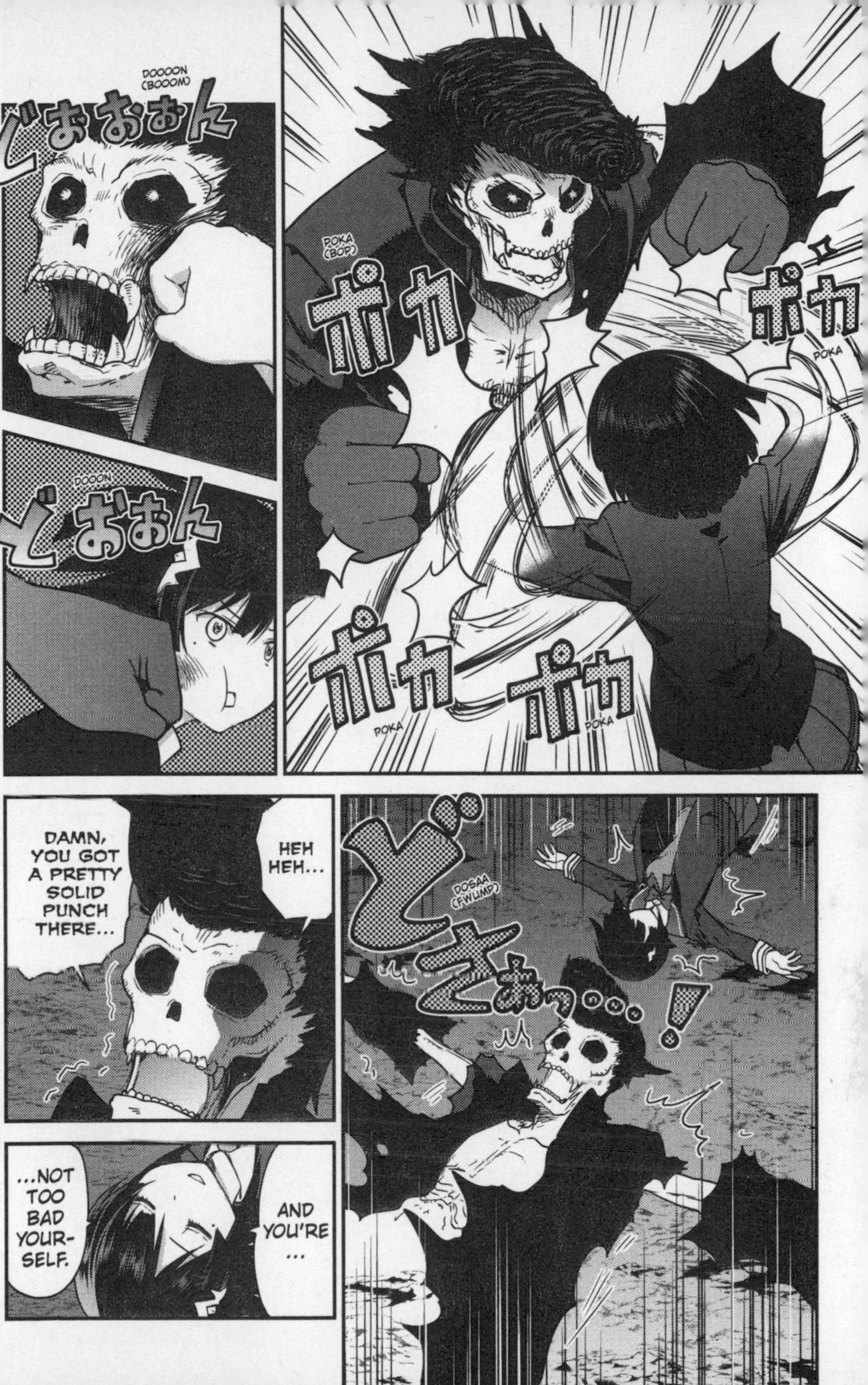
ポカ
POKA
POKA (BOP)
ポカ
ポカ
POKA
ポカー
POKA
DOOOON (BOOOM)
どぉぉぉん
DOOON
どぉぉん
DOSAA (FWUMP)
どさぁっ…！
HEH HEH...
DAMN, YOU GOT A PRETTY SOLID PUNCH THERE...
AND YOU'RE ...
...NOT TOO BAD YOURSELF.

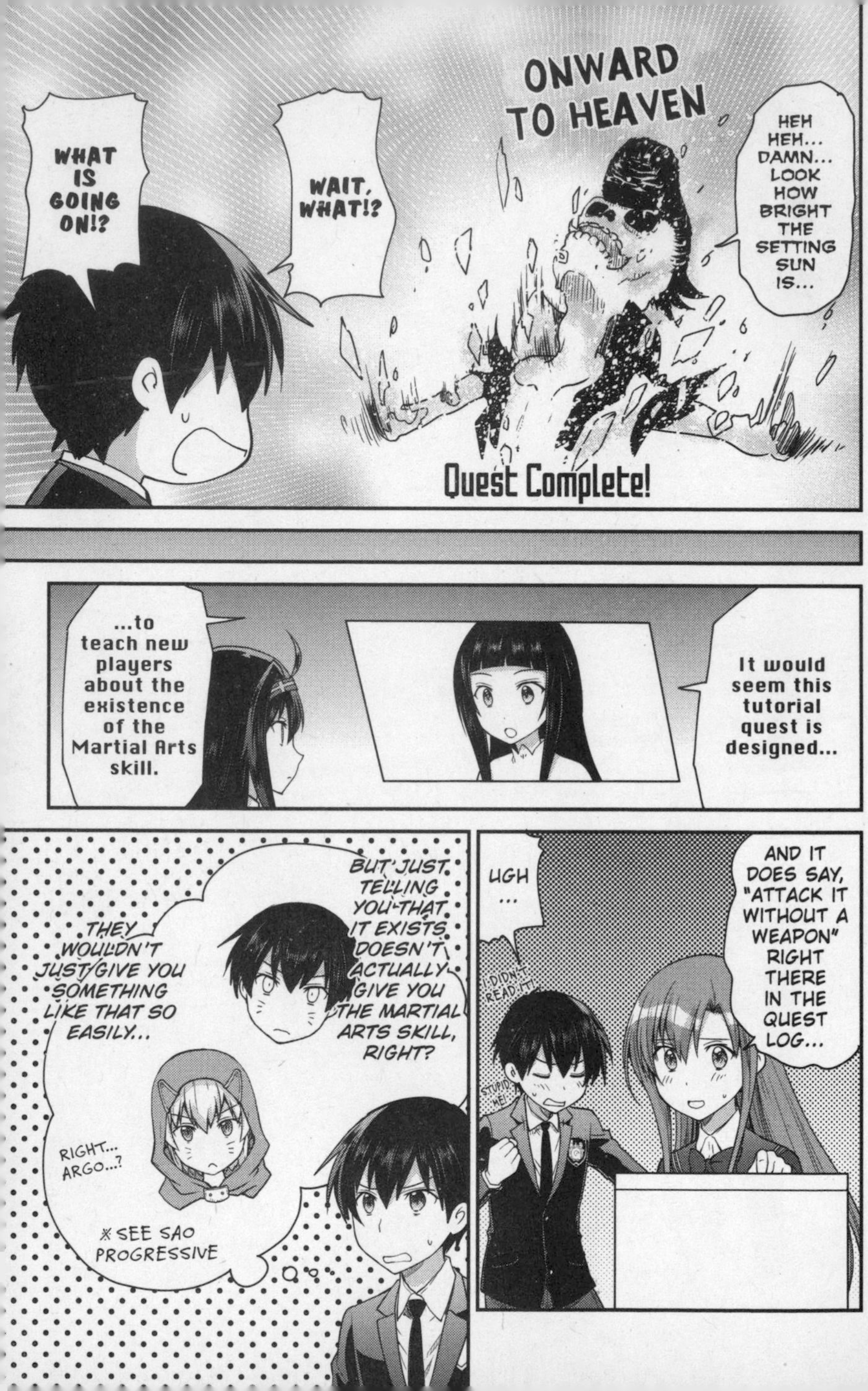
ONWARD TO HEAVEN
HEH HEH... DAMN... LOOK HOW BRIGHT THE SETTING SUN IS...
WAIT, WHAT!?
WHAT IS GOING ON!?
Quest Complete!
It would seem this tutorial quest is designed...
...to teach new players about the existence of the Martial Arts skill.
AND IT DOES SAY, "ATTACK IT WITHOUT A WEAPON" RIGHT THERE IN THE QUEST LOG...
UGH ...
I DIDN'T READ IT
STUPID ME!
BUT JUST TELLING YOU THAT IT EXISTS DOESN'T ACTUALLY GIVE YOU THE MARTIAL ARTS SKILL, RIGHT?
THEY WOULDN'T JUST GIVE YOU SOMETHING LIKE THAT SO EASILY...
RIGHT... ARGO...?
※SEE SAO PROGRESSIVE

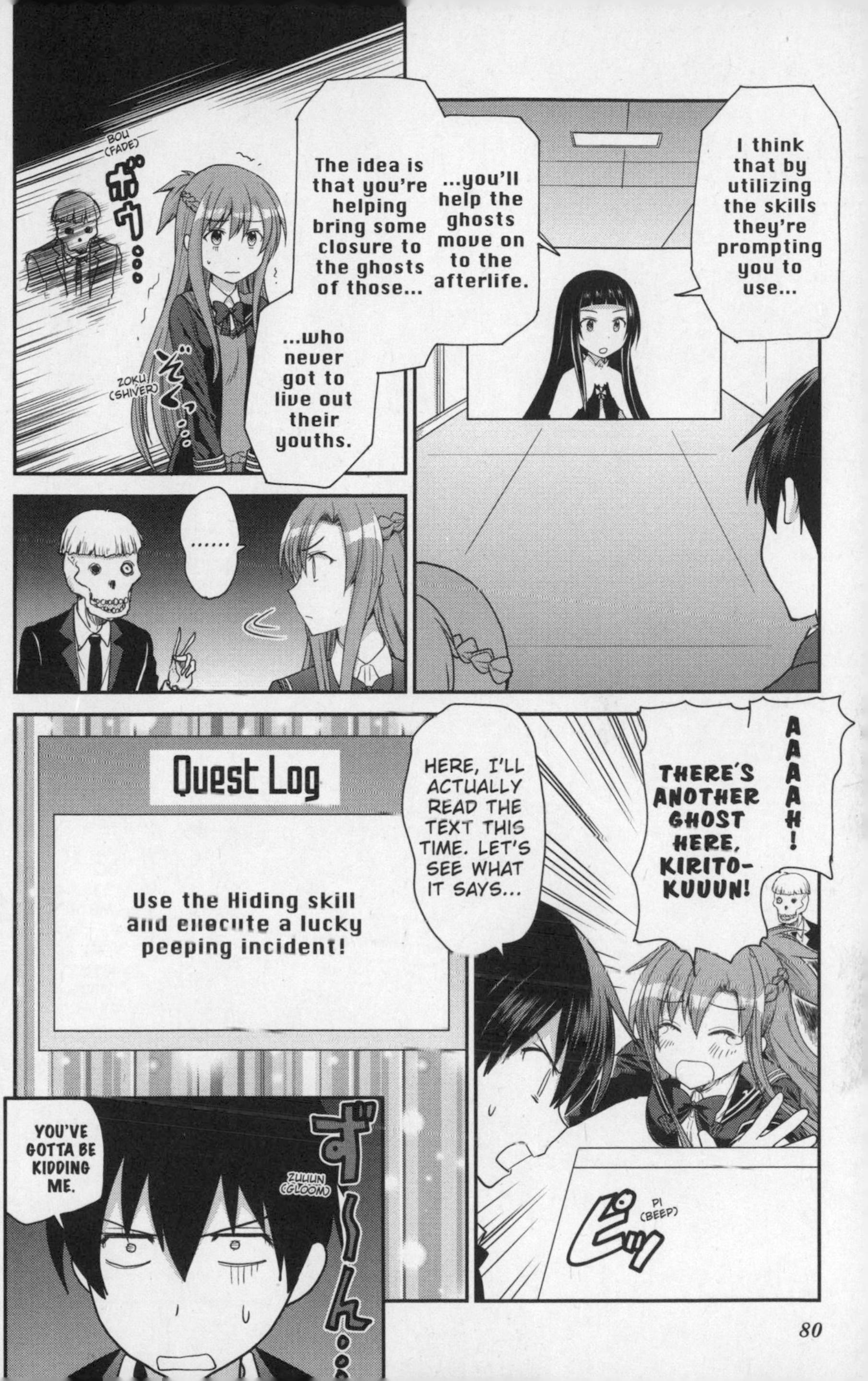
I think that by utilizing the skills they're prompting you to use...
...you'll help the ghosts move on to the afterlife.
The idea is that you're helping bring some closure to the ghosts of those...
BOU (FADE)
...who never got to live out their youths.
ZOKU (SHIVER)
......
AAAAH!
THERE'S ANOTHER GHOST HERE, KIRITO-KUUUN!
HERE, I'LL ACTUALLY READ THE TEXT THIS TIME. LET'S SEE WHAT IT SAYS...
PI (BEEP)
Quest Log
Use the Hiding skill and execute a lucky peeping incident!
ZUUUN (GLOOM)
YOU'VE GOTTA BE KIDDING ME.

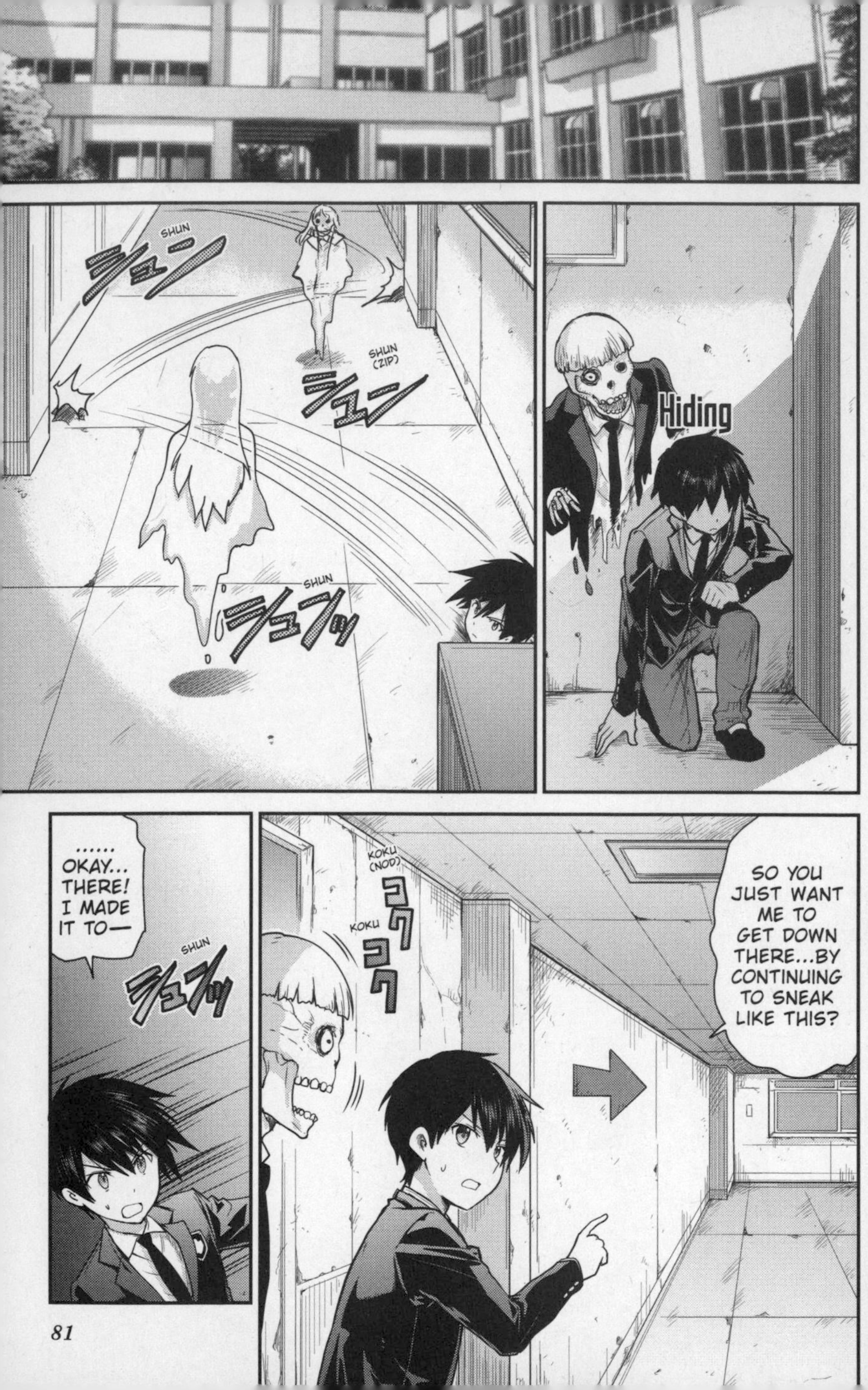
Hiding
SHUN
シュン
SHUN (ZIP)
シュン
SHUN
シュフッ
SO YOU JUST WANT ME TO GET DOWN THERE...BY CONTINUING TO SNEAK LIKE THIS?
KOKU (NOD)
コク
KOKU
コク
...... OKAY... THERE! I MADE IT TO—
SHUN
シュフッ

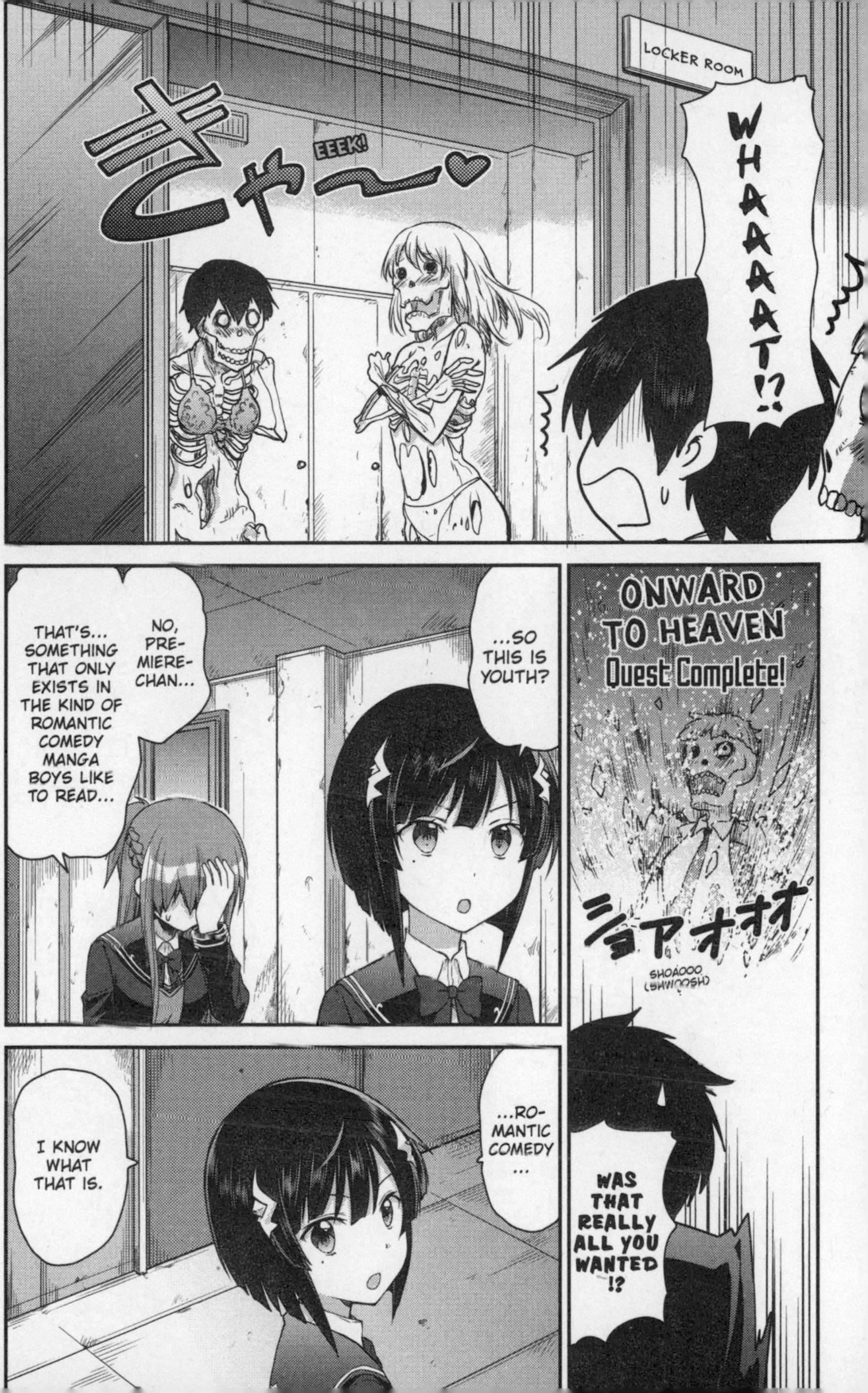
LOCKER ROOM
WHAAAAT!?
きゃ～♥
EEEK!
ONWARD TO HEAVEN Quest Complete!
ショアオオオ
SHOAOOO (SHWOOSH)
...SO THIS IS YOUTH?
NO, PREMIERE-CHAN...
THAT'S... SOMETHING THAT ONLY EXISTS IN THE KIND OF ROMANTIC COMEDY MANGA BOYS LIKE TO READ...
WAS THAT REALLY ALL YOU WANTED!?
...ROMANTIC COMEDY...
I KNOW WHAT THAT IS.

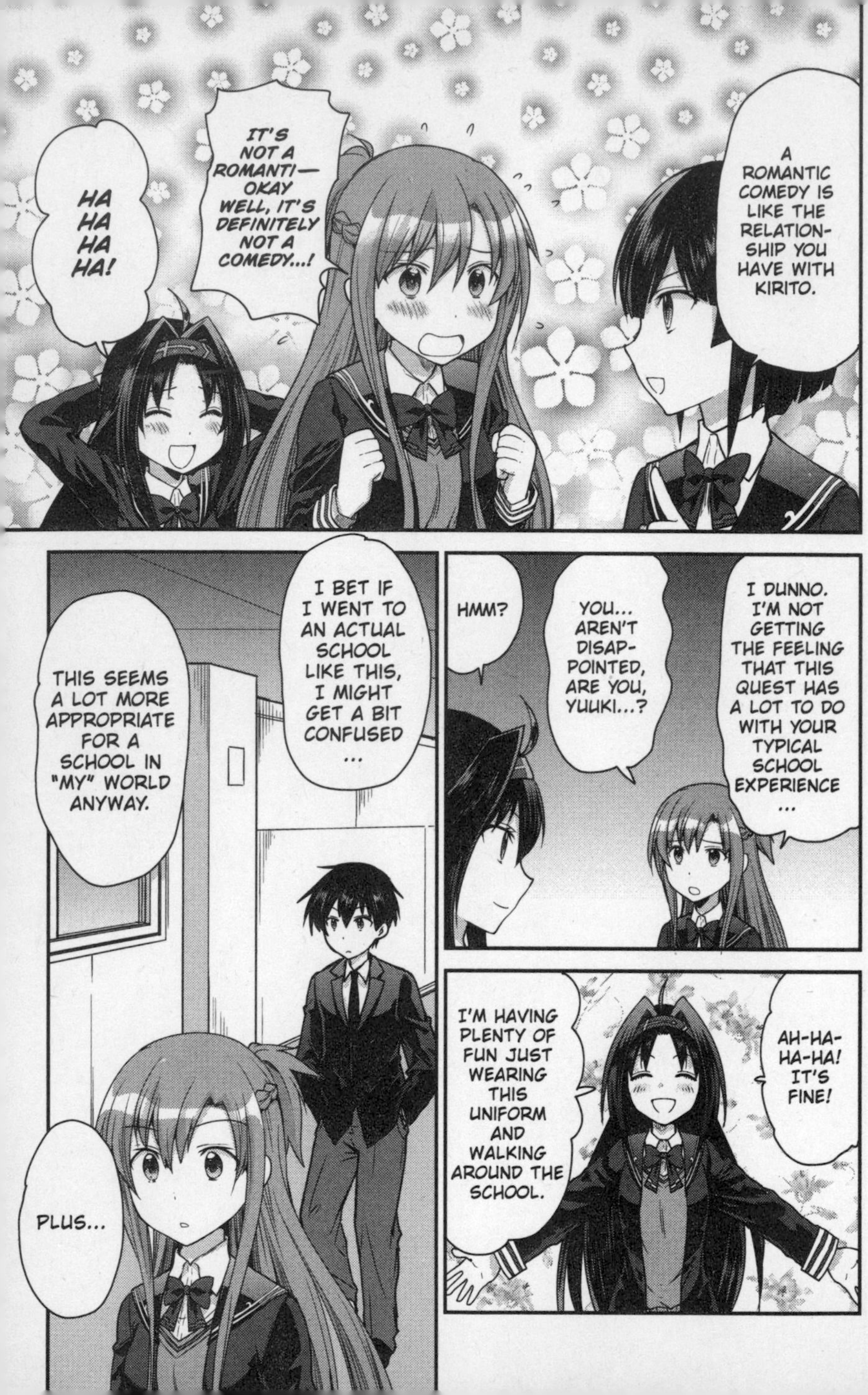
A ROMANTIC COMEDY IS LIKE THE RELATIONSHIP YOU HAVE WITH KIRITO.
IT'S NOT A ROMANTI— OKAY WELL, IT'S DEFINITELY NOT A COMEDY...!
HA HA HA HA!
I DUNNO. I'M NOT GETTING THE FEELING THAT THIS QUEST HAS A LOT TO DO WITH YOUR TYPICAL SCHOOL EXPERIENCE...
YOU... AREN'T DISAPPOINTED, ARE YOU, YUUKI...?
HMM?
AH-HA-HA-HA! IT'S FINE!
I'M HAVING PLENTY OF FUN JUST WEARING THIS UNIFORM AND WALKING AROUND THE SCHOOL.
I BET IF I WENT TO AN ACTUAL SCHOOL LIKE THIS, I MIGHT GET A BIT CONFUSED...
THIS SEEMS A LOT MORE APPROPRIATE FOR A SCHOOL IN "MY" WORLD ANYWAY.
PLUS...

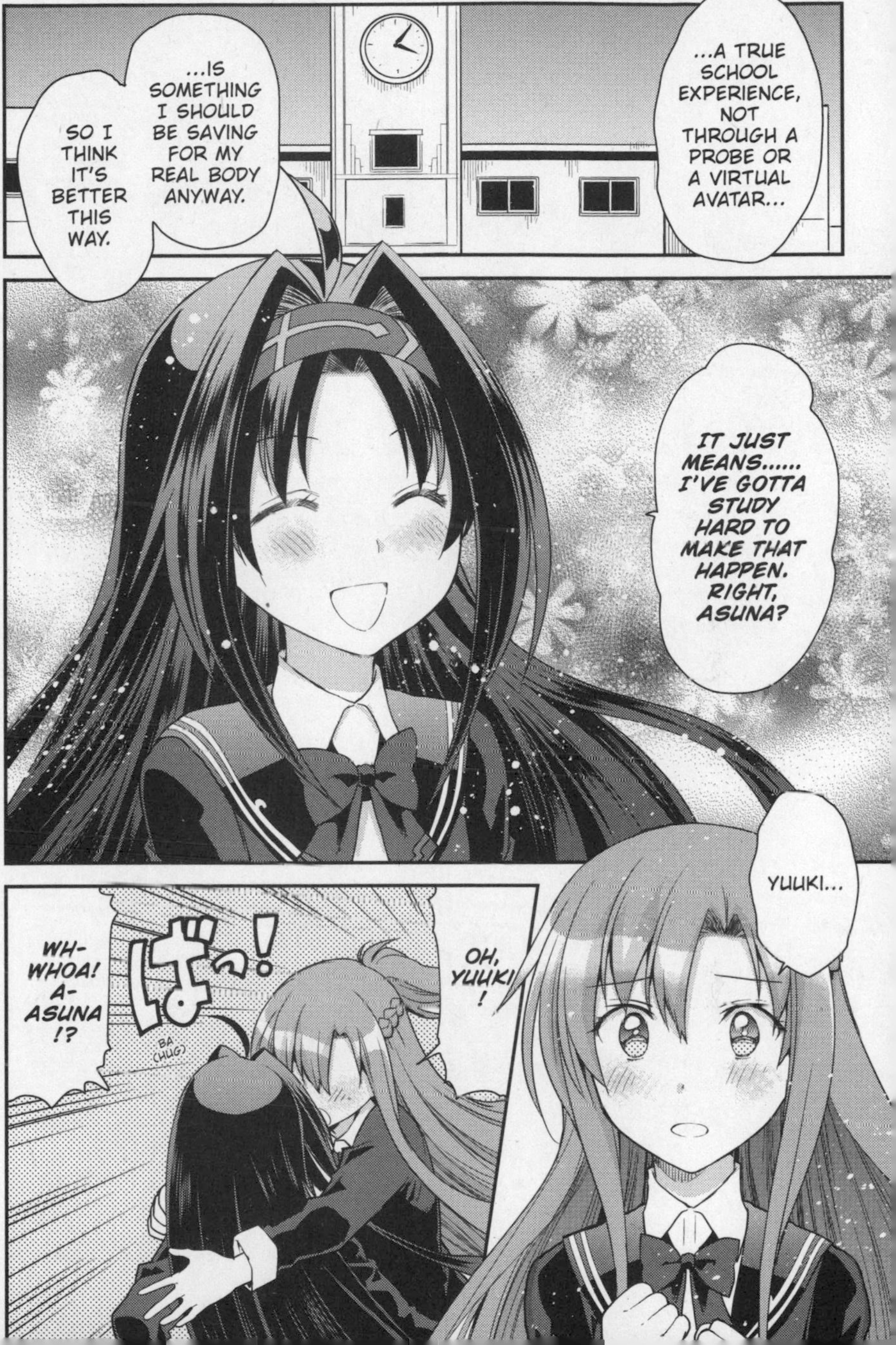
...A TRUE SCHOOL EXPERIENCE, NOT THROUGH A PROBE OR A VIRTUAL AVATAR...
...IS SOMETHING I SHOULD BE SAVING FOR MY REAL BODY ANYWAY.
SO I THINK IT'S BETTER THIS WAY.
IT JUST MEANS...... I'VE GOTTA STUDY HARD TO MAKE THAT HAPPEN. RIGHT, ASUNA?
YUUKI...
OH, YUUKI!
ばっ!
BA (HUG)
WH-WHOA! A-ASUNA!?

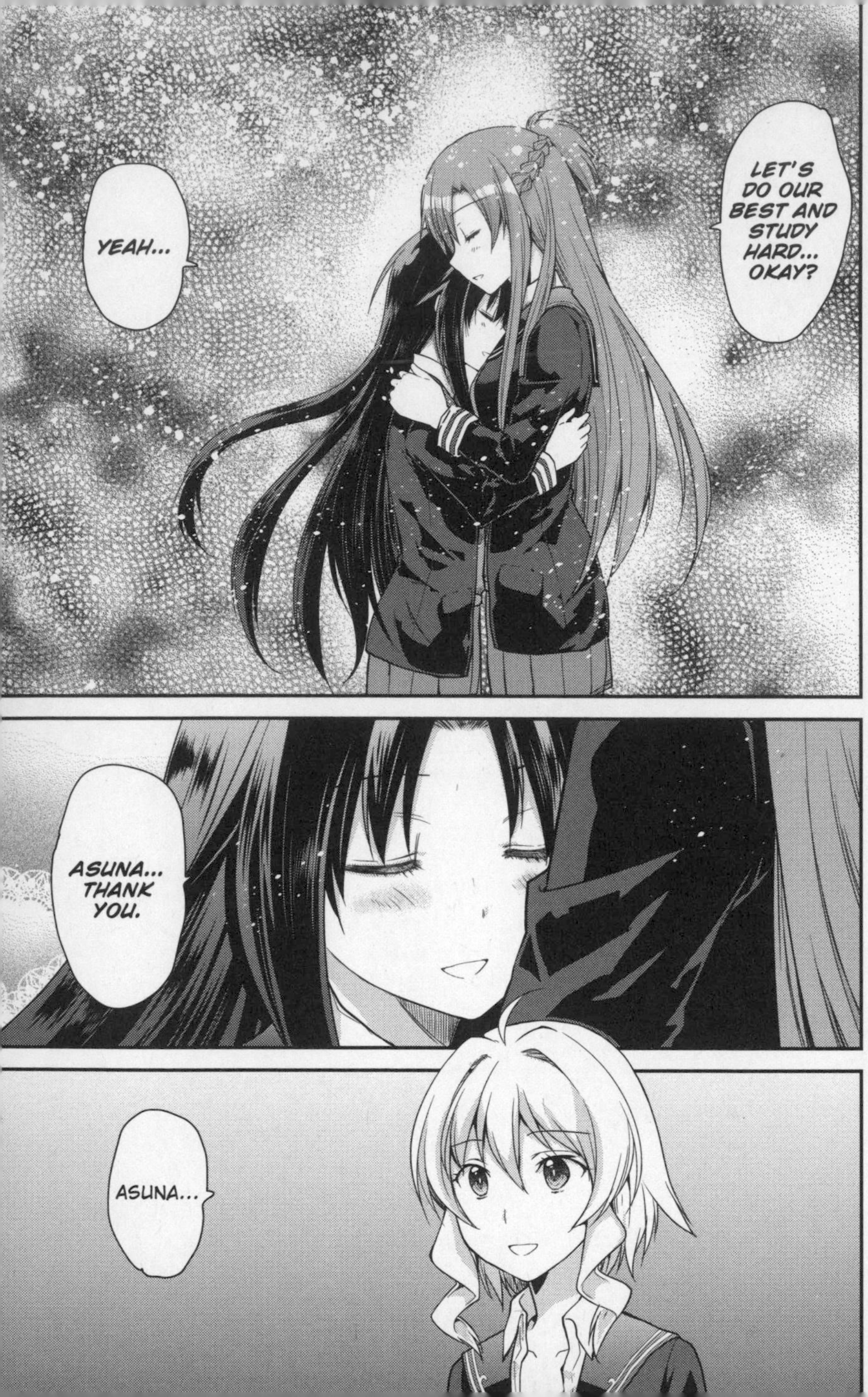
LET'S DO OUR BEST AND STUDY HARD... OKAY?
YEAH...
ASUNA... THANK YOU.
ASUNA...

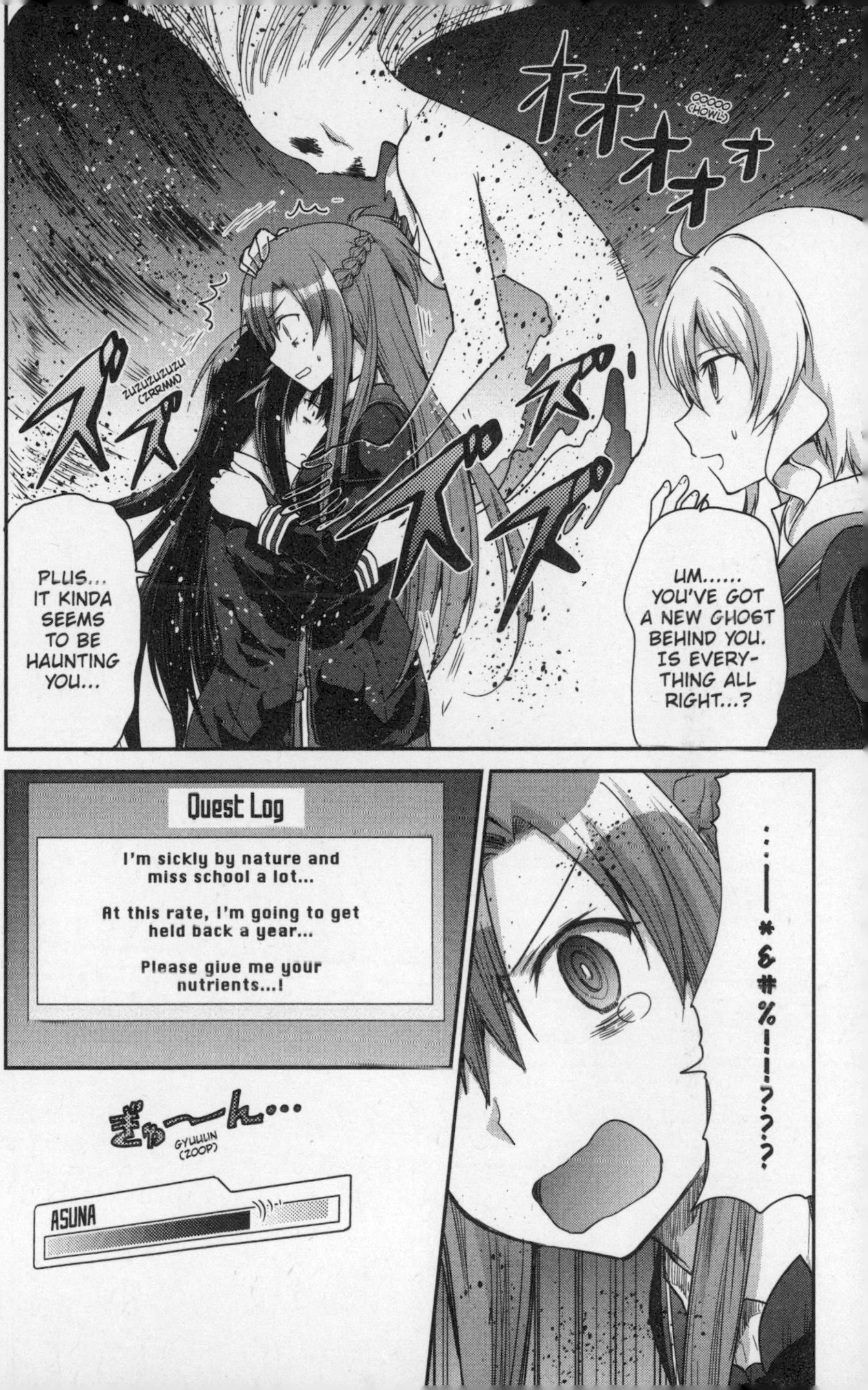
オオオオオ
OOOOO (HOWL)
UM...... YOU'VE GOT A NEW GHOST BEHIND YOU. IS EVERYTHING ALL RIGHT...?
ZUZUZUZUZU (ZRRMM)
PLUS... IT KINDA SEEMS TO BE HAUNTING YOU...
...—*&#%!!?!?!?
Quest Log
I'm sickly by nature and miss school a lot...
At this rate, I'm going to get held back a year...
Please give me your nutrients...!
ぎゅ〜ん…
GYUUUN (ZOOP)
ASUNA

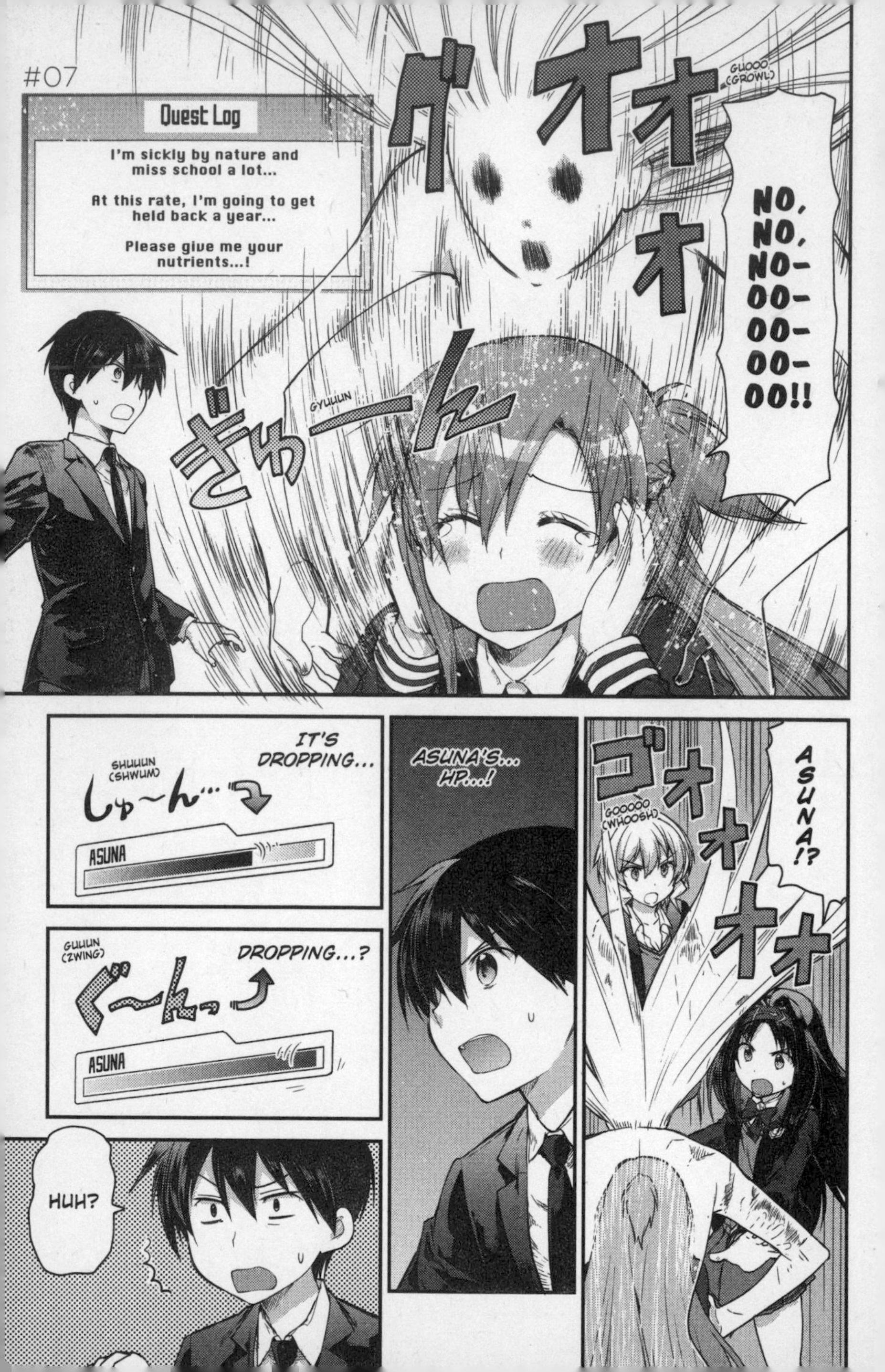

#07
GUOOO (GROWL)
グオオ
NO, NO, NO-OO-OO-OO-OO!!
Quest Log
I'm sickly by nature and miss school a lot...
At this rate, I'm going to get held back a year...
Please give me your nutrients...!
GYUUUN
ぎゅーん
ASUNA!?
GOOOOO (WHOOSH)
ゴオオオ
ASUNA'S... HP...!
IT'S DROPPING...
SHUUUN (SHWUM)
しゅ～ん…
ASUNA
DROPPING...?
GUUUN (ZWING)
ぐ～んっ
ASUNA
HUH?

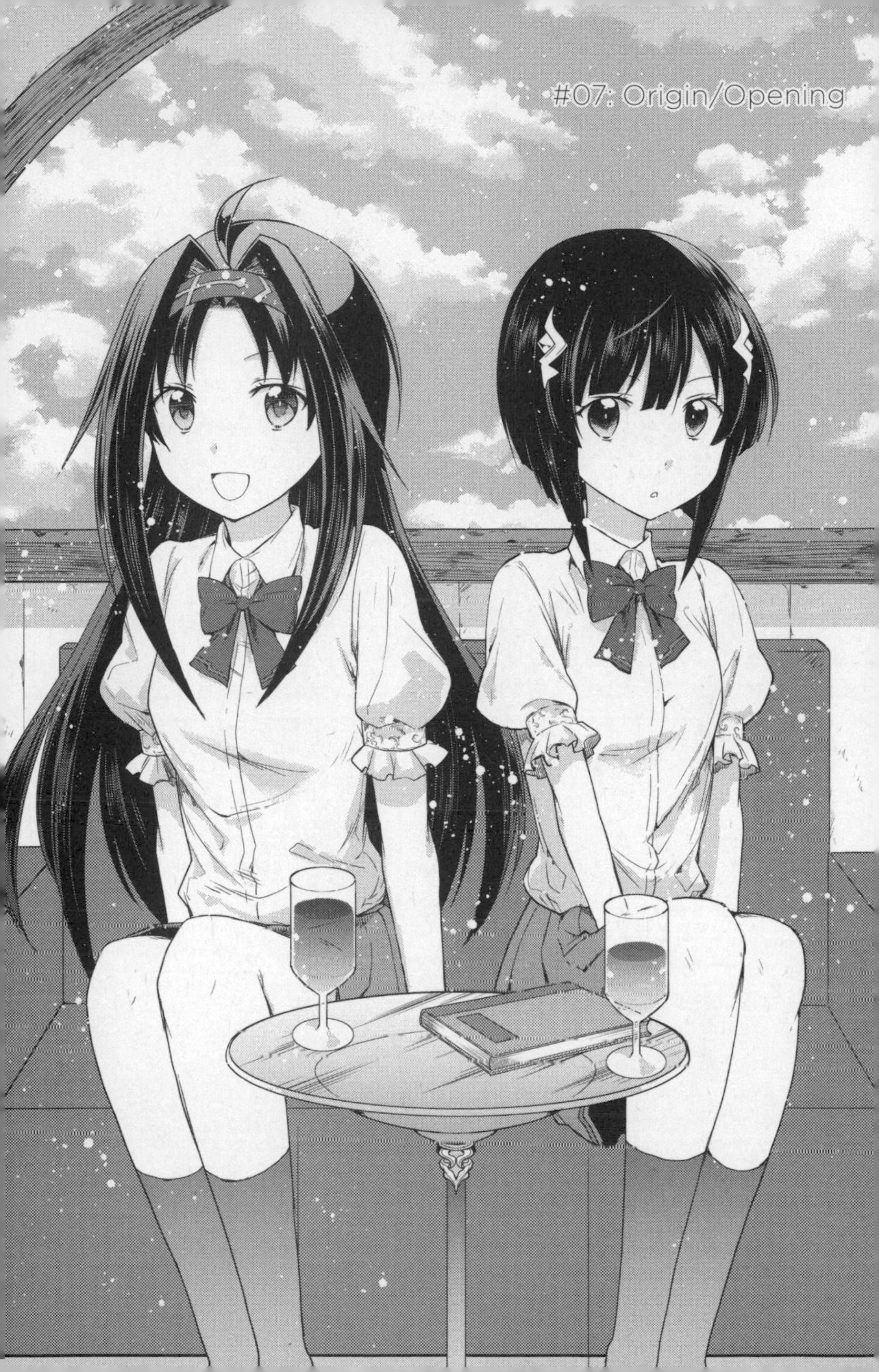
#07: Origin/Opening

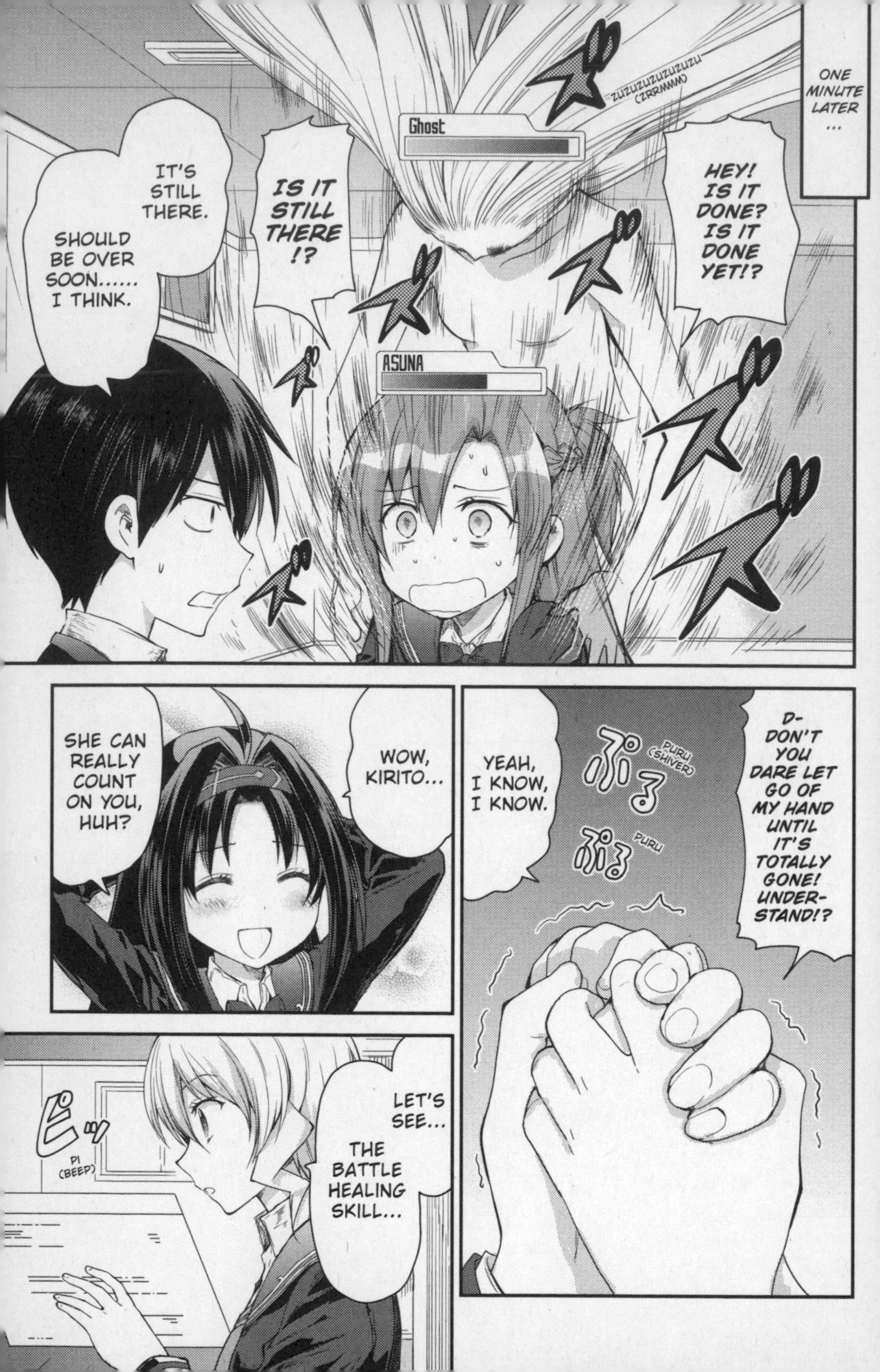
ONE MINUTE LATER...
HEY! IS IT DONE? IS IT DONE YET!?
ZUZUZUZUZUZUZU (ZRRMMM)
Ghost
ASUNA
IS IT STILL THERE!?
IT'S STILL THERE.
SHOULD BE OVER SOON...... I THINK.
D-DON'T YOU DARE LET GO OF MY HAND UNTIL IT'S TOTALLY GONE! UNDERSTAND!?
ぷる PURU (SHIVER)
ぷる PURU
YEAH, I KNOW, I KNOW.
WOW, KIRITO...
SHE CAN REALLY COUNT ON YOU, HUH?
LET'S SEE... THE BATTLE HEALING SKILL...
ピッ PI (BEEP)

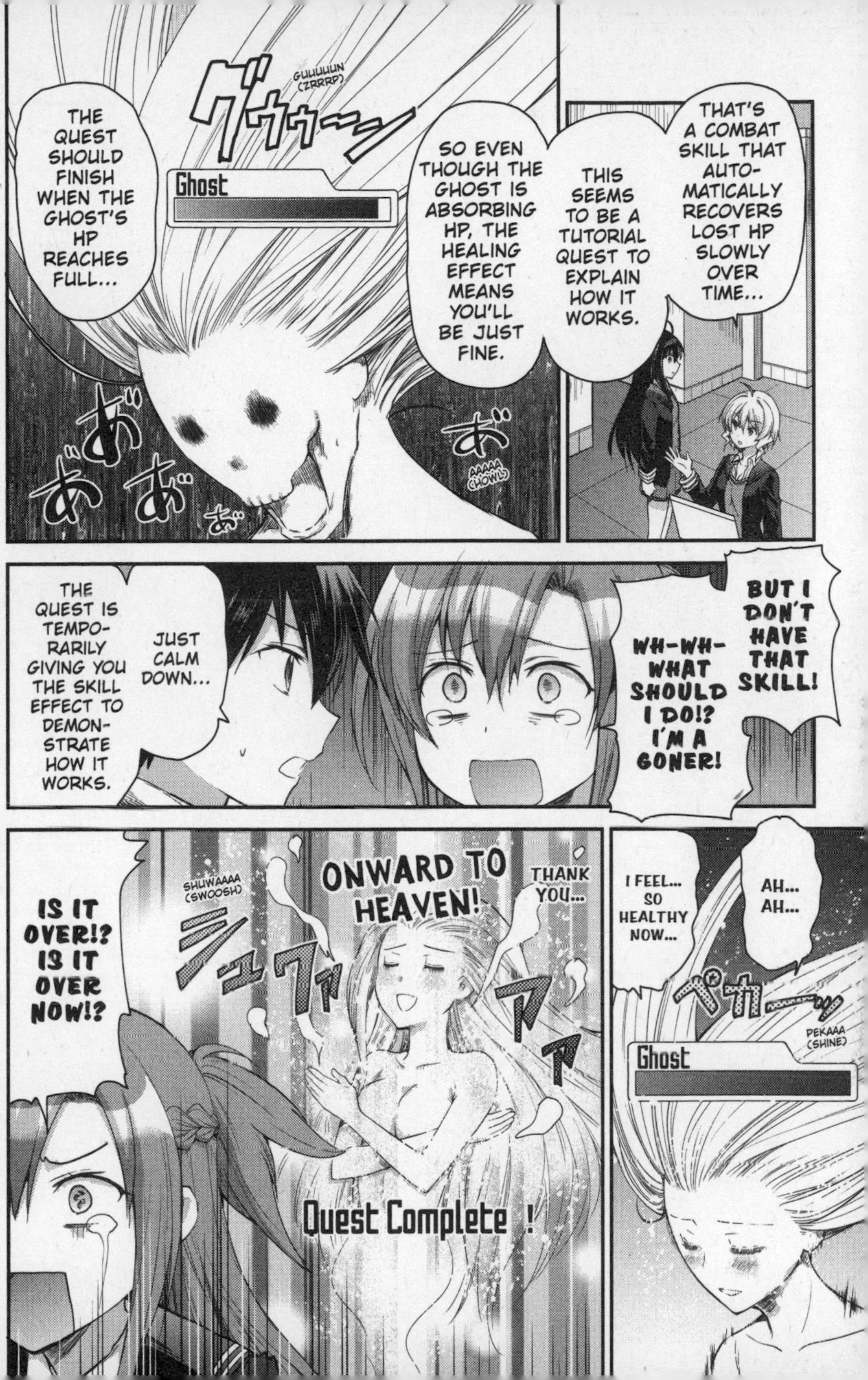
THAT'S A COMBAT SKILL THAT AUTO-MATICALLY RECOVERS LOST HP SLOWLY OVER TIME...
THIS SEEMS TO BE A TUTORIAL QUEST TO EXPLAIN HOW IT WORKS.
SO EVEN THOUGH THE GHOST IS ABSORBING HP, THE HEALING EFFECT MEANS YOU'LL BE JUST FINE.
GUUUUUN (ZRRRP)
Ghost
THE QUEST SHOULD FINISH WHEN THE GHOST'S HP REACHES FULL...
AAAAA (HOWL)
BUT I DON'T HAVE THAT SKILL!
WH-WH-WHAT SHOULD I DO!? I'M A GONER!
JUST CALM DOWN...
THE QUEST IS TEMPO-RARILY GIVING YOU THE SKILL EFFECT TO DEMON-STRATE HOW IT WORKS.
AH... AH...
I FEEL... SO HEALTHY NOW...
PEKAAA (SHINE)
Ghost
THANK YOU...
ONWARD TO HEAVEN!
SHUWAAAA (SWOOSH)
IS IT OVER!? IS IT OVER NOW!?
Quest Complete !

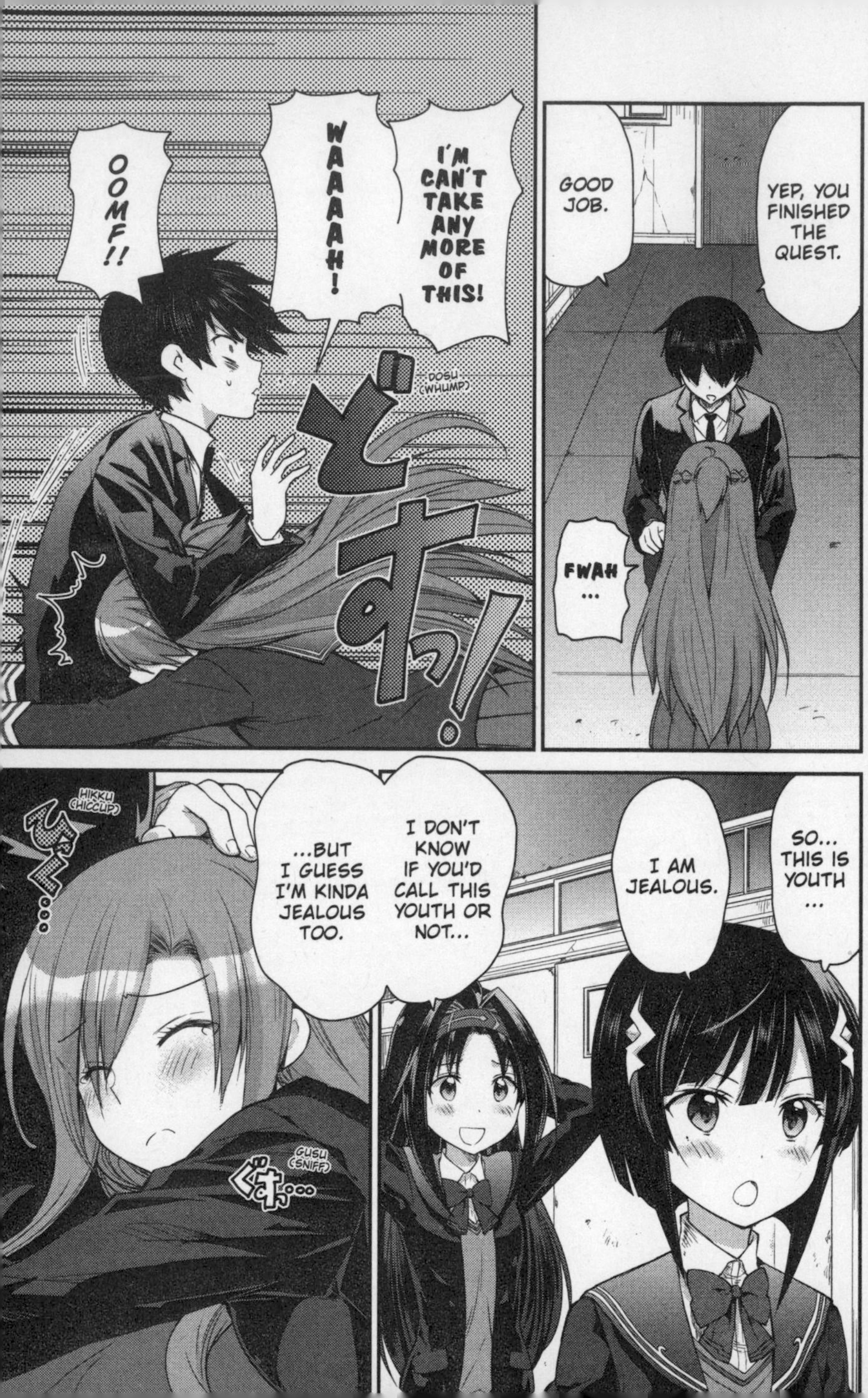
YEP, YOU FINISHED THE QUEST.
GOOD JOB.
FWAH ...
I'M CAN'T TAKE ANY MORE OF THIS!
WAAAAAH!
OOMF!!
DOSU (WHUMP)
SO... THIS IS YOUTH ...
I AM JEALOUS.
I DON'T KNOW IF YOU'D CALL THIS YOUTH OR NOT...
...BUT I GUESS I'M KINDA JEALOUS TOO.
HIKKU (HICCUP)
GUSU (SNIFF)

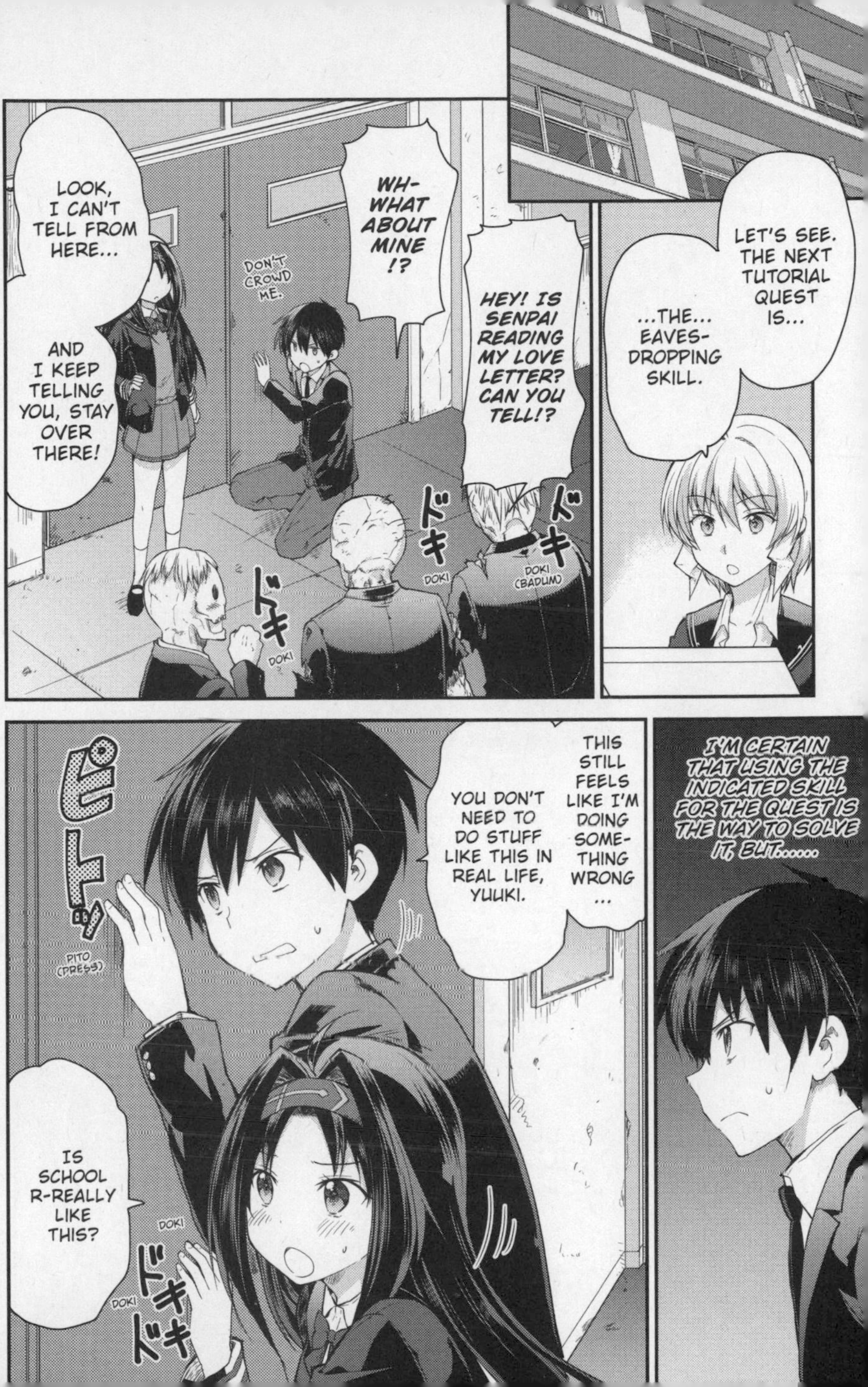
LET'S SEE. THE NEXT TUTORIAL QUEST IS...
...THE... EAVES-DROPPING SKILL.
HEY! IS SENPAI READING MY LOVE LETTER? CAN YOU TELL!?
WH-WHAT ABOUT MINE!?
DON'T CROWD ME.
LOOK, I CAN'T TELL FROM HERE...
AND I KEEP TELLING YOU, STAY OVER THERE!
ドキ
DOKI (BADUM)
ドキ
DOKI
ドキ
DOKI
I'M CERTAIN THAT USING THE INDICATED SKILL FOR THE QUEST IS THE WAY TO SOLVE IT, BUT......
THIS STILL FEELS LIKE I'M DOING SOME-THING WRONG...
YOU DON'T NEED TO DO STUFF LIKE THIS IN REAL LIFE, YUUKI.
ピトッ
PITO (PRESS)
IS SCHOOL R-REALLY LIKE THIS?
DOKI
ドキ
DOKI
ドキ

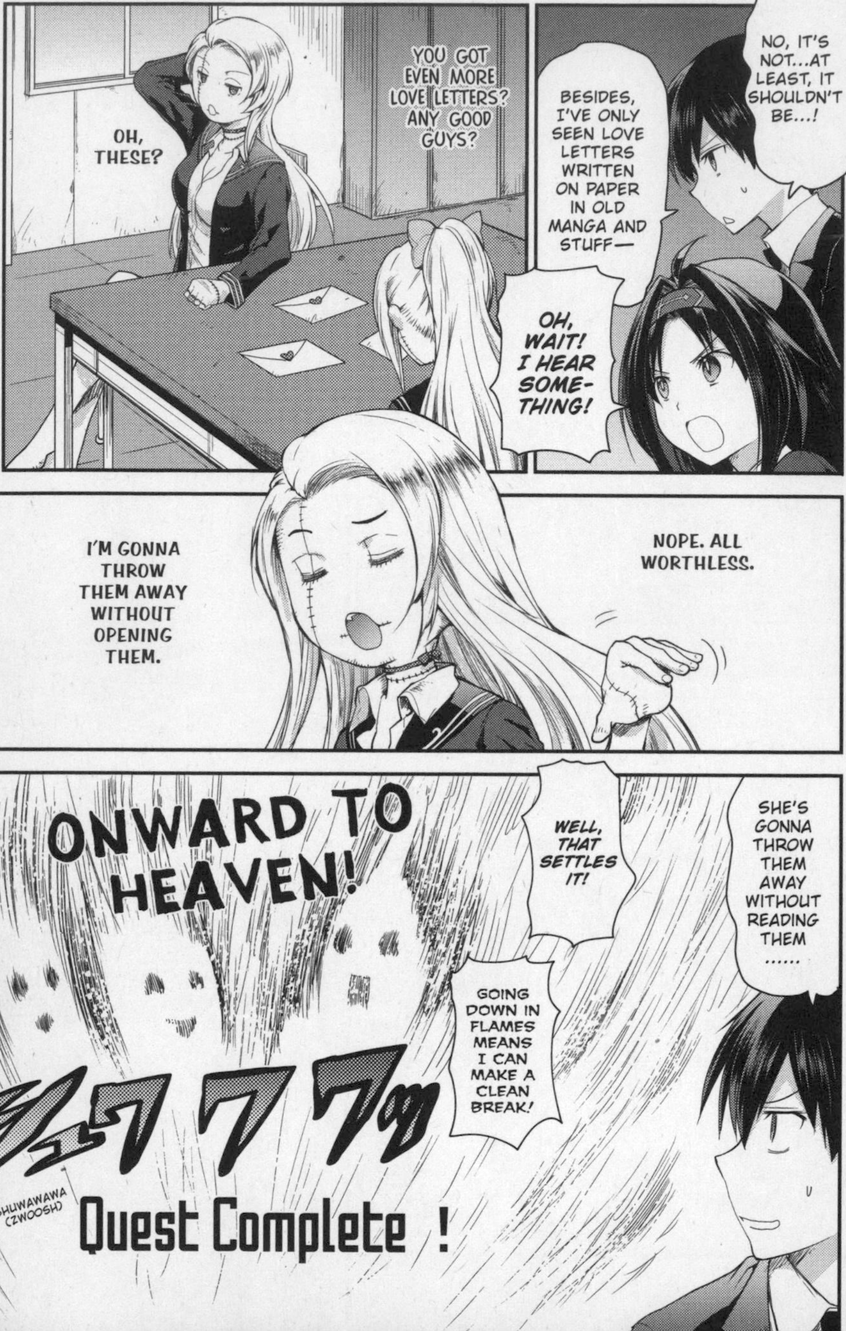
NO, IT'S NOT...AT LEAST, IT SHOULDN'T BE...!
BESIDES, I'VE ONLY SEEN LOVE LETTERS WRITTEN ON PAPER IN OLD MANGA AND STUFF—
OH, WAIT! I HEAR SOME-THING!
YOU GOT EVEN MORE LOVE LETTERS? ANY GOOD GUYS?
OH, THESE?
NOPE. ALL WORTHLESS.
I'M GONNA THROW THEM AWAY WITHOUT OPENING THEM.
SHE'S GONNA THROW THEM AWAY WITHOUT READING THEM......
WELL, THAT SETTLES IT!
GOING DOWN IN FLAMES MEANS I CAN MAKE A CLEAN BREAK!
ONWARD TO HEAVEN!
SHUWAWAWA (ZWOOSH)
Quest Complete !

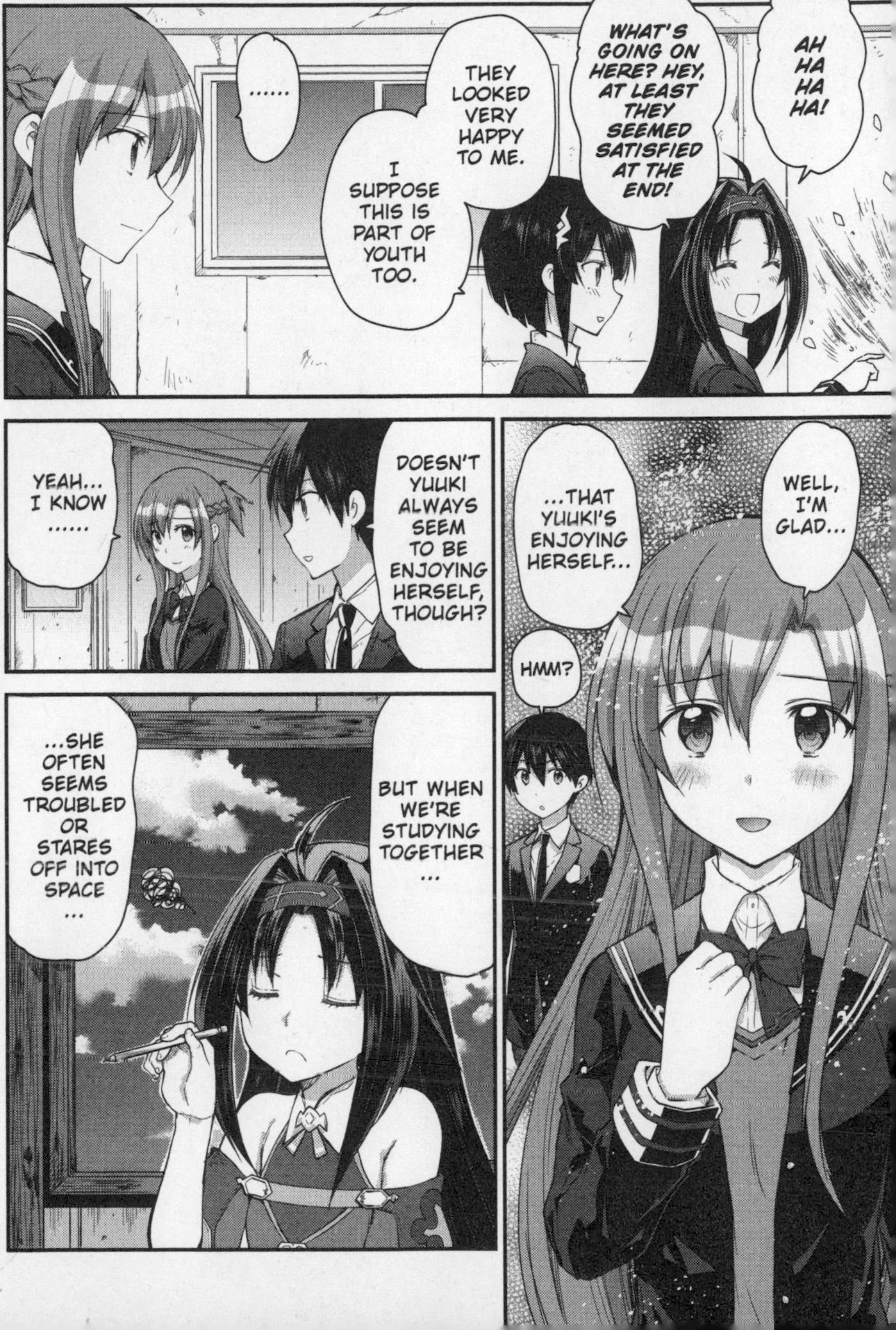
AH HA HA HA!
WHAT'S GOING ON HERE? HEY, AT LEAST THEY SEEMED SATISFIED AT THE END!
THEY LOOKED VERY HAPPY TO ME.
I SUPPOSE THIS IS PART OF YOUTH TOO.
......
WELL, I'M GLAD...
...THAT YUUKI'S ENJOYING HERSELF...
HMM?
DOESN'T YUUKI ALWAYS SEEM TO BE ENJOYING HERSELF, THOUGH?
YEAH... I KNOW ......
BUT WHEN WE'RE STUDYING TOGETHER ...
...SHE OFTEN SEEMS TROUBLED OR STARES OFF INTO SPACE ...

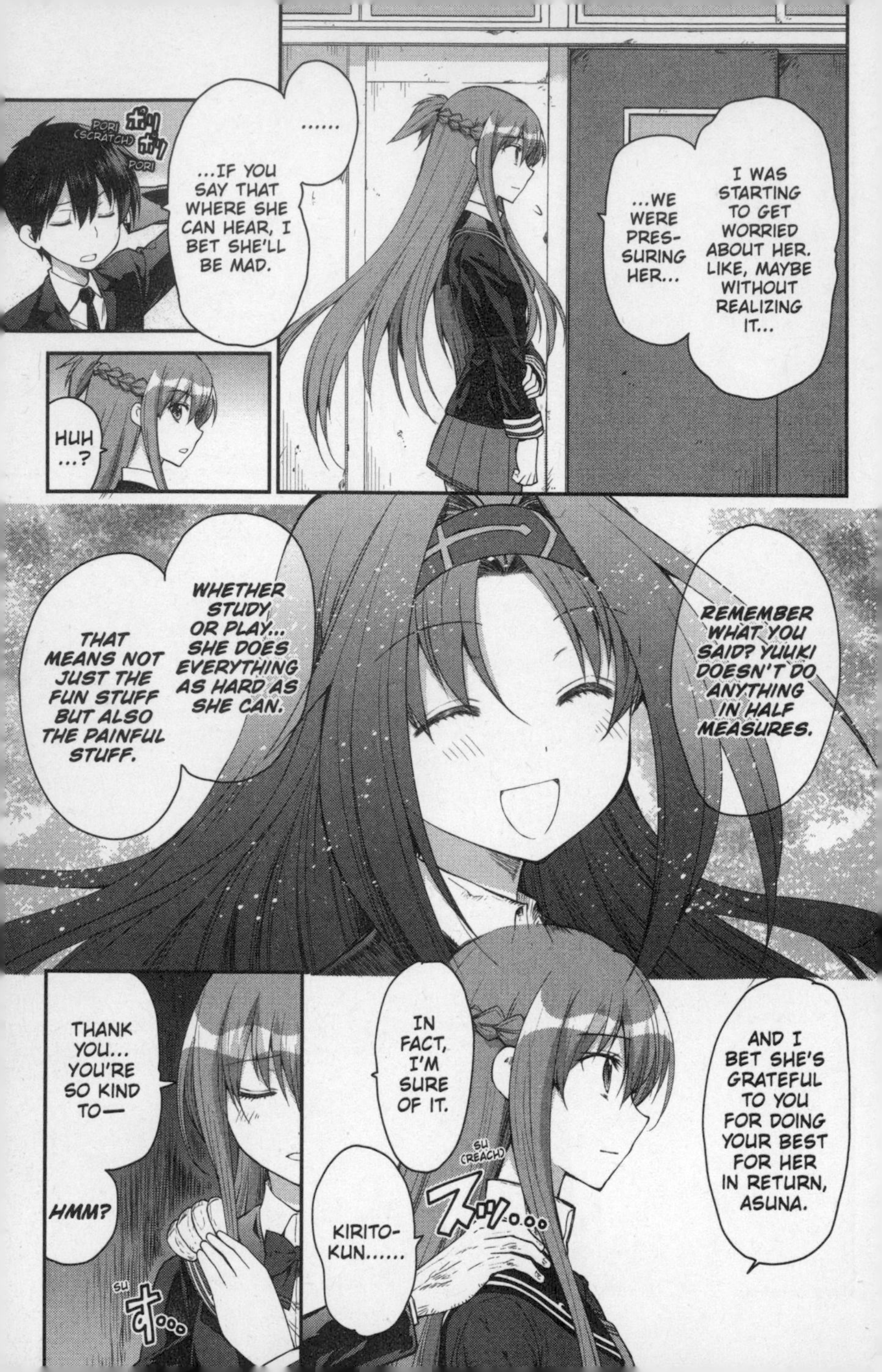
I WAS STARTING TO GET WORRIED ABOUT HER. LIKE, MAYBE WITHOUT REALIZING IT...
...WE WERE PRES-SURING HER...
......
PORI (SCRATCH) PORI
...IF YOU SAY THAT WHERE SHE CAN HEAR, I BET SHE'LL BE MAD.
HUH ...?
REMEMBER WHAT YOU SAID? YUUKI DOESN'T DO ANYTHING IN HALF MEASURES.
WHETHER STUDY OR PLAY... SHE DOES EVERYTHING AS HARD AS SHE CAN.
THAT MEANS NOT JUST THE FUN STUFF BUT ALSO THE PAINFUL STUFF.
AND I BET SHE'S GRATEFUL TO YOU FOR DOING YOUR BEST FOR HER IN RETURN, ASUNA.
IN FACT, I'M SURE OF IT.
SU (REACH)
KIRITO-KUN......
THANK YOU... YOU'RE SO KIND TO—
HMM?
SU

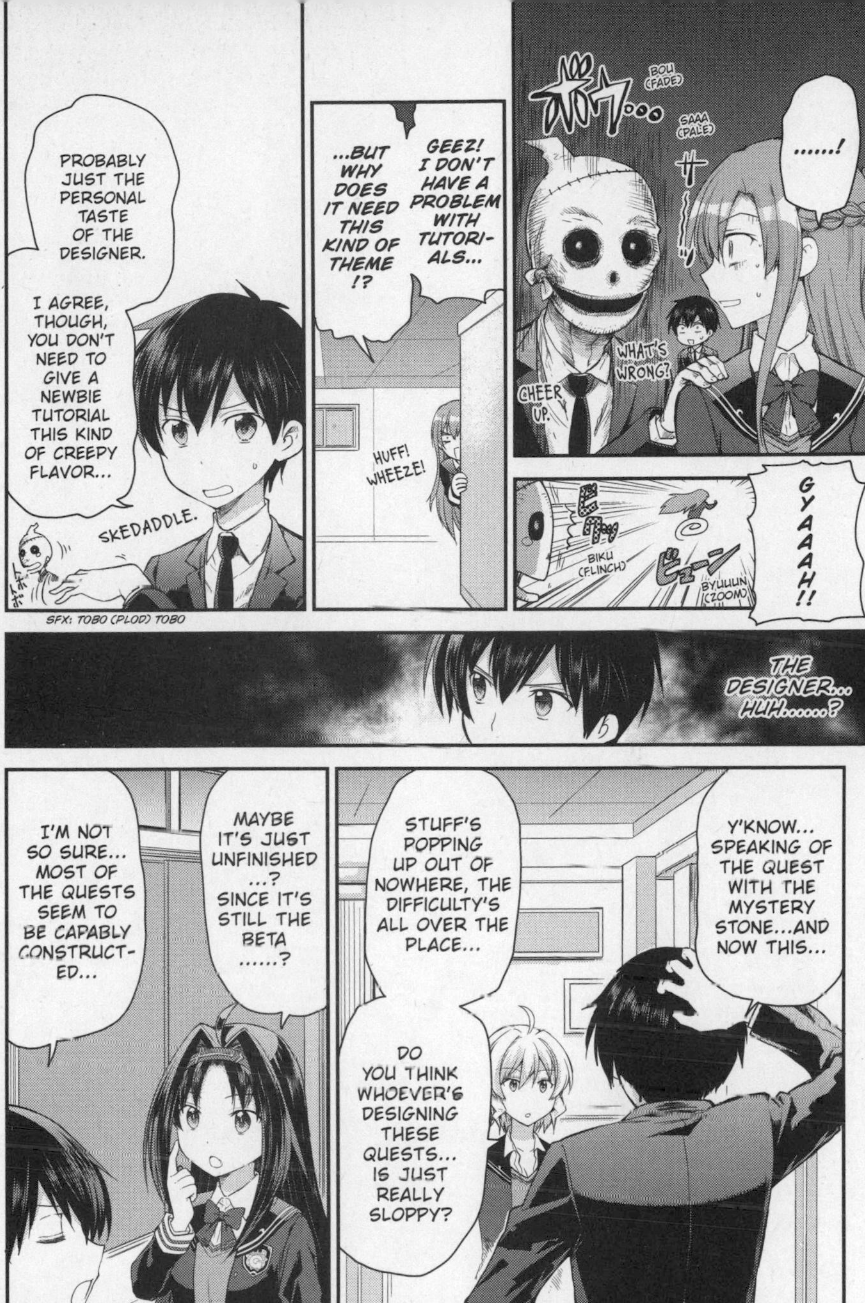
......!
SAAA (PALE)
BOU (FADE)
WHAT'S WRONG?
CHEER UP.
GYAAAH!!
BIKU (FLINCH)
BYUUUN (ZOOM)
GEEZ! I DON'T HAVE A PROBLEM WITH TUTORIALS...
...BUT WHY DOES IT NEED THIS KIND OF THEME !?
HUFF! WHEEZE!
PROBABLY JUST THE PERSONAL TASTE OF THE DESIGNER.
I AGREE, THOUGH, YOU DON'T NEED TO GIVE A NEWBIE TUTORIAL THIS KIND OF CREEPY FLAVOR...
SKEDADDLE.
SFX: TOBO (PLOD) TOBO
THE DESIGNER... HUH......?
Y'KNOW... SPEAKING OF THE QUEST WITH THE MYSTERY STONE...AND NOW THIS...
STUFF'S POPPING UP OUT OF NOWHERE, THE DIFFICULTY'S ALL OVER THE PLACE...
DO YOU THINK WHOEVER'S DESIGNING THESE QUESTS... IS JUST REALLY SLOPPY?
MAYBE IT'S JUST UNFINISHED ...? SINCE IT'S STILL THE BETA ......?
I'M NOT SO SURE... MOST OF THE QUESTS SEEM TO BE CAPABLY CONSTRUCTED...

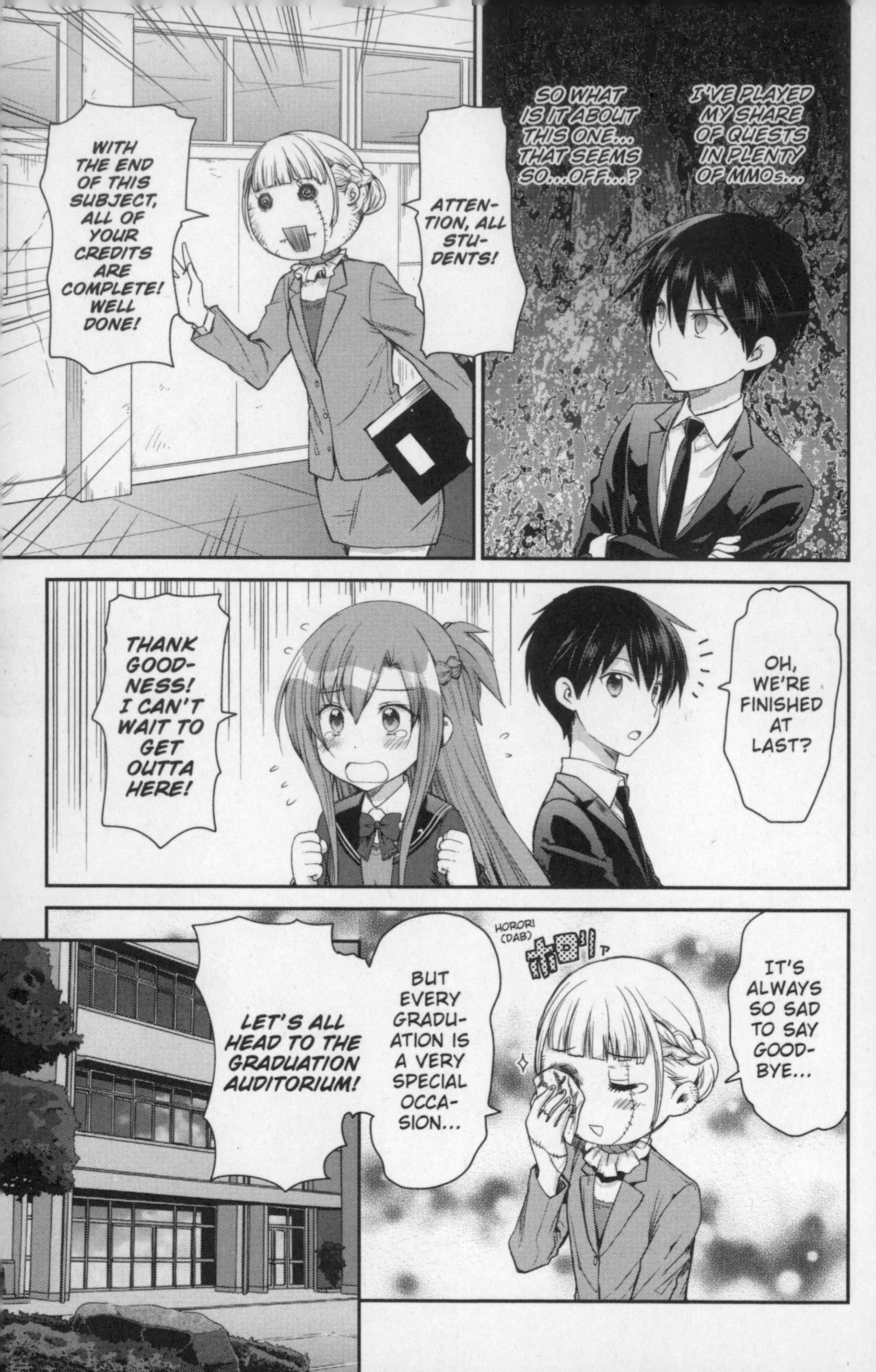
I'VE PLAYED MY SHARE OF QUESTS IN PLENTY OF MMOs...
SO WHAT IS IT ABOUT THIS ONE... THAT SEEMS SO...OFF...?
ATTENTION, ALL STUDENTS!
WITH THE END OF THIS SUBJECT, ALL OF YOUR CREDITS ARE COMPLETE! WELL DONE!
OH, WE'RE FINISHED AT LAST?
THANK GOODNESS! I CAN'T WAIT TO GET OUTTA HERE!
HORORI (DAB)
IT'S ALWAYS SO SAD TO SAY GOODBYE...
BUT EVERY GRADUATION IS A VERY SPECIAL OCCASION...
LET'S ALL HEAD TO THE GRADUATION AUDITORIUM!

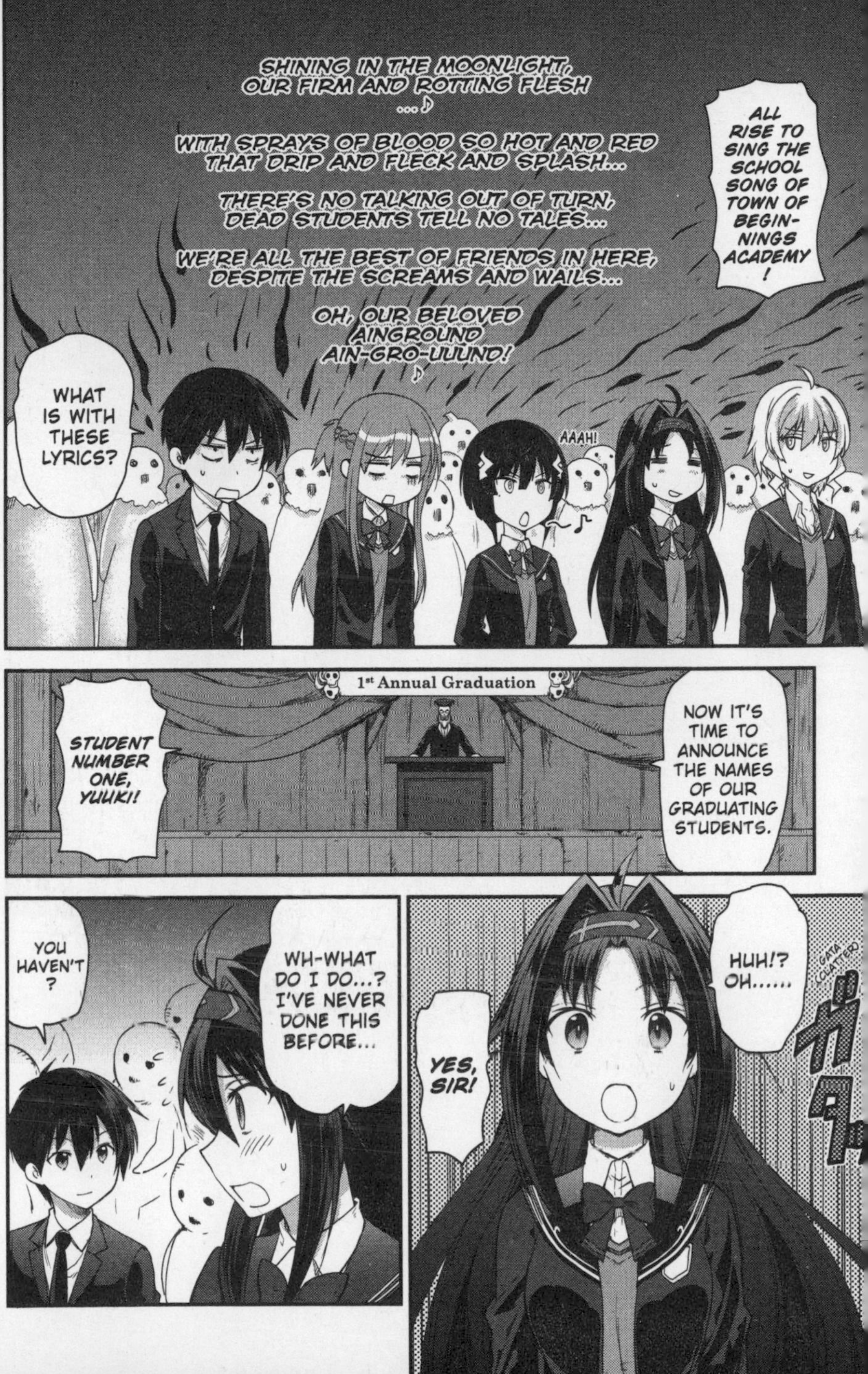
ALL RISE TO SING THE SCHOOL SONG OF TOWN OF BEGINNINGS ACADEMY!
SHINING IN THE MOONLIGHT, OUR FIRM AND ROTTING FLESH ...♪
WITH SPRAYS OF BLOOD SO HOT AND RED THAT DRIP AND FLECK AND SPLASH...
THERE'S NO TALKING OUT OF TURN, DEAD STUDENTS TELL NO TALES...
WE'RE ALL THE BEST OF FRIENDS IN HERE, DESPITE THE SCREAMS AND WAILS...
OH, OUR BELOVED AINGROUND AIN-GRO-UUUND! ♪
AAAH!
WHAT IS WITH THESE LYRICS?
1st Annual Graduation
NOW IT'S TIME TO ANNOUNCE THE NAMES OF OUR GRADUATING STUDENTS.
STUDENT NUMBER ONE, YUUKI!
GATA (CLATTER)
HUH!? OH......
YES, SIR!
WH-WHAT DO I DO...? I'VE NEVER DONE THIS BEFORE...
YOU HAVEN'T?

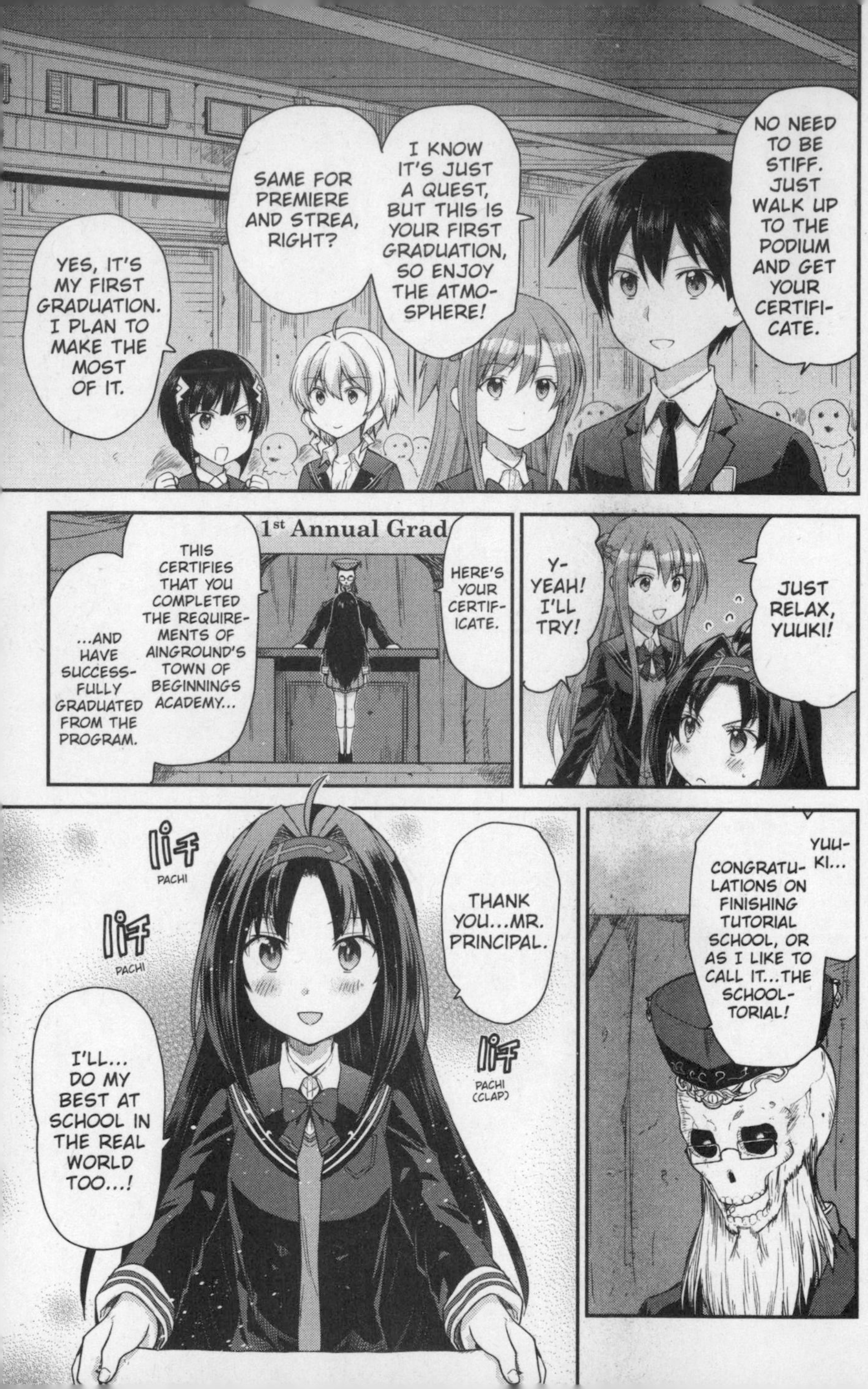
NO NEED TO BE STIFF. JUST WALK UP TO THE PODIUM AND GET YOUR CERTIFICATE.
I KNOW IT'S JUST A QUEST, BUT THIS IS YOUR FIRST GRADUATION, SO ENJOY THE ATMOSPHERE!
SAME FOR PREMIERE AND STREA, RIGHT?
YES, IT'S MY FIRST GRADUATION. I PLAN TO MAKE THE MOST OF IT.
JUST RELAX, YUUKI!
Y-YEAH! I'LL TRY!
1st Annual Grad
HERE'S YOUR CERTIFICATE.
THIS CERTIFIES THAT YOU COMPLETED THE REQUIREMENTS OF AINGROUND'S TOWN OF BEGINNINGS ACADEMY...
...AND HAVE SUCCESSFULLY GRADUATED FROM THE PROGRAM.
YUUKI...
CONGRATULATIONS ON FINISHING TUTORIAL SCHOOL, OR AS I LIKE TO CALL IT...THE SCHOOLTORIAL!
THANK YOU...MR. PRINCIPAL.
PACHI
PACHI
PACHI (CLAP)
I'LL... DO MY BEST AT SCHOOL IN THE REAL WORLD TOO...!

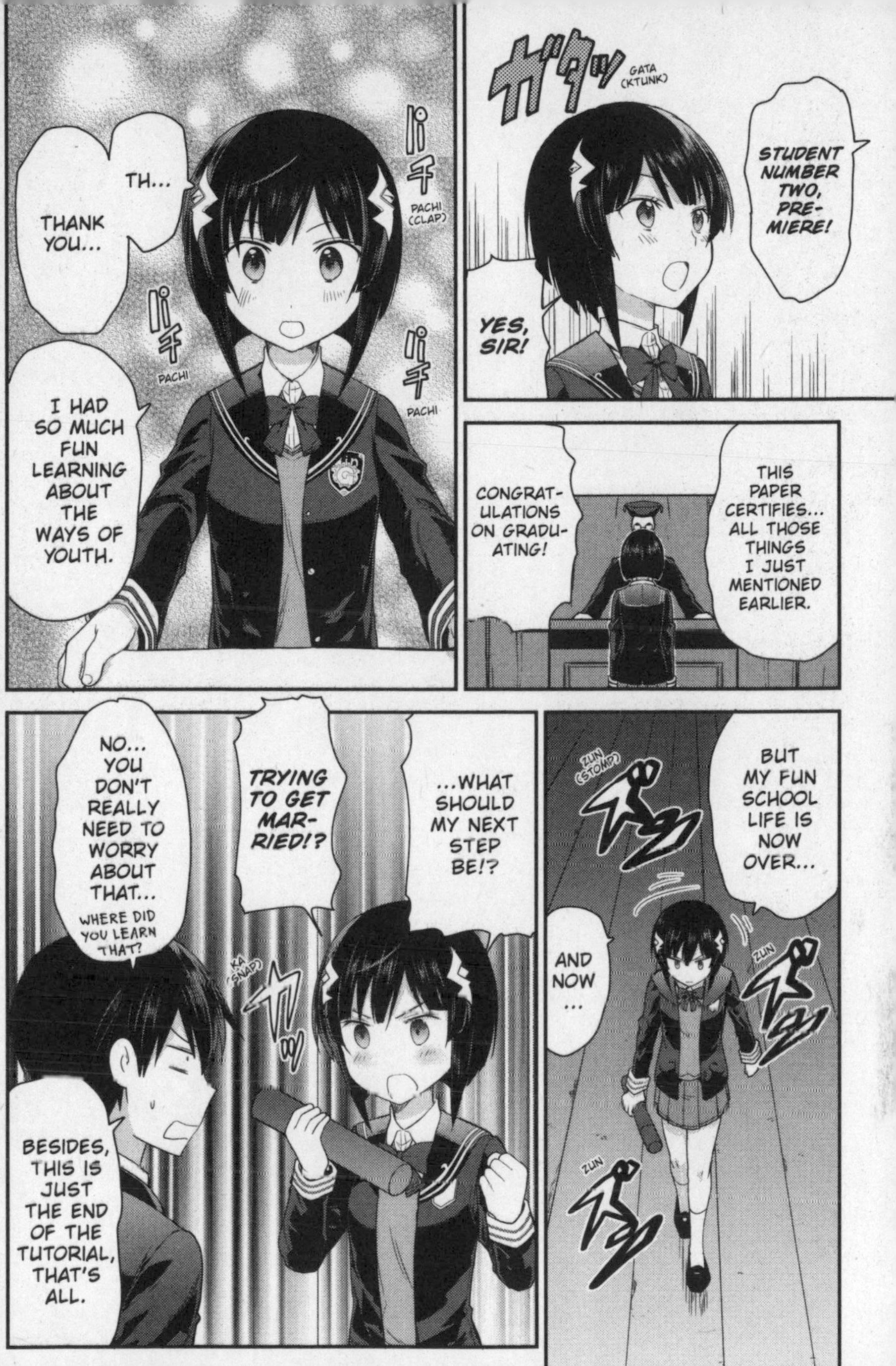
ガタッ
GATA (KTUNK)
STUDENT NUMBER TWO, PRE-MIERE!
YES, SIR!
THIS PAPER CERTIFIES... ALL THOSE THINGS I JUST MENTIONED EARLIER.
CONGRAT-ULATIONS ON GRADU-ATING!
パチ
PACHI (CLAP)
TH...
THANK YOU...
パチ
PACHI
パチ
PACHI
I HAD SO MUCH FUN LEARNING ABOUT THE WAYS OF YOUTH.
BUT MY FUN SCHOOL LIFE IS NOW OVER...
ZUN (STOMP)
AND NOW ...
ZUN
ZUN
...WHAT SHOULD MY NEXT STEP BE!?
TRYING TO GET MAR-RIED!?
NO... YOU DON'T REALLY NEED TO WORRY ABOUT THAT...
WHERE DID YOU LEARN THAT?
KA (SNAP)
BESIDES, THIS IS JUST THE END OF THE TUTORIAL, THAT'S ALL.

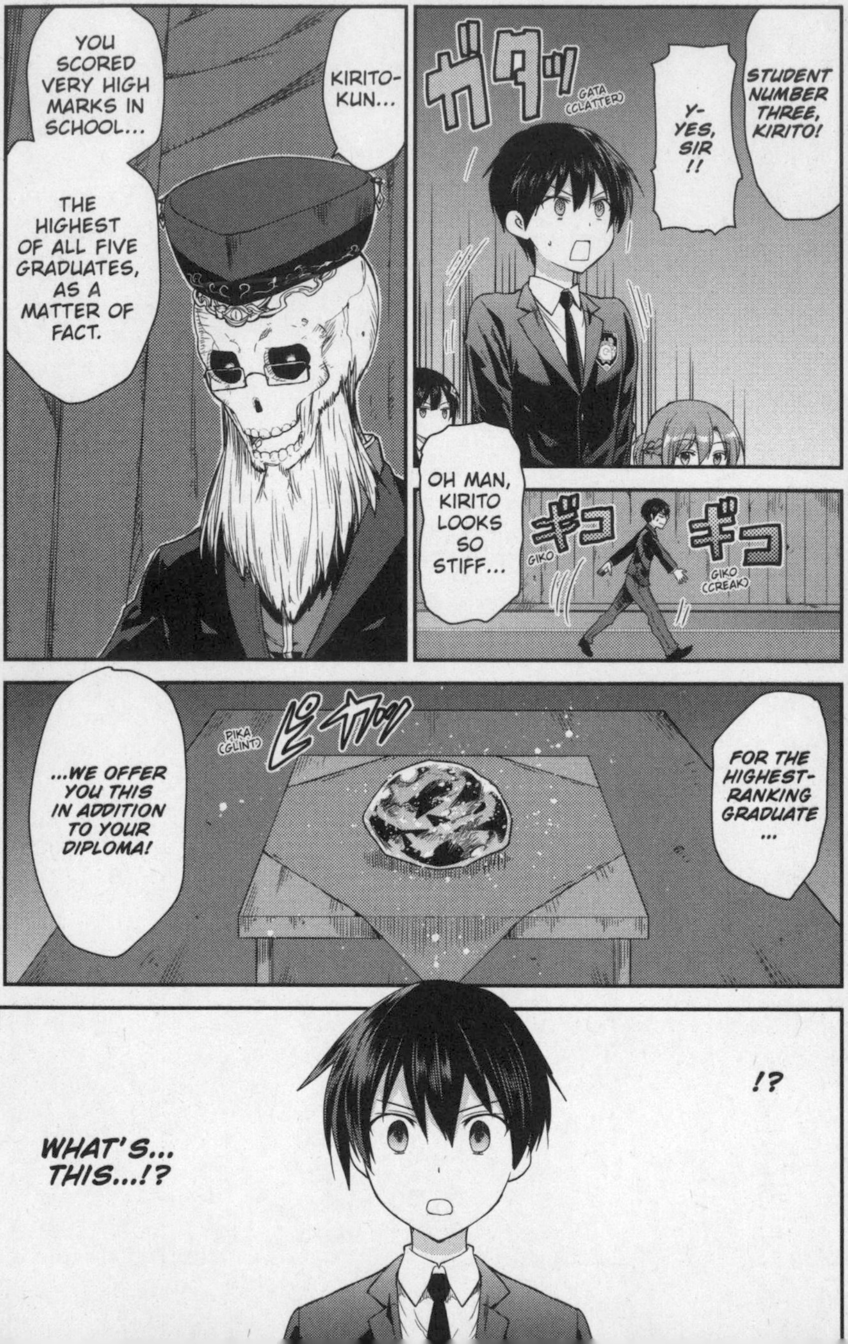
STUDENT NUMBER THREE, KIRITO!
Y-YES, SIR !!
GATA (CLATTER)
OH MAN, KIRITO LOOKS SO STIFF...
GIKO (CREAK)
GIKO
KIRITO-KUN...
YOU SCORED VERY HIGH MARKS IN SCHOOL...
THE HIGHEST OF ALL FIVE GRADUATES, AS A MATTER OF FACT.
FOR THE HIGHEST-RANKING GRADUATE ...
PIKA (GLINT)
...WE OFFER YOU THIS IN ADDITION TO YOUR DIPLOMA!
!?
WHAT'S... THIS...!?

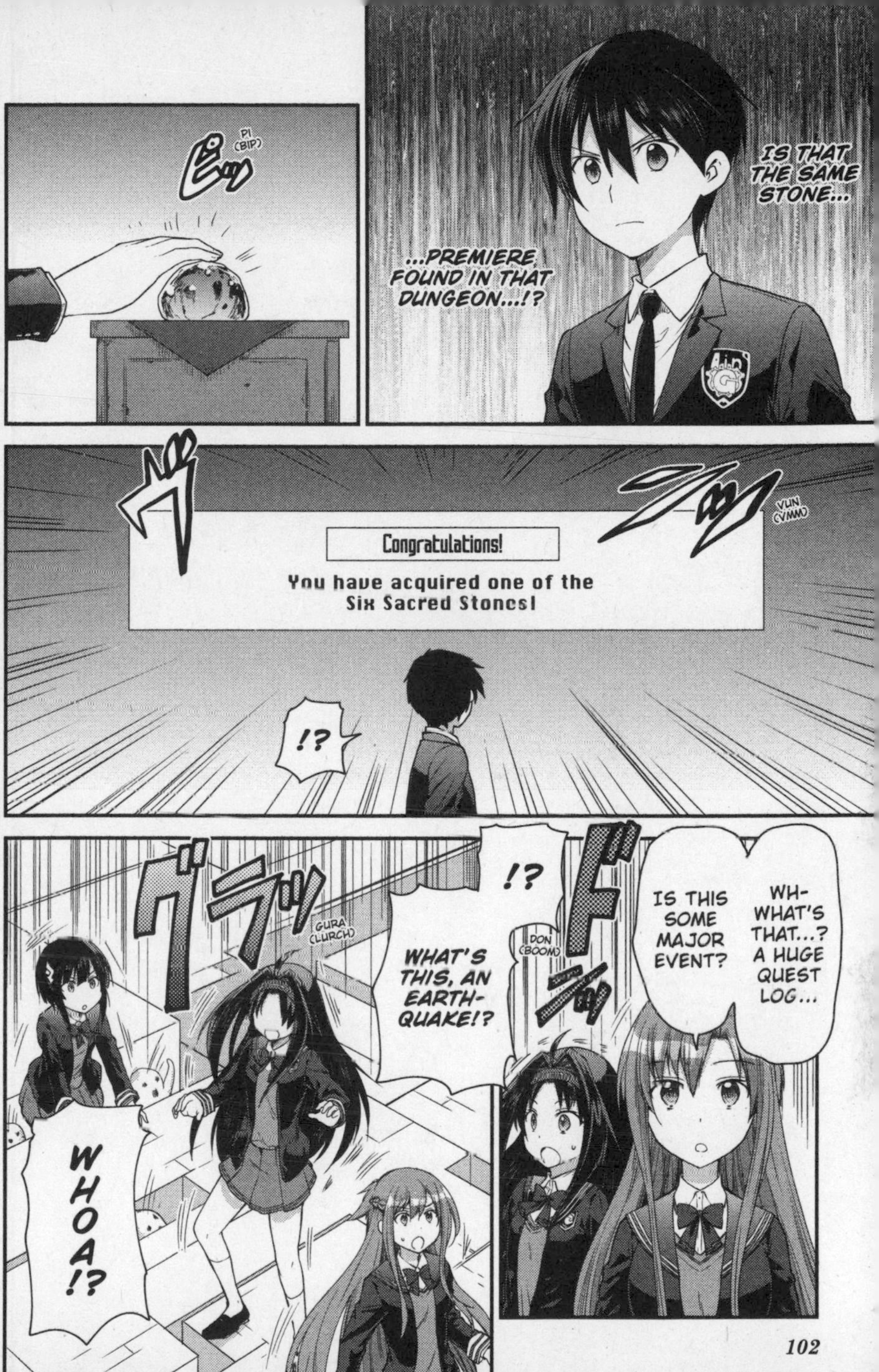
IS THAT THE SAME STONE...
...PREMIERE FOUND IN THAT DUNGEON...!?
PI (BIP)
VUN (VMM)
Congratulations!
You have acquired one of the Six Sacred Stones!
!?
WH-WHAT'S THAT...? A HUGE QUEST LOG...
IS THIS SOME MAJOR EVENT?
DON (BOOM)
!?
WHAT'S THIS, AN EARTHQUAKE!?
GURA (LURCH)
WHOA!?

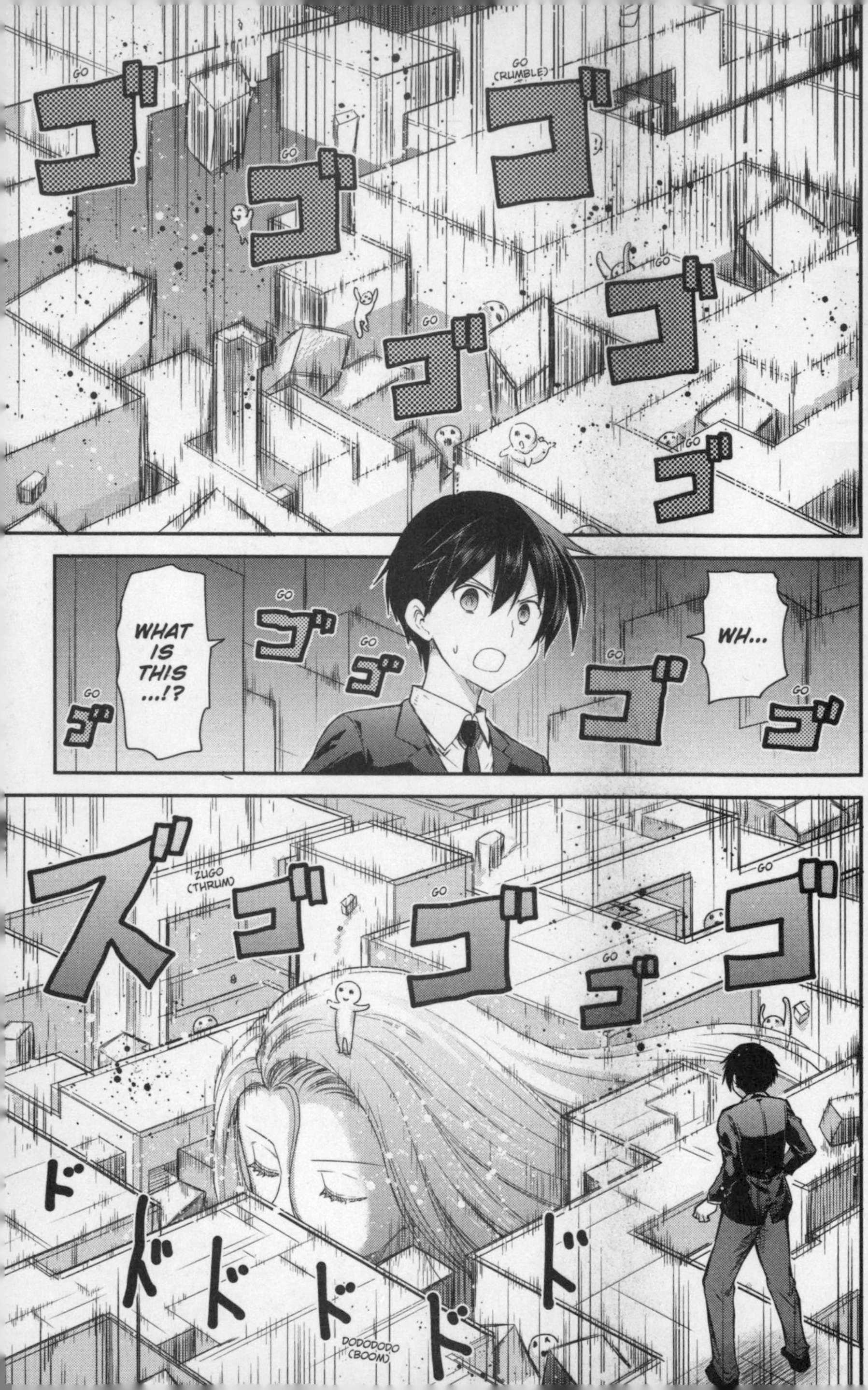
ゴ
GO
(RUMBLE)
ゴ
GO
ゴ
GO
ゴ
GO
ゴ
GO
ゴ
GO
ゴ
GO
WH...
ゴ
GO
ゴ
GO
WHAT IS THIS ...!?
ゴ
GO
ゴ
GO
ゴ
GO
ゴ
GO
ゴ
GO
ズゴ
ZUGO
(THRUM)
ドドドドド
DODODODO
(BOOM)

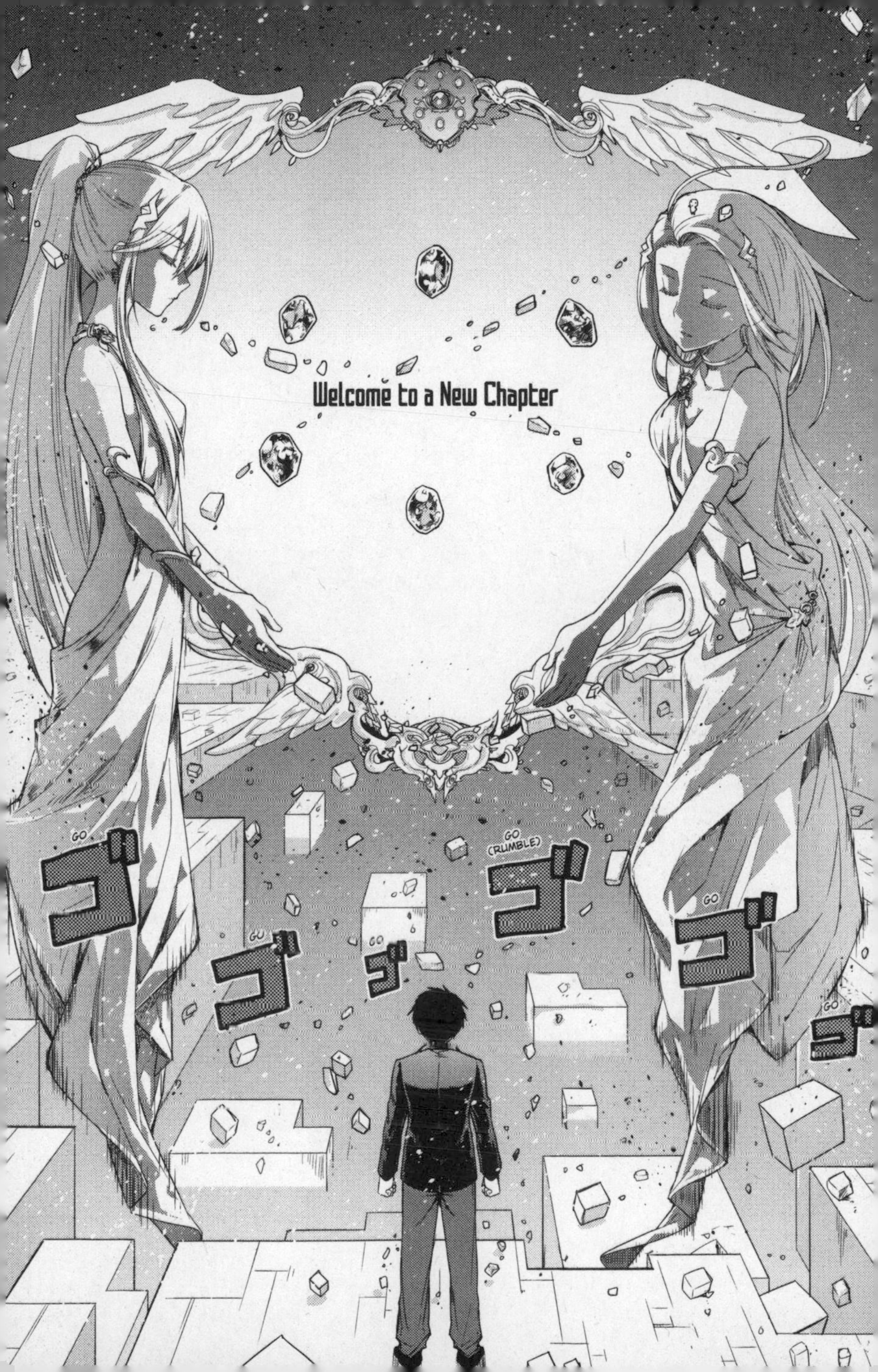
Welcome to a New Chapter
GO (RUMBLE) ゴ
GO ゴ
GO ゴ
GO ゴ
GU ゴ
GO ゴ

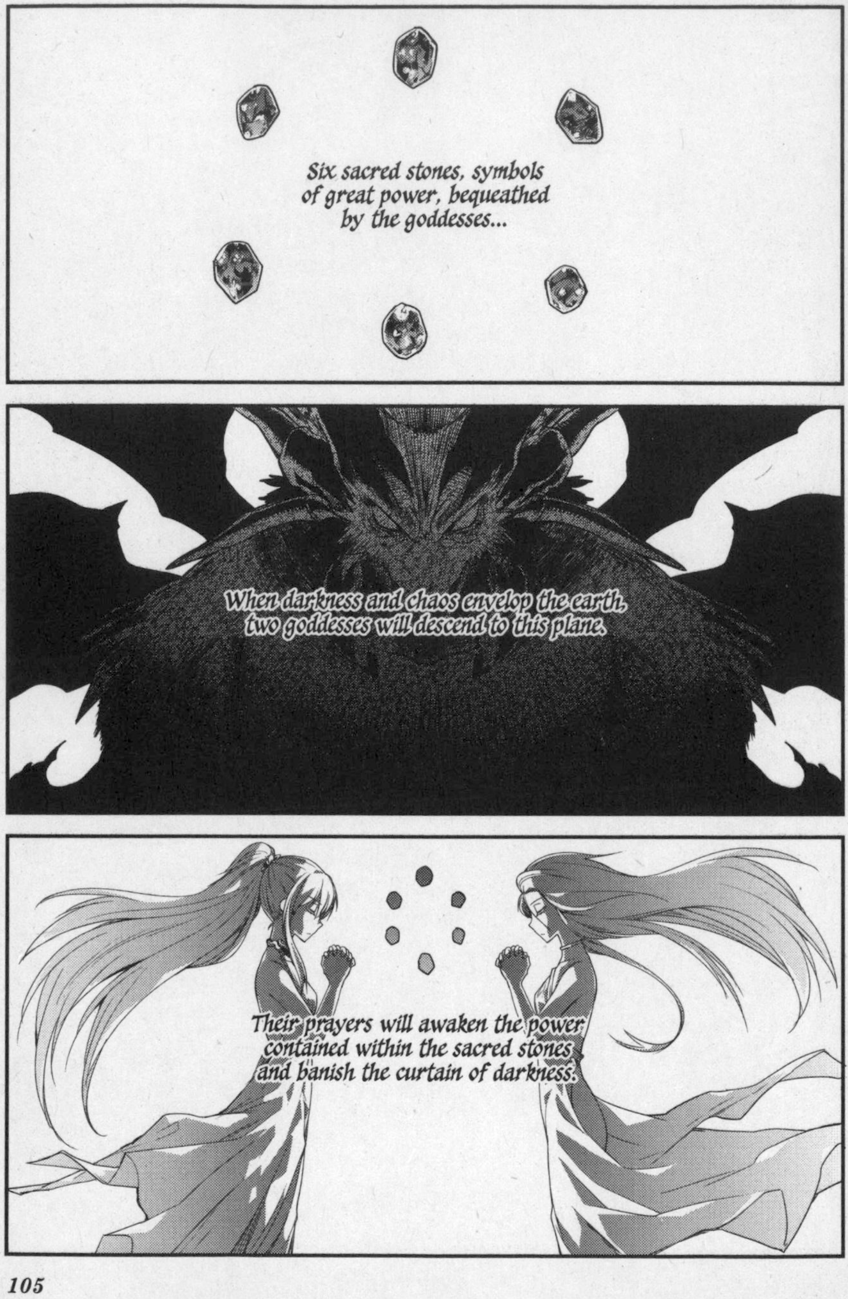
Six sacred stones, symbols of great power, bequeathed by the goddesses...
When darkness and chaos envelop the earth, two goddesses will descend to this plane.
Their prayers will awaken the power contained within the sacred stones and banish the curtain of darkness.

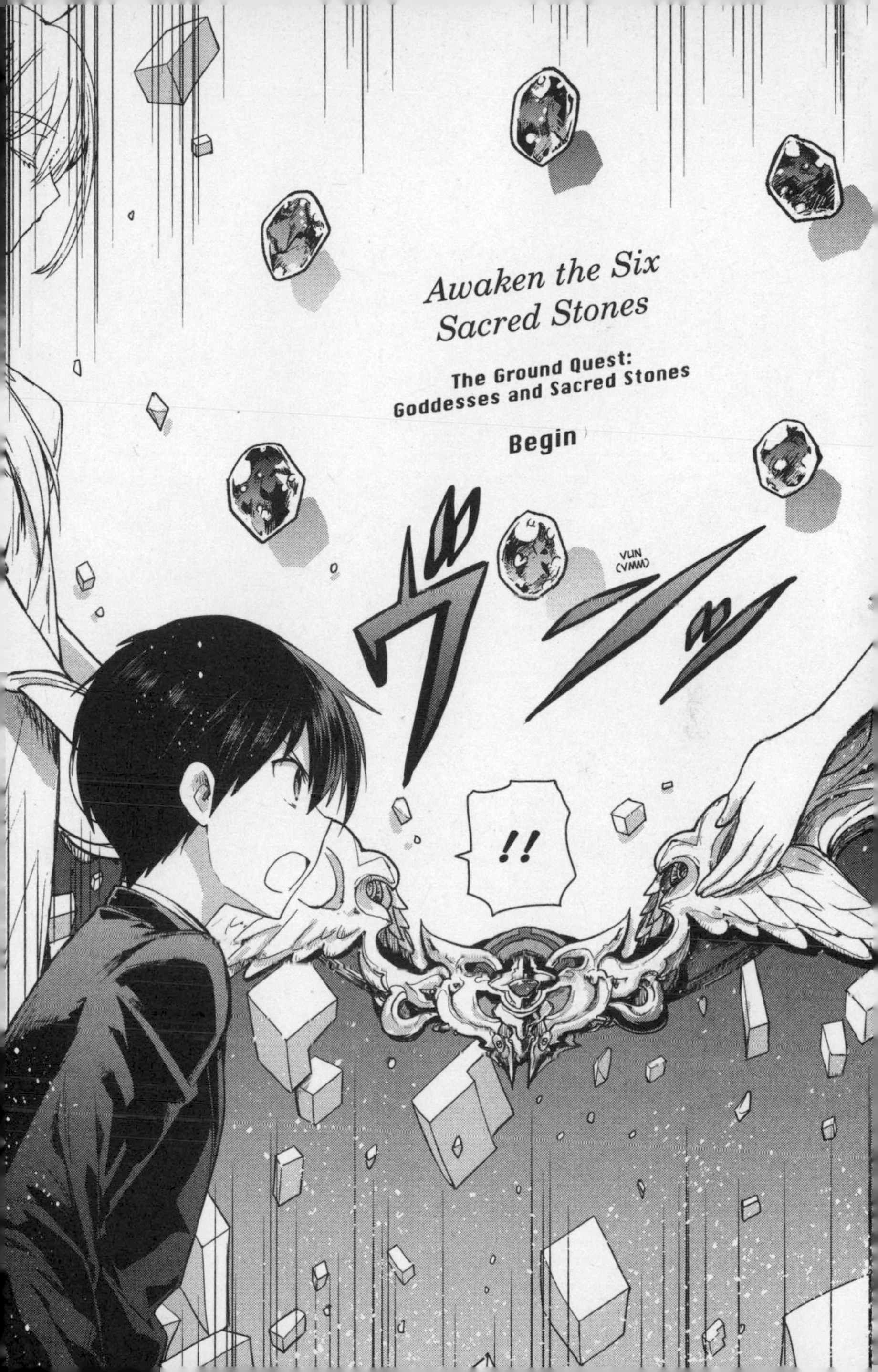
Awaken the Six Sacred Stones
The Ground Quest: Goddesses and Sacred Stones
Begin
VUN (VMM)
!!

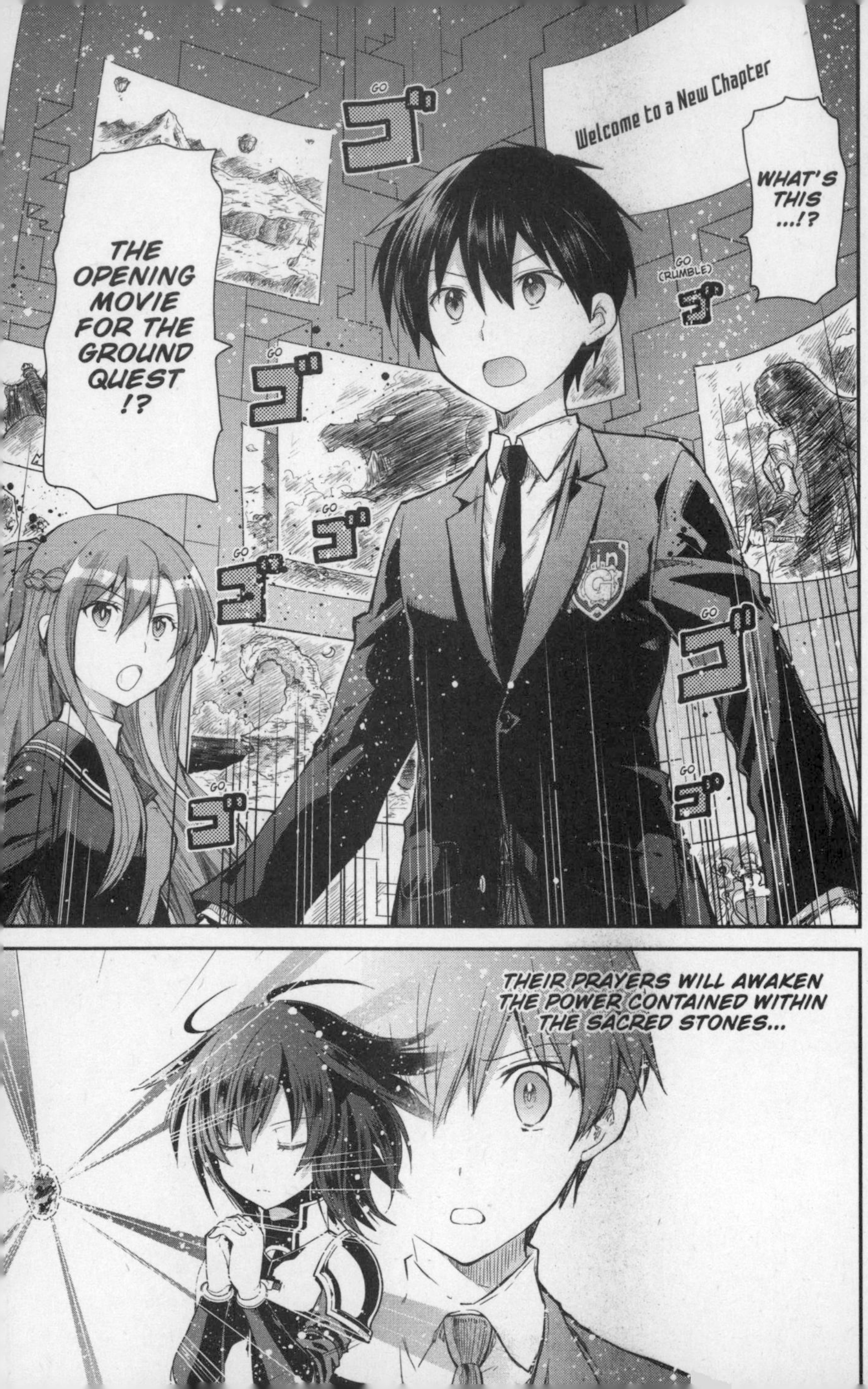
Welcome to a New Chapter
WHAT'S THIS ...!?
GO ゴ
GO (RUMBLE) ゴ
THE OPENING MOVIE FOR THE GROUND QUEST !?
GO ゴ
GO ゴ
GO ゴ
GO ゴ
GO ゴ
GO ゴ
THEIR PRAYERS WILL AWAKEN THE POWER CONTAINED WITHIN THE SACRED STONES...

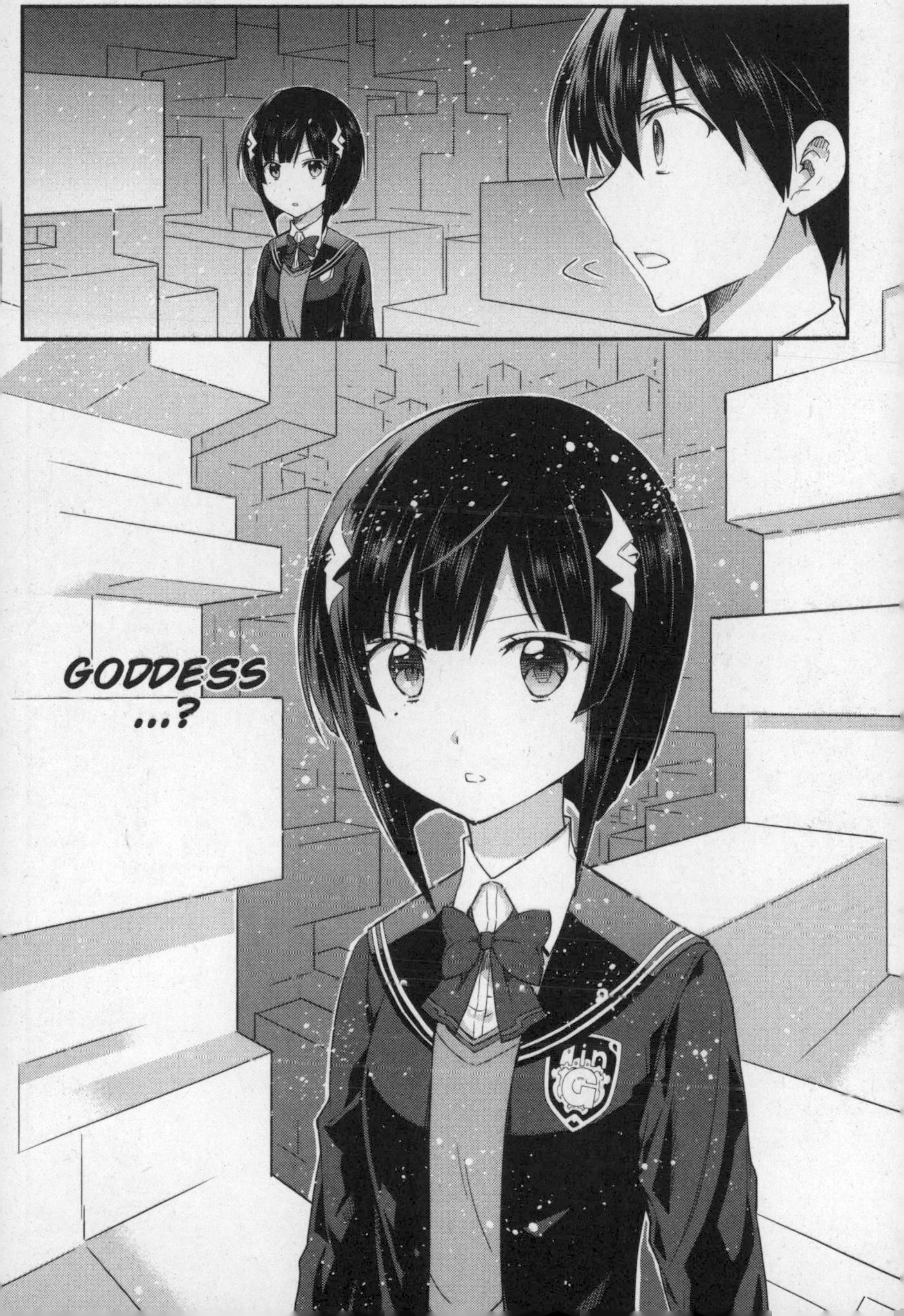
GODDESS
...?

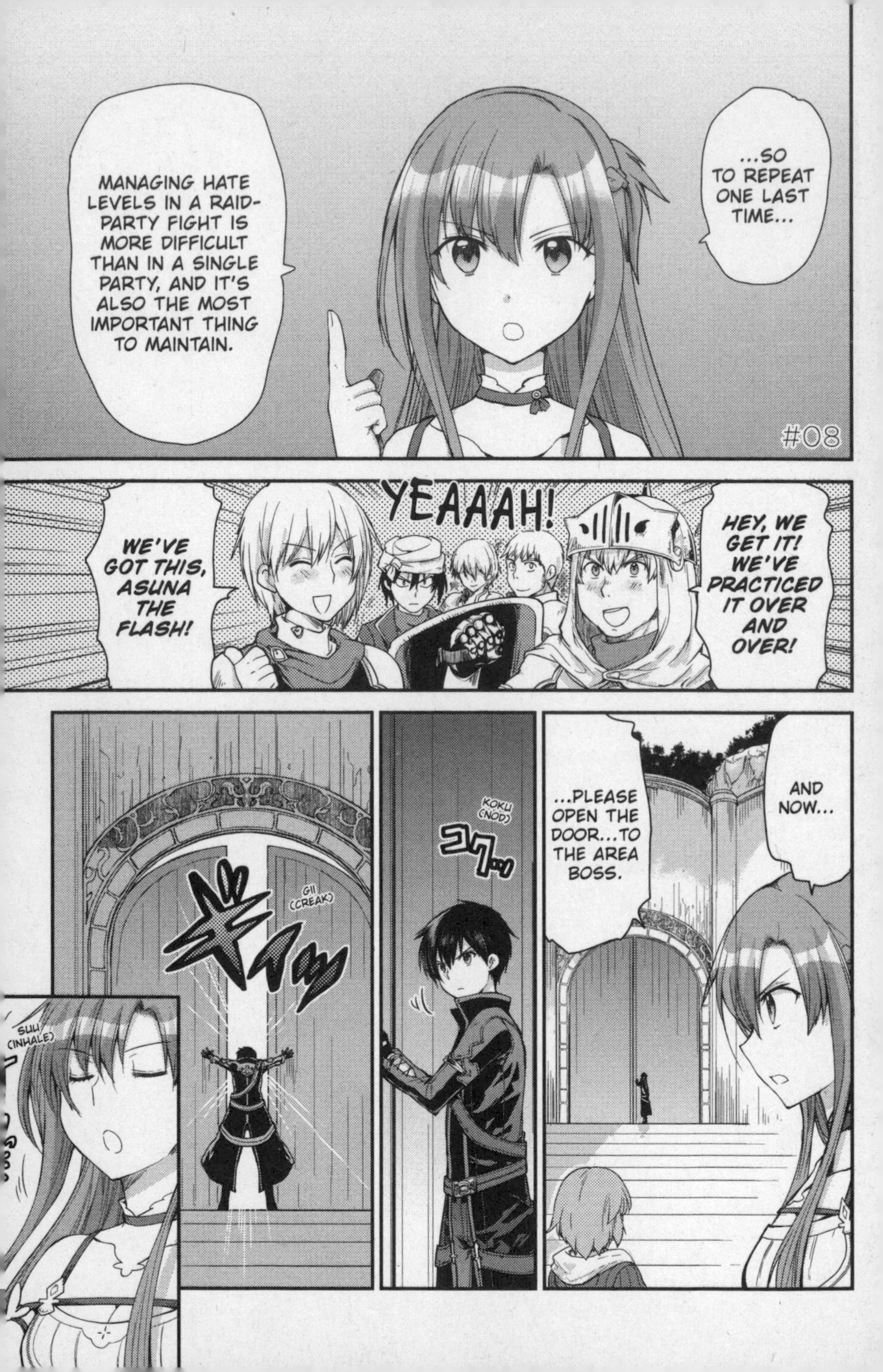
...SO TO REPEAT ONE LAST TIME...
MANAGING HATE LEVELS IN A RAID-PARTY FIGHT IS MORE DIFFICULT THAN IN A SINGLE PARTY, AND IT'S ALSO THE MOST IMPORTANT THING TO MAINTAIN.
#08
HEY, WE GET IT! WE'VE PRACTICED IT OVER AND OVER!
YEAAAH!
WE'VE GOT THIS, ASUNA THE FLASH!
AND NOW...
...PLEASE OPEN THE DOOR...TO THE AREA BOSS.
KOKU (NOD)
GII (CREAK)
SUU (INHALE)

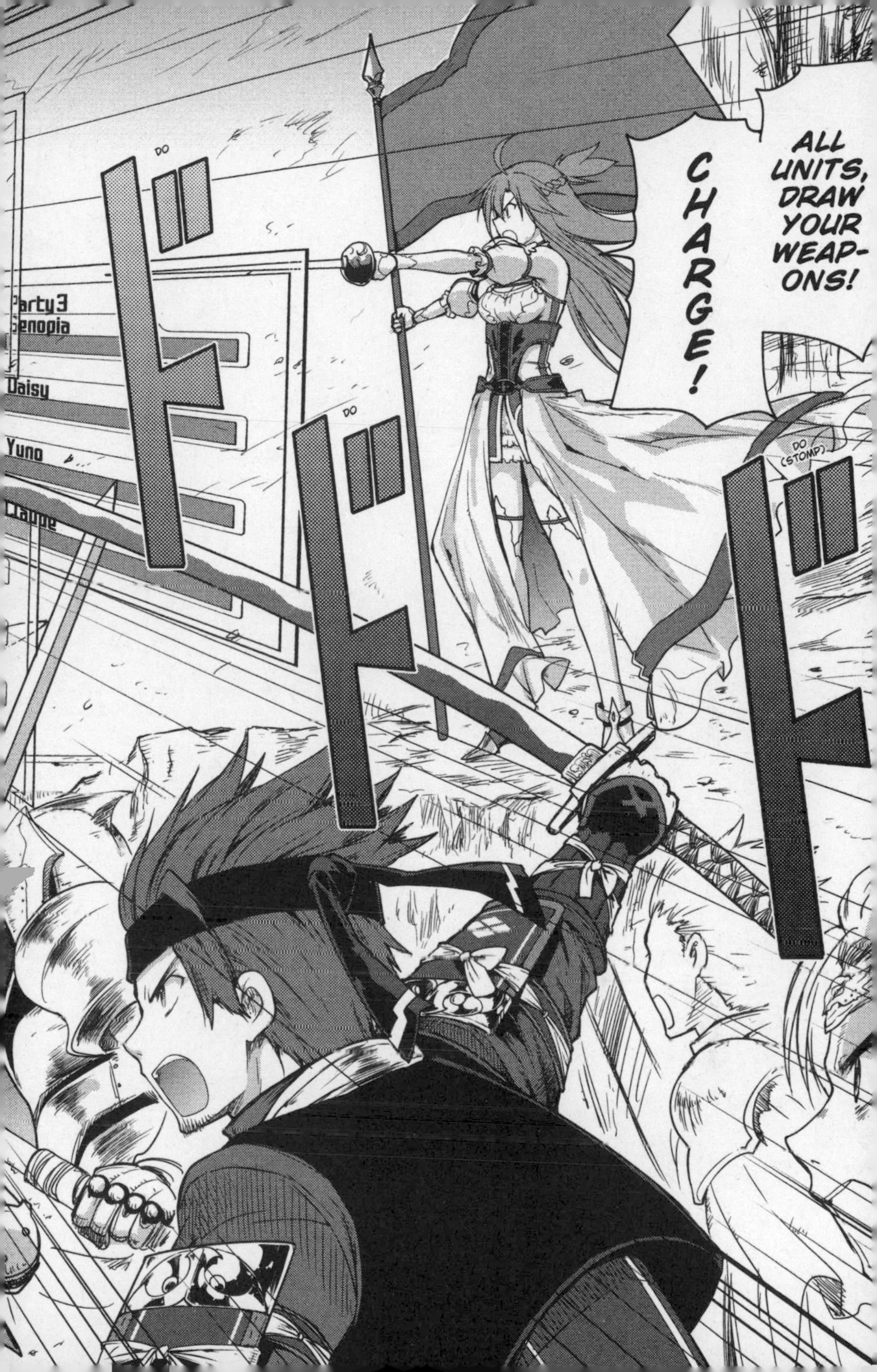
ALL UNITS, DRAW YOUR WEAPONS!
CHARGE!
DO
DO
DO (STOMP)
Party3
Senopia
Daisy
Yuno
Claupe

#08: Raid Boss

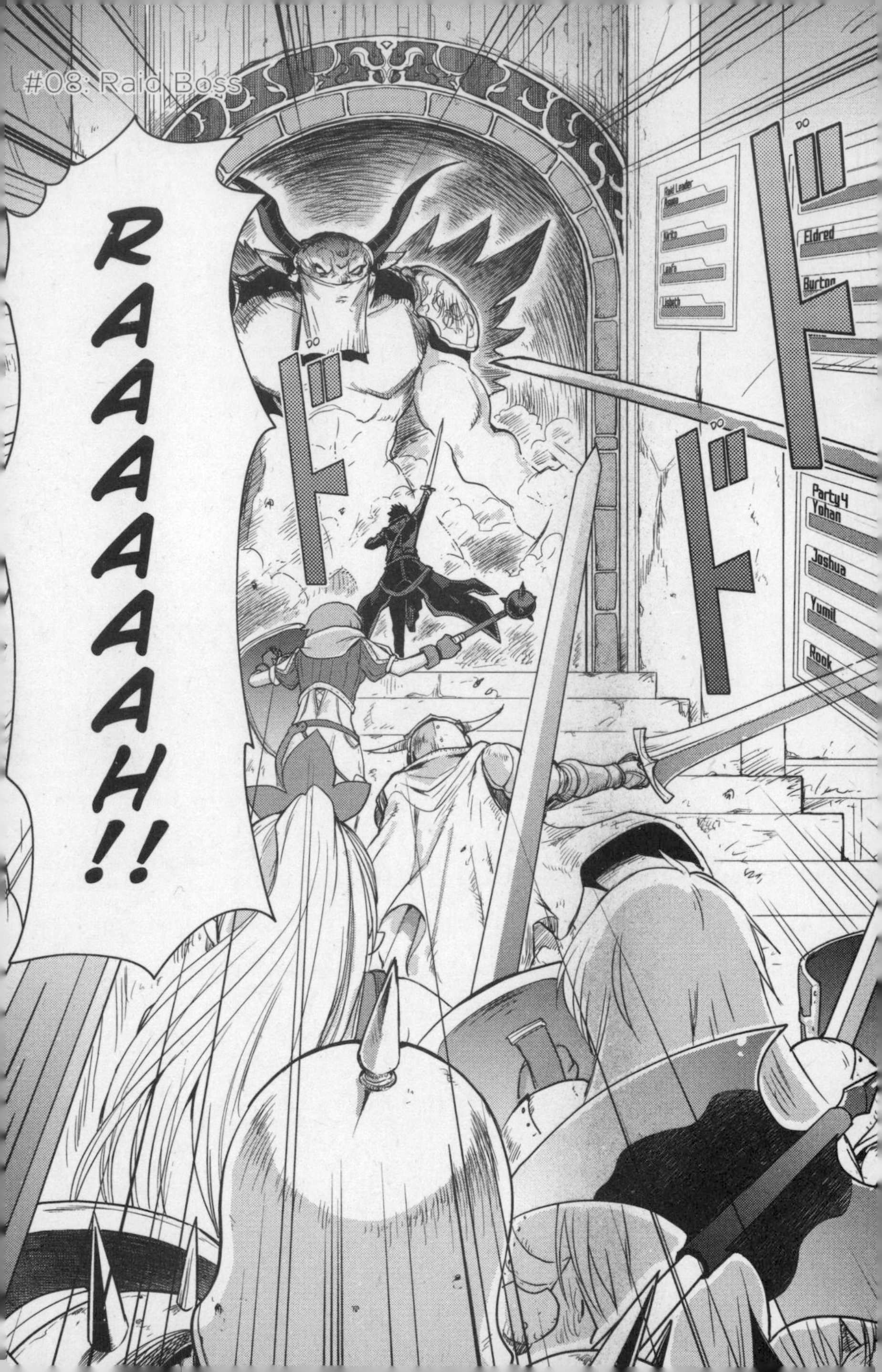
DO
DO
Raid Leader
Asuna
Kirito
Leafa
Lisbeth
Eldred
Burton
Party 4
Yohan
Joshua
Yumil
Rook
DO
RAAAAAAH!!

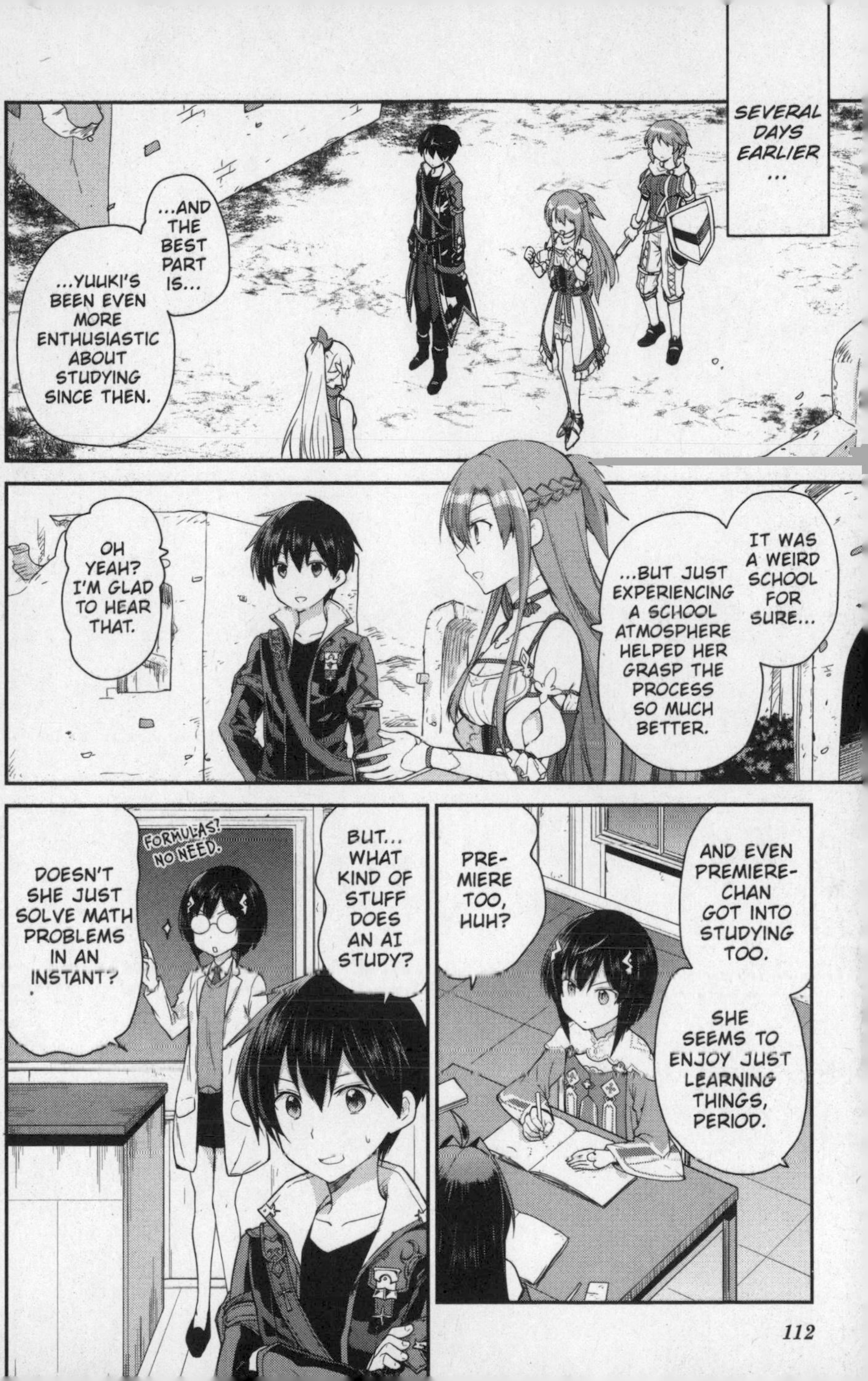
SEVERAL DAYS EARLIER ...
...AND THE BEST PART IS...
...YUUKI'S BEEN EVEN MORE ENTHUSIASTIC ABOUT STUDYING SINCE THEN.
IT WAS A WEIRD SCHOOL FOR SURE...
...BUT JUST EXPERIENCING A SCHOOL ATMOSPHERE HELPED HER GRASP THE PROCESS SO MUCH BETTER.
OH YEAH? I'M GLAD TO HEAR THAT.
AND EVEN PREMIERE-CHAN GOT INTO STUDYING TOO.
SHE SEEMS TO ENJOY JUST LEARNING THINGS, PERIOD.
PRE-MIERE TOO, HUH?
BUT... WHAT KIND OF STUFF DOES AN AI STUDY?
FORMULAS? NO NEED.
DOESN'T SHE JUST SOLVE MATH PROBLEMS IN AN INSTANT?

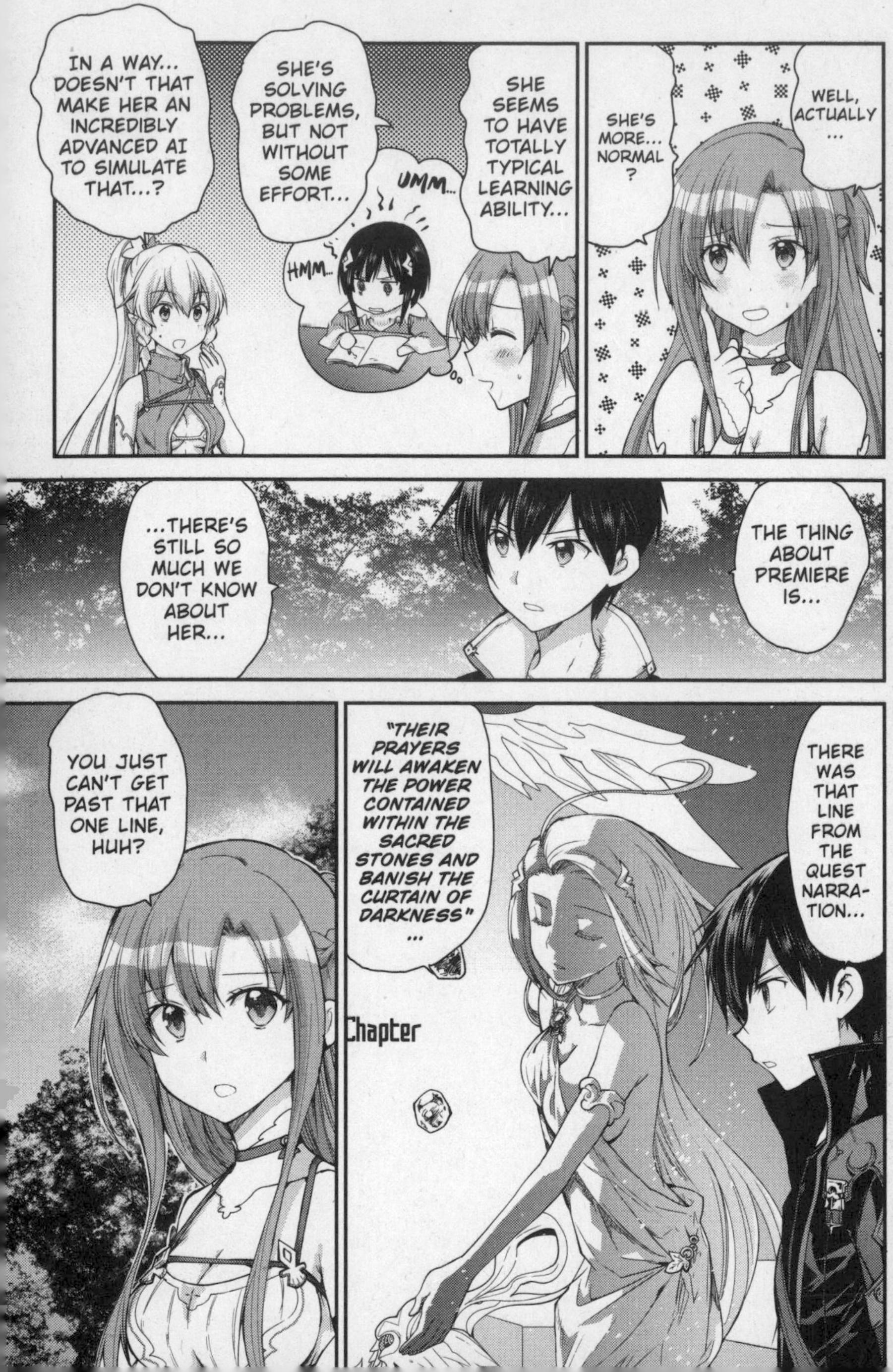
WELL, ACTUALLY...
SHE'S MORE... NORMAL?
SHE SEEMS TO HAVE TOTALLY TYPICAL LEARNING ABILITY...
SHE'S SOLVING PROBLEMS, BUT NOT WITHOUT SOME EFFORT...
UMM...
HMM...
IN A WAY... DOESN'T THAT MAKE HER AN INCREDIBLY ADVANCED AI TO SIMULATE THAT...?
THE THING ABOUT PREMIERE IS...
...THERE'S STILL SO MUCH WE DON'T KNOW ABOUT HER...
THERE WAS THAT LINE FROM THE QUEST NARRATION...
"THEIR PRAYERS WILL AWAKEN THE POWER CONTAINED WITHIN THE SACRED STONES AND BANISH THE CURTAIN OF DARKNESS"...
Chapter
YOU JUST CAN'T GET PAST THAT ONE LINE, HUH?

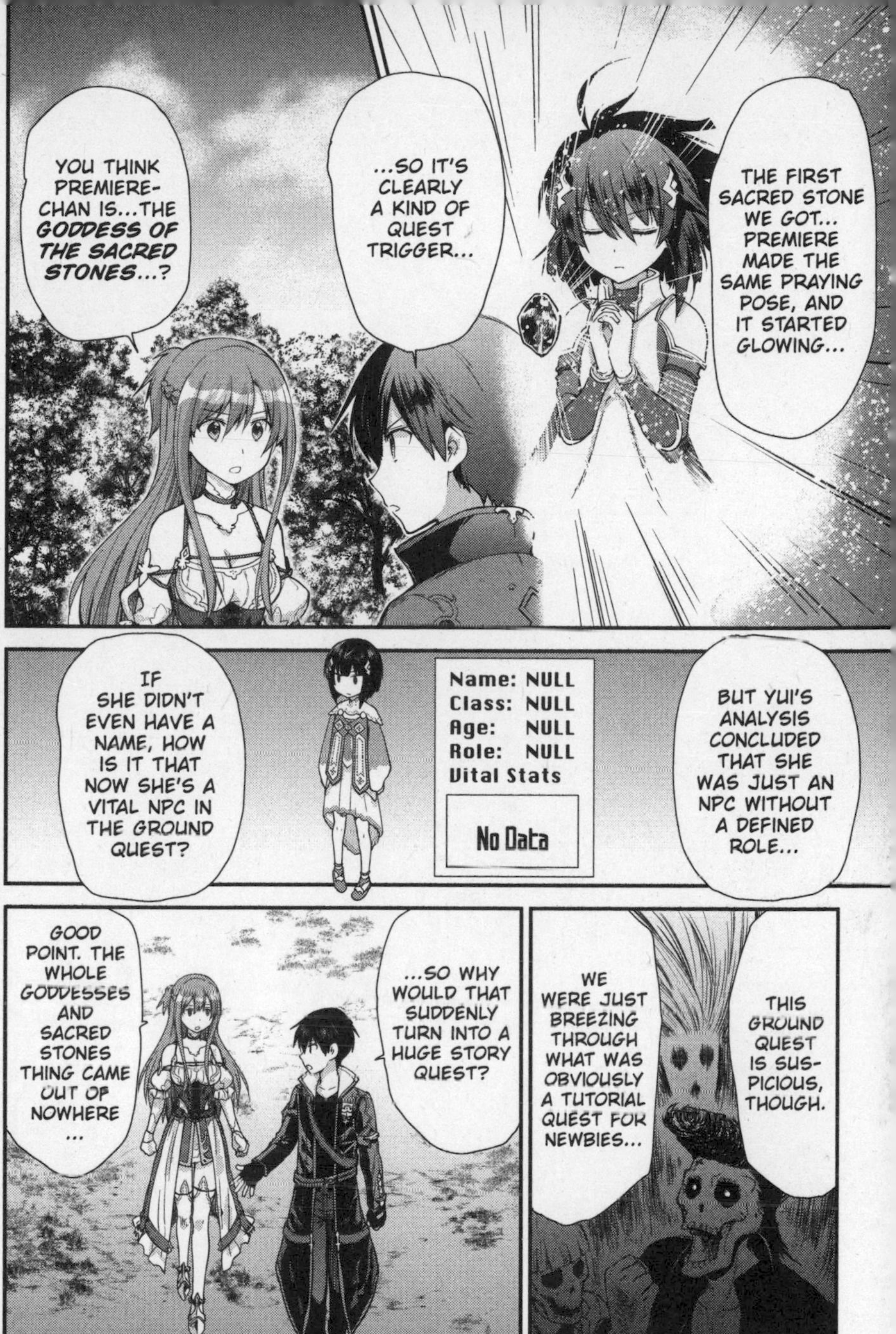
THE FIRST SACRED STONE WE GOT... PREMIERE MADE THE SAME PRAYING POSE, AND IT STARTED GLOWING...
...SO IT'S CLEARLY A KIND OF QUEST TRIGGER...
YOU THINK PREMIERE-CHAN IS...THE *GODDESS OF THE SACRED STONES...?*
BUT YUI'S ANALYSIS CONCLUDED THAT SHE WAS JUST AN NPC WITHOUT A DEFINED ROLE...
Name: NULL
Class: NULL
Age: NULL
Role: NULL
Vital Stats
No Data
IF SHE DIDN'T EVEN HAVE A NAME, HOW IS IT THAT NOW SHE'S A VITAL NPC IN THE GROUND QUEST?
THIS GROUND QUEST IS SUS-PICIOUS, THOUGH.
WE WERE JUST BREEZING THROUGH WHAT WAS OBVIOUSLY A TUTORIAL QUEST FOR NEWBIES...
...SO WHY WOULD THAT SUDDENLY TURN INTO A HUGE STORY QUEST?
GOOD POINT. THE WHOLE GODDESSES AND SACRED STONES THING CAME OUT OF NOWHERE...

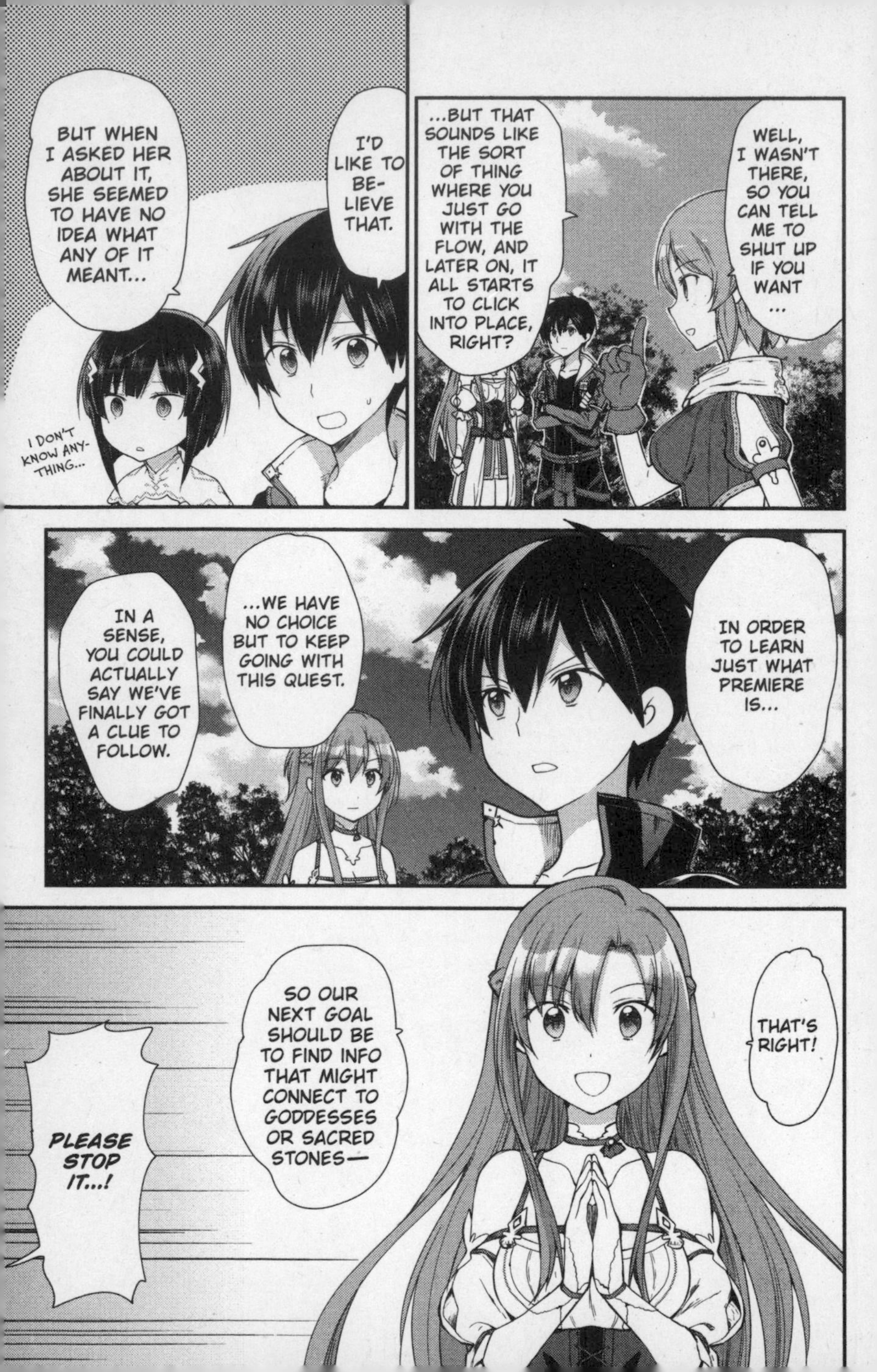
WELL, I WASN'T THERE, SO YOU CAN TELL ME TO SHUT UP IF YOU WANT...
...BUT THAT SOUNDS LIKE THE SORT OF THING WHERE YOU JUST GO WITH THE FLOW, AND LATER ON, IT ALL STARTS TO CLICK INTO PLACE, RIGHT?
I'D LIKE TO BE-LIEVE THAT.
BUT WHEN I ASKED HER ABOUT IT, SHE SEEMED TO HAVE NO IDEA WHAT ANY OF IT MEANT...
I DON'T KNOW ANY-THING...
IN ORDER TO LEARN JUST WHAT PREMIERE IS...
...WE HAVE NO CHOICE BUT TO KEEP GOING WITH THIS QUEST.
IN A SENSE, YOU COULD ACTUALLY SAY WE'VE FINALLY GOT A CLUE TO FOLLOW.
THAT'S RIGHT!
SO OUR NEXT GOAL SHOULD BE TO FIND INFO THAT MIGHT CONNECT TO GODDESSES OR SACRED STONES—
PLEASE STOP IT...!

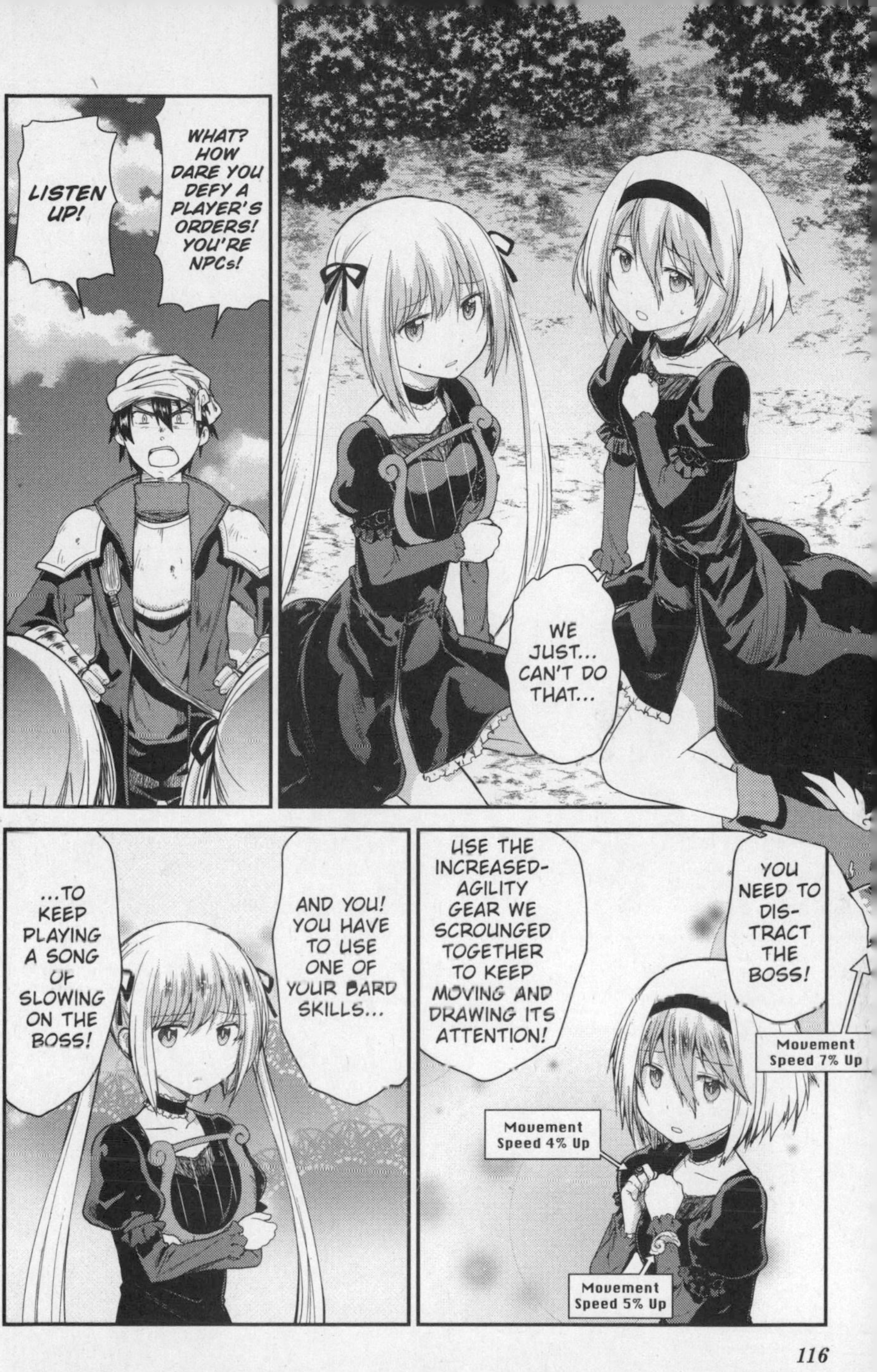
WE JUST... CAN'T DO THAT...
WHAT? HOW DARE YOU DEFY A PLAYER'S ORDERS! YOU'RE NPCs!
LISTEN UP!
YOU NEED TO DIS-TRACT THE BOSS!
USE THE INCREASED-AGILITY GEAR WE SCROUNGED TOGETHER TO KEEP MOVING AND DRAWING ITS ATTENTION!
Movement Speed 7% Up
Movement Speed 4% Up
Movement Speed 5% Up
AND YOU! YOU HAVE TO USE ONE OF YOUR BARD SKILLS...
...TO KEEP PLAYING A SONG OF SLOWING ON THE BOSS!

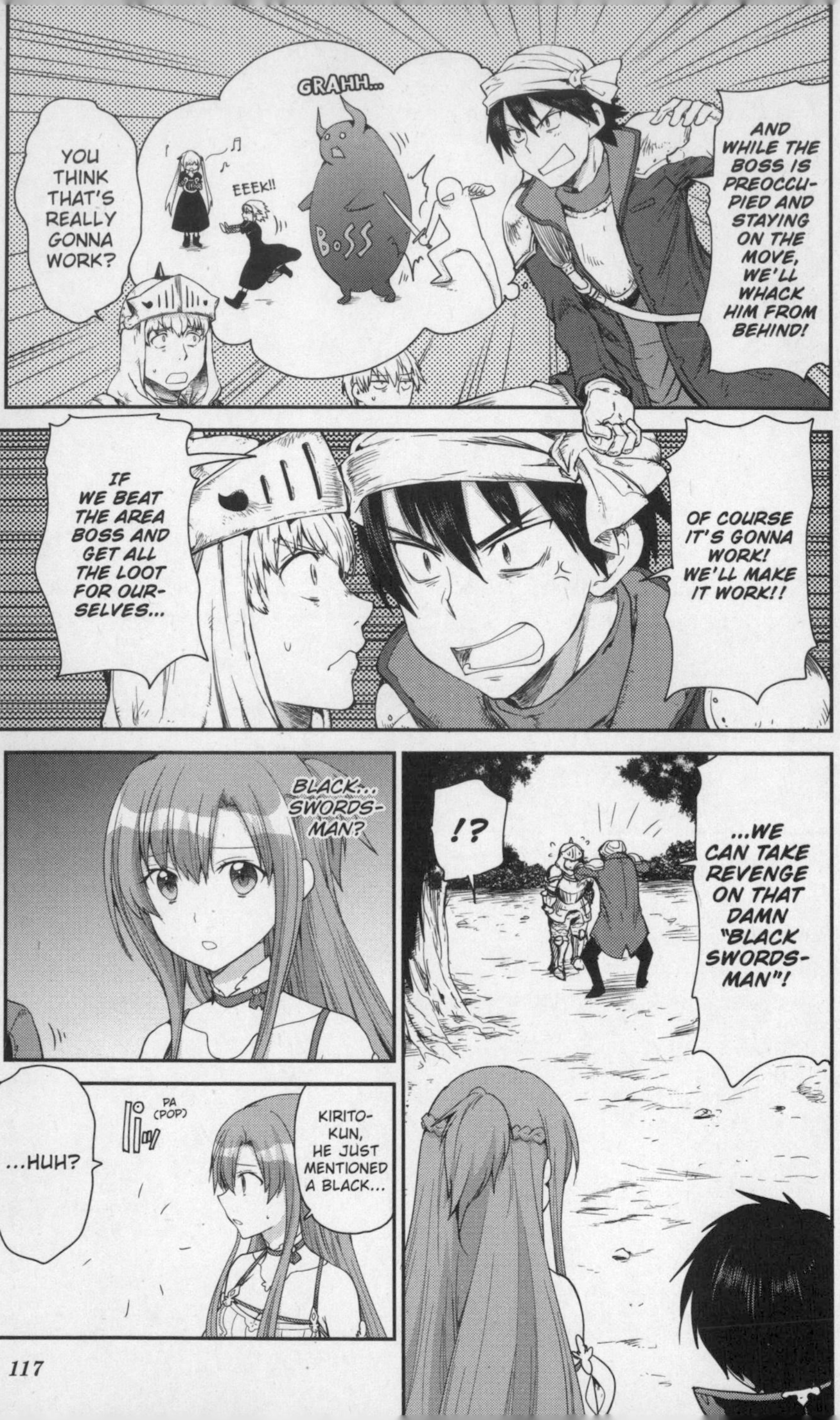
AND WHILE THE BOSS IS PREOCCUPIED AND STAYING ON THE MOVE, WE'LL WHACK HIM FROM BEHIND!
GRAHH...
EEEK!!
B.SS
YOU THINK THAT'S REALLY GONNA WORK?
OF COURSE IT'S GONNA WORK! WE'LL MAKE IT WORK!!
IF WE BEAT THE AREA BOSS AND GET ALL THE LOOT FOR OURSELVES...
...WE CAN TAKE REVENGE ON THAT DAMN "BLACK SWORDSMAN"!
!?
BLACK... SWORDSMAN?
KIRITO-KUN, HE JUST MENTIONED A BLACK...
PA (POP)
...HUH?

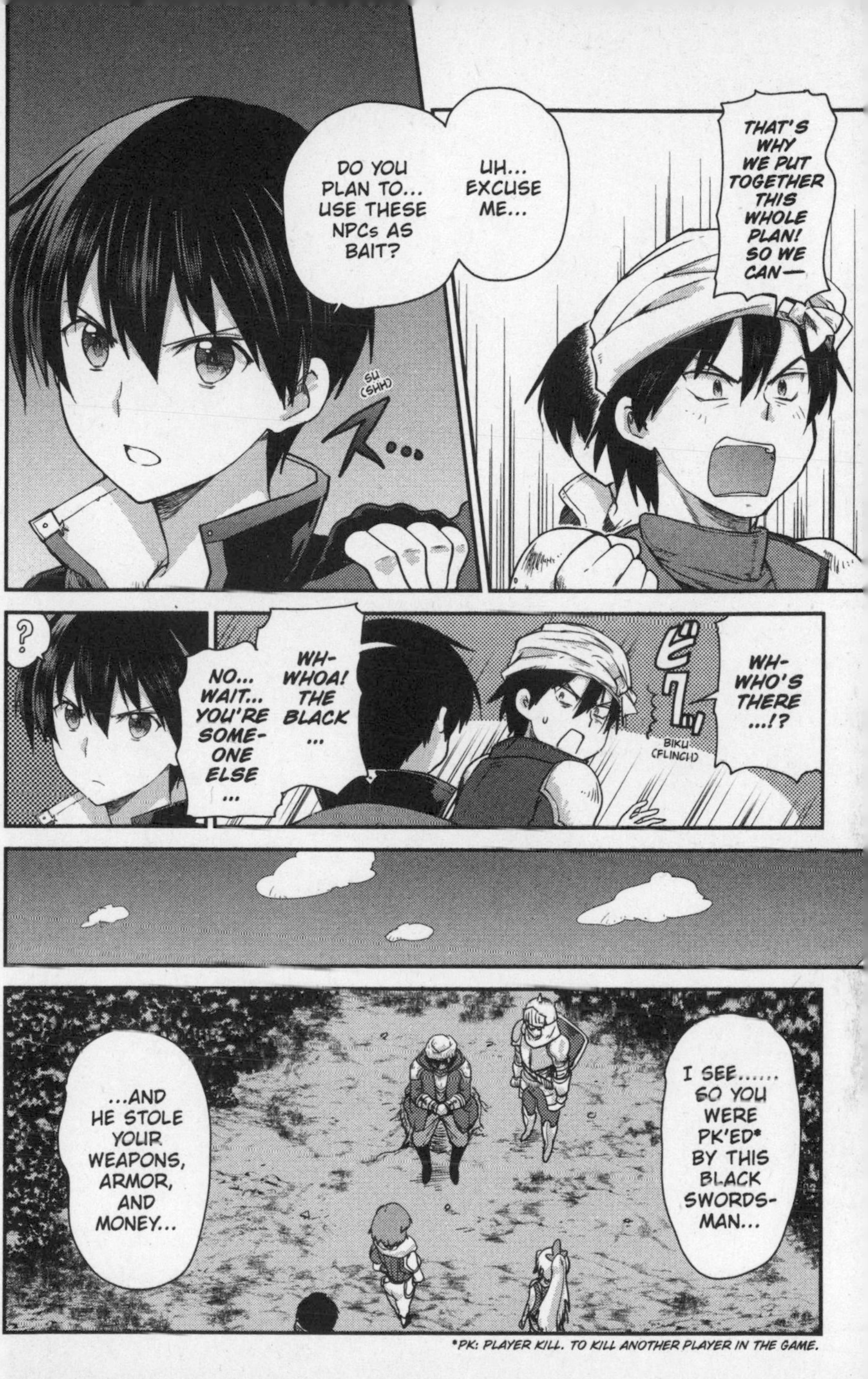
THAT'S WHY WE PUT TOGETHER THIS WHOLE PLAN! SO WE CAN—
UH... EXCUSE ME...
DO YOU PLAN TO... USE THESE NPCs AS BAIT?
SU (SHH)
WH- WHO'S THERE ...!?
BIKU (FLINCH)
WH- WHOA! THE BLACK ...
NO... WAIT... YOU'RE SOME-ONE ELSE ...
?
I SEE...... SO YOU WERE PK'ED* BY THIS BLACK SWORDS-MAN...
...AND HE STOLE YOUR WEAPONS, ARMOR, AND MONEY...

*PK: PLAYER KILL. TO KILL ANOTHER PLAYER IN THE GAME.

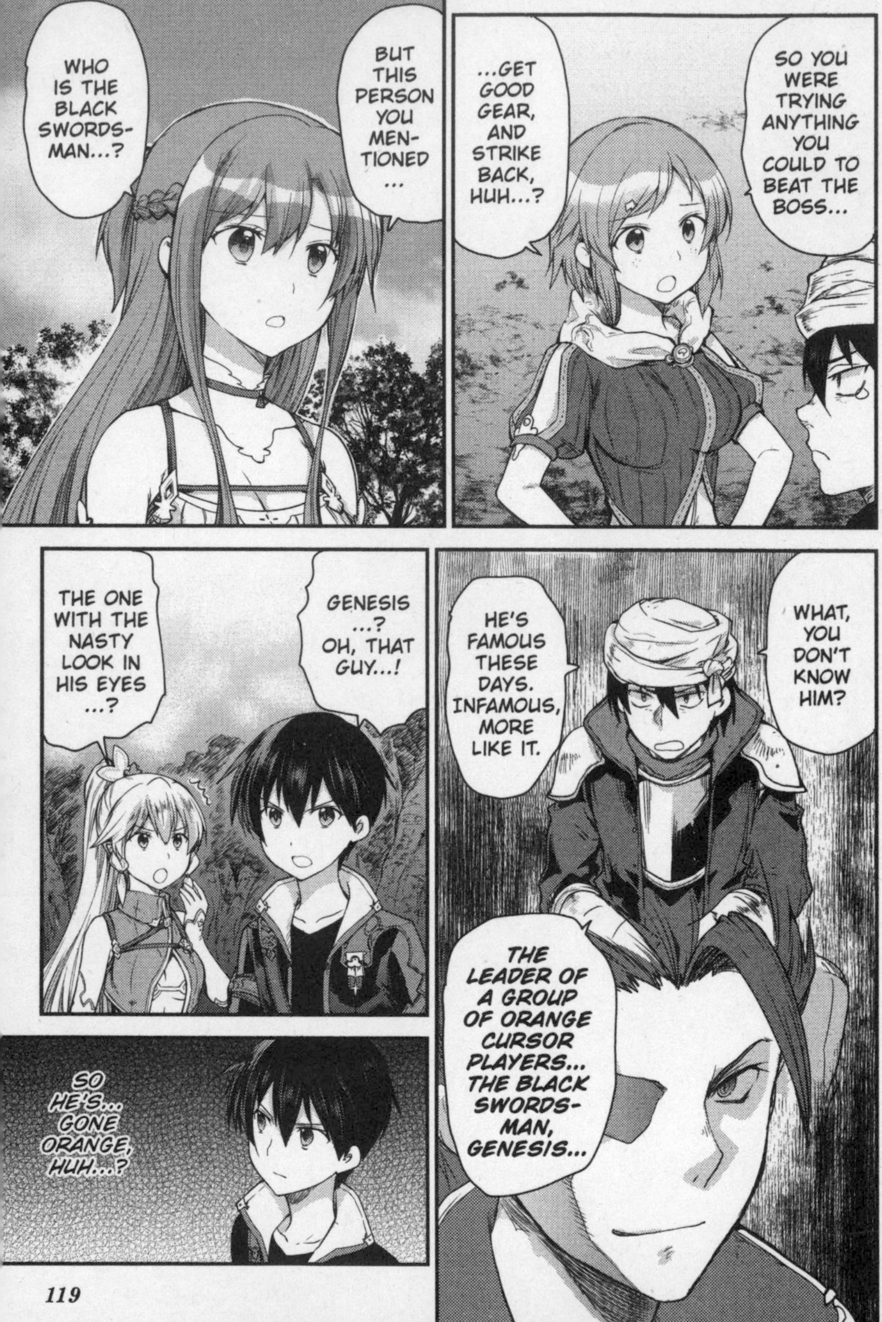

SO YOU WERE TRYING ANYTHING YOU COULD TO BEAT THE BOSS...
...GET GOOD GEAR, AND STRIKE BACK, HUH...?
BUT THIS PERSON YOU MENTIONED...
WHO IS THE BLACK SWORDSMAN...?
WHAT, YOU DON'T KNOW HIM?
HE'S FAMOUS THESE DAYS. INFAMOUS, MORE LIKE IT.
THE LEADER OF A GROUP OF ORANGE CURSOR PLAYERS... THE BLACK SWORDSMAN, GENESIS...
GENESIS...? OH, THAT GUY...!
THE ONE WITH THE NASTY LOOK IN HIS EYES...?
SO HE'S... GONE ORANGE, HUH...?

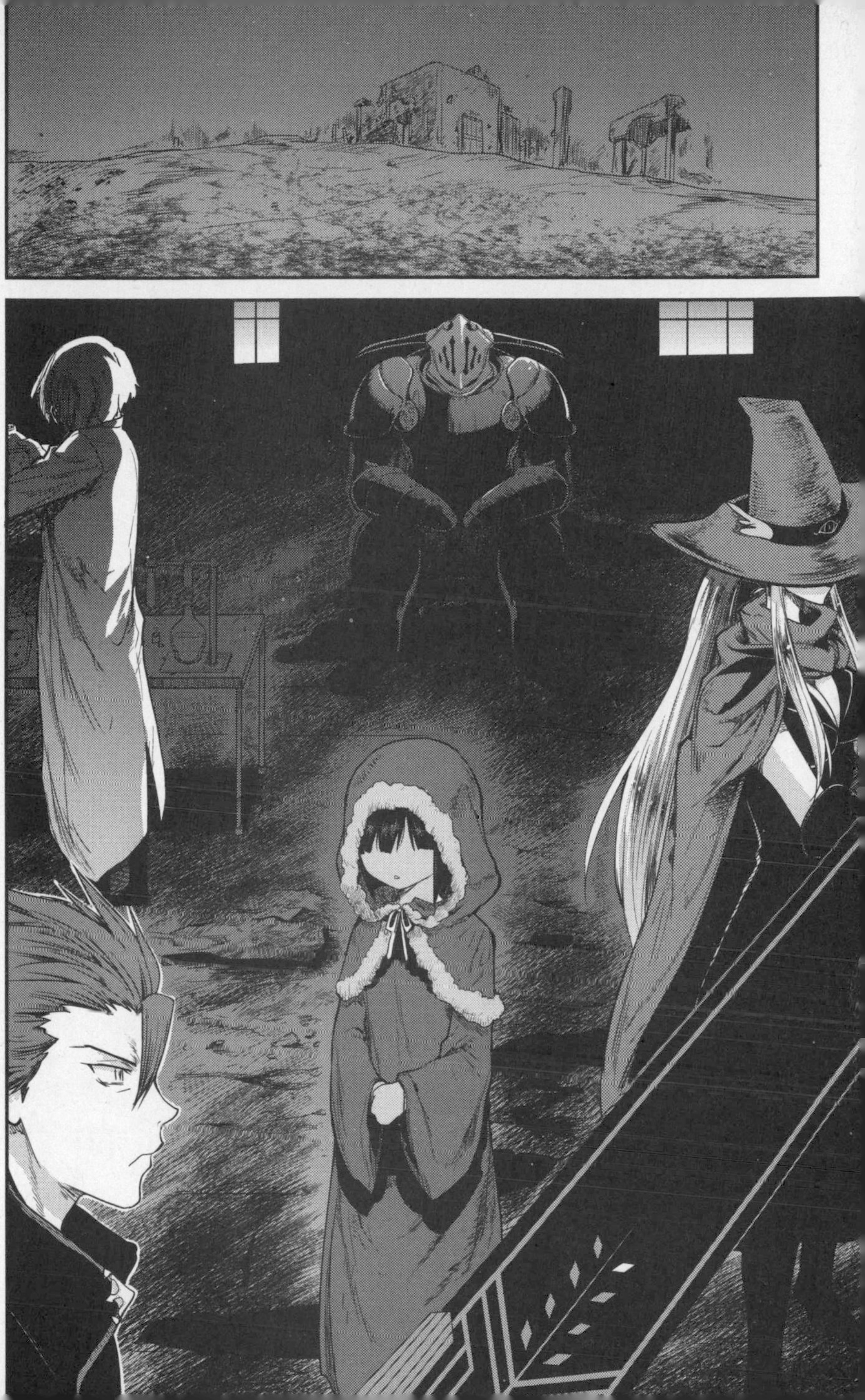

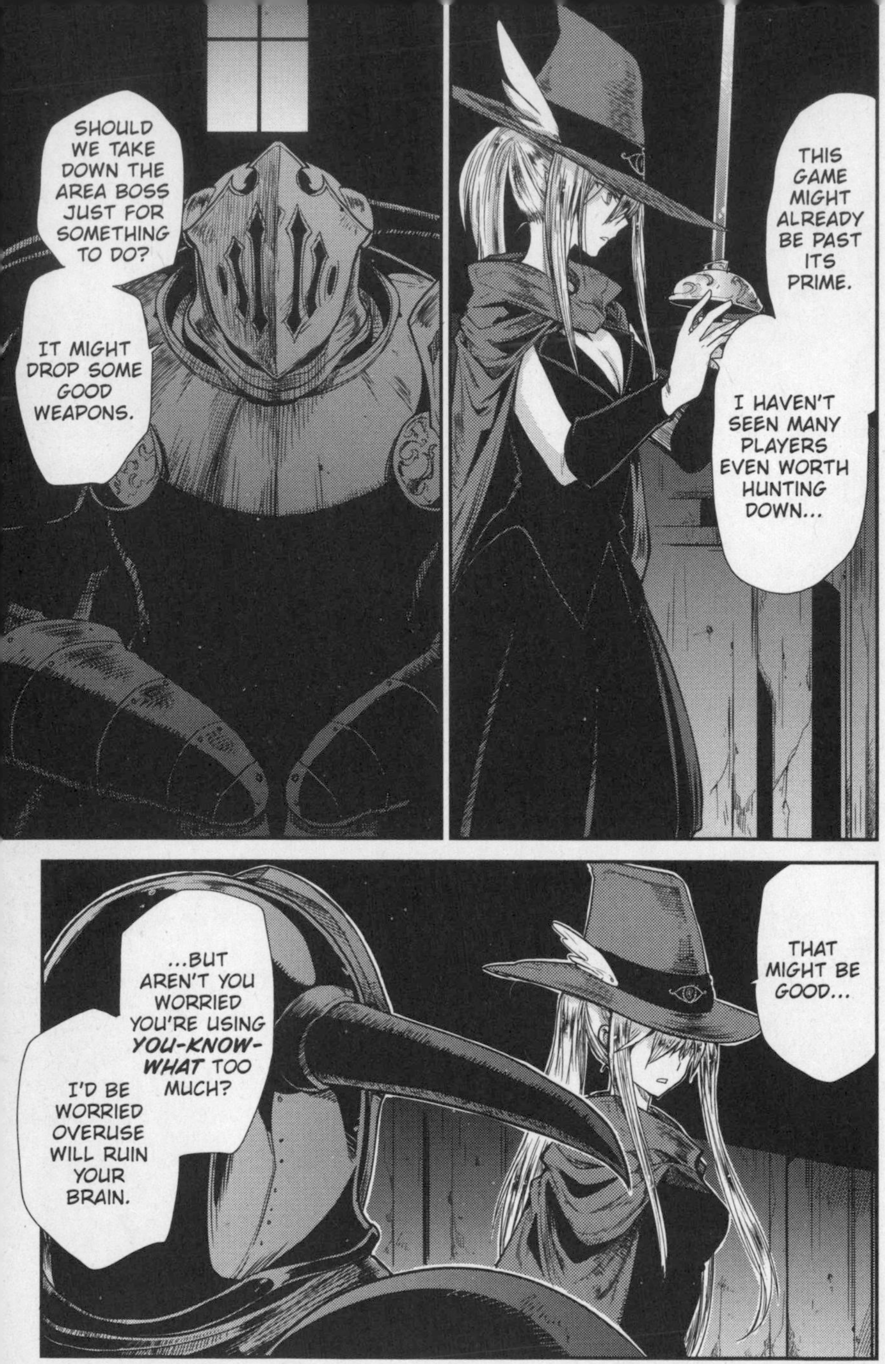
THIS GAME MIGHT ALREADY BE PAST ITS PRIME.
I HAVEN'T SEEN MANY PLAYERS EVEN WORTH HUNTING DOWN...
SHOULD WE TAKE DOWN THE AREA BOSS JUST FOR SOMETHING TO DO?
IT MIGHT DROP SOME GOOD WEAPONS.
THAT MIGHT BE GOOD...
...BUT AREN'T YOU WORRIED YOU'RE USING ***YOU-KNOW-WHAT*** TOO MUCH?
I'D BE WORRIED OVERUSE WILL RUIN YOUR BRAIN.

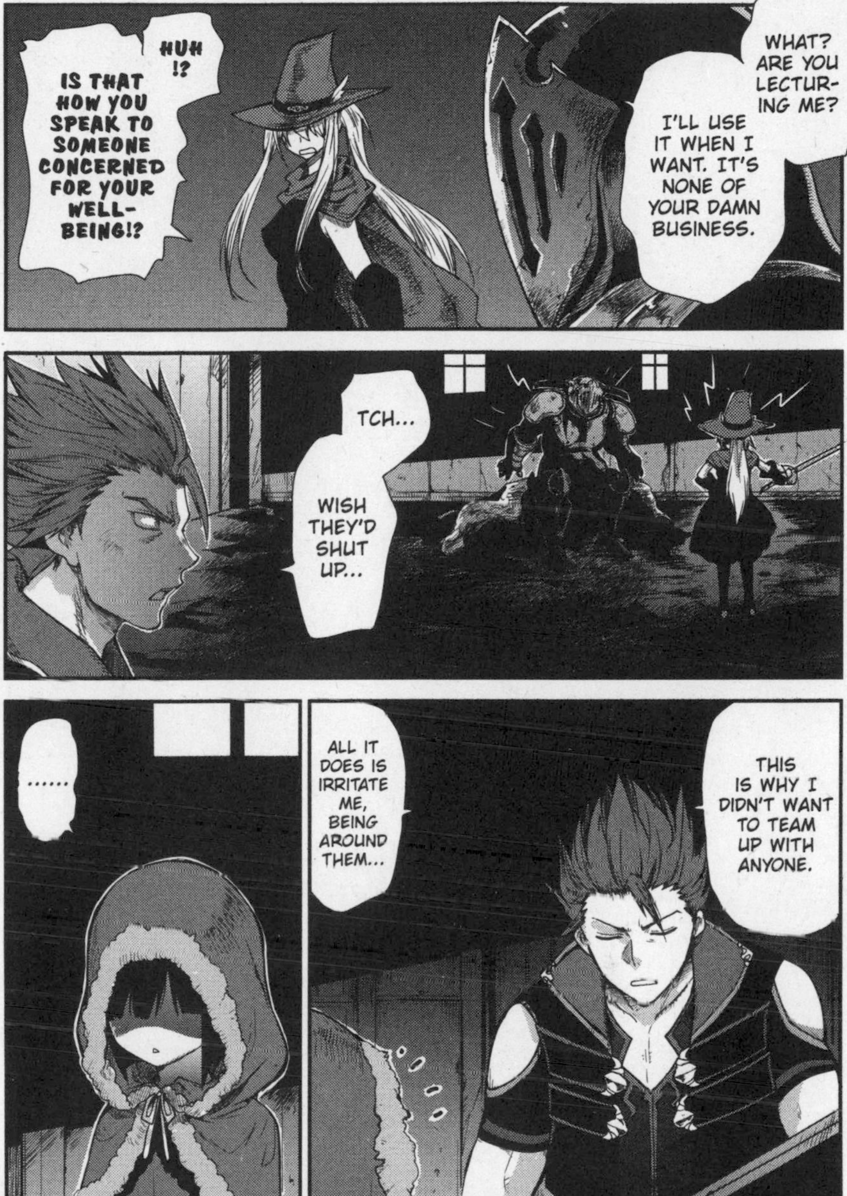
WHAT? ARE YOU LECTURING ME?
I'LL USE IT WHEN I WANT. IT'S NONE OF YOUR DAMN BUSINESS.
HUH!?
IS THAT HOW YOU SPEAK TO SOMEONE CONCERNED FOR YOUR WELL-BEING!?
TCH...
WISH THEY'D SHUT UP...
THIS IS WHY I DIDN'T WANT TO TEAM UP WITH ANYONE.
ALL IT DOES IS IRRITATE ME, BEING AROUND THEM...
......

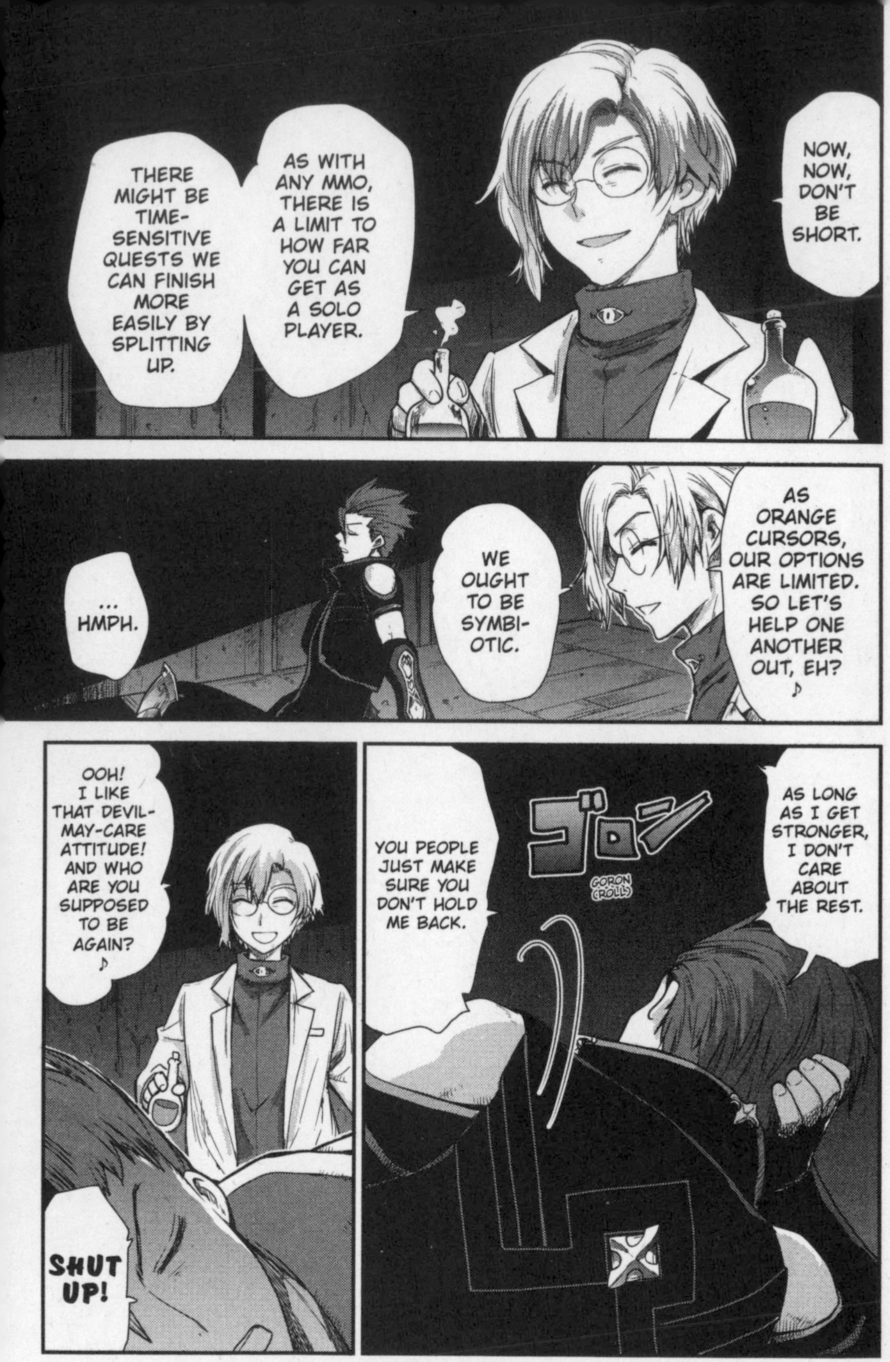
NOW, NOW, DON'T BE SHORT.
AS WITH ANY MMO, THERE IS A LIMIT TO HOW FAR YOU CAN GET AS A SOLO PLAYER.
THERE MIGHT BE TIME-SENSITIVE QUESTS WE CAN FINISH MORE EASILY BY SPLITTING UP.
AS ORANGE CURSORS, OUR OPTIONS ARE LIMITED. SO LET'S HELP ONE ANOTHER OUT, EH? ♪
WE OUGHT TO BE SYMBIOTIC.
... HMPH.
AS LONG AS I GET STRONGER, I DON'T CARE ABOUT THE REST.
ゴロン
GORON (ROLL)
YOU PEOPLE JUST MAKE SURE YOU DON'T HOLD ME BACK.
OOH! I LIKE THAT DEVIL-MAY-CARE ATTITUDE! AND WHO ARE YOU SUPPOSED TO BE AGAIN? ♪
SHUT UP!

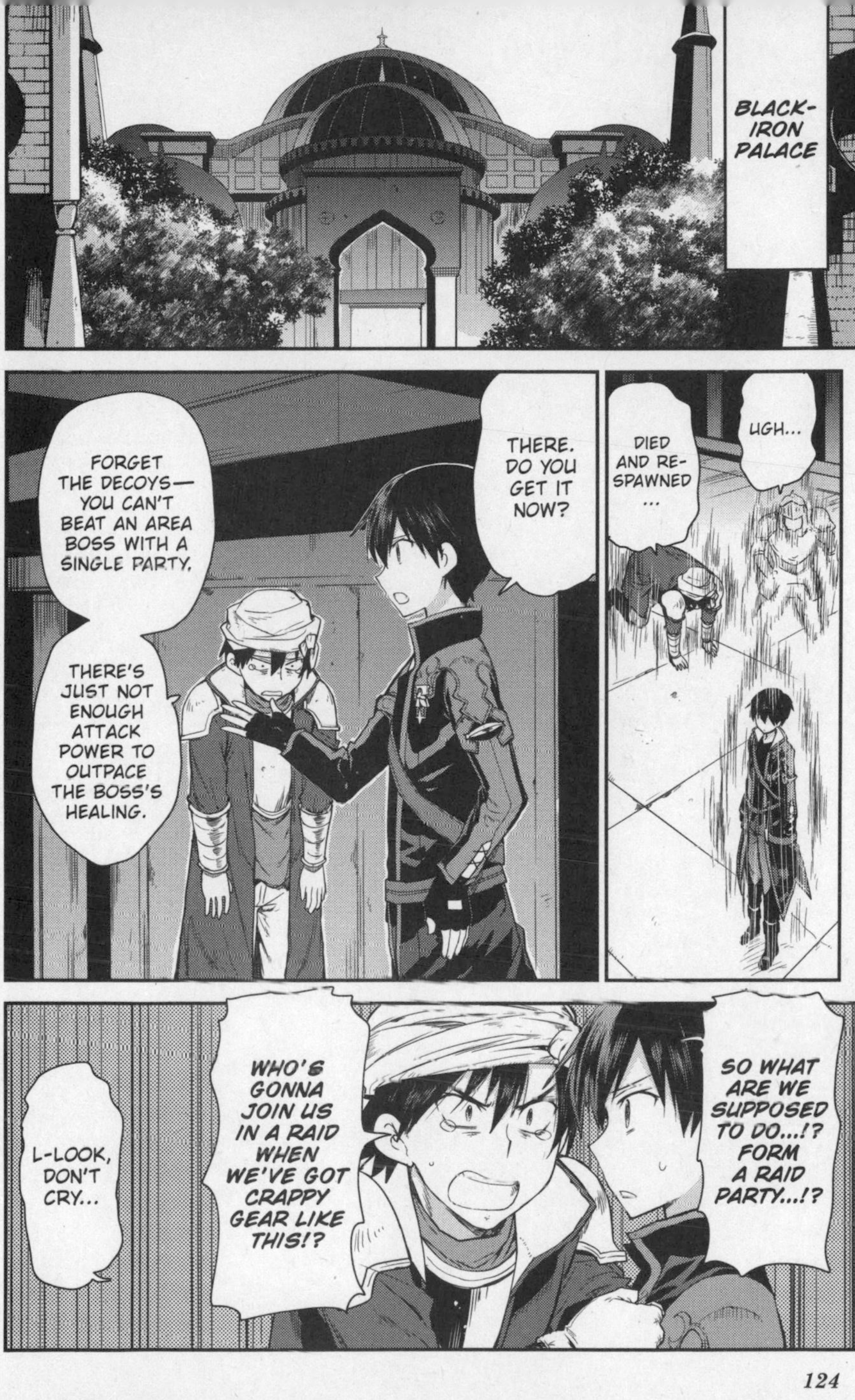
BLACK-IRON PALACE
UGH...
DIED AND RE-SPAWNED ...
THERE. DO YOU GET IT NOW?
FORGET THE DECOYS—YOU CAN'T BEAT AN AREA BOSS WITH A SINGLE PARTY.
THERE'S JUST NOT ENOUGH ATTACK POWER TO OUTPACE THE BOSS'S HEALING.
SO WHAT ARE WE SUPPOSED TO DO...!? FORM A RAID PARTY...!?
WHO'S GONNA JOIN US IN A RAID WHEN WE'VE GOT CRAPPY GEAR LIKE THIS!?
L-LOOK, DON'T CRY...

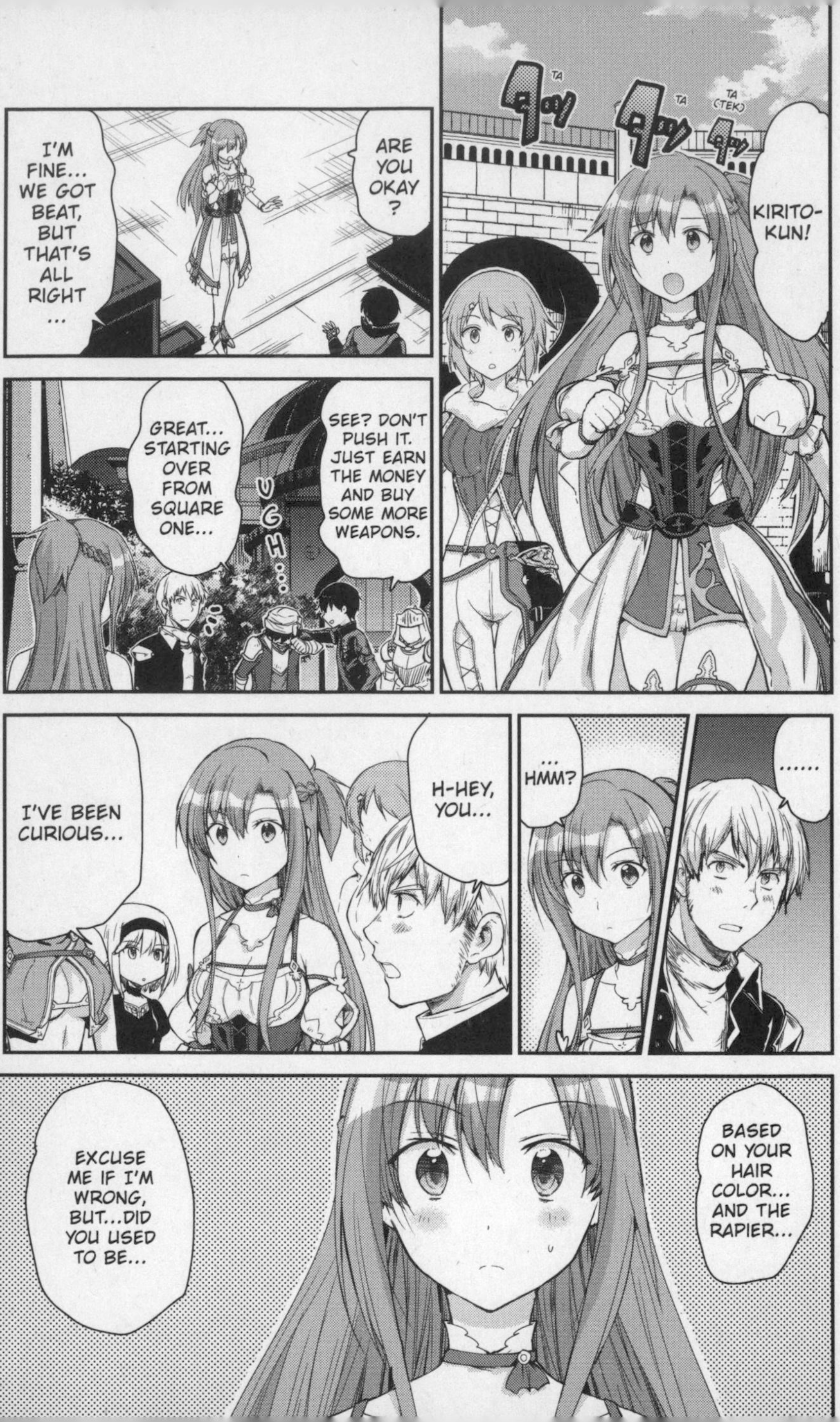
TA
TA
TA (TEK)
KIRITO-KUN!
ARE YOU OKAY?
I'M FINE... WE GOT BEAT, BUT THAT'S ALL RIGHT...
SEE? DON'T PUSH IT. JUST EARN THE MONEY AND BUY SOME MORE WEAPONS.
UGH...
GREAT... STARTING OVER FROM SQUARE ONE...
......
...HMM?
H-HEY, YOU...
I'VE BEEN CURIOUS...
BASED ON YOUR HAIR COLOR... AND THE RAPIER...
EXCUSE ME IF I'M WRONG, BUT...DID YOU USED TO BE...

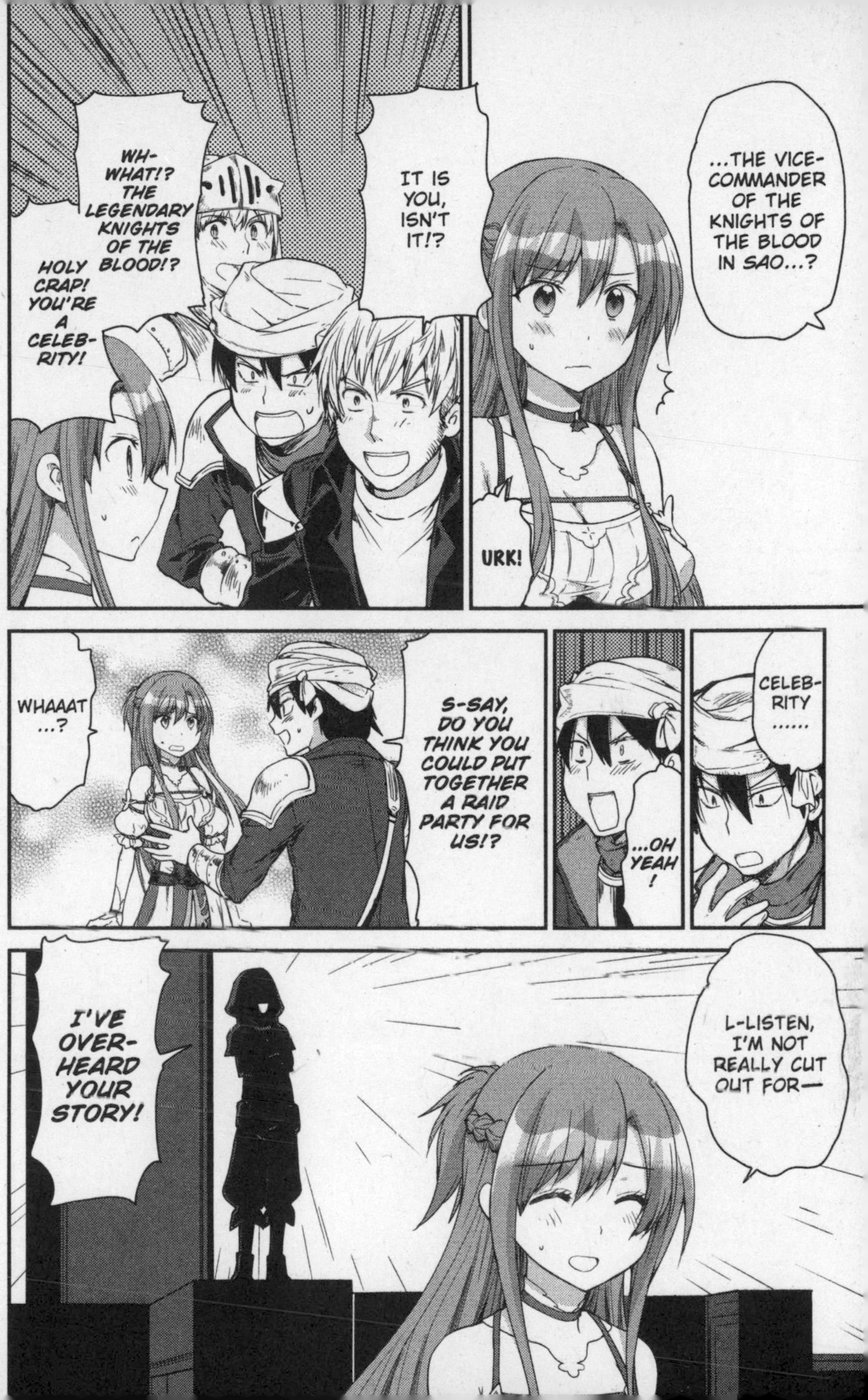
...THE VICE-COMMANDER OF THE KNIGHTS OF THE BLOOD IN SAO...?
URK!
IT IS YOU, ISN'T IT!?
WH-WHAT!? THE LEGENDARY KNIGHTS OF THE BLOOD!?
HOLY CRAP! YOU'RE A CELEBRITY!
CELEBRITY......
...OH YEAH!
S-SAY, DO YOU THINK YOU COULD PUT TOGETHER A RAID PARTY FOR US!?
WHAAAT...?
L-LISTEN, I'M NOT REALLY CUT OUT FOR—
I'VE OVERHEARD YOUR STORY!

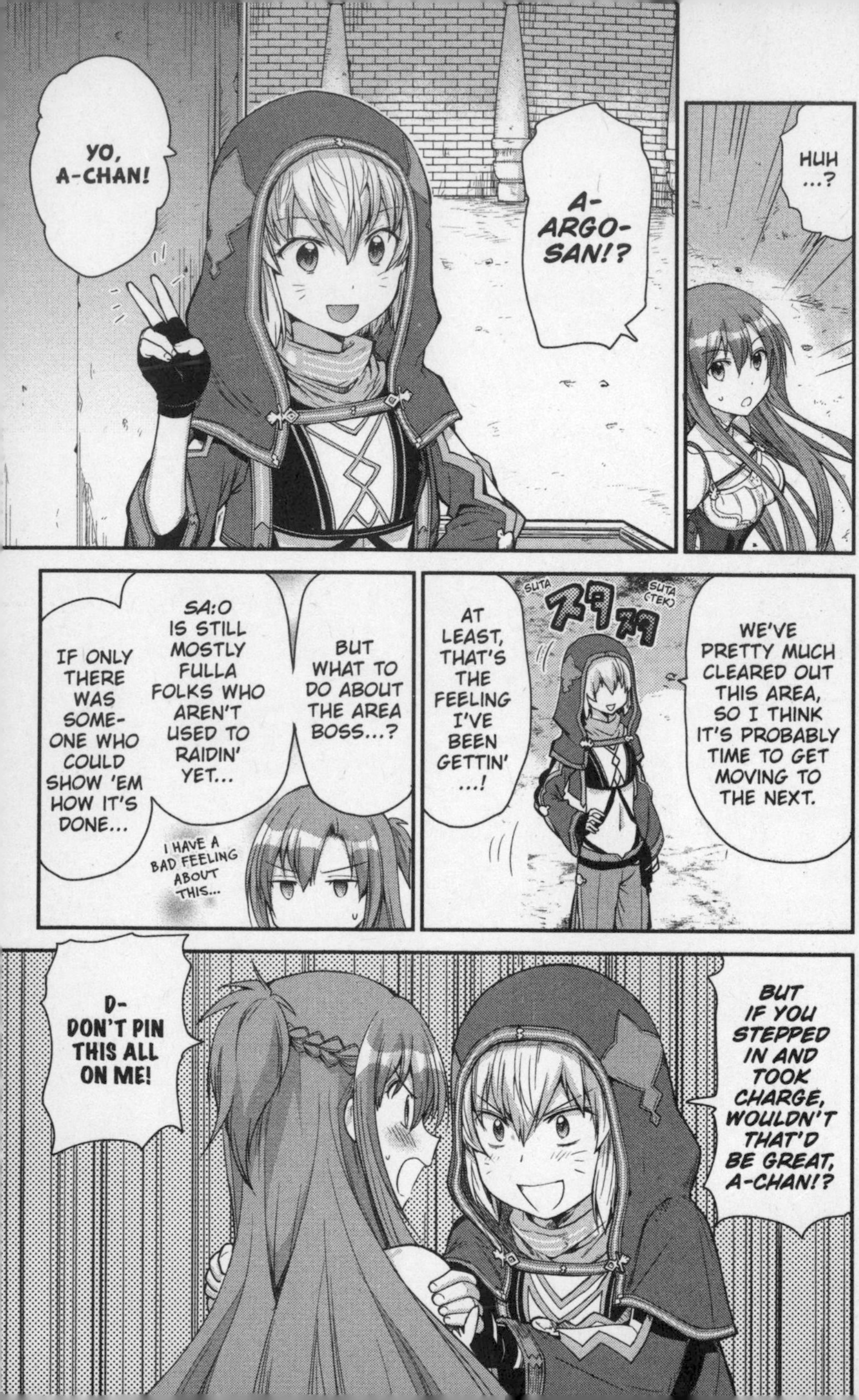

HUH ...?
A-ARGO-SAN!?
YO, A-CHAN!
SUTA SUTA (TEK)
スタスタ
WE'VE PRETTY MUCH CLEARED OUT THIS AREA, SO I THINK IT'S PROBABLY TIME TO GET MOVING TO THE NEXT.
AT LEAST, THAT'S THE FEELING I'VE BEEN GETTIN' ...!
BUT WHAT TO DO ABOUT THE AREA BOSS...?
SA:O IS STILL MOSTLY FULLA FOLKS WHO AREN'T USED TO RAIDIN' YET...
IF ONLY THERE WAS SOME-ONE WHO COULD SHOW 'EM HOW IT'S DONE...
I HAVE A BAD FEELING ABOUT THIS...
BUT IF YOU STEPPED IN AND TOOK CHARGE, WOULDN'T THAT'D BE GREAT, A-CHAN!?
D-DON'T PIN THIS ALL ON ME!

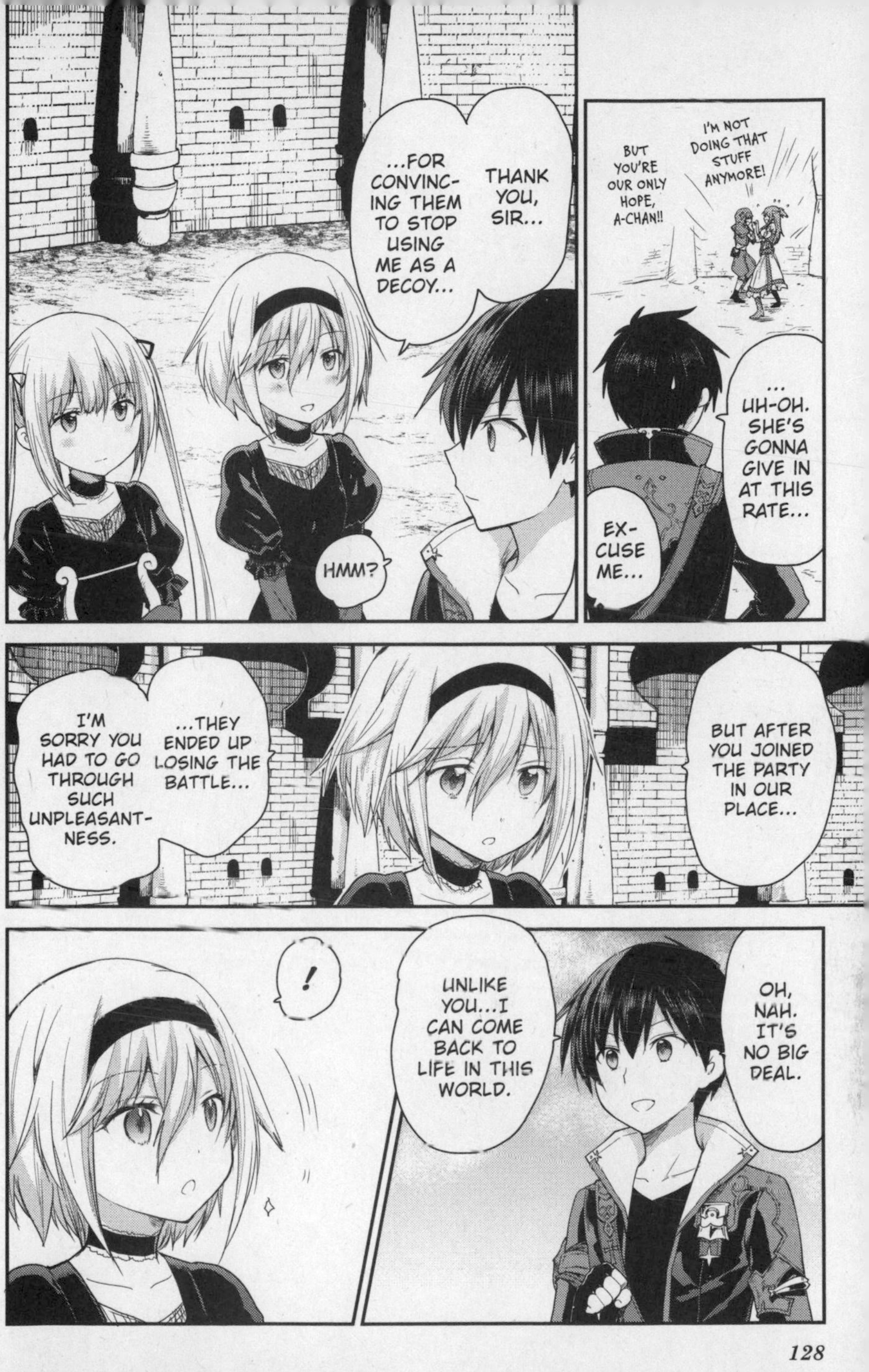
I'M NOT DOING THAT STUFF ANYMORE!
BUT YOU'RE OUR ONLY HOPE, A-CHAN!!
...UH-OH. SHE'S GONNA GIVE IN AT THIS RATE...
EXCUSE ME...
THANK YOU, SIR...
...FOR CONVINCING THEM TO STOP USING ME AS A DECOY...
HMM?
BUT AFTER YOU JOINED THE PARTY IN OUR PLACE...
...THEY ENDED UP LOSING THE BATTLE...
I'M SORRY YOU HAD TO GO THROUGH SUCH UNPLEASANTNESS.
OH, NAH. IT'S NO BIG DEAL.
UNLIKE YOU...I CAN COME BACK TO LIFE IN THIS WORLD.
!

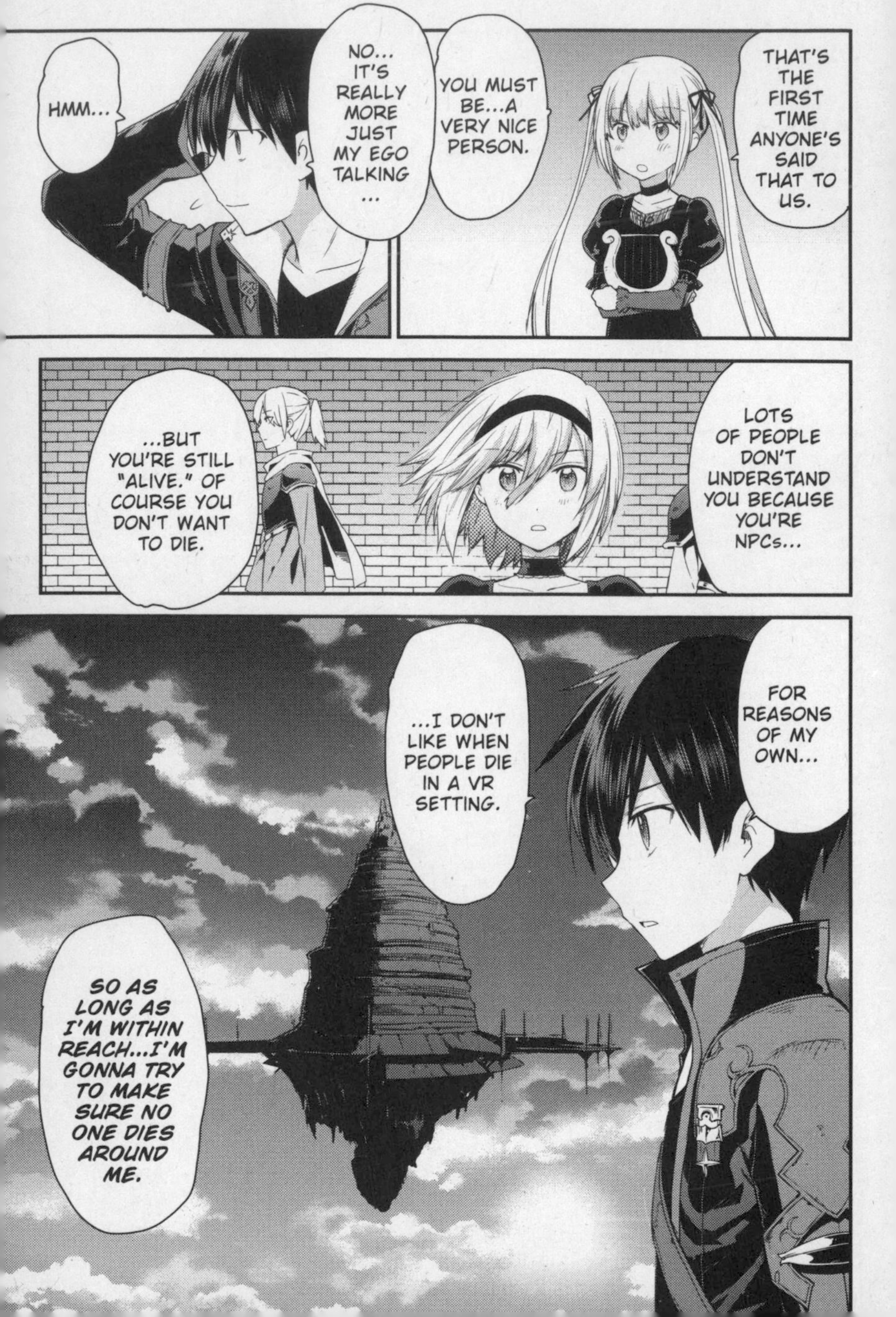
THAT'S THE FIRST TIME ANYONE'S SAID THAT TO US.
YOU MUST BE...A VERY NICE PERSON.
NO... IT'S REALLY MORE JUST MY EGO TALKING...
HMM...
LOTS OF PEOPLE DON'T UNDERSTAND YOU BECAUSE YOU'RE NPCs...
...BUT YOU'RE STILL "ALIVE." OF COURSE YOU DON'T WANT TO DIE.
FOR REASONS OF MY OWN...
...I DON'T LIKE WHEN PEOPLE DIE IN A VR SETTING.
SO AS LONG AS I'M WITHIN REACH...I'M GONNA TRY TO MAKE SURE NO ONE DIES AROUND ME.

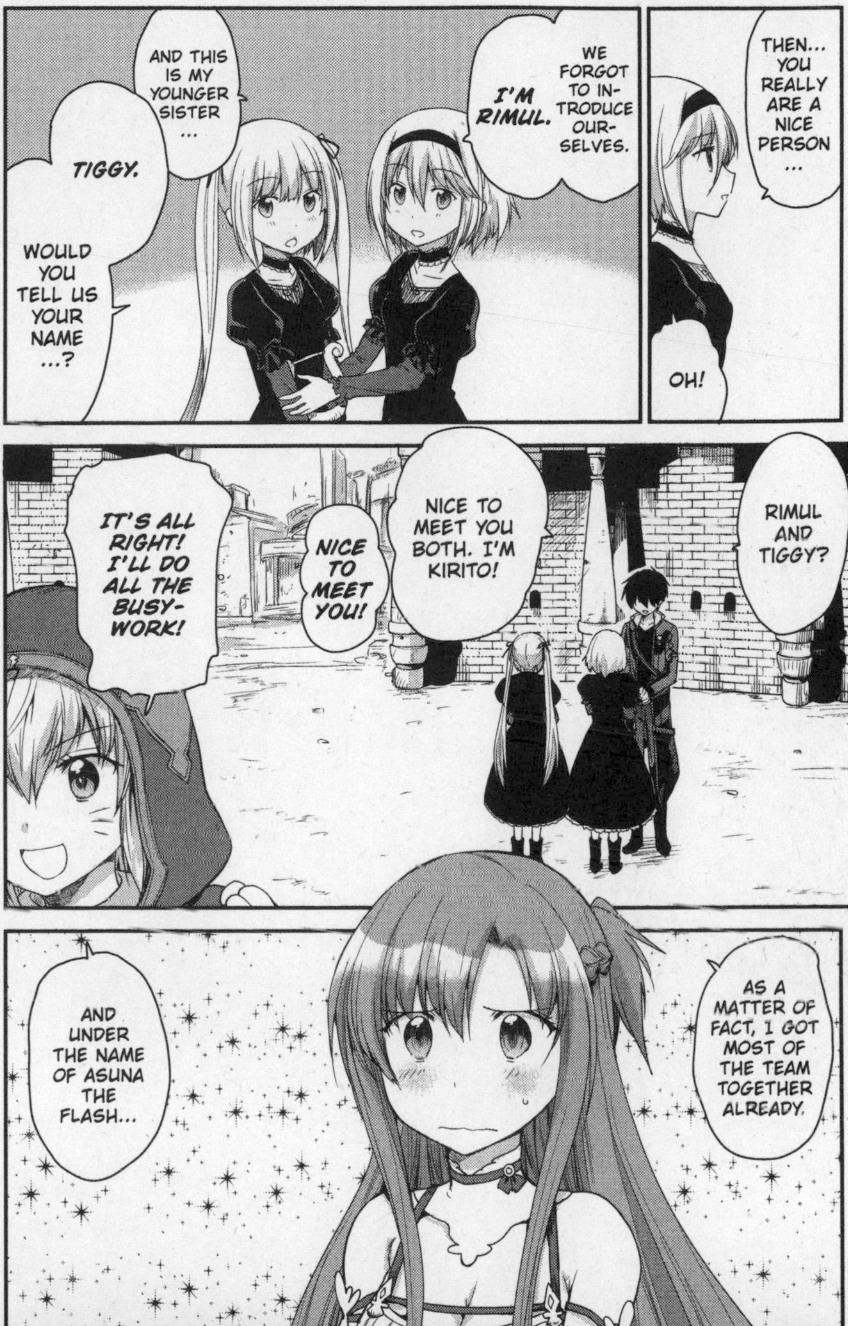
THEN... YOU REALLY ARE A NICE PERSON ...
OH!
WE FORGOT TO IN-TRODUCE OUR-SELVES.
I'M RIMUL.
AND THIS IS MY YOUNGER SISTER ...
TIGGY.
WOULD YOU TELL US YOUR NAME ...?
RIMUL AND TIGGY?
NICE TO MEET YOU BOTH. I'M KIRITO!
NICE TO MEET YOU!
IT'S ALL RIGHT! I'LL DO ALL THE BUSY-WORK!
AS A MATTER OF FACT, I GOT MOST OF THE TEAM TOGETHER ALREADY.
AND UNDER THE NAME OF ASUNA THE FLASH...

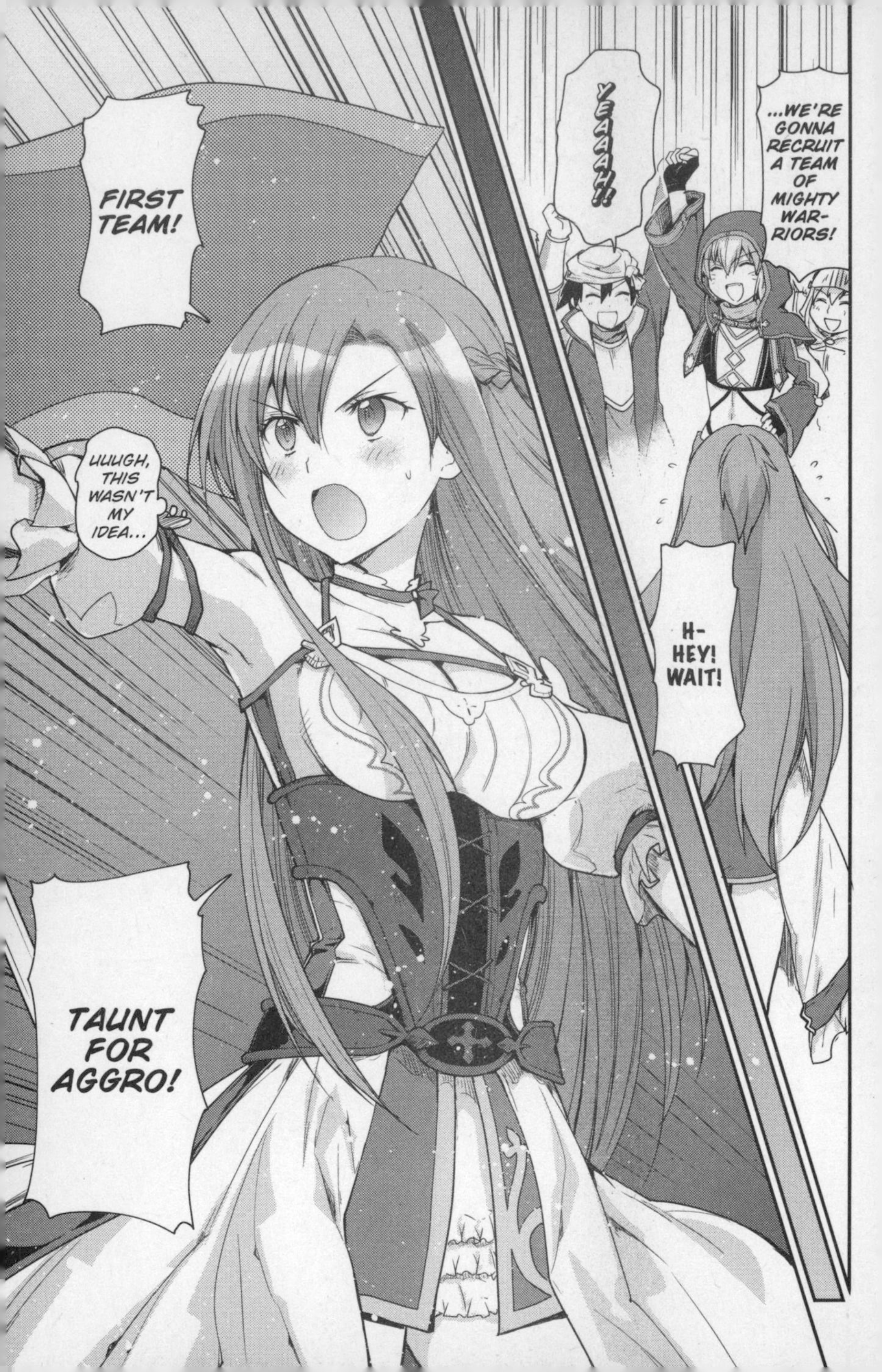
...WE'RE GONNA RECRUIT A TEAM OF MIGHTY WAR-RIORS!
YEAAAAH!!
H-HEY! WAIT!
FIRST TEAM!
UUUGH, THIS WASN'T MY IDEA...
TAUNT FOR AGGRO!

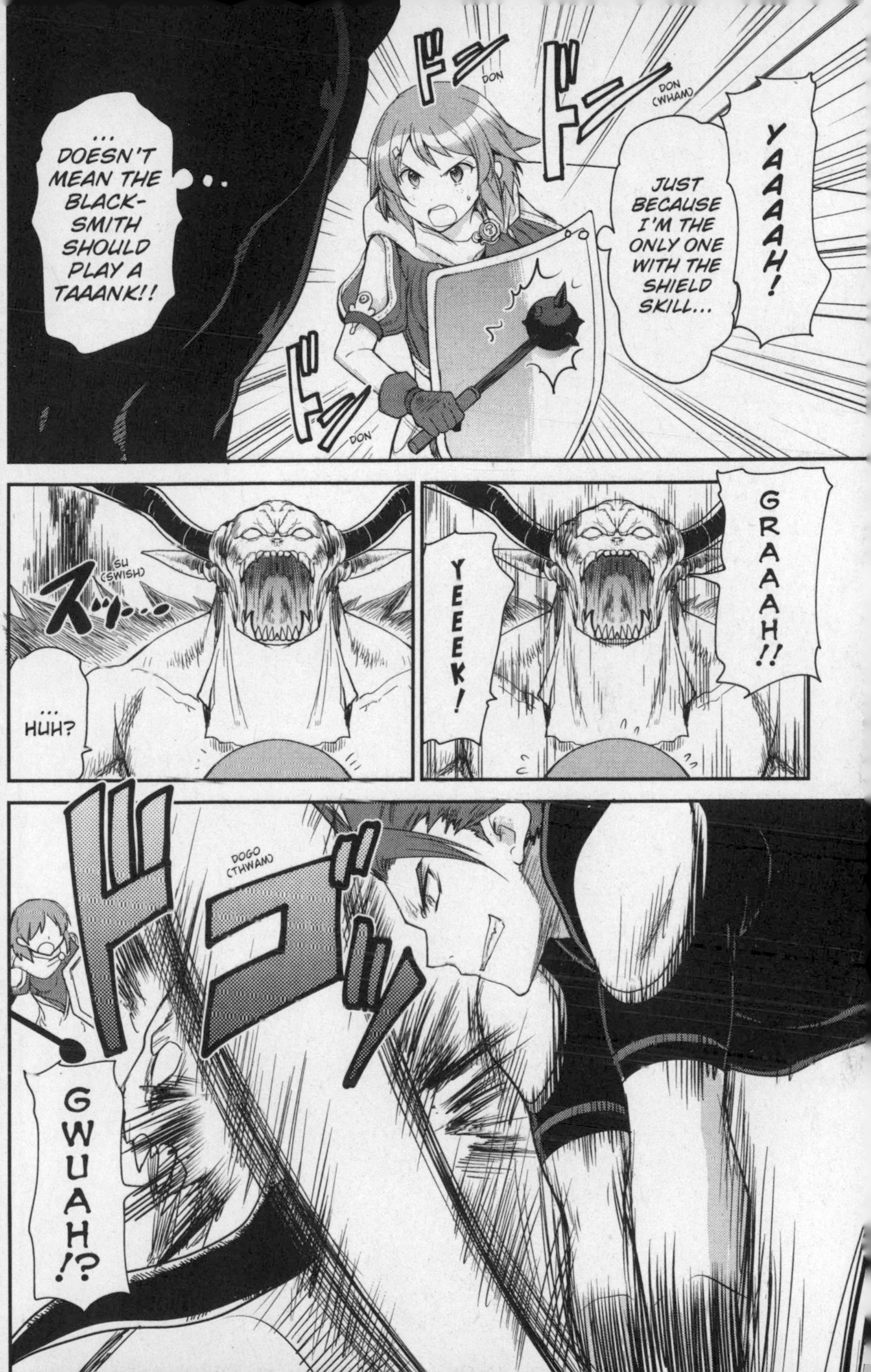
YAAAAH!
DON (WHAM)
DON
JUST BECAUSE I'M THE ONLY ONE WITH THE SHIELD SKILL...
...DOESN'T MEAN THE BLACK-SMITH SHOULD PLAY A TAAANK!!
DON
GRAAAAH!!
YEEEK!
SU (SWISH)
...HUH?
DOGO (THWAM)
GWUAH!?

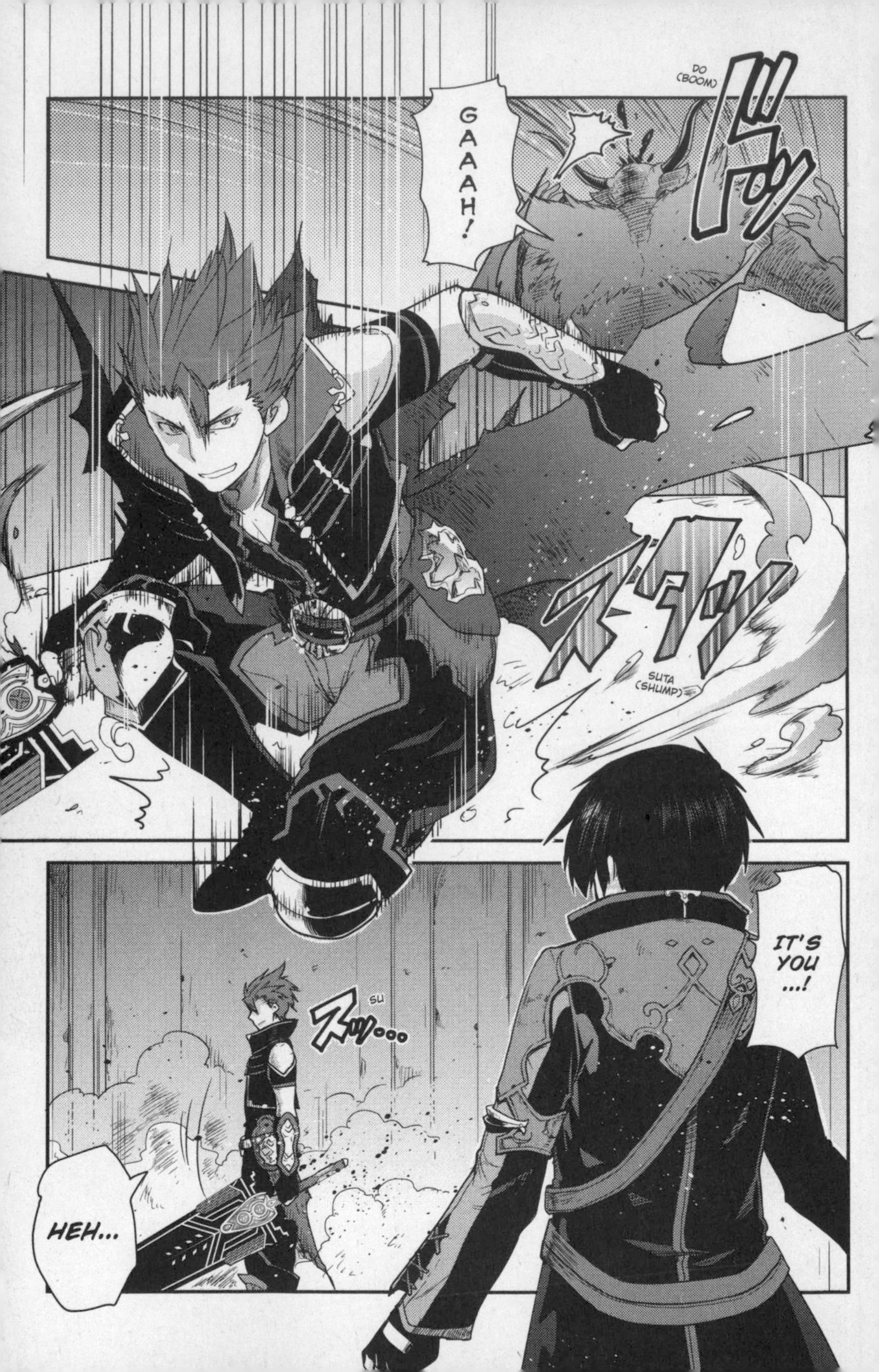
DO (BOOM)
GAAAH!
SUTA (SHUMP)
IT'S YOU ...!
SU
HEH...

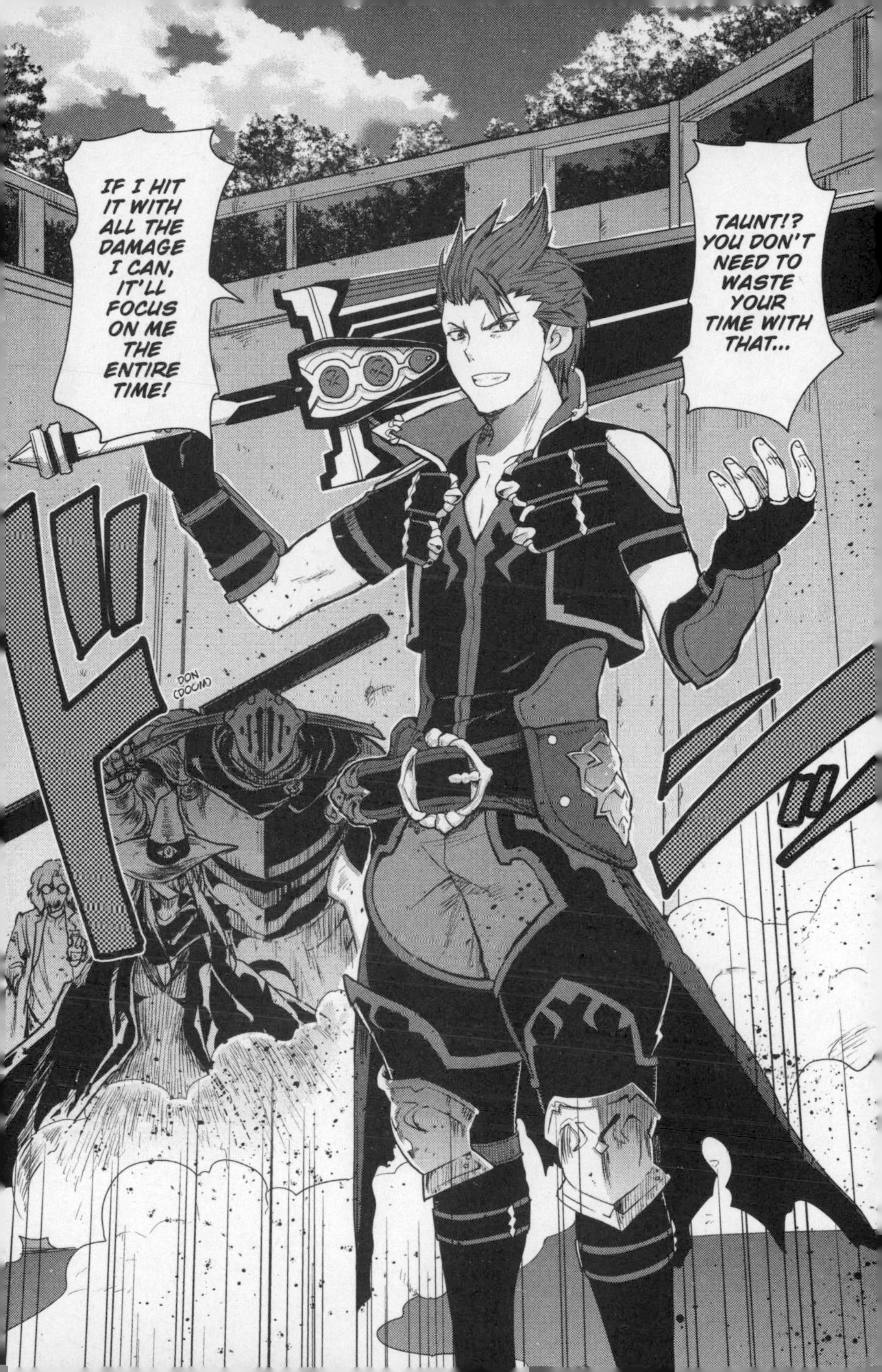
TAUNT!? YOU DON'T NEED TO WASTE YOUR TIME WITH THAT...
IF I HIT IT WITH ALL THE DAMAGE I CAN, IT'LL FOCUS ON ME THE ENTIRE TIME!
DON (DOOM)

#09: Orange Cursor

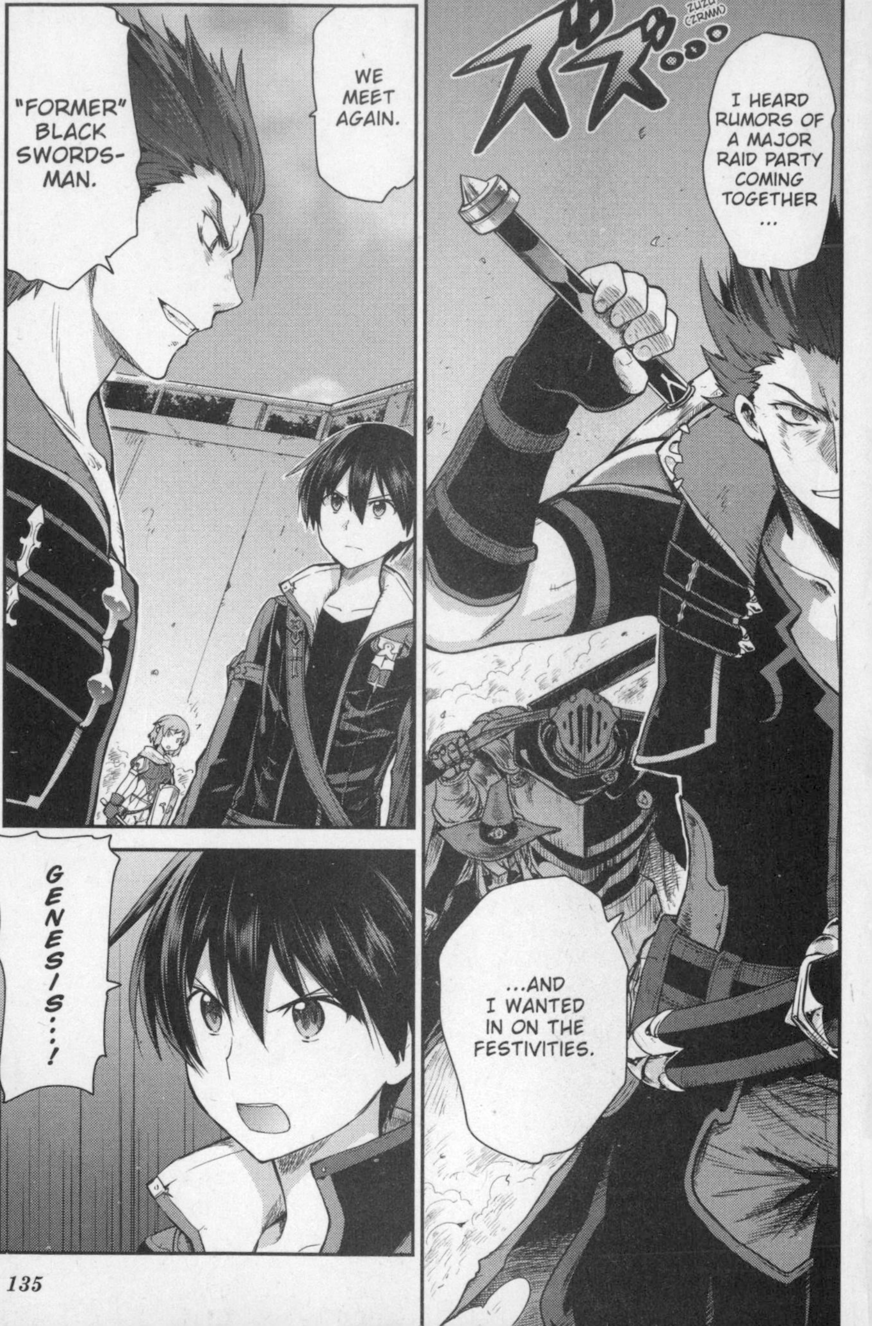
ZUZU (ZRMM)
I HEARD RUMORS OF A MAJOR RAID PARTY COMING TOGETHER...
...AND I WANTED IN ON THE FESTIVITIES.
WE MEET AGAIN.
"FORMER" BLACK SWORDS-MAN.
GENESIS...!

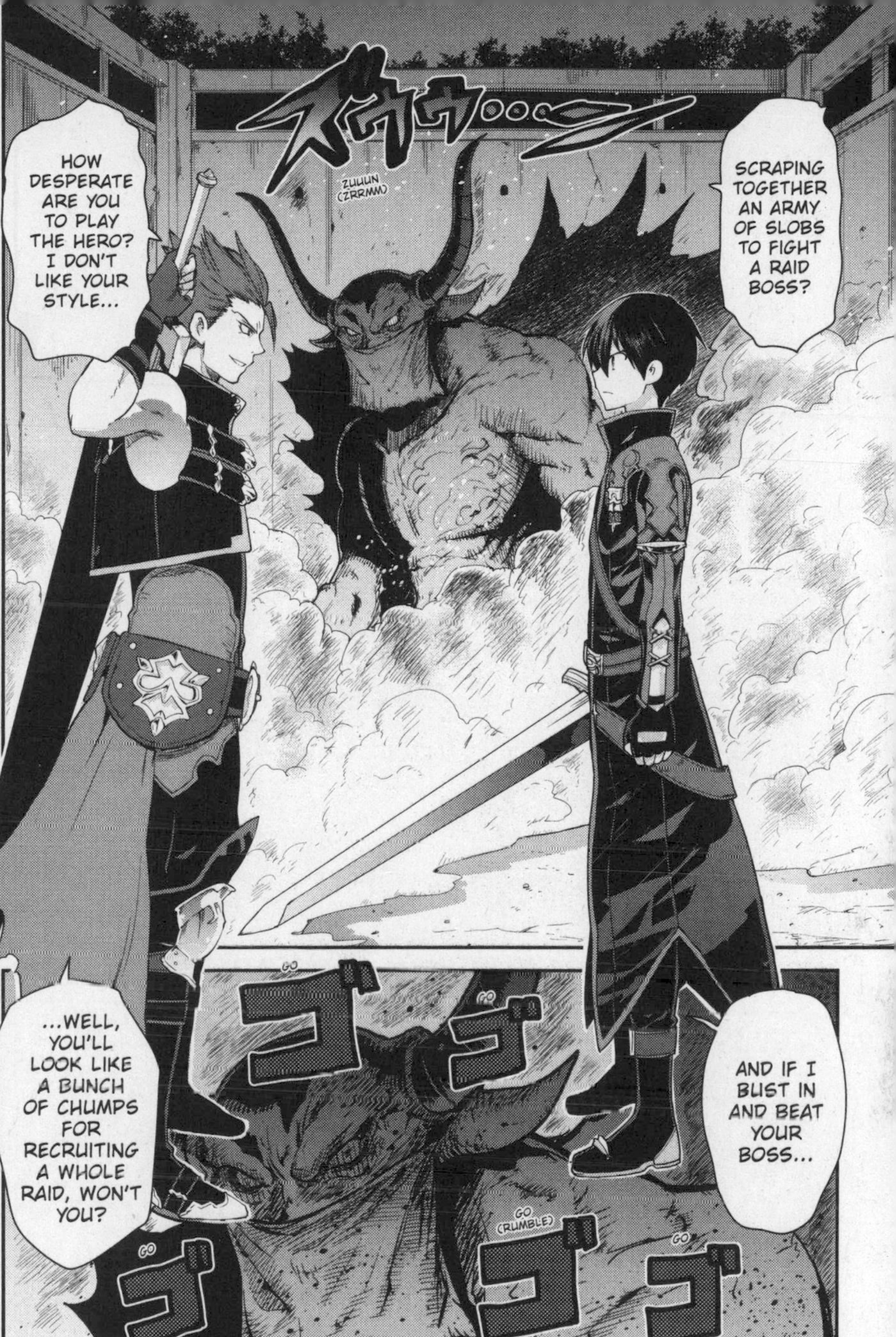
ZUUUN (ZRRMM)
SCRAPING TOGETHER AN ARMY OF SLOBS TO FIGHT A RAID BOSS?
HOW DESPERATE ARE YOU TO PLAY THE HERO? I DON'T LIKE YOUR STYLE...
GO
GO
AND IF I BUST IN AND BEAT YOUR BOSS...
...WELL, YOU'LL LOOK LIKE A BUNCH OF CHUMPS FOR RECRUITING A WHOLE RAID, WON'T YOU?
GO
GO (RUMBLE)
GO

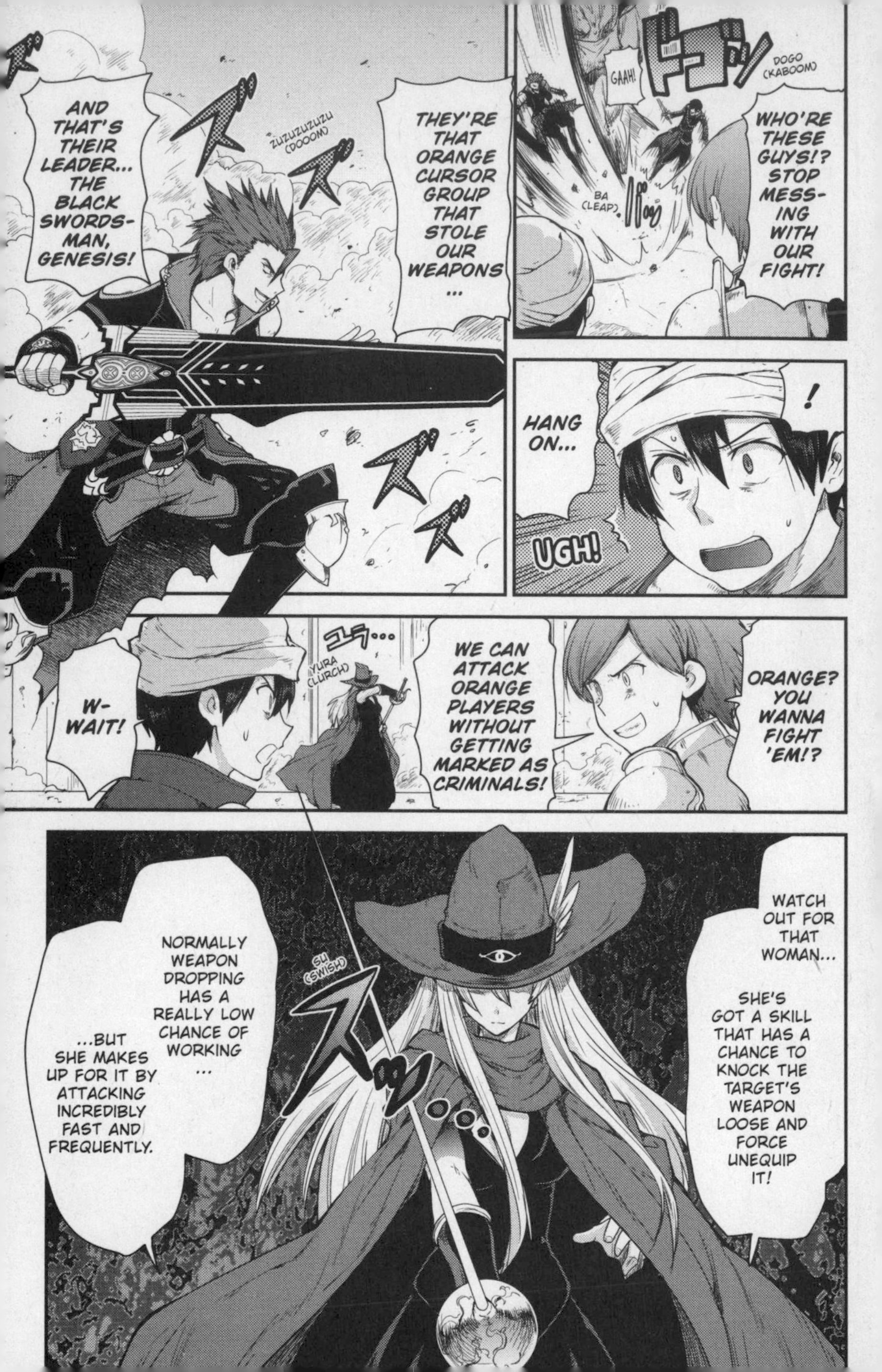

DOGO (KABOOM)
GAAH!
WHO'RE THESE GUYS!? STOP MESS-ING WITH OUR FIGHT!
BA (LEAP)
!
HANG ON...
UGH!
THEY'RE THAT ORANGE CURSOR GROUP THAT STOLE OUR WEAPONS...
ZUZUZUZUZU (DOOOM)
AND THAT'S THEIR LEADER... THE BLACK SWORDS-MAN, GENESIS!
ORANGE? YOU WANNA FIGHT 'EM!?
WE CAN ATTACK ORANGE PLAYERS WITHOUT GETTING MARKED AS CRIMINALS!
YURA (CLURCH)
W-WAIT!
WATCH OUT FOR THAT WOMAN...
SHE'S GOT A SKILL THAT HAS A CHANCE TO KNOCK THE TARGET'S WEAPON LOOSE AND FORCE UNEQUIP IT!
SU (SWISH)
NORMALLY WEAPON DROPPING HAS A REALLY LOW CHANCE OF WORKING...
...BUT SHE MAKES UP FOR IT BY ATTACKING INCREDIBLY FAST AND FREQUENTLY.

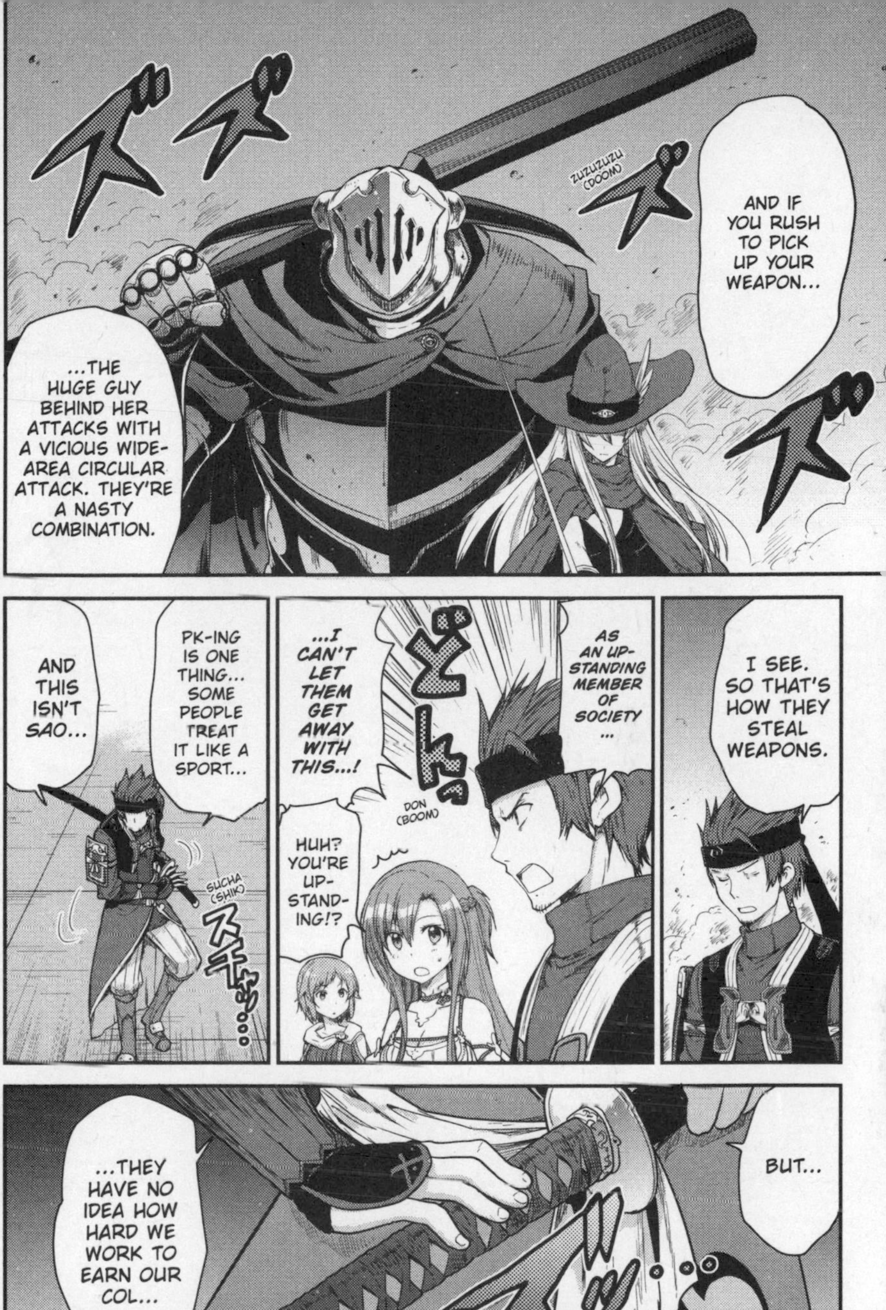
AND IF YOU RUSH TO PICK UP YOUR WEAPON...
ZUZUZUZU (DOOM)
...THE HUGE GUY BEHIND HER ATTACKS WITH A VICIOUS WIDE-AREA CIRCULAR ATTACK. THEY'RE A NASTY COMBINATION.
I SEE. SO THAT'S HOW THEY STEAL WEAPONS.
AS AN UP-STANDING MEMBER OF SOCIETY...
...I CAN'T LET THEM GET AWAY WITH THIS...!
DON (BOOM)
HUH? YOU'RE UP-STANDING!?
PK-ING IS ONE THING... SOME PEOPLE TREAT IT LIKE A SPORT...
AND THIS ISN'T SAO...
SUCHA (SHIK)
BUT...
...THEY HAVE NO IDEA HOW HARD WE WORK TO EARN OUR COL...
ZU (ZMMF)

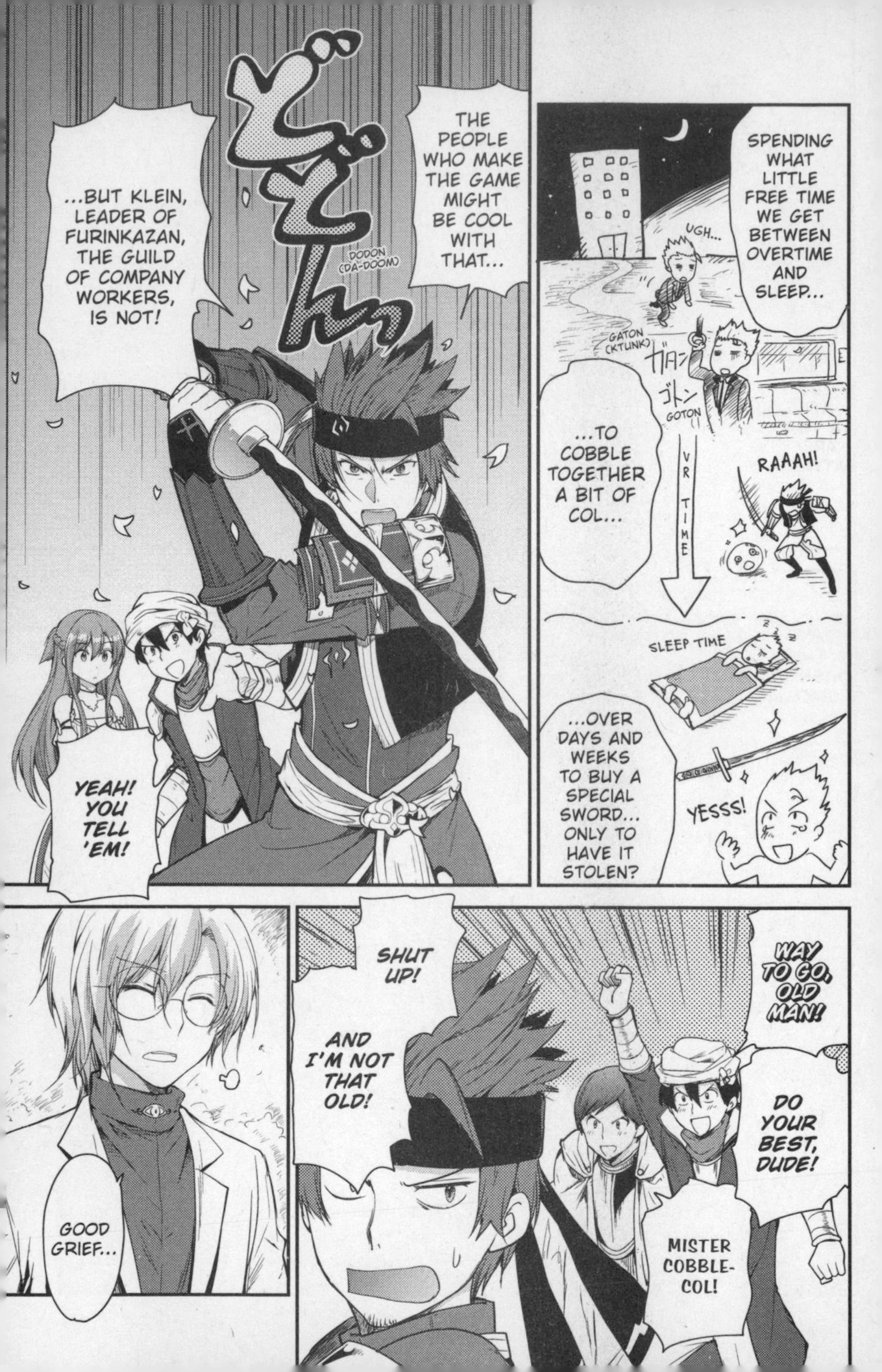
SPENDING WHAT LITTLE FREE TIME WE GET BETWEEN OVERTIME AND SLEEP...
UGH...
ガタン
GATON (KTUNK)
ゴトン
GOTON
...TO COBBLE TOGETHER A BIT OF COL...
VR TIME
RAAAH!
SLEEP TIME
...OVER DAYS AND WEEKS TO BUY A SPECIAL SWORD... ONLY TO HAVE IT STOLEN?
YESSS!
THE PEOPLE WHO MAKE THE GAME MIGHT BE COOL WITH THAT...
どどん
DODON (DA-DOOM)
...BUT KLEIN, LEADER OF FURINKAZAN, THE GUILD OF COMPANY WORKERS, IS NOT!
YEAH! YOU TELL 'EM!
WAY TO GO, OLD MAN!
SHUT UP!
DO YOUR BEST, DUDE!
AND I'M NOT THAT OLD!
MISTER COBBLE-COL!
GOOD GRIEF...

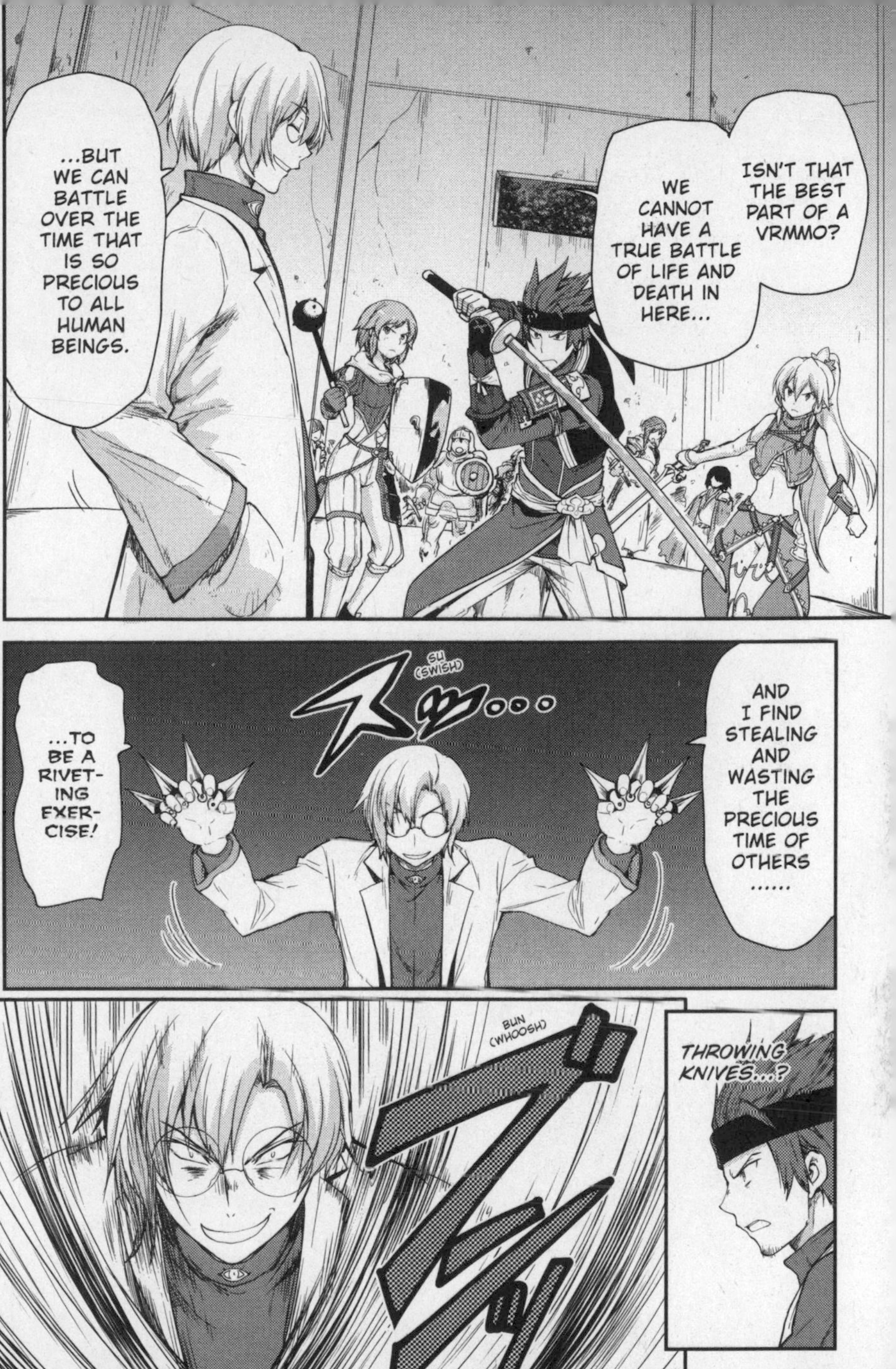
ISN'T THAT THE BEST PART OF A VRMMO?
WE CANNOT HAVE A TRUE BATTLE OF LIFE AND DEATH IN HERE...
...BUT WE CAN BATTLE OVER THE TIME THAT IS SO PRECIOUS TO ALL HUMAN BEINGS.
SU (SWISH)
AND I FIND STEALING AND WASTING THE PRECIOUS TIME OF OTHERS ......
...TO BE A RIVETING EXERCISE!
THROWING KNIVES...?
BUN (WHOOSH)

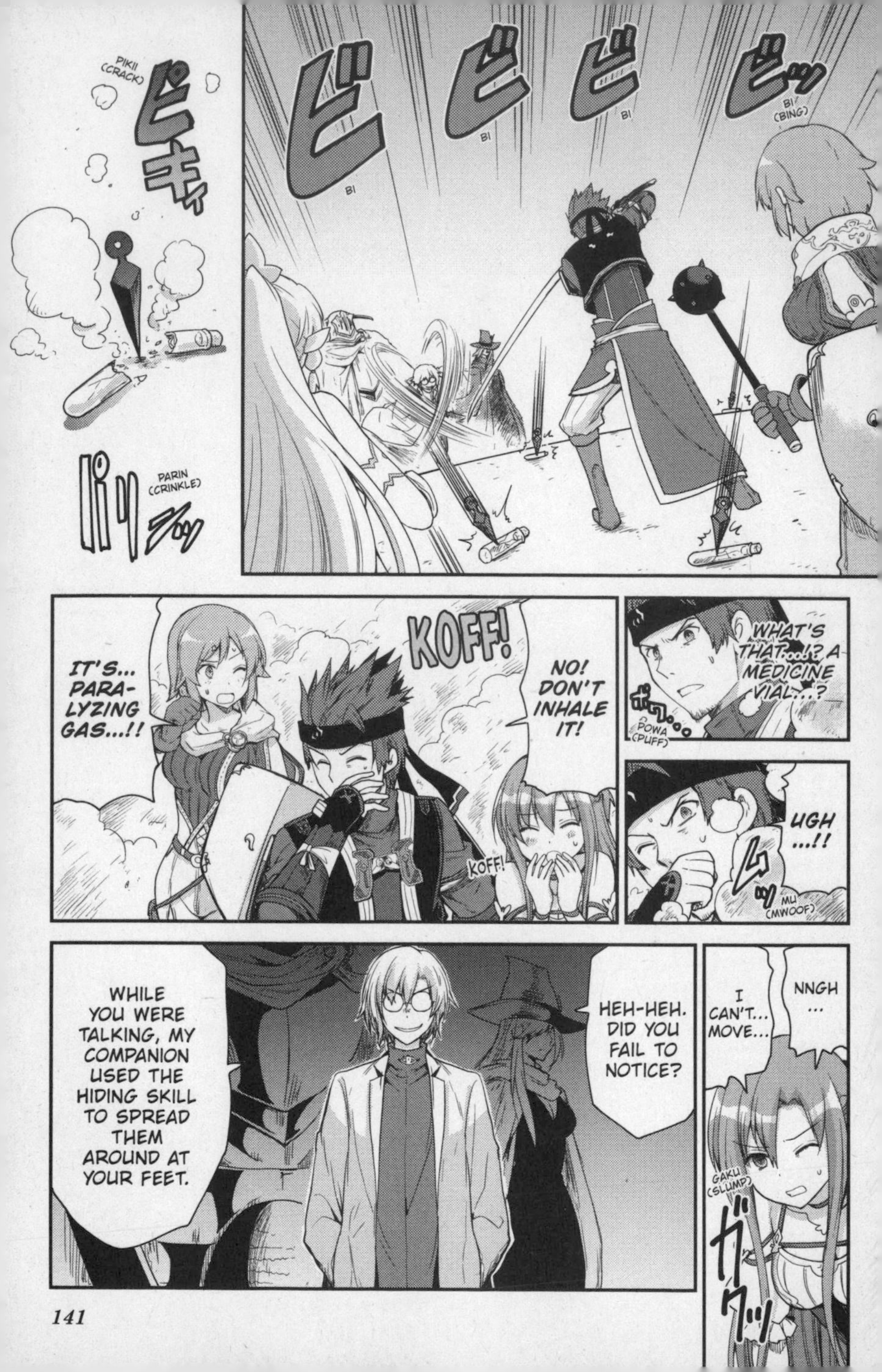
BI (BING)
BI
BI
BI
PIKII (CRACK)
PARIN (CRINKLE)
WHAT'S THAT...!? A MEDICINE VIAL...?
POWA (PUFF)
UGH ...!!
MU (MWOOF)
KOFF!
NO! DON'T INHALE IT!
IT'S... PARA-LYZING GAS...!!
KOFF!
NNGH ...
I CAN'T... MOVE...
GAKU (SLUMP)
HEH-HEH. DID YOU FAIL TO NOTICE?
WHILE YOU WERE TALKING, MY COMPANION USED THE HIDING SKILL TO SPREAD THEM AROUND AT YOUR FEET.

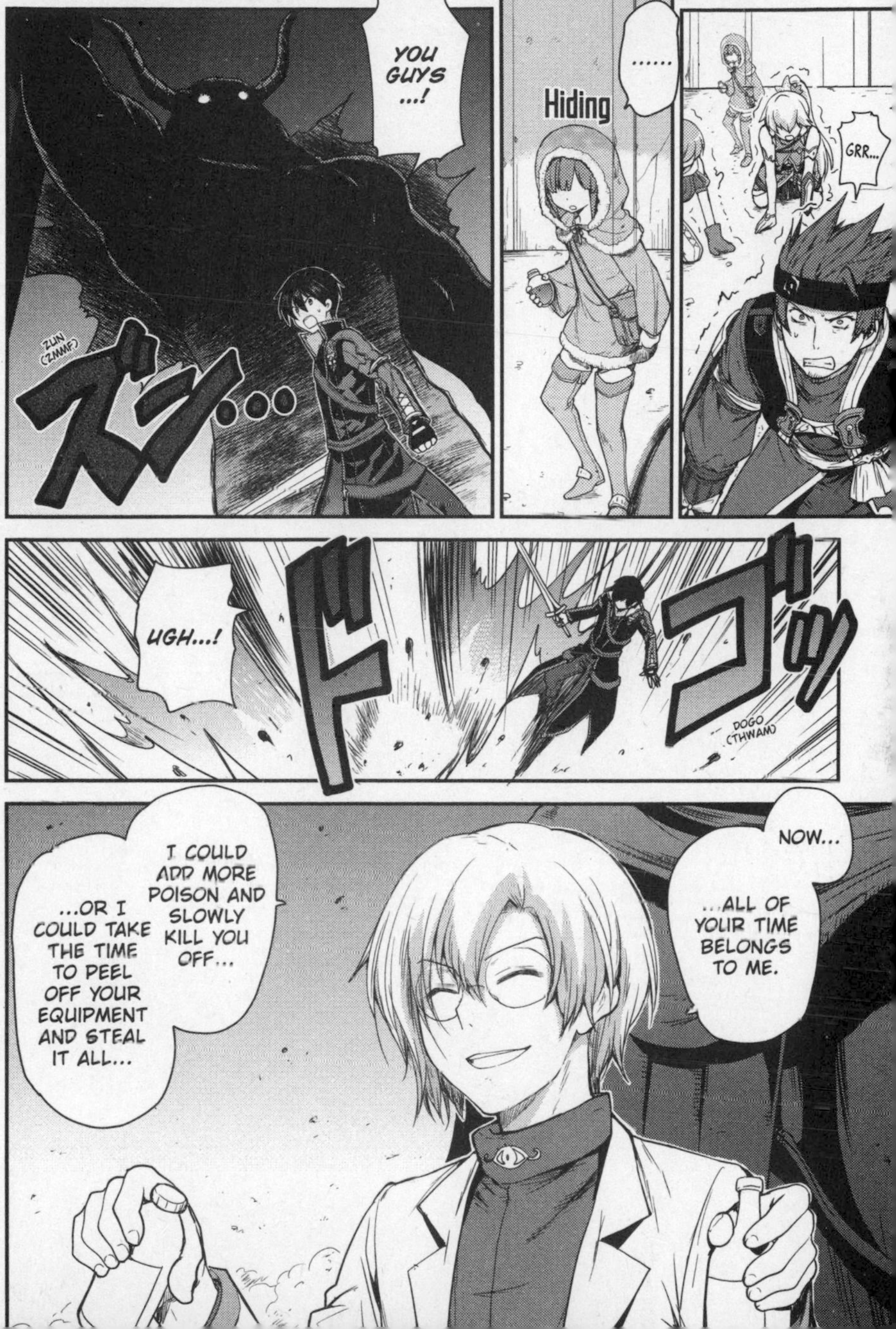
GRR...
Hiding
......
YOU GUYS ...!
ズン…
ZUN (ZMMF)
ドゴッ
DOGO (THWAM)
UGH...!
NOW...
...ALL OF YOUR TIME BELONGS TO ME.
I COULD ADD MORE POISON AND SLOWLY KILL YOU OFF...
...OR I COULD TAKE THE TIME TO PEEL OFF YOUR EQUIPMENT AND STEAL IT ALL...

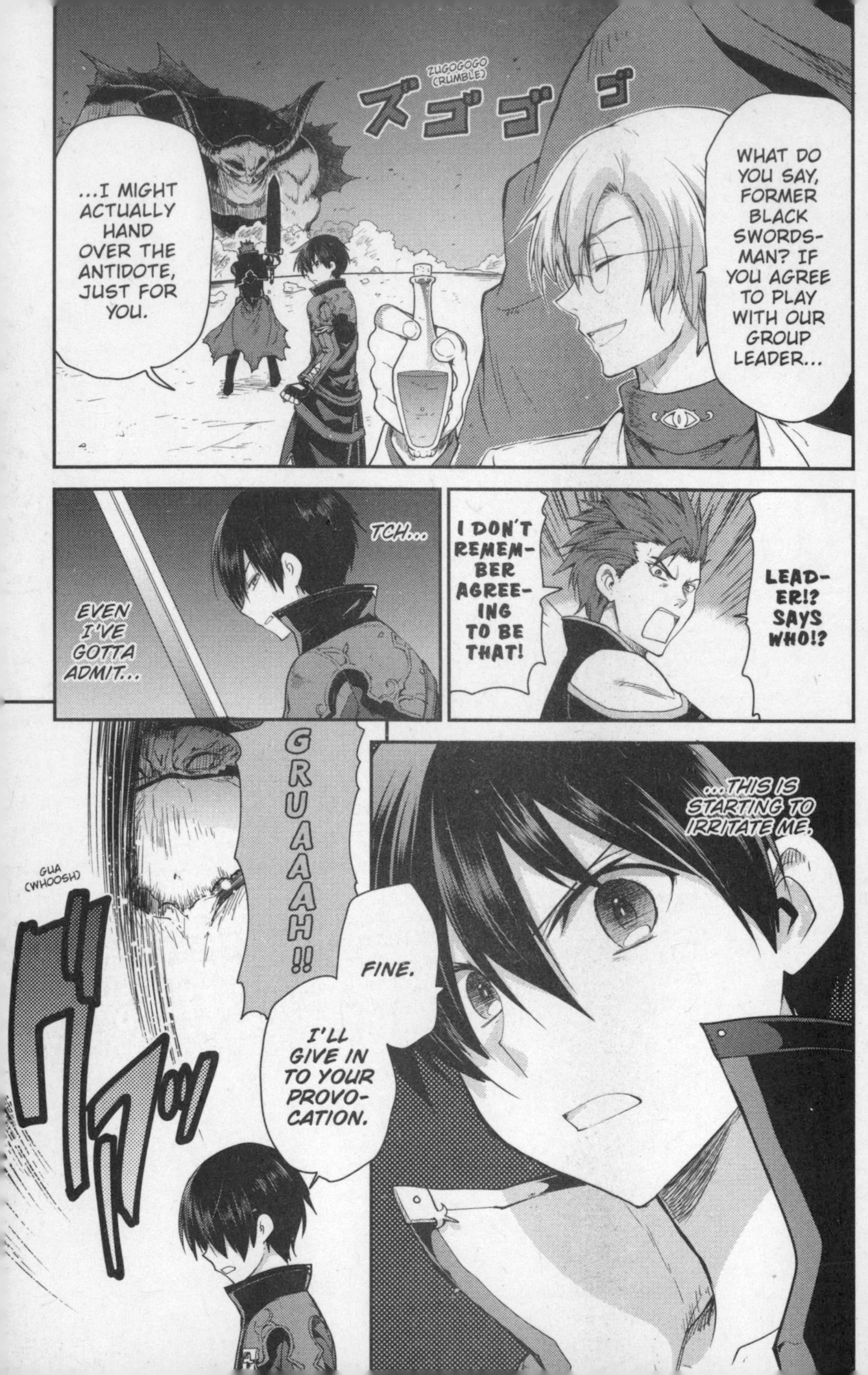
ZUGOGOGO (RUMBLE)
WHAT DO YOU SAY, FORMER BLACK SWORDS-MAN? IF YOU AGREE TO PLAY WITH OUR GROUP LEADER...
...I MIGHT ACTUALLY HAND OVER THE ANTIDOTE, JUST FOR YOU.
LEADER!? SAYS WHO!?
I DON'T REMEMBER AGREEING TO BE THAT!
TCH...
EVEN I'VE GOTTA ADMIT...
...THIS IS STARTING TO IRRITATE ME.
GRUAAAAH!!
GUA (WHOOSH)
FINE.
I'LL GIVE IN TO YOUR PROVOCATION.

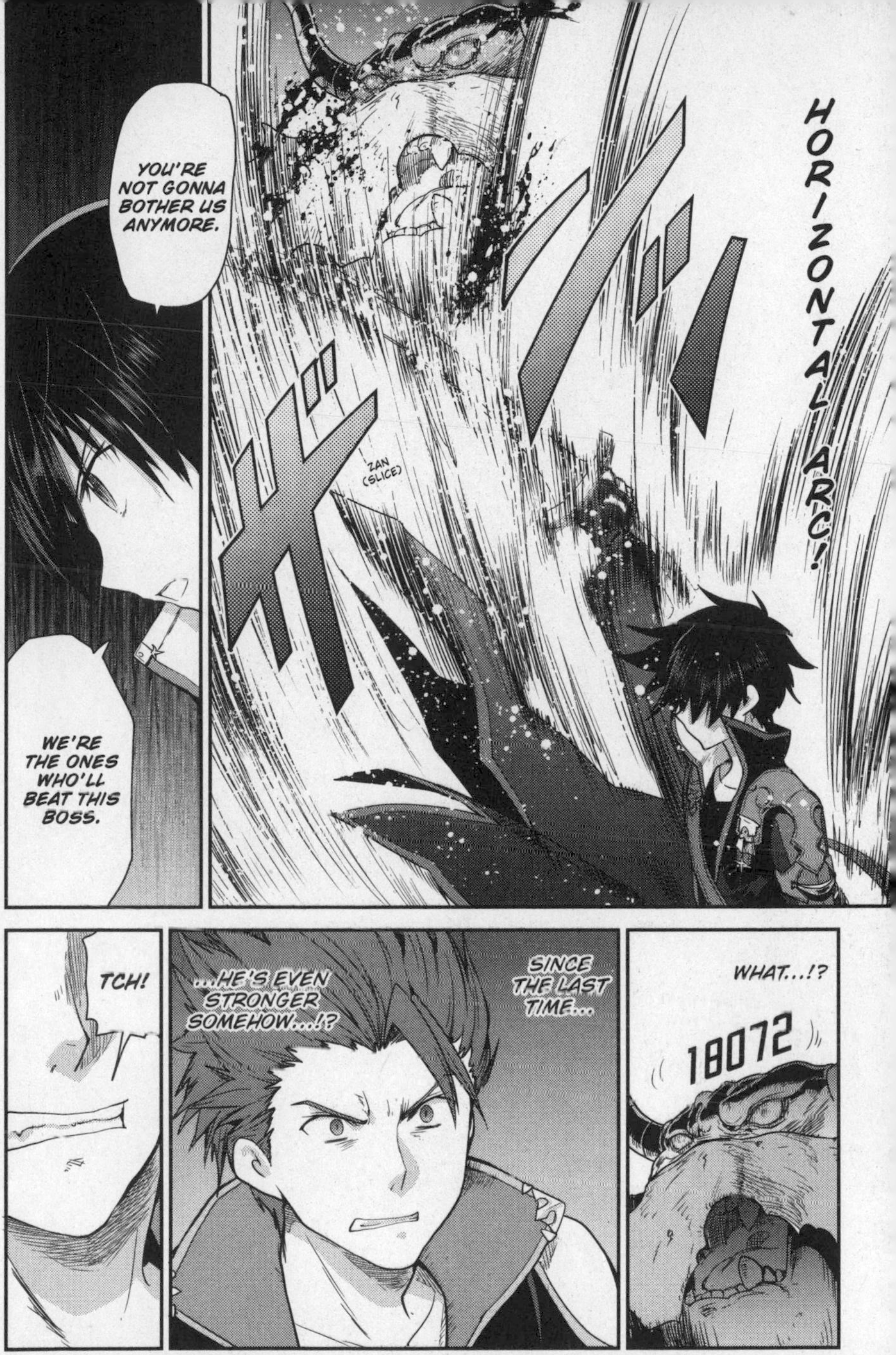
HORIZONTAL ARC!
ZAN (SLICE)
YOU'RE NOT GONNA BOTHER US ANYMORE.
WE'RE THE ONES WHO'LL BEAT THIS BOSS.
WHAT...!?
18072
SINCE THE LAST TIME...
...HE'S EVEN STRONGER SOMEHOW...!?
TCH!

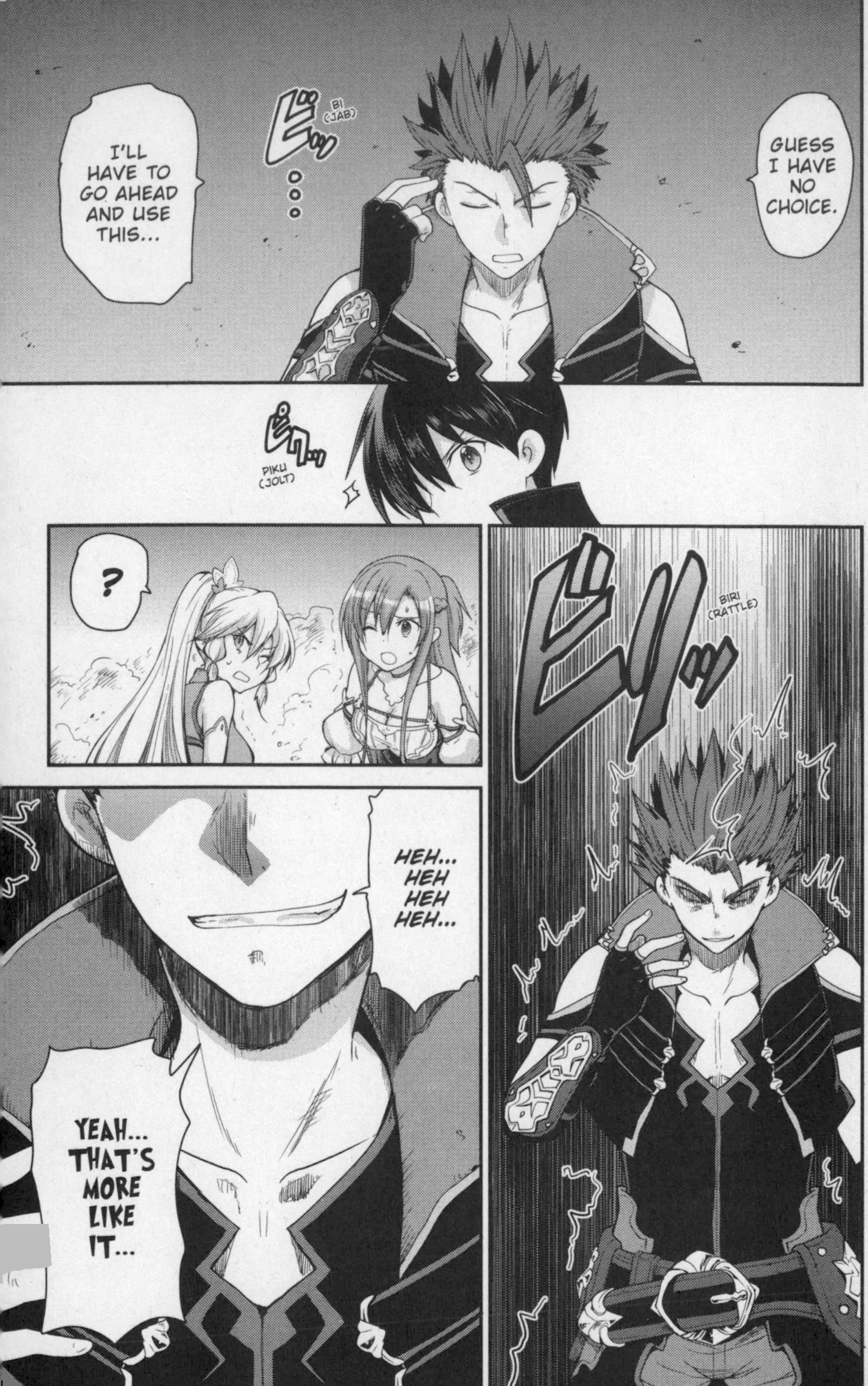
GUESS I HAVE NO CHOICE.
BI (JAB)
I'LL HAVE TO GO AHEAD AND USE THIS...
PIKU (JOLT)
BIRI (RATTLE)
?
HEH... HEH HEH HEH...
YEAH... THAT'S MORE LIKE IT...

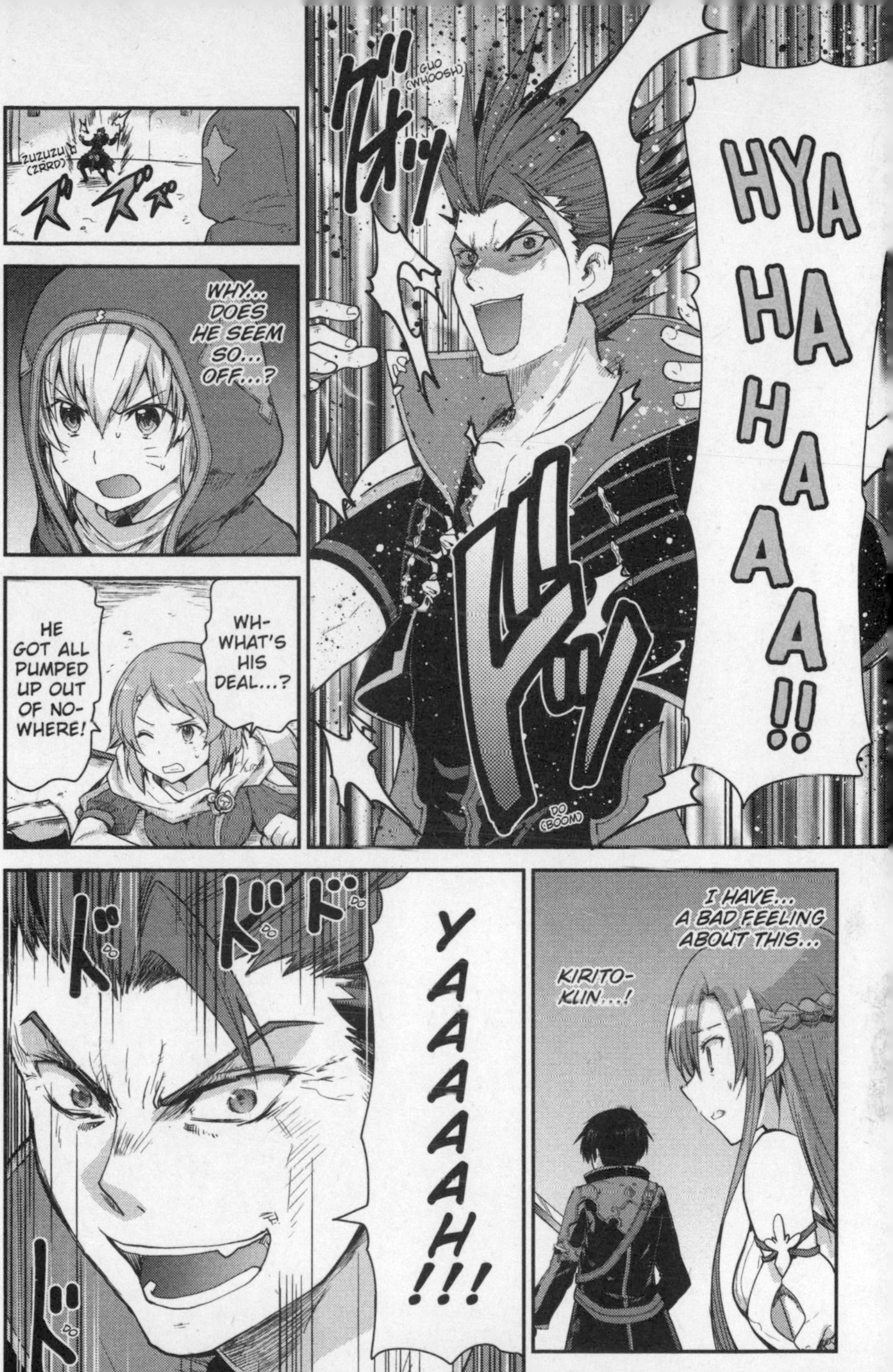
HYA HA HA HAAA!!
GUO (WHOOSH)
DO (BOOM)
ZUZUZU (ZRRD)
WHY... DOES HE SEEM SO... OFF...?
WH-WHAT'S HIS DEAL...?
HE GOT ALL PUMPED UP OUT OF NO-WHERE!
I HAVE... A BAD FEELING ABOUT THIS...
KIRITO-KLIN...!
YAAAAAAH!!!
DO
DO
DO
DO

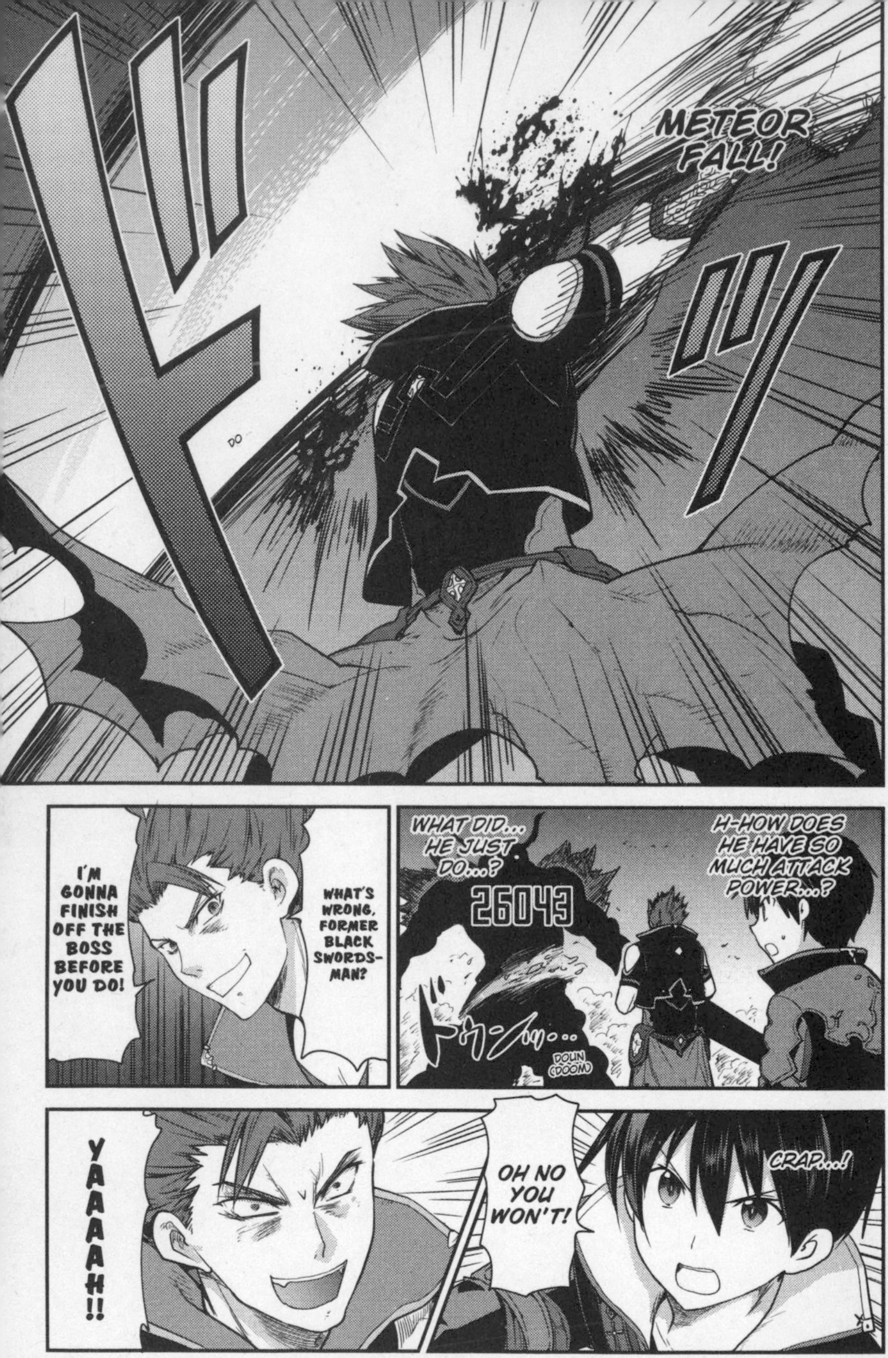
METEOR FALL!
DO...
H-HOW DOES HE HAVE SO MUCH ATTACK POWER...?
WHAT DID... HE JUST DO...?
26043
DOUN (DOOM)
WHAT'S WRONG, FORMER BLACK SWORDS-MAN?
I'M GONNA FINISH OFF THE BOSS BEFORE YOU DO!
CRAP...!
OH NO YOU WON'T!
YAAAAAH!!

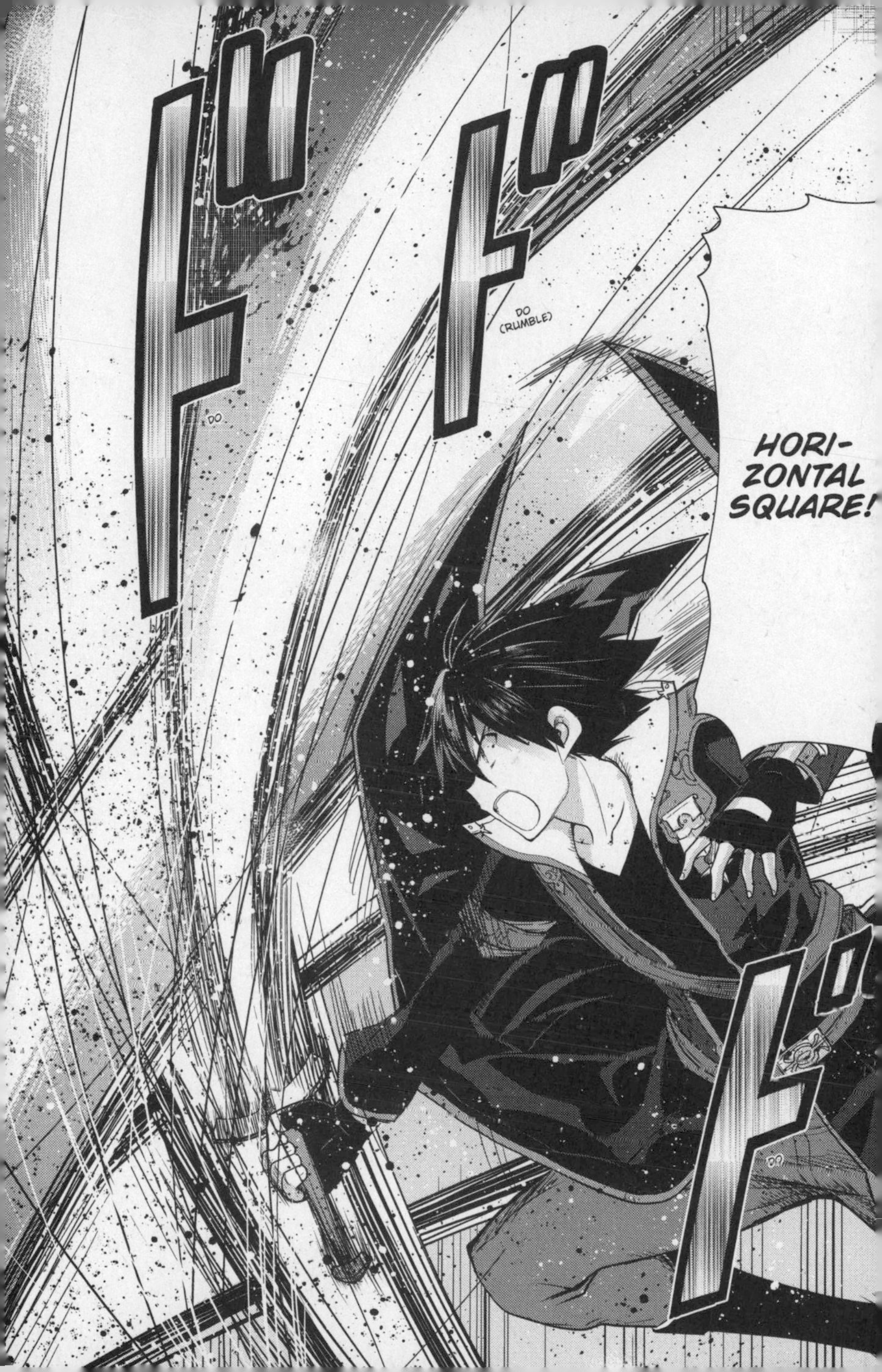
HORI-
ZONTAL
SQUARE!
DO
(RUMBLE)
DO
DO

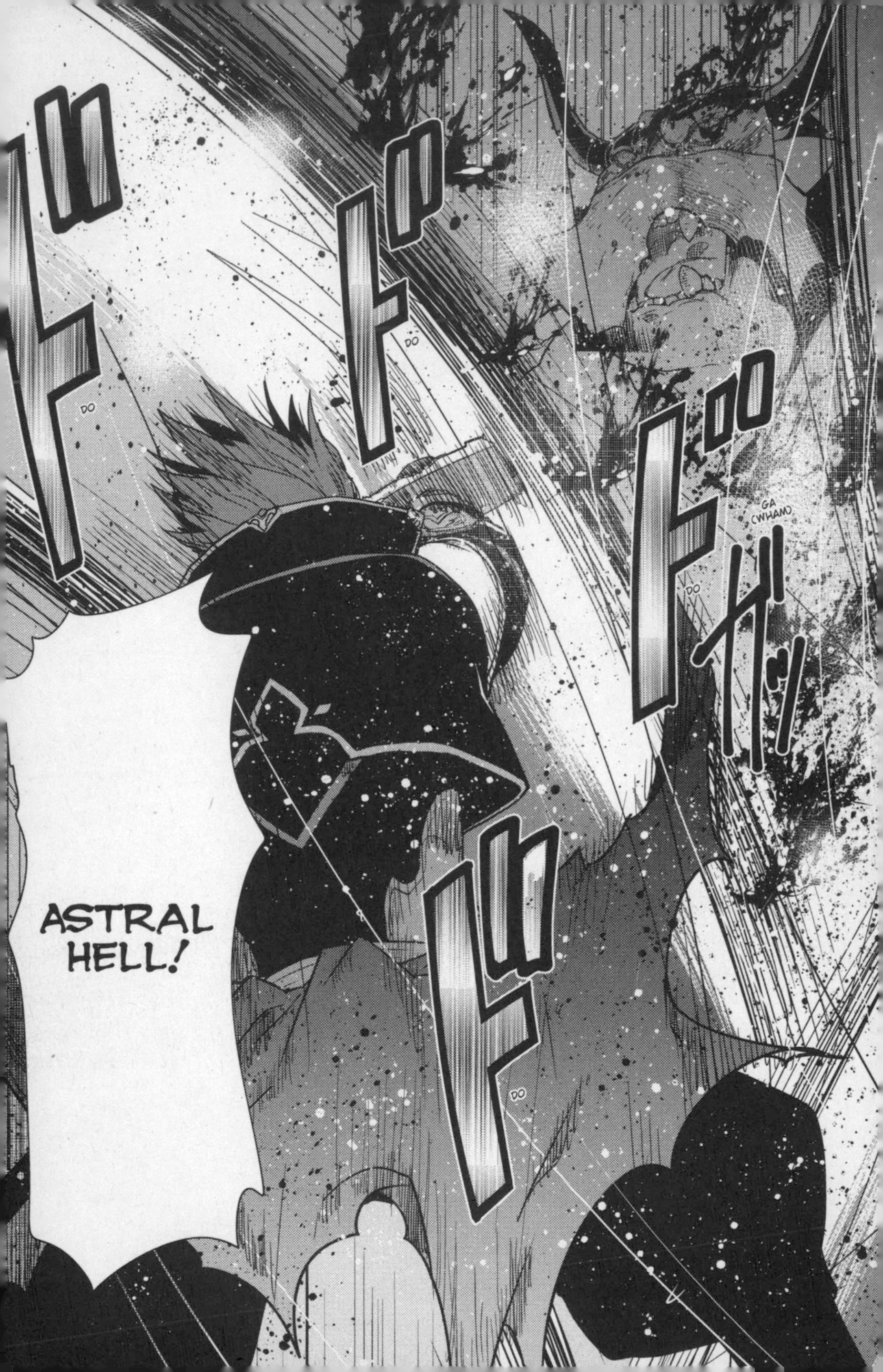
GA (WHAM)
DO
DO
DO
ASTRAL HELL!
DO

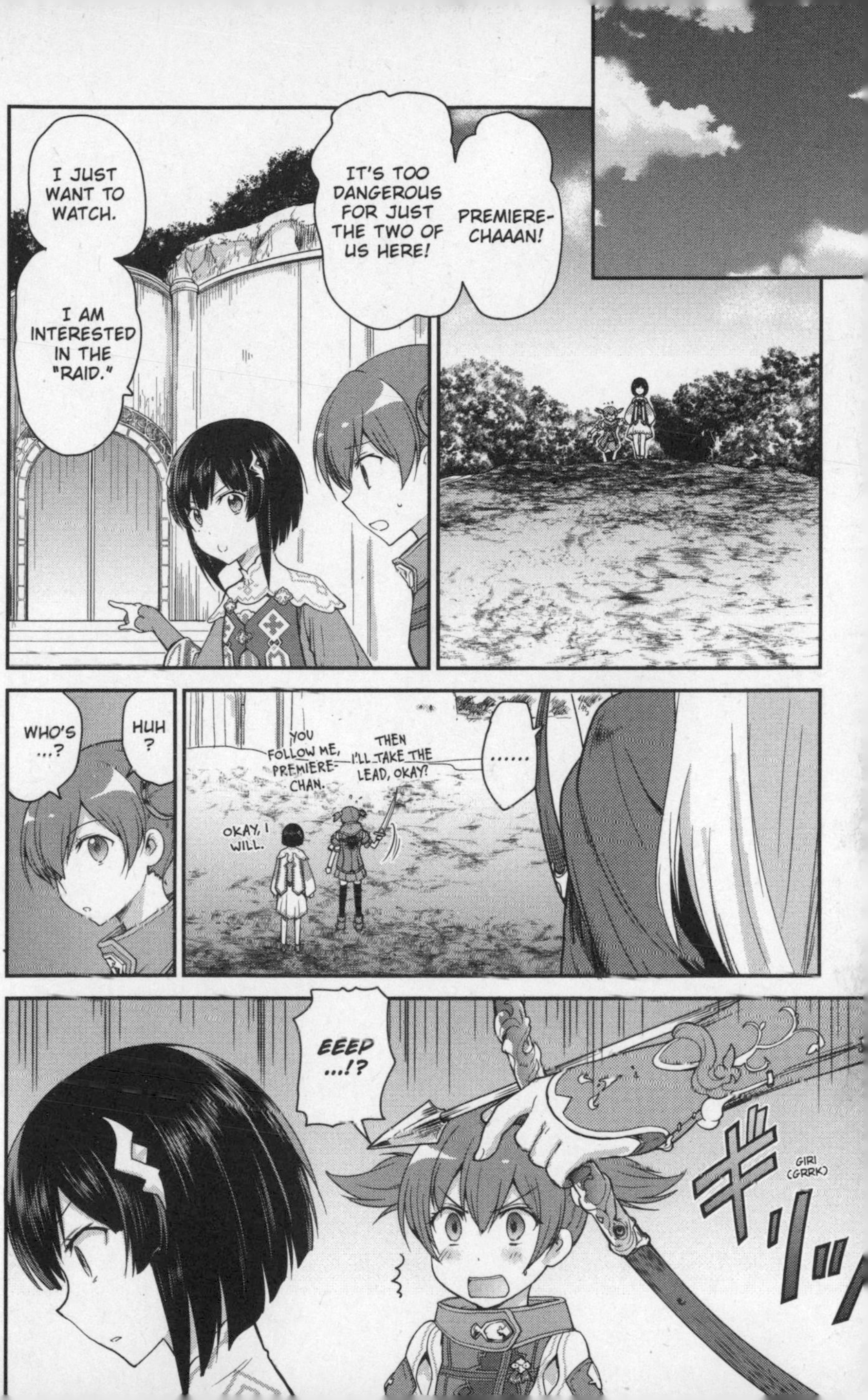
PREMIERE-CHAAAN!
IT'S TOO DANGEROUS FOR JUST THE TWO OF US HERE!
I JUST WANT TO WATCH.
I AM INTERESTED IN THE "RAID."
......
THEN I'LL TAKE THE LEAD, OKAY?
YOU FOLLOW ME, PREMIERE-CHAN.
OKAY, I WILL.
HUH?
WHO'S ...?
EEEP ...!?
GIRI (GRRK)

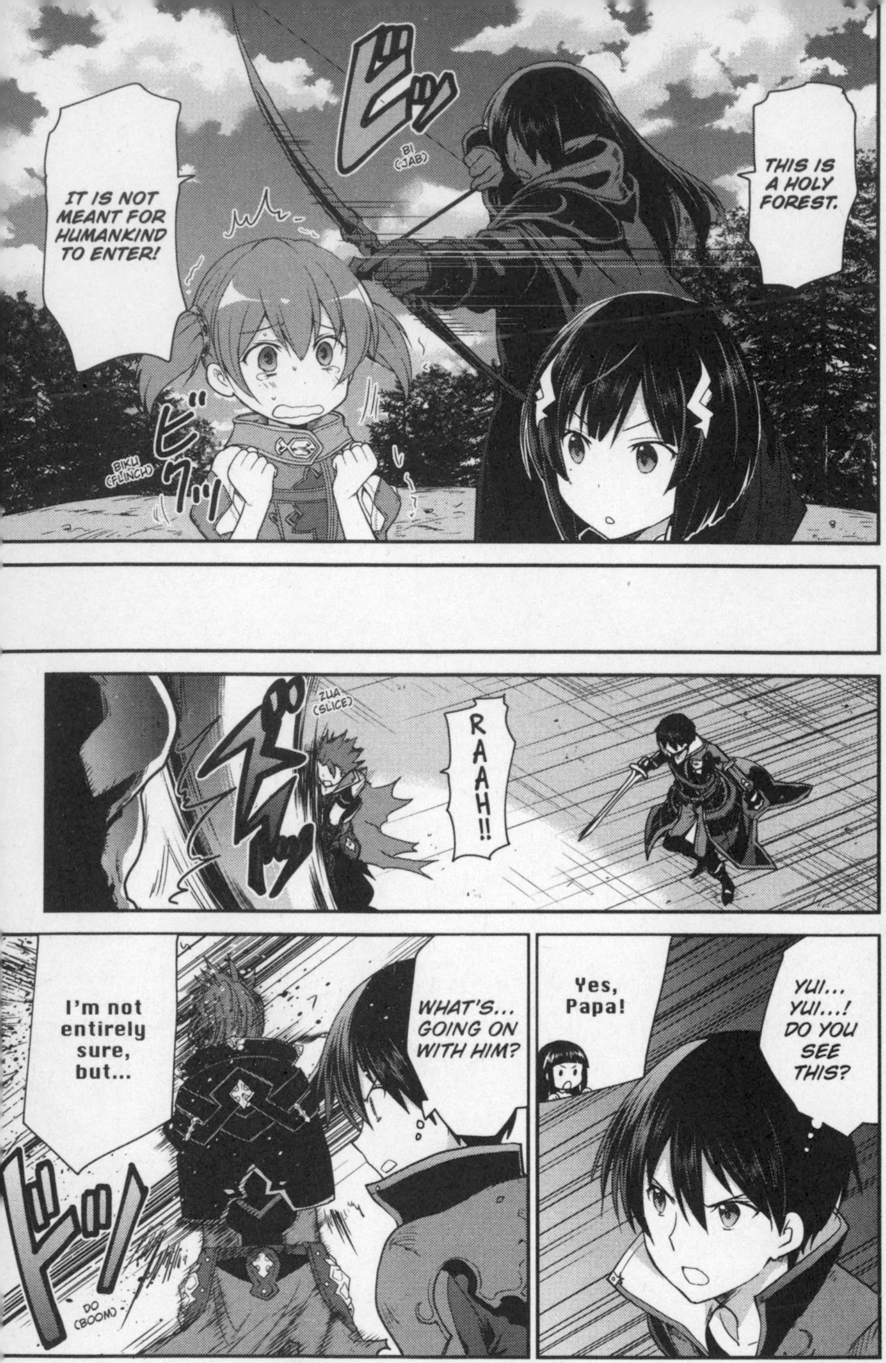
THIS IS A HOLY FOREST.
BI (JAB)
IT IS NOT MEANT FOR HUMANKIND TO ENTER!
BIKU (FLINCH)
ZUA (SLICE)
RAAH!!
YUI... YUI...! DO YOU SEE THIS?
Yes, Papa!
WHAT'S... GOING ON WITH HIM?
I'm not entirely sure, but...
DO (BOOM)

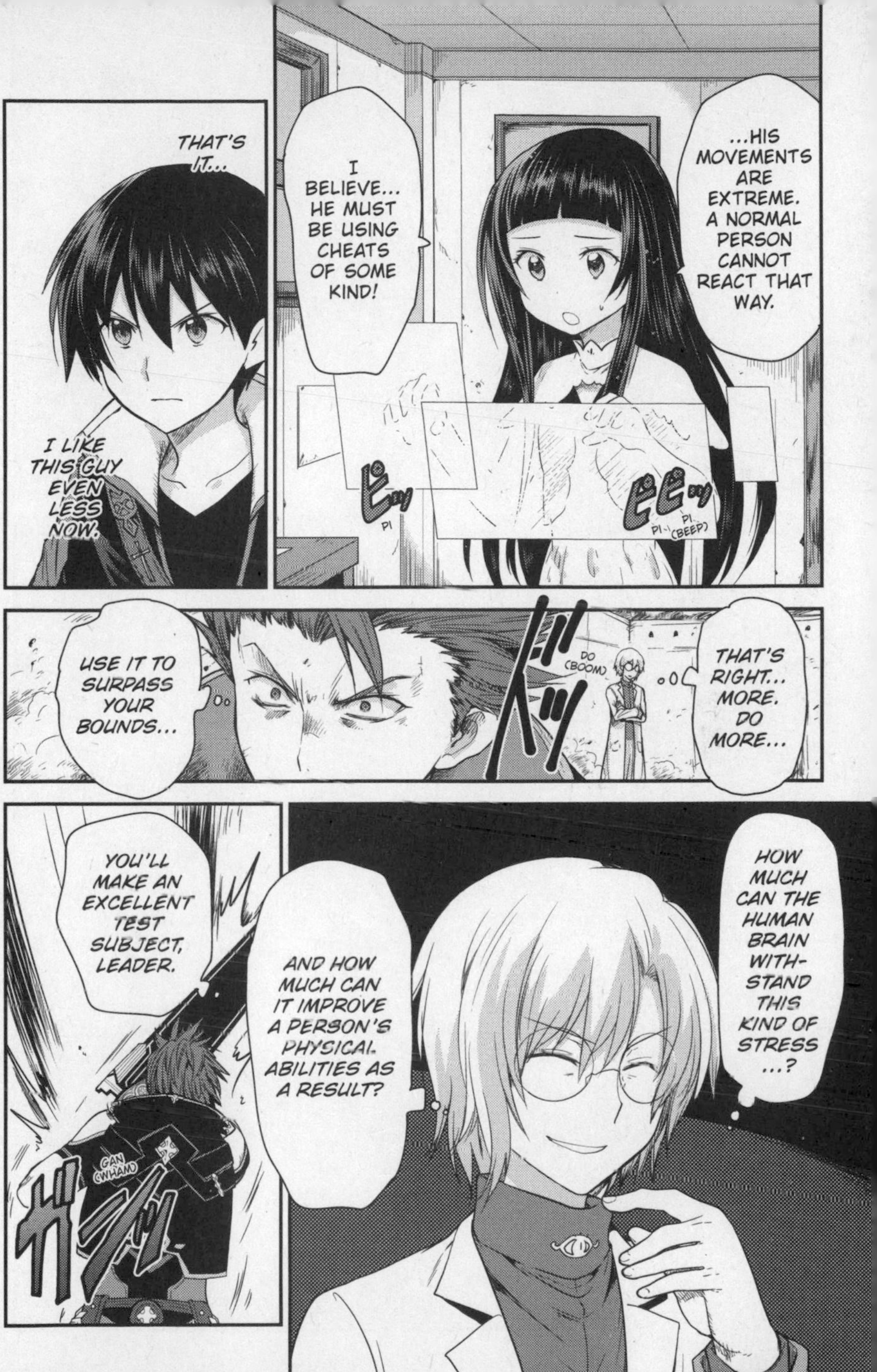
...HIS MOVEMENTS ARE EXTREME. A NORMAL PERSON CANNOT REACT THAT WAY.
I BELIEVE... HE MUST BE USING CHEATS OF SOME KIND!
PI PI (BEEP)
PI
THAT'S IT...
I LIKE THIS GUY EVEN LESS NOW.
THAT'S RIGHT... MORE. DO MORE...
DO (BOOM)
USE IT TO SURPASS YOUR BOUNDS...
HOW MUCH CAN THE HUMAN BRAIN WITH-STAND THIS KIND OF STRESS...?
AND HOW MUCH CAN IT IMPROVE A PERSON'S PHYSICAL ABILITIES AS A RESULT?
YOU'LL MAKE AN EXCELLENT TEST SUBJECT, LEADER.
GAN (WHAM)

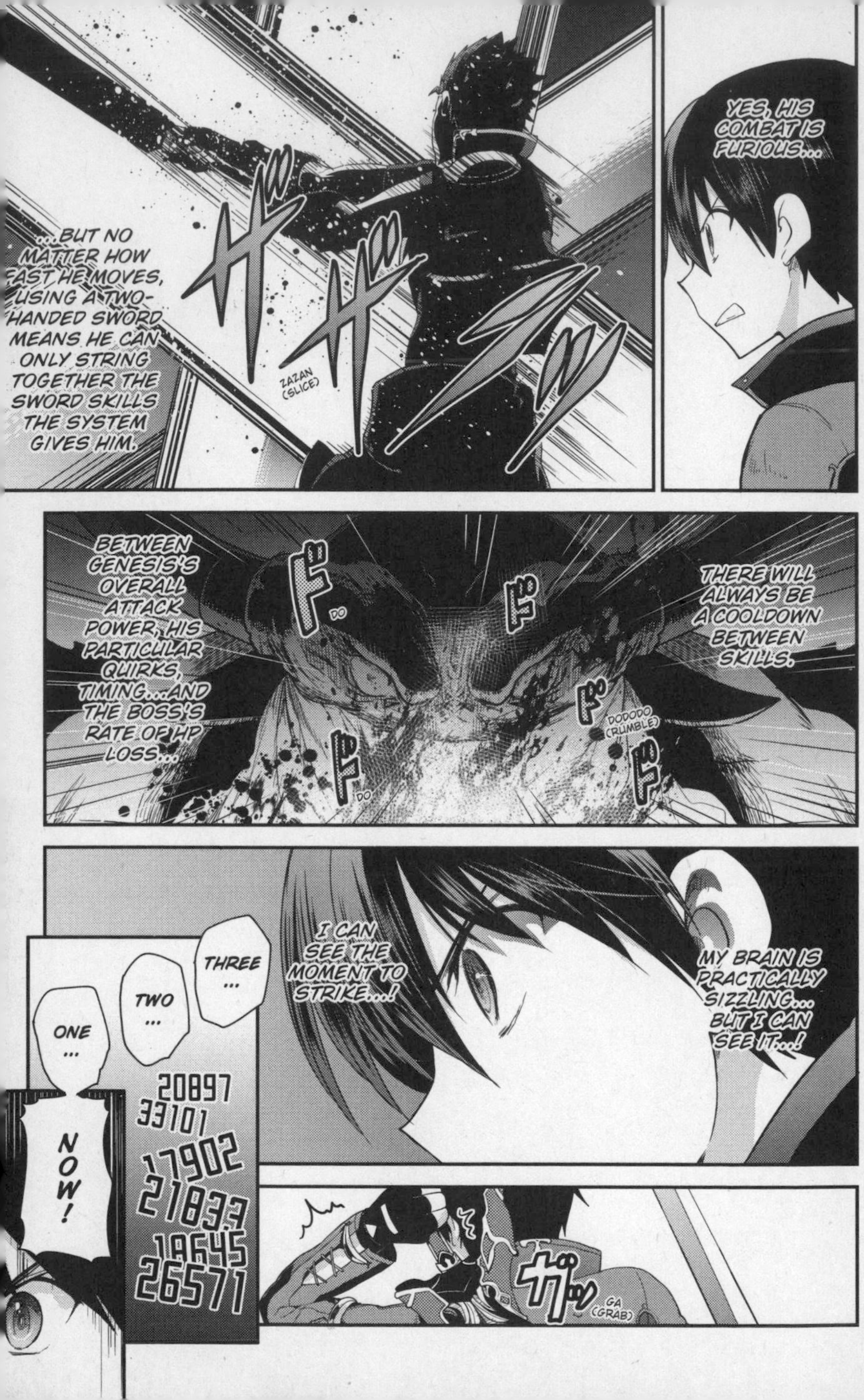
YES, HIS COMBAT IS FURIOUS...
...BUT NO MATTER HOW FAST HE MOVES, USING A TWO-HANDED SWORD MEANS HE CAN ONLY STRING TOGETHER THE SWORD SKILLS THE SYSTEM GIVES HIM.
ZAZAN (SLICE)
THERE WILL ALWAYS BE A COOLDOWN BETWEEN SKILLS.
BETWEEN GENESIS'S OVERALL ATTACK POWER, HIS PARTICULAR QUIRKS, TIMING...AND THE BOSS'S RATE OF HP LOSS...
DO
DODODO (RUMBLE)
DO
MY BRAIN IS PRACTICALLY SIZZLING... BUT I CAN SEE IT...!
I CAN SEE THE MOMENT TO STRIKE...!
THREE ...
TWO ...
ONE ...
20897
33101
17902
21833
19645
26571
NOW!
GA (GRAB)

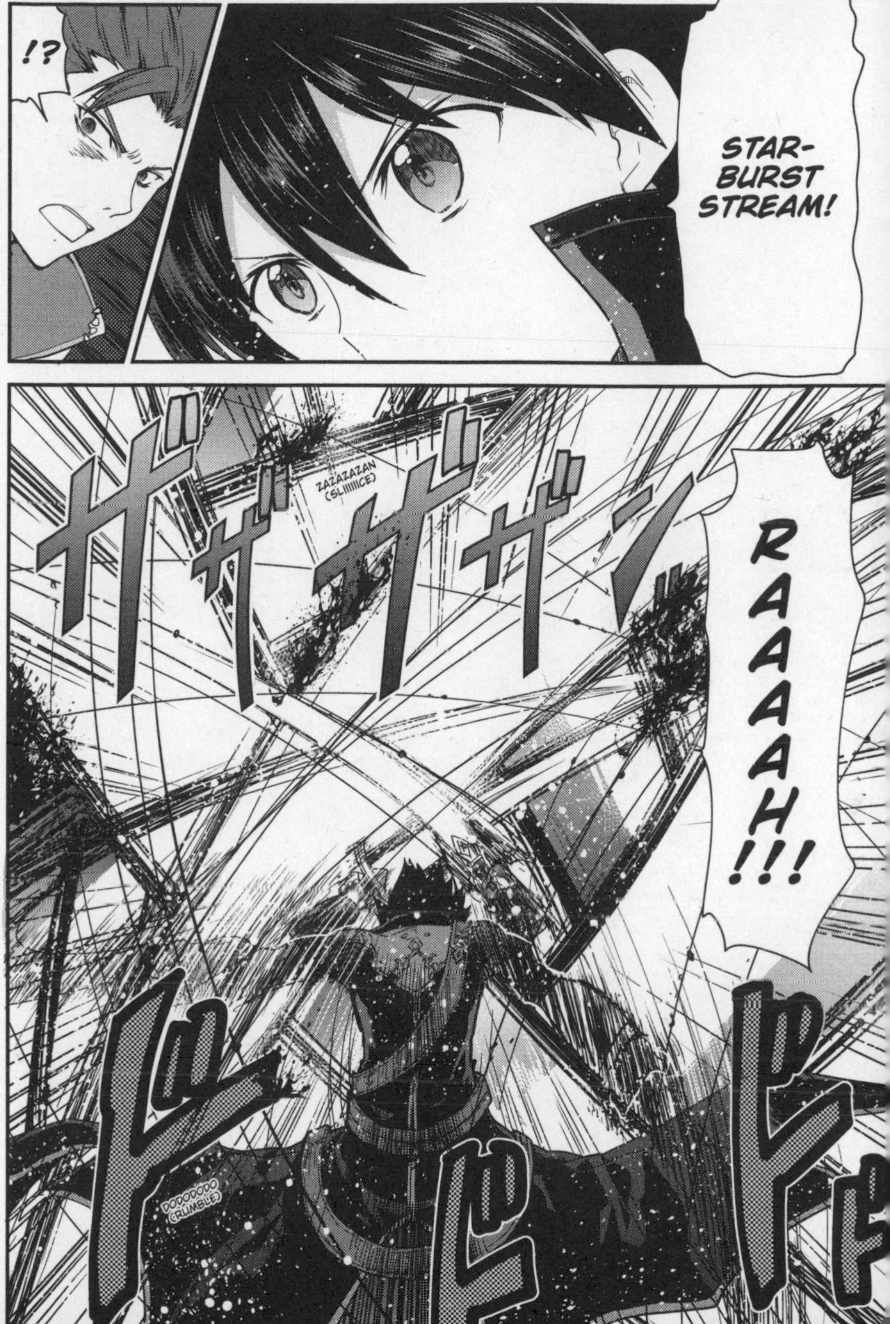
STAR-BURST STREAM!
!?
RAAAAAH!!!
ザザザザン
ZAZAZAZAN (SLIIIIIICE)
ドドドドド
DODODODO (RUMBLE)

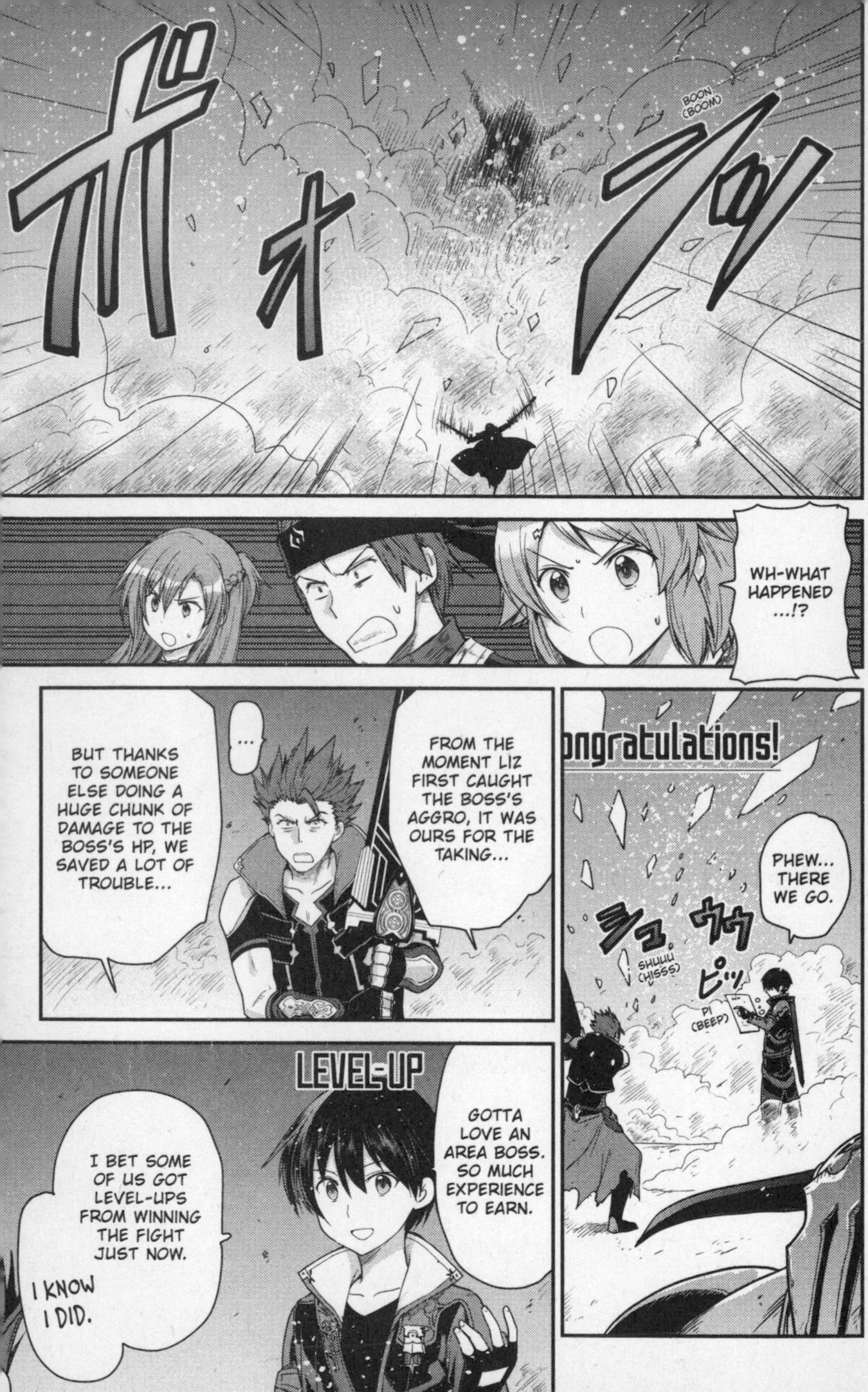

ボォンッ
BOON (BOOM)
WH-WHAT HAPPENED ...!?
ongratulations!
PHEW... THERE WE GO.
シュウウ
SHUUU (HISSS)
ピッ
PI (BEEP)
...
FROM THE MOMENT LIZ FIRST CAUGHT THE BOSS'S AGGRO, IT WAS OURS FOR THE TAKING...
BUT THANKS TO SOMEONE ELSE DOING A HUGE CHUNK OF DAMAGE TO THE BOSS'S HP, WE SAVED A LOT OF TROUBLE...
LEVEL-UP
GOTTA LOVE AN AREA BOSS. SO MUCH EXPERIENCE TO EARN.
I BET SOME OF US GOT LEVEL-UPS FROM WINNING THE FIGHT JUST NOW.
I KNOW I DID.

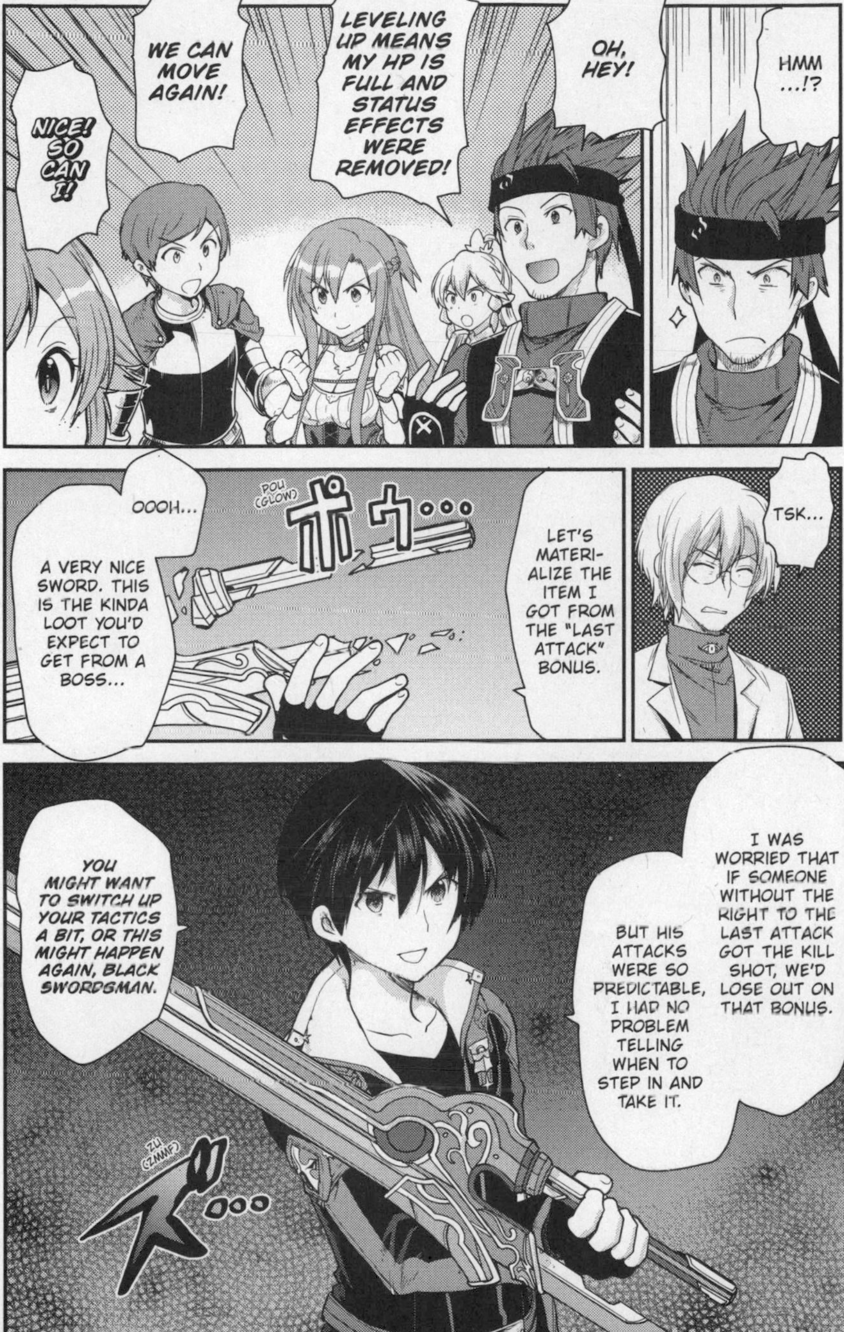
HMM ...!?
OH, HEY!
LEVELING UP MEANS MY HP IS FULL AND STATUS EFFECTS WERE REMOVED!
WE CAN MOVE AGAIN!
NICE! SO CAN I!
TSK...
LET'S MATERI-ALIZE THE ITEM I GOT FROM THE "LAST ATTACK" BONUS.
POU (GLOW)
ポウ…
OOOH...
A VERY NICE SWORD. THIS IS THE KINDA LOOT YOU'D EXPECT TO GET FROM A BOSS...
I WAS WORRIED THAT IF SOMEONE WITHOUT THE RIGHT TO THE LAST ATTACK GOT THE KILL SHOT, WE'D LOSE OUT ON THAT BONUS.
BUT HIS ATTACKS WERE SO PREDICTABLE, I HAD NO PROBLEM TELLING WHEN TO STEP IN AND TAKE IT.
YOU MIGHT WANT TO SWITCH UP YOUR TACTICS A BIT, OR THIS MIGHT HAPPEN AGAIN, BLACK SWORDSMAN.
ZU (ZWNNG)
ズ…

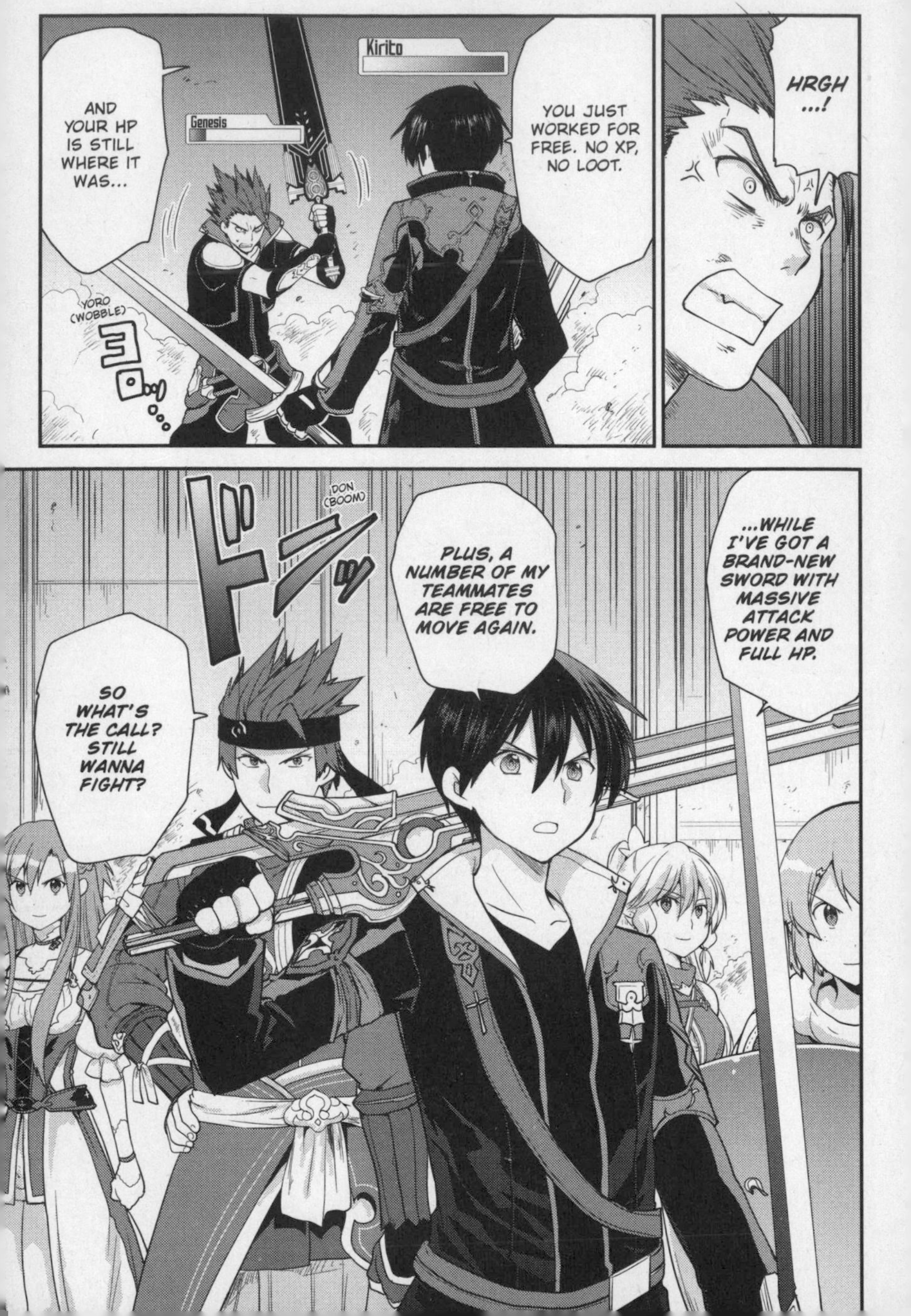
HRGH ...!
YOU JUST WORKED FOR FREE. NO XP, NO LOOT.
Kirito
AND YOUR HP IS STILL WHERE IT WAS...
Genesis
YORO (WOBBLE)
...WHILE I'VE GOT A BRAND-NEW SWORD WITH MASSIVE ATTACK POWER AND FULL HP.
PLUS, A NUMBER OF MY TEAMMATES ARE FREE TO MOVE AGAIN.
DON (BOOM)
SO WHAT'S THE CALL? STILL WANNA FIGHT?

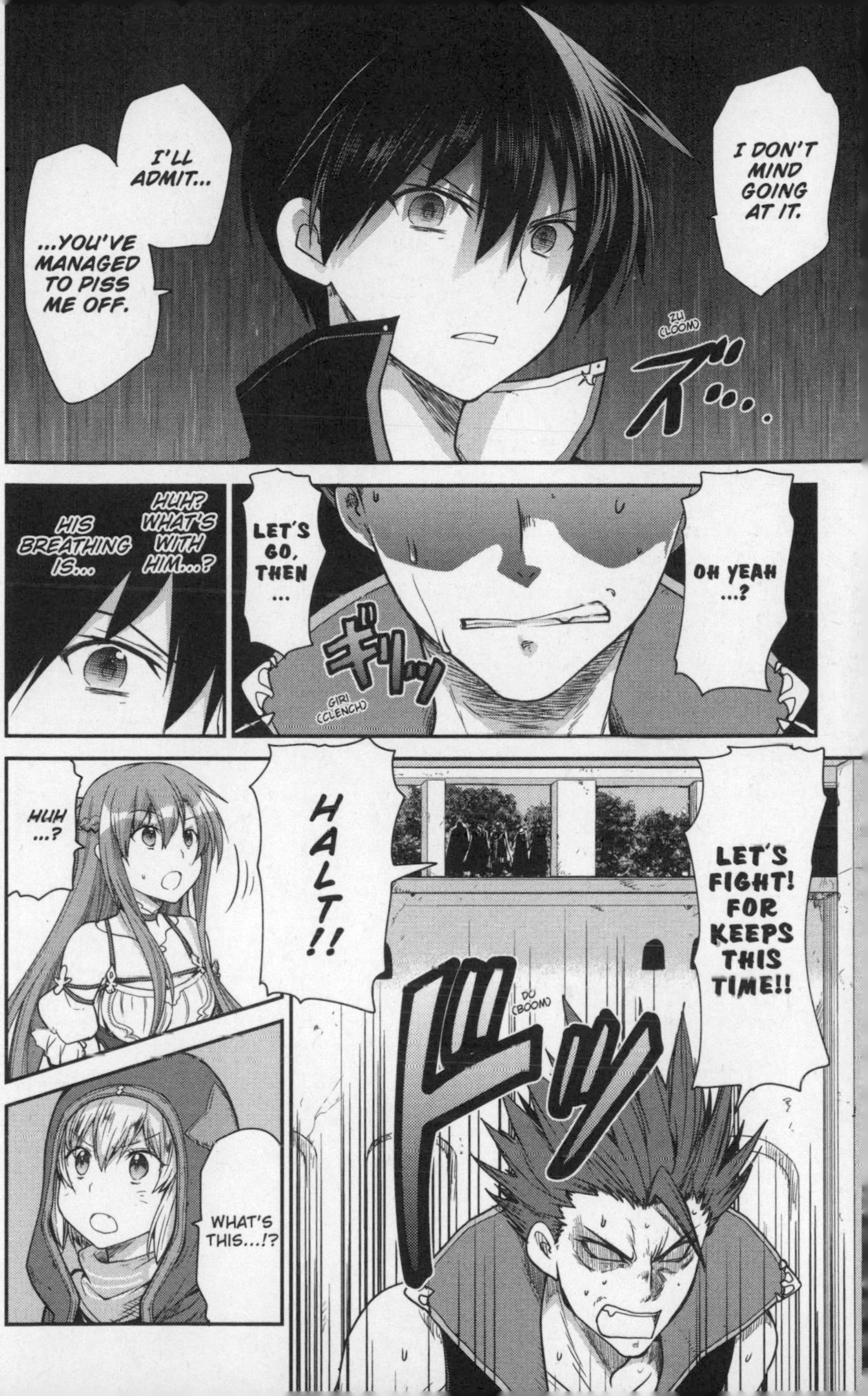
I DON'T MIND GOING AT IT.
I'LL ADMIT...
...YOU'VE MANAGED TO PISS ME OFF.
ZU (LOOM)
OH YEAH ...?
LET'S GO, THEN ...
GIRI (CLENCH)
HUH? WHAT'S WITH HIM...?
HIS BREATHING IS...
LET'S FIGHT! FOR KEEPS THIS TIME!!
HALT!!
DU (BOOM)
HUH ...?
WHAT'S THIS...!?

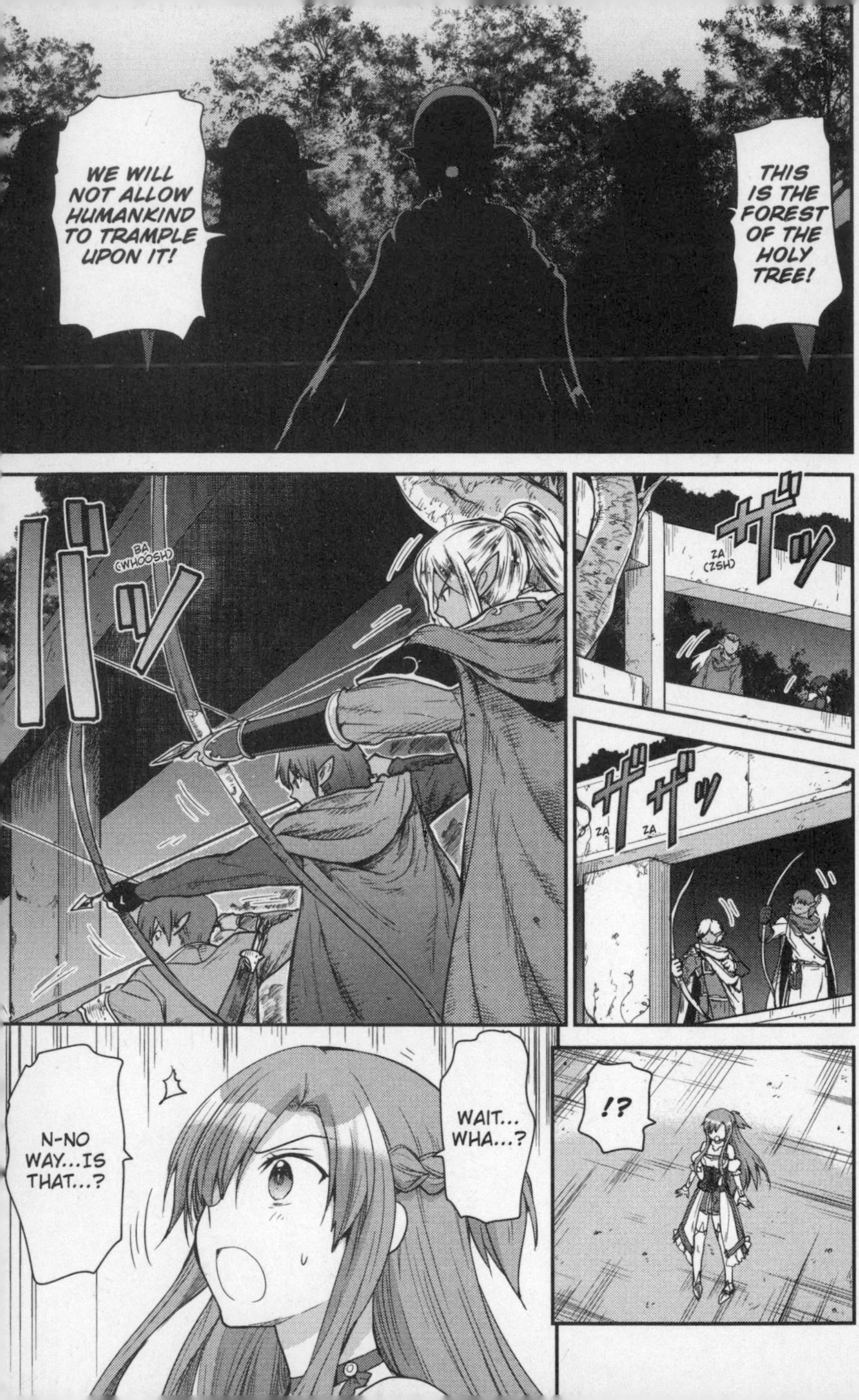
THIS IS THE FOREST OF THE HOLY TREE!
WE WILL NOT ALLOW HUMANKIND TO TRAMPLE UPON IT!
ザッ
ZA (ZSH)
ザザッ
ZA
ZA
バッ
BA (WHOOSH)
!?
WAIT... WHA...?
N-NO WAY...IS THAT...?

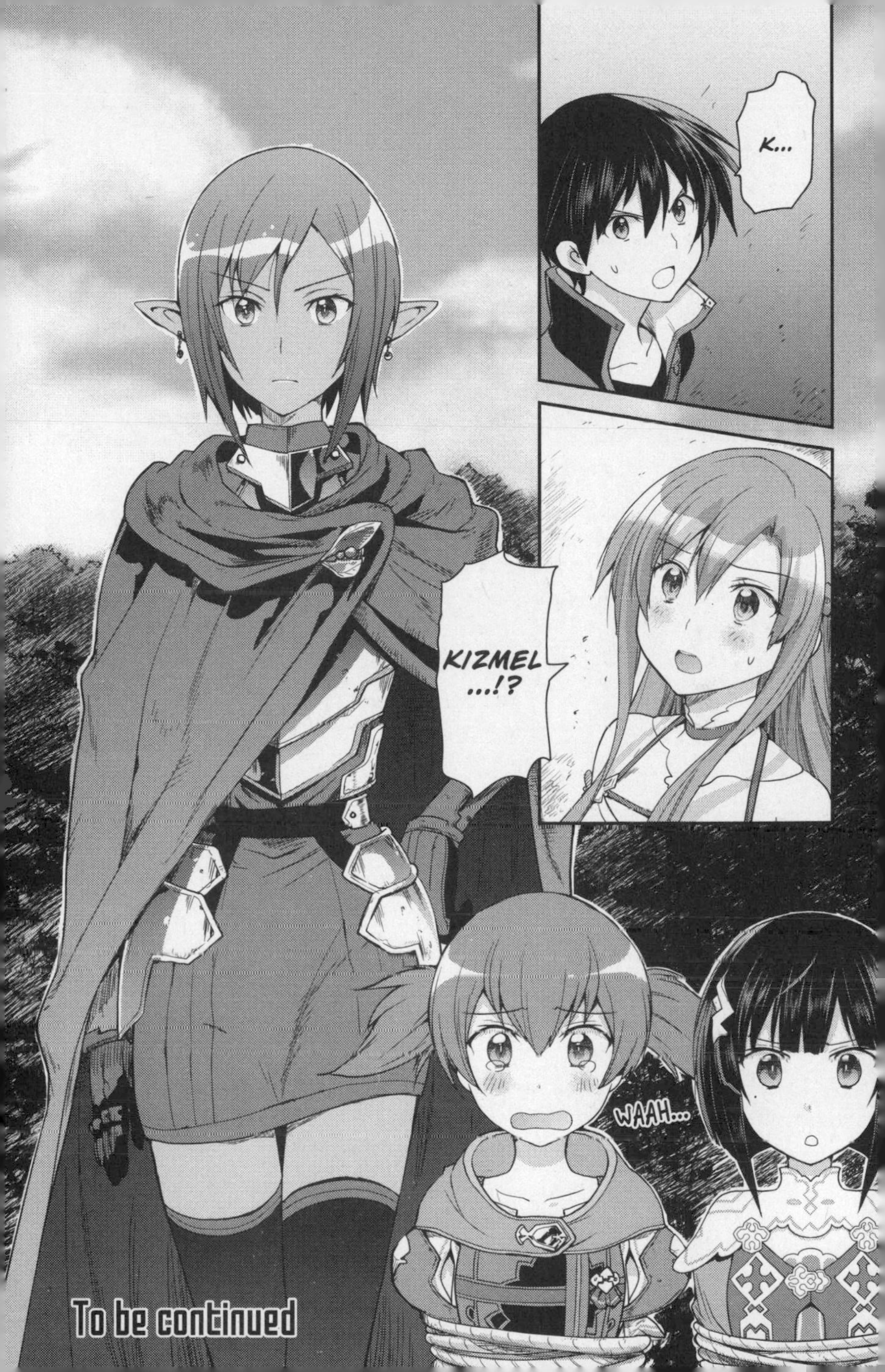
K...
KIZMEL ...!?
WAAH...
To be continued

VOLUME 2 AFTERWORD

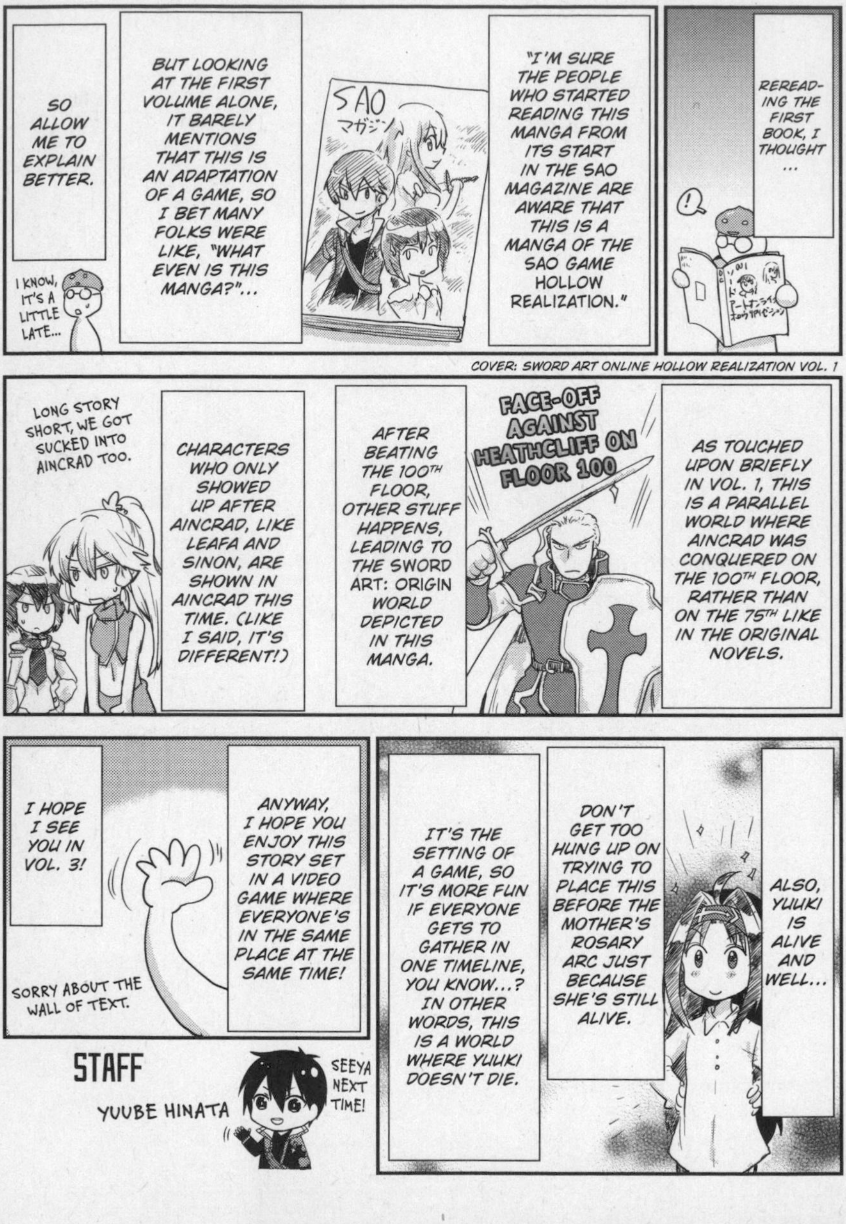
REREADING THE FIRST BOOK, I THOUGHT...
!
"I'M SURE THE PEOPLE WHO STARTED READING THIS MANGA FROM ITS START IN THE SAO MAGAZINE ARE AWARE THAT THIS IS A MANGA OF THE SAO GAME HOLLOW REALIZATION."
SAO マガジン
BUT LOOKING AT THE FIRST VOLUME ALONE, IT BARELY MENTIONS THAT THIS IS AN ADAPTATION OF A GAME, SO I BET MANY FOLKS WERE LIKE, "WHAT EVEN IS THIS MANGA?"...
SO ALLOW ME TO EXPLAIN BETTER.
I KNOW, IT'S A LITTLE LATE...
COVER: SWORD ART ONLINE HOLLOW REALIZATION VOL. 1
AS TOUCHED UPON BRIEFLY IN VOL. 1, THIS IS A PARALLEL WORLD WHERE AINCRAD WAS CONQUERED ON THE 100TH FLOOR, RATHER THAN ON THE 75TH LIKE IN THE ORIGINAL NOVELS.
FACE-OFF AGAINST HEATHCLIFF ON FLOOR 100
AFTER BEATING THE 100TH FLOOR, OTHER STUFF HAPPENS, LEADING TO THE SWORD ART: ORIGIN WORLD DEPICTED IN THIS MANGA.
CHARACTERS WHO ONLY SHOWED UP AFTER AINCRAD, LIKE LEAFA AND SINON, ARE SHOWN IN AINCRAD THIS TIME. (LIKE I SAID, IT'S DIFFERENT!)
LONG STORY SHORT, WE GOT SUCKED INTO AINCRAD TOO.
ALSO, YUUKI IS ALIVE AND WELL...
DON'T GET TOO HUNG UP ON TRYING TO PLACE THIS BEFORE THE MOTHER'S ROSARY ARC JUST BECAUSE SHE'S STILL ALIVE.
IT'S THE SETTING OF A GAME, SO IT'S MORE FUN IF EVERYONE GETS TO GATHER IN ONE TIMELINE, YOU KNOW...? IN OTHER WORDS, THIS IS A WORLD WHERE YUUKI DOESN'T DIE.
ANYWAY, I HOPE YOU ENJOY THIS STORY SET IN A VIDEO GAME WHERE EVERYONE'S IN THE SAME PLACE AT THE SAME TIME!
I HOPE I SEE YOU IN VOL. 3!
SORRY ABOUT THE WALL OF TEXT.
SEEYA NEXT TIME!
STAFF
YUUBE HINATA

SWORD ART ONLINE: HOLLOW REALIZATION ②

ART: TOMO HIROKAWA
ORIGINAL STORY: REKI KAWAHARA
CHARACTER DESIGN: abec
STORY SUPERVISION: BANDAI NAMCO ENTERTAINMENT

Translation: Stephen Paul   Lettering: Brndn Blakeslee

This book is a work of fiction. Names, characters, places, and incidents are the product of the author's imagination or are used fictitiously. Any resemblance to actual events, locales, or persons, living or dead, is coincidental.

SWORD ART ONLINE -HOLLOW REALIZATION- Vol. 2
© 2017 REKI KAWAHARA/TOMO HIROKAWA
© 2016 REKI KAWAHARA/PUBLISHED BY KADOKAWA CORPORATION
ASCII MEDIA WORKS/SAO MOVIE Project
© 2014 REKI KAWAHARA/PUBLISHED BY KADOKAWA CORPORATION
ASCII MEDIA WORKS/SAOII Project
© BANDAI NAMCO Entertainment Inc.
First published in Japan in 2017 by KADOKAWA CORPORATION, Tokyo.
English translation rights arranged with KADOKAWA CORPORATION, Tokyo,
through Tuttle-Mori Agency, Inc., Tokyo.

English translation © 2019 by Yen Press, LLC

Yen Press
1290 Avenue of the Americas
New York, NY 10104

Visit us at yenpress.com
facebook.com/yenpress
twitter.com/yenpress
yenpress.tumblr.com
instagram.com/yenpress

First Yen Press Edition: February 2019

Yen Press is an imprint of Yen Press, LLC.
The Yen Press name and logo are trademarks of Yen Press, LLC.

The publisher is not responsible for websites (or their content) that are not owned by the publisher.

Library of Congress Control Number: 2018950180

ISBNs: 978-1-9753-2788-0 (paperback)
        978-1-9753-2789-7 (ebook)

10 9 8 7 6 5 4 3 2 1

WOR

Printed in the United States of America